Social and Psychological Dimensions of Personal Debt
and the Debt Industry

Also by Serdar M. Değirmencioğlu

SOME STILL MORE EQUAL THAN OTHERS: Or Equal Opportunities for All (*editor*)

Also by Carl Walker

DEMOCRATISING DISTRESS: Reforming Approaches to Suffering through the Accounts of the Everyday Mental Health Work Being Undertaken in Our Communities (*co-author*)

COMMUNITY PSYCHOLOGY AND THE ECONOMICS OF MENTAL HEALTH: Global Perspectives (*co-editor*)

ON THE SICK: Work and the Mental Health Crisis in Britain (*co-author*)

DEPRESSION AND GLOBALISATION: The Politics of Mental Health in the 21st Century

PSYCHODERMATOLOGY (*co-author*)

UNDERSTANDING SKIN PROBLEMS (*co-author*)

Social and Psychological Dimensions of Personal Debt and the Debt Industry

Edited by

Serdar M. Değirmencioğlu
Doğuş University, Turkey

Carl Walker
University of Brighton, UK

Selection, introduction and editorial content © Serdar M. Değirmencioğlu and Carl Walker 2015
Individual chapters © Respective authors 2015

All rights reserved. No reproduction, copy or transmission of this publication may be made without written permission.

No portion of this publication may be reproduced, copied or transmitted save with written permission or in accordance with the provisions of the Copyright, Designs and Patents Act 1988, or under the terms of any licence permitting limited copying issued by the Copyright Licensing Agency, Saffron House, 6–10 Kirby Street, London EC1N 8TS.

Any person who does any unauthorized act in relation to this publication may be liable to criminal prosecution and civil claims for damages.

The authors have asserted their rights to be identified as the authors of this work in accordance with the Copyright, Designs and Patents Act 1988.

First published 2015 by
PALGRAVE MACMILLAN

Palgrave Macmillan in the UK is an imprint of Macmillan Publishers Limited, registered in England, company number 785998, of Houndmills, Basingstoke, Hampshire RG21 6XS.

Palgrave Macmillan in the US is a division of St Martin's Press LLC, 175 Fifth Avenue, New York, NY 10010.

Palgrave Macmillan is the global academic imprint of the above companies and has companies and representatives throughout the world.

Palgrave® and Macmillan® are registered trademarks in the United States, the United Kingdom, Europe and other countries.

ISBN 978–1–137–40778–8

This book is printed on paper suitable for recycling and made from fully managed and sustained forest sources. Logging, pulping and manufacturing processes are expected to conform to the environmental regulations of the country of origin.

A catalogue record for this book is available from the British Library.

A catalog record for this book is available from the Library of Congress.

For Anna and Andrew. We write this in the hope that your world looks better than ours

CW

For Çiğdem. Without your support, I would not have the strength to stand the neoliberal tidal wave

SMD

Contents

List of Tables and Figures ix

Acknowledgements x

Notes on Contributors xi

Introduction 1
Carl Walker and Serdar M. Değirmencioğlu

Part I Austerity, Financialisation and Serial Asset Extraction: Understanding Institutionalised Suffering

1 Debt in the Everyday Lives of 100 Families Experiencing Urban Poverty in New Zealand 19
Darrin Hodgetts, Emily Garden, Shiloh Groot and Kerry Chamberlain

2 All Roads Lead to Finance: A Critical Overview of Debt in the USA 39
Daniel G. Cooper and Bradley D. Olson

3 The Impact of the Swiss Franc Loans Crisis on Croatian Households 61
Petra Rodik

4 The Consequences of Evictions in Spain 84
Aïda Ballester, Moisés Carmona, Rubén David Fernández, Ana González, Johanna Jiménez, Elies Martínez, Irene Moulas, Laura Peret and Carolina Viano

5 The Experiences of Individuals in Debt during an Era of Extreme Austerity in Greece 101
Alexandra Papamichail and Petros Mizamidis

Part II The Public Face of the Debt Industry: Discourse and Wellbeing

6 Debt Dynamics in the UK and Beyond: How Propaganda Impedes Effective Political Action 123
Mark Burton

7 The Social Construction of "Indebted Man": Economic Crisis, Discursive Violence and the Role of Mass Media in Italy — 138
Adriano Zamperini and Marialuisa Menegatto

8 Chasing Happiness through Personal Debt: An Example of Neoliberal Influence in Norwegian Society — 160
Salman Türken, Erik Carlquist and Henry Allen

9 "Financial Capability" Considered from a Community Psychology-Informed Process in the North East of England — 180
Jacqui Lovell and Jacqui Akhurst

10 The Indebted Individual: Dominant Discourses and Alternative Understandings of Personal Debt in the UK — 203
Paul Hanna, Liz Cunningham and Carl Walker

Part III Political Histories of Personal Debt: Managed Decline, the Debt Industry and Wellbeing

11 Online Peer-to-Peer Lending as a New Profit Industry and Debt Trap — 225
Ceylan Cizmeli and Mert Demir

12 Thinking about the Personal Debt Industry: Voices from Puerto Rico — 241
Dolores S. Miranda Gierbolini and Ida de Jesús Collazo

13 Personal Debt in Third-World Latin American Society — 256
Douglas Marlon Arévalo Mira

14 The Personal Debt Industry: Racist Debt Practices and Pasifika Peoples in New Zealand — 268
Bruce Curtis and Cate Curtis

Conclusion: Thoughts for the Future — 288
Carl Walker

Index — 298

Tables and Figures

Tables

6.1	Composition of debt, by category, for selected countries, expressed as a percentage of GDP	128
6.2	Government debt: propaganda and reality	131
7.1	Number of articles per year of the corpus	148

Figures

3.1	Bank loans to households	64
3.2	The structure of foreign-currency loans to households	65
3.3	Share of different loan types within Swiss franc-denominated loans outstanding	67
3.4	Instalment increase	70
3.5	The self-assessment of the probability of foreclosure – debtors with Swiss franc-denominated housing loans ($n = 854$)	71
6.1	UK government debt as a percentage of GDP over the last 110 years	126
6.2	Composition of debt, by category, for selected countries, expressed as a percentage of GDP	127

Acknowledgements

Carl Walker thanks the University of Brighton for the award of a research sabbatical which facilitated the editing of this book.

Bruce Curtis and Cate Curtis acknowledge the financial support of the Europe Institute, University of Auckland. Bruce is deeply indebted to them for their support of a project that began examining exhortations to politeness in the public sphere and has been expressed here, in part, as an examination of damaged identities.

Darrin Hodgetts, Shiloh Groot, Kerry Chamberlain and Emily Garden acknowledge that the Family 100 Project was initiated and funded by the Auckland City Mission.

Petra Rodik thanks Karin Doolan, Nicole Kwiatkowski, Branka Lukačević-Gregić, Tomislav Prpić, Andrea Gerenčer, Mihailo Radosavljević and the editors of this book. She is grateful for their useful feedback and kind help, both with the survey that she conducted in early 2012 as a Franc Association activist and with preparing her chapter.

Alexandre Papamichail and Petros Mizamidis thank Sotiria Gkatziou for assistance with editing their chapter.

Adriano Zamperini and Marialuisa Menegatto acknowledge the financial support of the Coop School of Montelupo – National Institute of Training for Consumer Cooperatives, Florence, Italy. They thank Enrico Parsi and his colleagues from the Coop School of Monetelupo for their invaluable comments on earlier drafts of their chapter.

Douglas Marlon Arévalo Mira would like to give special thanks to Camilia Carolina Acevedo Paz, who supported the translation of his chapter.

Contributors

Jacqui Akhurst is Professor of Community Psychology at York St John University, UK. She is particularly interested in collaborative and participatory action research in community settings. She holds a master's in counselling psychology and a PhD in psychotherapy, and she has experience of the practice–research interface in both the UK and South Africa. She is the immediate past chair of the Community Psychology Section of the British Psychological Society and has an honorary position at the University of KwaZulu Natal, South Africa.

Henry Allen is an independent researcher and part-time lecturer. He holds a PhD in political science from the University of East Anglia, UK. In order to carry out this research he received an ESRC scholarship through the Centre for Competition Policy. His research interests are in public administration, interest organisations, the media and research methods.

Aïda Ballester is a social worker with experience of planning, implementing, coordinating and evaluating programmes that are focused on children. She is interested in educational intervention based on participation and innovative models with adolescents and youth at risk of exclusion. She holds a master's in social and educational interventions from the Universitat de Barcelona, Spain, and is a member of the Apropa't project.

Mark Burton is a visiting professor at Manchester Metropolitan University, UK. He previously worked in community intellectual disability services and in various professional and management roles, emphasising the link between practice with the social conditions within which people live, and using a variety of frameworks from the critical social sciences to inform this. Since retirement he has described himself as a scholar-activist, working on a variety of environmental, economic and political issues, and he is a member of the Steady State Manchester collective, which promotes the alternative post-growth model of economy and society in the context of post-industrial Greater Manchester. He is co-author of *Critical Community Psychology*.

Erik Carlquist is a clinical and social psychologist. He is a member of the cultural and community psychology group at the Department of Psychology, University of Oslo, Norway. His research encompasses the psychology of language, communication and the cultural transmission of knowledge and ideology. He is connected to the Oslo Ideology Project and the Eudaimonic and Hedonic Happiness Investigation, the latter being an ongoing international project to study the cultural diversity of wellbeing representations.

Kerry Chamberlain is Professor of Social and Health Psychology at Massey University in Auckland, New Zealand. He is a critical health psychologist whose research focuses on health and the everyday, with specific interests in disadvantage, medications, media, materiality, mundane ailments and food, and in innovative qualitative research methodology. He has published widely on health issues and qualitative research matters. He is co-author of *Health Psychology: A Critical Introduction*, associate editor for *Psychology & Health* and the *British Journal of Health Psychology*, and an editorial board member of several other journals. He is a fellow of the European Health Psychology Society, and an executive committee member of the International Society for Critical Health Psychology.

Ceylan Cizmeli is a former Fulbright scholar. She holds a PhD in social and health psychology from Stony Brook University, USA. She is working as a full-time faculty member at the State University of New York at Oswego, USA. Her research focuses on examining the validity and reliability of multidimensional models of stress and violence among diverse groups, differences in health outcomes accounted for by individual and contextual factors, and stability and change across time in the occurrence of stress-related reactions and violent behaviours.

Daniel G. Cooper is an urban affairs researcher with a background in urban planning and community psychology. He is Associate Director of the Institute on Public Safety and Social Justice at the Adler School in Chicago, USA. His research interests include housing, community and economic development, urban politics, community organising, mass incarceration and urban inequality. Much of his work is done in collaboration with grassroots coalitions that are working to improve disadvantaged neighbourhoods through collective impact and policy change.

Liz Cunningham is Senior Lecturer in Community Research and Practice at the University of Brighton, UK. Her key interests include the development of culturally appropriate psychology, the use of participatory action research, social and community development, and oral history/narrative methods.

Bruce Curtis is Senior Lecturer in Sociology at the University of Auckland, New Zealand. He is interested in the analysis and critique of late capitalism, neoliberalism and neocolonialism.

Cate Curtis is Senior Lecturer in Psychology at the University of Waikato, New Zealand. Prior to her current post, she worked within community organisations, focusing on the areas of disadvantaged women and youth, and (un)employment.

Serdar M. Değirmencioğlu is Professor of Developmental and Community Psychology at Doğuş University, Turkey. He is a public scholar and outspoken advocate of children's rights. He has written on for-profit higher education, militarism and martyrdom, and young people's participation. He is President of the European Community Psychology Association.

Ida de Jesús Collazo is a professor at the Department of Economics, Faculty of Social Sciences, University of Puerto Rico, Río Piedras Campus, where she teaches macroeconomic theory, the political economy of capitalism, the history of economic thought, the economics of Puerto Rico and the economics of education. She studied economics at the University of Puerto Rico, Río Piedras Campus and at The New School for Social Research at New York, USA. She was formerly Director of the Department of Economics and Dean of the Faculty of Social Sciences.

Mert Demir is a PhD candidate in finance at the City University of New York (CUNY), USA. His research focuses on the role of corporate non-financial performance and disclosure on corporate financing decisions and firm valuation. He is a research associate in the corporate social responsibility-sustainability monitor project at the Weissman Center for International Business at Baruch College, CUNY, and he also teaches courses on financial management and futures and forward markets at the college.

xiv Notes on Contributors

Rubén David Fernández is a social community psychologist, a professor and researcher in the social psychology departments of the universities of Barcelona and Girona, Spain. He is a founder partner of the ETCS cooperative in Barcelona. His research topics include participatory methodologies, empowerment, community health, community art practices, social psychology and applied IAP.

Emily Garden is Project Officer for the Auckland City Mission Family 100 Project, which followed 100 Auckland families living in long-term hardship over the course of a year. She holds a master's in sociology and cultural studies from Goldsmiths College, University of London, UK, and a BA in visual communication from Auckland University of Technology, New Zealand. She has a keen interest in issues of social justice, including poverty and inequality, stigma, discrimination and representation. She has worked for community mental health groups and for the Ministry of Health's Like Minds, Like Mine project. She also taught for several years at Auckland University of Technology.

Ana González is a member of the Apropa't project. She holds a master's in psychosocial intervention from the University of Barcelona. Her professional experience focuses on collectives that are at risk of exclusion, in relation to both intellectual disability and immigration. She has a special interest in gender and women's studies.

Shiloh Groot is Lecturer in Social Psychology at the University of Auckland, New Zealand. She is an interdisciplinary and indigenous social scientist who works in the fields of indigenous worldviews and communities, resilience, sex work, urban poverty and health. She is co-chair of the Māori Caucus for the New Zealand Coalition to End Homelessness, where she advises on the expansion of research strategies that will inform the development of national policy and service provision.

Paul Hanna is a chartered psychologist and Lecturer in Sustainable Tourism at the University of Surrey, UK. His research interests include identity, wellbeing, sustainability and pro-environmental behaviours. His work has been published in a range of journals, including *GeoJournal, Journal of Consumer Culture, Theory & Psychology, Qualitative Research, Qualitative Research in Psychology* and *Environmental Economics*. He is currently working on a range of research projects exploring spatial, affective, social and individual elements of sustainable behaviour in relation to leisure and tourism.

Darrin Hodgetts is Professor of Societal Psychology at Massey University. Prior to his current academic appointment, he held posts at Memorial University, Canada, in community health, the London School of Economics and Political Sciences, UK, in media and communications, and the University of Waikato, New Zealand, in community psychology. He conducts participative research on urban poverty, health inequalities, social class and homelessness.

Johanna Jiménez is a member of the Apropa't project and a volunteer in the Psychosocial Unit of Medecins Sans Frontieres (MSF). She holds a master's in psychosocial intervention from the University of Barcelona. Her professional experience focuses on administrative management, research related to personal agency and empowerment in adolescents, and psychosocial intervention in humanitarian labour. She has an interest in community intervention, empowerment, social in/exclusion and international cooperation.

Jacqui Lovell is a PhD candidate in community psychology in her final year at York St John University. She is using visual methodology and in particular bodymapping and participatory video production in her research in partnership with diverse people who experience social exclusion. She is a self-employed community psychologist, a permaculturist and a social activist living and working in the North East of England. She is committed to working for social change in equal partnership with people at the bottom of the social hierarchy and to this end is an active member of the Edge Fund, a radical funding organisation, and the National Service User Network.

Elies Martínez is a member of the Apropa't project and actively monitors interventions with children and youth groups. She holds a master's in psychosocial intervention from the University of Barcelona. She has experience working as a social educator in a foster care centre for minors in Valencia, Spain.

Marialuisa Menegatto is a clinical and community psychologist, psychotherapist and PhD candidate in human science and philosophy in the Department of Psychology, Pedagogy and Philosophy at Verona University, Italy. Her research interests include social conflict and practices of reconciliation, forms of exclusion and violence, human rights and social justice, war and peace, and interpersonal and interethnic relationships.

Douglas Marlon Arévalo Mira holds a master's in community psychology from Universidad Centroamericana "José Simeón Cañas" in San Salvador, El Salvador, where he has been working since 2003 as manager of the research laboratory of the Psychology Department. He has worked as a lecturer at several Salvadoran universities, including Universidad Centroamericana, Universidad Jose Matias Delgado and Universidad Francisco Gavidia. His research interests include leisure-time management among university students, psychosocial trauma following the 2009 Honduran coup and self-inflicted violence. He is the coordinator of a research group that focuses on the living conditions of youth in rural areas in the north of the country.

Dolores S. Miranda Gierbolini is a professor in the Graduate Psychology Program at the University of Puerto Rico. She is a former president of the Puerto Rico Psychology Association and chairperson of the Department of Psychology and Faculty Representative on the university's board of trustees. She has dedicated most of her academic work to grassroots socioeconomic community movements and higher education.

Petros Mizamidis is a software engineer and holds an MSc in computer games and entertainment from Goldsmiths, University of London. He has many years of experience dealing with the marginalisation of vulnerable people in Greece and a personal interest in social constructions of individuals living in poverty.

Moises Carmona Monferrer is Professor of Social Psychology in the Universitat de Barcelona and a member of the Research Group Community and Cultural Psychology. His research topics include community action, empowerment, art in community and IAP (Participatory Action Research) (PAR).

Irene Moulas is a member of the Apropa't project. She holds a master's in psychosocial intervention from the University of Barcelona. She has experience of working with groups that are at risk of social exclusion. She has participated in the organising committee of the 4th International Conference of Community Psychology.

Bradley D. Olson is a community psychologist, activist and consultant. He is an associate professor at National Louis University, USA, and co-chair of its community psychology PhD programme. His research areas include human rights, non-violence and mixed methods research. He is a founder of the Coalition for an Ethical Psychology, former chair of the American Psychological Association divisions for Social Justice, past president of Psychologists for Social Responsibility and past president of the Society for the Study of Peace, Conflict and Violence. He is currently co-editor of the Community Psychology book series.

Alexandra Papamichail is a psychology graduate registered with the British Psychological Society and she holds a master's in psychology from the University of Bristol, UK. Her research experience is in the association of socioeconomic factors (e.g. unemployment and social stigma) with mental health. She is undertaking a doctoral study on adolescents who are violent towards their parents, investigating the contribution of psychological and social factors to this phenomenon.

Laura Peret is a member of the Apropa't project. She holds a master's in psychosocial intervention from the University of Barcelona. Her research focuses on leisure time with children, psychosocial intervention in collectives at risk of social exclusion and victims of gender violence. She has an interest in international cooperation, gender and women's studies, and child soldiers.

Petra Rodik is an associate professor in the Department of Sociology, Faculty of Humanities and Social Sciences, University of Zagreb, Croatia. Her publications include *The Social Role of the Military: Discourse on Croatian Armed Forces 1991–2008* and (co-authored with Srbljinović and Penzar) *Formal Models of Social Conflicts*. She has participated in the campaign against illegitimate private debt in Croatia. Her research interests include economic sociology and qualitative research methods.

Salman Türken is a doctoral candidate in the Department of Psychology, University of Oslo. As a cultural, community and critical psychologist, he is interested in investigations of discourse and subjectivity, globalisation, ideology and neoliberalism. He is connected to the Oslo Ideology Project and is also a member of the COST (European Cooperation in Science and Technology) Action entitled "Social psychological dynamics of historical representations in the enlarged European Union".

Carolina Viano is Project Director of the non-governmental organisation Volunteers Psychologists in Chile. She holds a master's in law and public policy on childhood, adolescence and family from the University of Diego Portales, Chile, and a master's in psychosocial intervention from the University of Barcelona. She has participated in various projects and research related to public policies for social integration.

Carl Walker is Principal Lecturer in Psychology at the University of Brighton, UK. His research work in recent years has focused on the structural relationship between forms of social inequality and mental distress. He is a member of the British Psychological Society select committee for community psychology and coordinates a European Community Psychology Association Task Force on austerity politics and mental health across Europe.

Adriano Zamperini is Professor of Psychology in Interpersonal Relationships, Psychology of Violence and Psychology of Social Discomfort at the University of Padua, Italy, where he is also the Director of the Center of Research for Migration and Intercultural Studies. He is a member of the scientific board at the Andrea Devoto Institute Foundation based in Florence, Italy. His fields of research in social psychology include solidarity and indifference, social justice and human rights, social exclusion and ostracism, interpersonal and collective conflicts, war and peace, and the psychology of health.

Introduction

Carl Walker and Serdar M. Değirmencioğlu

> another thing we do is once the customer has got a loan we have to phone them once they've done six payments, between six and twelve months and do a loan review but really what the bank is trying to do is try and sell them another loan.
>
> Bank worker

> Since last November my husband's started having anxiety attacks and he would sort of start retching and he'd have a nose bleed... he's now been on anti-anxiety tablets for over a year and he's still retching because of this (the communications from collectors).
>
> Debt client

> It's very rarely that we will see clients that had just mismanaged their money, who over committed liberally beyond their means, it's rare.
>
> Charity debt advisor

There have of late been numerous attempts to make sense of the increasingly global upward trends in personal debt. This is perhaps unsurprising when we consider the ways in which the 2008 global financial crisis has thrown a critical spotlight on a range of seemingly interrelated personal debt events. Recently we have seen reports of the return of the formerly common trend of imprisoning poor and working-class US citizens who are not able to pay their debts (Roberts, 2014). Some 77% of US households are in serious debt, with one in seven people being pursued by a debt collector (Ross, 2013). The UK is currently witnessing steady growth in personal debt, which appears to show little sign of abating (Walker et al., 2014). Indeed, this increase is a growing problem in a number of countries (European Parliament Directorate

General for Internal Policies, 2010). Research across 20 European nations suggests that consumer mortgage and non-mortgage loans totalled EUR 9.08 trillion at the end of 2011, up from EUR 8.03 trillion in 2007 (Benn, 2012). Commenting on the findings, the director of Finaccord said:

> In most countries, the idea that households are shoring up their financial situation by paying off loans is simply not correct. Rather, the value of outstanding consumer debt is a structural feature of many economies and for a lot of individuals it is simply not possible for them to manage without it.
>
> (Benn, 2012)

The existence of sustained problems of acute poverty and hunger in many countries across the globe can be understood as having particular consequences for experiences of personal debt as they are increasing not only in many countries in Africa and Latin America but also in the liberal democracies of the global North (Dear et al., 2013). We have seen the recent movement to institute popular debt audits in more than 18 countries in order to ascertain both the extent and the legitimacy of public debt (Keuchevan, 2014). Strike Debt!, an activist network, launched the Rolling Jubilee to buy cheap debts on secondary markets and by doing so raised USD500,000 in a matter of weeks. This was enough to eliminate almost USD15 million worth of debt in one year. Most of the abolished debts had been generated from emergency room visits (Ross, 2013). Debt, both public and personal, appears to be an issue of growing international concern.

As such there have been a number of recent attempts to make sense of the experiences of the people whose normal living costs require debt financing so that they can be met. Andrew Ross (2013) talks of describing such nation states as "creditocracies" and suggests that in recent years the sharpening conflict between creditor and debtor has become more meaningful than the traditional struggle between capital and labour. Keuchevan (2014) suggests that debt has come to be the governing principle of societies by taking the form of what Coco (2014) refers to as "debtfare" – that is, the prolonged interlocking payment obligations that operate as a socially constructed trap where debt institutions lock people's current and future life choices and possibilities into unequal, unfree and mobility-limiting capitalist relations. In the many countries that are experiencing debtfare, debt is culturally mapped by the twin disciplining discourses of religious morality and neoliberal personal responsibility that contribute to an institutionalised misrecognition of debtors as being solely responsible for their consequences in a marketised social world.

An understanding of the nature and function of personal debt needs a broader understanding of contemporary and historical economic conditions. It requires a consideration of capital not so much as a "thing" but as a process where money is perpetually sent in search of more money (Harvey, 2010), and it requires an interrogation of such flows of capital. Capitalism is a system that reproduces capital, through accumulation. To accumulate capital it is necessary to make profit. Whereas Ross (2013) makes a distinction between the dichotomies of capital/labour and creditor/debt, for LeBaron (2014), debt bondage in advanced capitalist countries is reflective of the general expansion in the power of debt as a form of labour discipline. Debt contributes to delayed retirement and the acceptance of ever-lower-paid jobs, especially for women. Here it can be understood as the cornerstone of neoliberal capitalist discipline, defining the parameters of incorporation and the exit from labour markets and reshaping daily lives in varying ways, both within and between nation states. As Turner (2008) argues, there has been a growing requirement by governing authorities to position personal debt as central to the success of consumer capitalist economies.

Neolioberalism can generally be understood as the dominant practices and discourses that emerged, albeit unevenly, around the early 1980s and which put a premium on market-based regulation (Roberts and Soederberg, 2014). "Always geographically and temporally specific, the variegated forms of neoliberalism encompass complex, contested, dynamic and often contradictory sets of structures and process that entail both ideological and disciplinary features" (p. 657). Hall and colleagues have suggested that the 2008 financial crisis has been used as a vehicle through which to entrench and embed the neoliberal model of governance, and a result of this there has been a steady and uncompromising assault on incomes, standards and the conditions of life (Hall et al., 2013), where financial centres operate as centres of wealth extraction rather than wealth creation.

Ritzer (1995) suggested that it was possible to view people as victims of a financial system that depended on their going deeply into debt and that itself grows wealthy as a result of this indebtedness. For Ritzer, modern neoliberal capitalism has come to depend on a high level of consumer indebtedness, having encountered natural limits in extracting cash from consumers. Montgomerie (2007) supports this contention, arguing that the development of asset-backed securities (ABSs) in the shadow banking system has in recent years served to augment the supply of credit that is available to overcome widespread income stagnation. ABSs are important in credit markets because they lighten equity requirements on issuers' balance sheets and allow the recycling of loan pools through off-balance sheet transactions which increase the supply of credit. However, they also bring about a bias among lenders towards targeting and acquiring persistent revolving debtors because the ability to issue an ABS is predicated on the existence of a certain proportion of unpaid balances. Hence in many countries we have seen the rise of the phenomenon of rapacious credit-selling with few regulatory restrictions, often mirrored by increasingly brutal debt-collection regimes for the growing number who find themselves unable to service their debts (Walker et al., 2012).

Debt as systemic violence

Hodgetts et al. (2013) suggest that the technocratic and bureaucratic debt processes that harm certain vulnerable groups of people as a matter of course can be understood as forms of a systemic violence that creates experiences of often profound subjective suffering in the form of depression, anxiety, anger and suicide (Fitch et al., 2007; Drentea and Reynolds, 2012). Debt has become highly profitable for banks that are seeking to deliver ever more elusive profits, and there has been an abrogation of responsibility from the political classes for the responsibility of debt growth (Griffiths, 2007). Indeed the very term "personal debt" is a misleading misnomer that comes to invisibilise state-sanctioned, industrialised bureaucracies of political violence.

There is indeed very little that is personal about personal debt. Rather, what the chapters in this book reveal is the variety of often similar and sometimes variegated ways in which neoliberal polities around the world have cohered in order to industrialise a systemic and prolonged asset extraction from a growing number of people who live in these countries. Personal debt is a symbolic chimera that functions to personalise profound structural inequalities. Serres' metaphor of the parasitical relation as a principle for the production of change in social relations (Brown and Stenner, 2009) is useful in helping to understand the way in which a variety of agencies, actors and discourses operate around the world in order to sustain and develop credit industries. Deregulation and privatised money systems have allowed for the emergence of a finance capital with the enhanced capacity to exploit and to extract profit (Mellor, 2010). This often involve practices that are akin to forms of social parasitism where host humans are acquired and cultivated, and where capital is extracted through a range of activities that maintain their status as sustainable revolving debtors (Walker, in press). Such systems provide a clear example of where the broader interests of society are subsumed by the needs and demands of the credit system. These forms of systemic asset extraction can be understood as collective forms of trauma (Moreira, 2003). To focus on symptoms of mental ill health or financial literacy in isolation from these industries is to misunderstand the collective and systemic nature of suffering and human indignity that are routinised through the debt industries.

However, that is not to simplify peoples' debt experiences as displays of passive victimhood where debtors are simply subject to forms of control and dependence (Burkitt, 2008). Rather, what this volume shows is that individuals and communities are not only subject to relations of control but also have capacities to reconstitute themselves within and through their social relations and to engage in political acts of resistance. If one is to draw out a central flaw in theorisations of debt experiences then it must be the failure to grasp the complexity of the intersections between markets and actions which stem from and are mediated by the body (Deville, 2012). What we have come to understand as mental health – that is, bodies, their reactions, emotions and responses – is not contained within corporeal vessels but are effects that are distributed across a range of sociotechnical apparatuses, sites and markets (Deville, 2012). Rather than simplistic understandings linking atomised, responsibilising experiences of debt and financial strain that impact self-contained emotions, the interaction between industrial apparatuses and embodied suffering requires a broader and more nuanced focus where affective relations and practices are deliberate and planned strategies of captation where ensembles of operations try to bind people to industrial agencies. Here, consumer debt organisations operate not just by obtaining and acting on information but also by seeking to transform peoples' very worlds using logics that are often invisible to debtors (Deville, 2012; Walker et al., 2014).

This book seeks to address Deville's (2013) call for the need to take seriously the intersection between social material processes and the generation and management of affect. Cochoy suggests a concerted study of how markets can become oriented towards embodied human states that range from habit to curiosity, weariness and temptation (Cochoy, 2007), and to understand not only practices of subjection that are inherent in neoliberal market relations but also the counterstrikes and forms of resistance to such abusive market orientations.

An exploration of the subjective experiences of national industries of debt is by definition an interrogation of hegemonic neoliberal discourse and practice, where the free individual of bourgeois ideology has been shaped by free-market fundamentalism and where peoples' thoughts and feelings are shaped in accordance with domineering individualistic norms (Layton, 2010). It is an interrogation of the various forms of private global governance that function to establish the credit-worthiness of national governments and in so doing discipline borrowing on financial markets and national fiscal strategies (McGrew, 2010).

This volume constitutes an attempt to bring together a range of theoretical and disciplinary lenses that have previously demarcated and atomised constituent parts of debt industries into questions of economics, psychology, sociology and politics. It seeks to allow us to understand embodied affective relations in the context of the practices of global governance that reproduce poverty, indebtedness and the creditor industries situated therein. To understand how important debt now is in terms of shaping peoples' lives requires an exploration of the international experiences of debtfare societies that are characterised by racial, gender and class-segregated lending, media constructions, discourses that are mixed and contradictory, discursive violence, extortion, commodification via entertainment, propaganda and home evictions. Debt industries need to be viewed in the context of the politics of radical austerity and where rational-actor models of classical economics are replaced by cultural explanations of social and organisational phenomena. There is a need for suffering and subjective experience to be understood as properties of supraindividual units of analysis that cannot be reduced to the direct consequences of individuals' attributes or motives. In exploring international debt industries, this book is interested in types of actor, organisational form and their relations, the nature of institutional logics and governance structures (Scott, 2004). Here we explore institutions of debt as historically developed patterns of social relations (Avgerou, 2004), and we pay attention to such aspects as the myths and visions that have captured the imagination of its participant actors and the institutional political mechanisms that perpetuate the norms of constituent actors and agencies. In so doing we will be better placed to make sense of the subjugated voices of those in sufferance (Avgerou, 2004).

Austerity, financialisation and serial asset extraction: Understanding institutionalised suffering

In 1986 a financial "Big Bang" linked London and New York, and brought the world's major financial markets into one trading system, thus constituting an integration of global and national financial markets

(Harvey, 2010). Since then we have seen the liberal economies of the global North and South both increasingly characterised by a growing reliance on financial markets and logics. Financial markets have thus come to exercise an increasing influence on political economies and society where firms, households and subjects have been oriented and disciplined by the pursuit of shareholder value (French and Kneale, 2012). Privatisation has swept around the globe in attempts to find more places to put surplus capital (Harvey, 2010). Financialisation, the pattern of accumulation in which profit-making increasingly occurs through financial channels and institutions (rather than trade and commodity production), has become increasingly dominant and enabled by neoliberal regulatory frameworks, apparatuses and organisations (Snider, 2014).

Moreover, we have seen the radical reconstitution of peoples' lives through the dominance of financialisation. One such reconstitution is the movement of personal and public debt to the centre of current economic orthodoxy. Debt is used by international institutions to force through economic policies which act against the interests of ordinary people (Dear et al., 2013) and where capital extraction from financial services institutions that require financial bailouts come with conditions to increase austerity, such as cuts in spending, increases in regressive taxes, privatisation and deregulation.

Part I of this book (chapters 1–5) focuses on the ways in which austerity and financialisation, as political and economic development strategies, have worked in different national contexts to impose a variety of forms of serial asset extraction from both nation states and the populations therein. It lays bare the psychosocial impacts of such regimes on the populations who frequently find themselves dehumanised, excluded, responsibilised and evicted from their homes.

Hodgetts, Garden, Groot and Chamberlain (Chapter 1) open by exploring the way in which personal debt in New Zealand is primarily a means by which the undeserving wealthy extract money from economically vulnerable groups in society. They focus on how debt has been associated with exploitative intergroup relations, increased servitude and the perpetuation of misery among economically vulnerable groups. Their chapter explores aspects of the relationship between 100 families experiencing urban poverty in Auckland, fringe lenders and welfare institutions. In terms of understanding the ways in which subjectivities of debt come to be constituted through particular economic regimes, they show that people who are forced to take on debt are dehumanised through the constructions of debtors as financially illiterate and frivolous beings who are responsible for their impoverished circumstances.

Cooper and Olson (Chapter 2) then provide a critical overview of the history and ecology of increased debt in the USA, from political economy to individual and community impacts. Their contribution examines US financialisation since the 1980s, and it provides a theoretical framework for understanding how this process has quickly led to radical inequality, the roll-back of public service provision and the explosion of new financial products that drive the financialisation of all aspects of life. It explores how psychological research has made rich contributions to the understanding of how debt impacts individuals and communities. The chapter concludes with a discussion of the role that psychology could play in a push for greater critical consciousness. Following this, Rodik (Chapter 3) places financialisation further under the spotlight by focusing on the impact of the so-called "Swiss francs loans" crisis in Croatia in order to demonstrate a recent case where loans denominated in Swiss francs, and vulnerable to currency fluctuations and high interest, mean that many households now face problems with the repayment of their significant, barely repayable, debt. In August 2011, bank clients with Swiss franc-denominated loans started a nongovernmental organisation called Franc Association that, together with the Croatian Alliance for Consumer Protection, filed a lawsuit against the eight largest Croatian banks. The crisis was the subject of intense public debate. This chapter provides a socioeconomic focus on what led so many households into debt-repayment problems and it presents clear quantitative evidence of the impact that the repayment burden has on peoples' lives.

Ballester, Monferrer, Fernández, González, Jiménez, Martínez, Moulas, Peret and Viano (Chapter 4) use the context of the increasing evictions in Spain to highlight one national example of the impacts of austerity economics as a solution to the structural economic impacts of financialisation. A housing bubble that was rendered invisible by governments and financial institutions and characterised by speculation and limited diversification ended with disastrous consequences for society and especially for the middle classes. This contribution focuses on exposing the various psychological repercussions that overwhelm families who are at risk of eviction, and it locates this suffering within the problematic response of the Spanish state to the post-crash eviction crisis that continues to blight so many lives. It discusses how the combination of limited fundamental human rights, shame, stigmatisation, fuel poverty, child malnutrition and evictions constitute different types of hidden poverty, but it also outlines a self-managed pilot project that is focused on improving resilience in families facing evictions.

Moving from Spain to Greece, Papamichail and Mizamidis (Chapter 5) use their contribution to further present experiences of indebtedness during an era of extreme austerity in Greece and the impacts on the wellbeing and mental suffering of the population. They employ a number of qualitative in-depth accounts to contribute to the debates about personal lived experiences of austerity regimes, where the extraction of public funds to repay international creditors, as a hallmark of the doctrine of neoliberal financialised economies, is privileged over the lives of stigmatised and suffering people whose structurally induced recourse to personal debt has become a common mode of everyday survival.

The public face of the debt industry: Discourse, propaganda and wellbeing

Relationships of power are manifest in daily life through language forms, myths and symbolic processes, and the professional language of politicians helps to shape public beliefs about what forms of behaviour and knowledge are acceptable (Edelman, 1985). By accepting the need for sophisticated ways through which to understand the operation of complicated social apparatuses (Miller and Rose, 2008, p. 3), Part II (chapters 6–10) explores dominant categories of debt discourse. It examines public discourse and propaganda where the economic endeavours of politicians and corporations are translated into the personal capacities, aspirations and disciplining of subjects. In this way we want not only to frame the way in which debt discourse and propaganda impact the mental life of human beings but also to explore how the complex social apparatuses that work to produce specific types of indebted individual can be contested, resisted and challenged.

Despite clearly instantiated and damaging practices of financialisation in recent years – including selling to poor people mortgages that have been crafted in such a way as to make default if not inevitable then very likely, taking on bets regarding how long it would take holders to default, and the packaging of the mortgage and bet together and selling them to institutional investors (Graeber, 2011) – political discourse about personal debt is still characterised by the dogged neoliberal insistence on unregulated markets and profligate states. Moreover, public constructions of human beings as rational, self-interested actors and the need for responsibilised citizens continue to be dominant. The last 30 years have seen the construction of a vast bureaucratic propaganda apparatus for the creation and maintenance of hopelessness, personal responsibility and inevitability that has denatured any sense of possible alternative futures to neoliberal hegemony (Graeber, 2011). Part II explores these apparatuses in a range of countries and begins to touch on alternative visions to replace what Bauman (2007) understands as the economics of excess, waste and deception and that facilitates change as an individual project.

By examining dominant accounts of debt, credit and money, and the underlying structural realities, Mark Burton builds upon the accounts of financialisation and austerity in Part I by situating the ideology and propaganda that support austerity policies within the continued rapacious accumulation strategy of transnational capital. His contribution (Chapter 6) explores the human and ecological consequences of the freedom of private financial institutions to create money and explores in detail the general failure to counter the austerity narrative. It finishes by outlining some key priorities and resources for an alternative politics.

Zamperini and Menegatto (Chapter 7) use a critical analysis of the Italian media to focus on how constructions of debt make inseparable the production of the debtor subject and their morality. Public constructions of debt have produced specific morality narratives where the unemployed, users of public services and entire populations come to be responsibilised for the transactions of often distant economic actors and institutions. This contribution looks at how the Italian mass media have been central in privileging sacrifice and guilt as appropriate responses to very specifically constructed discourses of crisis.

Türken, Carlquist and Allen (Chapter 8) then develop some of these themes through the context of televised public entertainment in Norway. Their contribution is a critical analysis that outlines the way in which the relationship between creditors and debtors is fundamentally social and political. It demonstrates how the social and political dimensions feature through an analysis of the Norwegian TV show *Luksesfellen* (The Luxury Trap). The chapter argues that reality TV programmes, or "debt TV", function as technologies of governmentality that notably produce and reproduce specific narratives that are associated with debt – principally that it is exclusively an individual financial problem, not a social or political one. It demonstrates how debt TV functions to discipline both the participants and, importantly, the audience into more "financially literate" subjects, and by extension more governable citizens.

Following the exposition of financially literate subjects disciplined through reality TV, Akhurst and Lovell (Chapter 9) then further explore the discourse of financial capability in the UK. They contextualise personal debt within recent political and economic practices that appear to have encouraged international financial institutions to create personal debt. They explore the way in which the individualised discourse of "financial capability" has been constructed by financial services agencies and which ascribes personal debt to individuals' lack of financial awareness and irresponsibility. Critically scrutinising a tool that is designed to measure "financial capability", the chapter outlines a community-based project with diverse people who have experienced social and economic exclusion and mental distress in the North East of England. By so doing it critiques the ideas that are embedded in the construct and raises awareness about the systemic character of the debt industry and the need for collective rather than individualised responses.

Hanna, Cunningham and Walker (Chapter 10) offer an account of individual indebtedness which attempts to explore the possibility of seeing debt differently. They draw on Foucault's understanding of power, knowledge and agency to provide a theoretical account of how individual indebtedness might be seen through an alternative lens. Their contribution draws on data from interviews with a range of stakeholders within the UK debt industry to highlight the "moments of resistance" that were discovered in the interview data in which alternative discourses come to the fore, facilitating an alternative construction of the problem of debt, and subsequently repositioning the "indebted individual" in a more sympathetic position. The chapter concludes by suggesting that attention needs to be paid to challenging banking policies, "educational" initiatives, financial discourses and the individualisation thesis proliferated in much of the mainstream psychology if we are to challenge the entrenched structural precursors of personal debt.

Political histories of personal debt: Managed decline, the debt industry and wellbeing

Wilkinson (2005, p. 18) suggests that "we should liken the injustice of health inequalities to that of a government that executed a significant proportion of its population without cause". This is because inequality is not a personal quality; rather, it is a quality of a nation state and so is largely determined by political, economic and ideological activity. The ways in which personal debt is integrated into peoples' psychological states is highly historically and socially structured where those who are trapped in cycles of poorly paid and poor-quality work and unemployment require credit to survive. Over time and across different continents, we have seen the way in which the value of labour has decreased as people have become more indebted, and where net household indebtedness is now chronic rather than episodic (Baragar and Chernomas, 2012). A share of household income is now allocated to servicing debt obligations. It is handed over to the financial sector through increasingly habitual interest payments, and these payments result in a reduction in the quantity of abstract labour time that workers can command from the wages that they receive.

In a number of countries we have seen average disposable incomes decline relative to gross domestic product growth (Leaver, 2013). Part III (chapters 11–14) offers a range of contributions that provide accounts of how such circumstances have developed in different historical and geographical contexts and shows how they are constrained and reproduced through historical relations of colonisation, and political and economic management. It also provides intuition for the future practices of critical scholars in terms of advocating an abandonment of the fictionalised and idealised ahistoricism narrative of what it is to be human and instead make potentially meaningful contributions to the historically and culturally mediated social oppression of personal debt (Martin Baro, 1994).

With its lower interest rates and easier access to credit, peer-to-peer (P2P) lending has rapidly emerged as an alternative to traditional lending for many troubled borrowers. Cizmeli and Demir (Chapter 11) take a closer look at the P2P lending industry in the USA and from an operational and regulatory perspective they review its underlying motivations and mechanisms, as well as its consequences for all actors involved. They argue that P2P lending is guided by the same neoliberal policies that contribute to the development and maintenance of problematic debt industries, and that it is thus a false flag solution to the problem of overindebtedness. The chapter concludes by discussing potential ways to disrupt the historical debt cycle by focusing on social, political and economic policies.

Dolores Miranda Gierbolini and Ida de Jesus Collazo (Chapter 12) explore the context of personal debt in Puerto Rico. This is positioned in terms of the historical legacy of crises of capitalism and Puerto Rico's status as a territory of the USA. A historical and contextual account of the current crises of personal debt, and the associated psychological burden, is located in the gap between personal income and personal consumption expenditure, and where Puerto Rican subjectivities have traditionally been mediated not only by local social economic forces but by histories of colonial identity politics that have served to complicate the psychological impact of personal debt. In this chapter the social construction of personal debt and its subjective impact are framed within the interrelations of global economic politics and the relation between the USA and the Puerto Rican debt industry.

Mira (Chapter 13) follows by providing a narrative case-study account of the way in which people experience debt in El Salvador. Their first contact with the banking system in the country is typically characterised by the provision of immediate credit with few requirements. Here the growth in personal debt is contextualised through a lens which considers not only deregulated credit markets but cultural and historical practices which often see family members taking on the debts of deceased family members. However, at the heart of these practices sits the basic imbalance between spending and revenue, a situation which is experienced not only at the domestic level but also at the national level.

The final contribution offers an account of debt extraction in New Zealand that is both historically and racially constituted. Curtis and Curtis (Chapter 14) note that the country was a first mover in combining "austerity" and low wages with the sale of public assets. They contextualise personal debt growth within a low-wage economy with declining measures of "affordability". Their contribution outlines structural elements of credit availability and, in particular, the racialisation of indebtedness as an example of Bauman's (2007) notion of flawed consumption. The role of psychology is discussed before the chapter finishes by suggesting ways of breaking the debt cycle.

References

Avgerou, C. (2004). IT as an institutional actor in developing countries. In Krishna, S. and Madon, S. (eds). *The Digital Challenge: Information Technology in the Development Context*. Aldershot: Ashgate Publishing, pp. 46–62.

Baragar, F. and Chernomas, R. (2012). Profits from production and profits from exchange: Financialisation, household debt and profitability in 21st century capitalism. *Science & Society*, 76(3), 319–339.

Bauman, Z. (2007). *Consuming Life*. Cambridge: Polity Press.

Brown, S. and Stenner, P. (2009). *Psychology without Foundations*. London: Sage.

Burkitt, I. (2008). Subjectivity, self and everyday life in contemporary capitalism. *Subjectivity*, 23, 236–245.

Cochoy, F. (2007). A brief theory on the capitation of publics: Understanding the market with little red riding hood. *Theory, Culture and Society*, 24(7–8), 203–223.

Coco, L. E. (2014). The cultural logics of bankruptcy abuse prevention and consumer protection act of 2005 Fiscal identities and financial failure. *Critical Sociology*, 40(5), 711–727.

Dear, J., Dear, P. and Jones, T. (2013). *Life and Debt: Global Studies of Debt and Resistance*. Jubilee Debt Campaign, http://www.eurodad.org/files/pdf/5253faf79b829.pdf.

Deville, J. (2012). Regenerating market attachments, consumer credit debt collection and the capture of affect. *Journal of Cultural Economy*, 5(4), 423.

Deville, J. (2013). Consumer credit default and collections: The shifting ontologies of market attachment. *Consumption Markets & Culture*, 25 October, http://www.tandfonline.com/doi/abs/10.1080/10253866.2013.849593.

Drentea, P. D. and Reynolds, J. R. (2012). Neither a borrower nor a lender be: The relative importance of debt and SES for mental health among older adults. *Journal of Aging and Health*, 24(4), 673.

Edelman, M. (1985). *The Symbolic Uses of Politics*. Chicago: University of Illinois Press.

European Parliament Directorate General for Internal Policies (2010). Household indebtedness in the EU. European Parliament, retrieved on May 4, 2011, http://www.europarl.europa.eu/document/activities/cont/201103/20110324 ATT16330/20110324ATT16330EN.pdf.

Fitch, C., Simpson, A., Collard, S. and Teasdale, M. (2007). Mental health and debt: Challenges for knowledge, practice and identity. *Journal of Psychiatric and Mental Health Nursing*, 14, 128–133.

French, S. and Kneale, J. (2012). Speculating on careless lives. *Journal of Cultural Economy*, 5(4), 391–406.

Graeber, D. (2011). *Debt: The First 5,000 Years*. New York: Melville House.

Griffiths, M. (2007). Consumer debt in Australia: Why banks will not turn their backs on profit. *International Journal of Consumer Studies*, 31, 230–236.

Hall, S., Massey, D. and Rustin, M. (2013). After Neoliberalism. The Kilburn Manifesto, http://www.lwbooks.co.uk/journals/soundings/pdfs/manifestoframing statement.pdf.

Harvey, D. (2010). *The Enigma of Capital and the Crises of Capitalism*. London: Profile Books.

Hodgetts, D., Chamberlin, K., Tankel, Y. and Groot, S. (2013). Researching poverty to make a difference: The need for reciprocity and advocacy in community research. *The Australian Community Psychologist*, 25(1), 46–59.

Keuchevan, R. (2014). The French are right: Tear up public debt – most of it is illegitimate anyway, retrieved on April 25, 2014 http://www.theguardian.com/commentisfree/2014/jun/09/french-public-debt-audit-illegitimate-working-class-internationalim.

Layton, L. (2010). Irrational exuberance: Neoliberal subjectivity and the perversion of truth. *Subjectivity*, 3(3), 303–322.

Leaver, A. (2013). Growth in whose interests? *Discover Society*, Issue 3, 3 December 2013, http://www.discoversociety.org/2013/12/03/growth-in-whose-interests/.

LeBaron, G. (2014). Reconceptualising debt bondage as a class-based form of labour discipline. *Critical Sociology*, 40(5), 763–780.

Martin-Baró, I. (1994). *Writings for a Liberation Psychology*. Cambridge: Harvard University Press.

McGrew, T. (2010). *The Links between Global Governance, UK Poverty and Welfare Policy*. York: The Joseph Rowntree Foundation.

Mellor, M. (2010). *The Future of Money: From Financial Crisis to Public Resource*. London: Pluto Press.

Miller, P. and Rose, N. (2008). *Governing the Present*. London: Polity Press.
Montgomerie, J. (2007). Financialization and consumption: An alternative account of rising consumer debt levels in Anglo-America. CRESC Working Paper Series. Manchester.
Moreira, V. (2003). Poverty and psychopathology. In Carr, S.C. and Sloan, T.S. (eds). *Poverty And Psychology: From Global Perspective to Local Practice*. New York: Springer.
Ritzer, G. (1995). *Expressing America: A Critique of the Global Credit Card Society*. New York: Pine Forge Press.
Roberts, A. (2014). Doing borrowed time: The state, the law and the coercive governance of "undeserving" debtors. *Critical Sociology*, 40(5), 669–687.
Roberts, A. and Soederberg, S. (2014). Politicising debt and denaturalising the "new normal". *Critical Sociology*, 40(5), 657–668.
Ross, A. (2013). *Creditocracy*. London: OR Books.
Scott, W. R. (2004). Institutional theory: Contributing to a theoretical research program. In Smith, K.G. and Hitt, M.A (eds). *Great Minds in Management: The Process of Theory Development*. Oxford: Oxford University Press, pp. 460–484.
Snider, L. (2014). Interrogating the algorithm: Debt derivatives and the social reconstruction of stock market trading. *Critical Sociology*, 40(5), 747–762.
Turner, G. (2008). *The Credit Crunch*. London: Pluto Press.
Walker, C. (in press). Psychology, social class and parasitic encounters in the UK debt industry. *Theory and Psychology*.
Walker, C., Cuningham, L., Hanna, P. and Ambrose, P. (2012). *Responsible Individuals and Irresponsible Institutions: A Report into Mental Health and the UK Credit Industry*. Brighton: University of Brighton.
Walker, C., Burton, M., Akhurst, J. and Degirmencioglu, S. M. (2014). Locked into the system? Critical community psychology approaches to personal debt in the context of crises of capital accumulation. *Journal of Community and Applied Social Psychology*, DOI: 10.1002/casp.2209, retrieved on November 13, 2014 http://onlinelibrary.wiley.com/doi/10.1002/casp.2209/.
Wilkinson, R. G. (2005). *The Impact of Inequality: How to Make Sick Societies Better*. London: Routledge.

Part I

Austerity, Financialisation and Serial Asset Extraction: Understanding Institutionalised Suffering

1
Debt in the Everyday Lives of 100 Families Experiencing Urban Poverty in New Zealand

Darrin Hodgetts, Emily Garden, Shiloh Groot and Kerry Chamberlain

Debt is at once a personal, relational and structural issue. Debt, as discussed in this chapter, involves debtors (who are stigmatised in society) and entrepreneurial fringe lenders. Concerns regarding debt, inequitable profiteering and associated servitude have taxed the intellectual capacity of societies for millennia. Debt has proved to be a site for struggle between rich and poor grounded in debates regarding interest, the seizure of persons and property, rebellion and amnesty (Graeber, 2011). Societies as far back as 2400 BC have addressed the social instabilities that stem from exploitative lending practices, wealth concentration for some lenders and deteriorations in living conditions and debt slavery for others through the introduction of jubilee or debt forgiveness periods (Hammurabi Code, 1762 BC). Forgiving "the poor" for the parasitic actions of lenders is something that barely registers as a realistic option today. Reluctance to forgive such debt is, in part, the product of a misguided morality, which binds debtors and dictates that they should pay "their" debts despite the predatory actions of lenders. It also reminds us that debt is seen differently by debtors and lenders. For the former it is often about survival and for the latter profit. Yet we almost exclusively hear the lenders' perspectives. This chapter challenges such symbolic power by engaging the perspective of debtors in New Zealand.

Ultimately, debt impoverishes; debt wounds; debt kills (Graeber, 2011; Walker, 2011; Sweet et al., 2013). These costs benefit the undeserving wealthy who, despite what they constantly tell us, have no more intelligence, talent or entrepreneurial zest than anyone else. Such people do not earn their money; they literally make money and exhibit a moral flexibility that allows them to exploit others for their own gains. This situation is particularly disturbing when we realise that debt is simply "the perversion of a promise. It is a promise corrupted by both math and violence" (Graeber, 2011, p. 391). Debt is a promise that families living in poverty often cannot afford to repay. Something has to give, and families that are experiencing the relational and health consequences of debt should not be the people who continue to pay more than their share. After all, sometimes we are all unable to keep our promises.

Societal-level processes are adversely affecting personal issues of debt that are explored in this chapter. In response to a growing national debt brought on by neoliberalism,[1] New Zealand is caught in a process of privatising communal assets, reducing welfare programmes, and higher living costs that drag more and more people into debt in order to survive. Austerity is the order of the day, for the poor at least. Reflecting on similar processes in the USA, *The Debt Resistors' Operation Manual* (2012, p. 52) states:

> mafia capitalism means that governments make cuts and the people have to go into debt to survive. The burden of sustaining "life" gets shifted from the state to the individual and household... Debt is a way of controlling us – making us weak, afraid and financially unstable.

As with many Organisation for Economic Co-operation and Development (OECD) states, increased disparities in income and rocketing personal debt among lower socioeconomic status groups in New Zealand are accompanied by a systematic dismantling of welfare supports that were established to reduce, or at least buffer people against, the harshest consequences of poverty (Hodgetts et al., 2013).

Conditionality, or the notion that support is only warranted for those who comply with punitive managerial controls (Bauman, 2005; Standing, 2011), is central to the efforts of the current New Zealand government to save NZD 1.6 billion (New Zealand dollars) in welfare spending by reducing dependency on government assistance (see http://www.national.org.nz/welfare-reforms.aspx, accessed 20 June 2012). Conditions for state-based support have been tightened and benefit payments are stopped if clients do not comply with reformed regulations (Bourdieu, 1998). A central technology here is intense economic control manifested through requirements for regular detailed professional budget scrutiny of household accounts. Current austerity measures exacerbate the dilemmas that are faced by families who are already living stressful and inadequately resourced lives (Boon and Farnsworth, 2011), around income insecurity, growing debt (Landvogt, 2006; Green, 2012), food insecurity (Dowler and O'Connor, 2012) and social exclusion (Boon and Farnsworth, 2011). Families whose incomes are insufficient to meet their basic requirements for food and shelter are increasingly being forced to access loans from fringe lenders in order to get by (Boon and Farnsworth, 2011; Walker, 2012; Hodgetts et al., 2013). Consequently, they face further inequities in that they are often charged interest rates upwards of 100% per annum. Until these fringe lenders are properly regulated and current austerity measures are reversed, New Zealand is left with growing inequality and debt-related instability, stress, hurt, pain and illness (cf. Graeber, 2011; Walker, 2011; Sweet et al., 2013).

As with many OECD nations, New Zealand is witnessing a rise in the precariat with people surviving on inadequate benefits, low wages, disrupted and part-time ("flexible") employment and debt (Standing, 2011). The debt industry has grown to exploit the situation of the precariat (cf. Walker, 2011). Psychology is implicated in these processes through the application of the dominant Anglo-US model of the self-regulating autonomous individual and corrective technologies directed at addressing the supposed personal deficits and enforcing conditionality in welfare provision (Cromby and Willis, in press; Walker, 2012; Hodgetts et al., 2013). Intense supervision based on behavioural principles is sold to the public as being central to the rehabilitation of the poor.

Our focus and broader project

This chapter documents how debt involves relationships between debtors, their families, retrenched welfare institutions and fringe lenders, and how it links the personal and the structural. We draw on insights from conversations about debt with 100 impoverished families in Auckland to explore the psychosocial impacts of debt. Our analysis offers further understandings of debt as relational from Simmel's (1908/1990) observation that money can "invade" kinship and social relations in ways that can dehumanise debtors and obscure the responsibilities of lenders. We document how debt may be used to sustain some relational practices but can also dissolve familial and community supports.

The Family100 project is located within the Auckland City Mission. It seeks to develop alternative understandings of families in need and to promote initiatives that better meet their requirements (Hodgetts et al., 2013). Households, contextualised within their familial and service networks, are the unit of analysis. Specifically, every two weeks over the period of a year, 100 householders spoke frankly with social workers about their experiences using a range of drawing[2] and interview exercises. The participating families were selected to be representative of families who were regularly accessing the mission's foodbank. The cohort consisted of 40% Māori, 25% Pacific Islander, 22% European and 13% Asian and other minority groups. We met with the social workers every week to conduct training, collaboratively develop research materials, review participant responses and ensure continuity in the project.

The materials for analysis consisted of discussion notes from the fortnightly interactions, various participant drawings and bimonthly recorded interviews. The concept of phronesis (practically orientated knowledge regarding how to address issues) (Flyvbjerg et al., 2012) was central to our analytic approach. People who are experiencing hardship have a stock of intimate, practical experiential knowledge of their situation (phronesis) that other people lack. Such experiential wisdom is not simply cognitive in nature; it is embodied in stress, humiliation, frustration, fear, depression and anxiety. Scholarly engagements with participants' knowledge of debt and their associated daily practices are centrally important in challenging the neoliberal structures that reproduce the structural inequities of a debt society (Graeber, 2011). A key consideration was how general (societal) structures and relationships are reproduced via particular (personal) situations (Hodgetts et al., 2013). In this regard, our work is informed by Simmel's (1903/1964) principle of emergence of social phenomena and his orientation towards looking locally in order to understand systemic elements of the sociocultural world within which people reside and make do.

Acceptance of debt as a reality of life in a reformed welfare state

Many participants found it impossible to imagine a life without debt. On a minority of occasions, debt is used to buy "discretionary" items, such as TVs. More often than not, debt is a means of responding to a chronic shortage of resources, addressing day-to-day expenses and coping with unanticipated expenses, such as funerals and illness scares. As Walker (2012, p. 535) notes, "problematic personal debt arises from a persistent disparity between income and expenditure, insecure labour market experiences and the financial impact of normal life events". Taking on debt allows people to obtain essential items that are necessary to sustain both life and relationships. Debt is where survival meets fringe lending. Below we establish the pragmatic requirement for families to take on debt and the role of budgeters in failing to address the structural causes of debt. We then consider how the abusive and punitive approach to welfare that is endemic in welfare agencies (Hodgetts et al., 2013), such as Work and Income New Zealand (WINZ), forces families to rely even more on exploitative fringe lenders.

Helen accesses fringe lenders to help her to cover her day-to-day expenses. She feels loyalty to these institutions that provide her with capital that she has no other means of accessing. Broader issues of exploitation, which she is very aware of, are less important to her than addressing her family's immediate needs and unexpected expenses. Her account situates debt in the context of inadequate welfare support and the futility of budgeting:

> What I do is I have Aotea Finance and they're the people that help me with car repairs or anything like that, and that's when WINZ (State welfare agency) isn't available... I tell you what, they've [Aotea Finance] saved my bacon a few times. There's all sorts – just the unforeseen costs that no one else will cater for. I even went to my budgeter and they got me to sign a contract saying that I wouldn't take any more finance out, and I told them I wouldn't sign. I actually wrote a clause in saying that unless you know someone that will do car repairs for free I am still with Aotea Finance until further notice and I will do a top up... I tried to get a bank loan, which is cheaper, as everyone knows, but I don't clear enough money a week because I'm on the minimum Domestic Purposes Benefit... I receive 386 per week. The rent itself is 380. There is no accountant, even a PhD, that can budget this... Now, why would anyone [WINZ] refer me to a budget agency given the situation?... The simple fact is when the expenditure exceeds the income, "I'm in trouble". That is basically why I am reliant on charity [food bank]... What's the option? The option here is borrow, which I have done, heavily in debt. Friends, families and no one wants to be a friend anymore. And rightfully so...

Such participants accept that they simply have to pay more to access the necessities in life and go into debt merely to survive. Their focus is on the immediate situation, and the pragmatic strategy of borrowing to survive requires an acceptance of exploitation. Most of our participants were engaged with budgeting services because they were required to be by WINZ, which often presented this as a punishment.

A few participants reported positive experiences with some budgeting services, where some budget advisors acted as advocates for clients and helping them to access their entitlements for government support. However, budgeting was generally presented by our participants as an exercise in "ticking boxes" that failed to address the base causes of their financial difficulties. Budget advisors were depicted as telling our participants not to take on any more debt with fringe lenders, but they offered little in terms of sustainable solutions to the structural causes of their clients' debts. Budgeting services were overwhelmingly presented as agents of control that worked for WINZ:

> I've come across some budgeting people that's just full of shit, they just write down everything what Work and Income [WINZ] wants to see and yet they don't actually budget for budgeting... At the end of the day, whatever she had written down on that piece of paper just didn't add up to our income... She writes up what WINZ wants to see and sends you off. She doesn't actually help in any way so if we fall short on food, nothing like that... We've got so many debts and the majority of it is loaning and things like that just to support us to get by the next day. It's just brought us to more debt on top of debts because we can't afford to pay it back... Yeah, it's too frustrating because their [government welfare] laws have changed and they need so much more from us. We only get so much on the benefit or whatever benefit we're on. The travelling for budgeting and everything else they want us to go collect, they don't think about the gas, how expensive it is and things like that. Instead of going to WINZ for help, we'd rather just go to finance companies, knowing that you're gonna be in debt again, but it's the easiest way to get money to feed your family at that time.
>
> (Kali)

As Kali demonstrates, "There is commonly confusion between financial competence and financial difficulty" (Landvogt, 2006, p. 2). The debts of these participants are less the product of financial incompetence and more the product of inadequate resourcing and exploitation (Walker, 2012). Families who are living in poverty have to be good money managers, although they are vulnerable to exploitation and crises that get them into further strife. In these extracts we get a sense of the almost frivolous nature of budgeting as a form of governance of the poor (cf. Walker, 2011). There are broader, sanitising implications of these processes. Forcing families to undergo budgeting by strangers signals how the money that families use is not their own (Zelizer, 1994): it belongs to the state or the lenders. This reflects the estrangement of families from society (Simmel, 1908/1978), particularly when family priority setting for spending is disrupted by the competing priorities of budgeters and WINZ. Intense budgeting and micromanagement of these household budgets works to transform poverty into an "arithmetic problem" around how much money is coming in and how much is going out (Simmel, 1908/1978).

In contextualising their debts, our participants invoke a lack of sympathy from WINZ regarding the realities of their situations and comment on abusive responses to their requests for assistance (Hodgetts et al., 2013). Many prefer loans from fringe lenders to advances from WINZ due to the arduous process involved in getting welfare assistance, the length of time to get support, feelings of shame and poor treatment from staff. Fringe lenders are more accessible than welfare support. A key strategy for neoliberal governments in avoiding their obligations regarding welfare support is to make it so difficult for families to access support that they give up and go elsewhere, thus relieving the pressure on the government's balance sheet (Bourdieu, 1998; Bauman, 2005). Welfare reforms mean that families are pushed away from the state and into the hands of fringe lenders:

> Because if I go to WINZ: "This is the situation, I need this, I need that." They said, "Oh, well, it's your own fault if you struggle more." And they decline it... You're asking WINZ for $150 because food is so expensive and then they'll turn around and say, "I'm sorry, we can only do $100.00." I'm saying, "Oh, my God". I told them the price of the milk powder is $33.00 and I give them a letter as well from hospital saying that my daughter was premature labour. And that $100.00 was only a packet of nappies, one formula and my kids' lunch for the week... Sometimes you just cry. When your kids are sick you just feel so helpless and you can't give them what they need... Can't take them to the park or anything because there's hardly no food to pack to take... WINZ expect me to run here and there and yet I told them, "I just finished giving birth. I can't run here and there. Please, I'm already over my limits..." I had my two girls in the car and I had to sleep at Seaside Park with a new-born... Then Child Youth and Family Services might think I'm a bad Mum, with a new-born and nine-year-old and take my kids.
>
> (Tara)

Even when in acute need, many participants report being denied adequate support from WINZ as a matter of course (Hodgetts et al., 2013). As a result, they turn to fringe lenders:

> Because all my [welfare] entitlements and everything were all used up I could no longer get extra assistance from WINZ. So, yeah, I got the clothes truck in there, got my kids new shoes, got them some blankets. There was just nowhere else for me to go and access any other help... I just couldn't afford to go out and buy in one go. And it's no credit check or anything like that so you get the approval, make a payment, they get their payment and then away the payments go. It's easy to accumulate dumb debt like that.
>
> (Tina)

Tina talks about a lack of adequate support from WINZ in meeting the basic necessities in life. Having to beg for food and charity is a demeaning experience for increasing numbers of people, both those living on benefits and the working poor (Dowler and O'Connor, 2012). Opting out of interactions with WINZ, like leaving abusive intimate relationships, can be frightening and have negative consequences, including becoming more vulnerable to fringe finance (Hodgetts et al., 2013). Both Tara and Tina are aware that they are forced to rely on debt to get by (Walker, 2012), even when they are also encouraged by institutions such as budgeting services to feel guilty about their situation. Forcing families to take on debt for basic necessities can be read as a form of indentured servitude. After all, it can take a lifetime to work off such debts. Buying things for one's children is also a way of feeling normal or at least ensuring that their children do not miss out. Debt allows for identity work and social inclusion. Through such processes, structural issues become personal and relational concerns (Simmel, 1903/1997).

There is an industry that lives off the poor and, according to our participants, workers within this industry are quite aggressive in encouraging debt. The fringe lending sector creates products that are designed to confuse debtors (*The Debt Resistors' Operations Manual*, 2012). Lenders rarely use the negative term "debt" and instead use the positive term "credit" (Bell, 1976). Lenders hook families with pre-approved lines of credit (debt) that do not require them to increase their weekly payments. Fringe lenders also provide advice on how families might succeed in obtaining loans by making it appear as though they have sufficient income to service more debt:

> Being a clothing truck, I had $8.00 left to pay on my account thingy. Clothes Truck came around and he told me that I'm in credit for 500. I didn't really understand that, but he said I'm in credit by 500, I can shop, and then keep my payments at $30.00 a week. And I said, "No, no, I just want to pay off that $8.00. I don't wanna be with you anymore." I didn't get anything so he left...In a way they're good, you can pay as you wear, or pay as you use. A lot of people out there need new shoes for your kids, the truck's coming up the road so you're gonna go shopping, cos that used to be such a big thrill for me and the kids, we could go just out to the end of the driveway, do our shopping and they're like, "Yeah, we got new cloths," it was easier and that's the trap. Them and loan sharks are a big trap.
>
> (Charlie)

Participants talk openly about the sales tactics of clothing trucks and finance companies. People tend to be well aware that clothing trucks were exploiting them, but they see purchasing from trucks on credit as their only option. In terms of employee advice to enable our participants to be able to take on debt, Jade refers to her interactions with a car dealer and finance company, and the common tropes that are used to give people access to more debt:

> A good example would be get two letters saying you've got two boarders and then I'll give you a car so it shows you've got more money...Even at Instant Finance they will ask you in a roundabout way, "Do you have any boarders?" Then you'll say, "No," and they go, "Do you wanna get a boarder?" I'll be, "Yeah, more money, of course, anyone would want more money." "Find someone to board with you and then get a letter from them." Or they'll ask the person that wants a loan that's a boarder to get a letter off the person that they're living with saying they don't pay any money so all the money they get goes to them. So, that shows they can afford to get whatever they're applying for...Yes, they mislead you and they also tell you how to go about making the paperwork look good for the creditor so they accept your application.

It is evident from such accounts that debt is proactively encouraged in an unregulated market, where companies can prey on the poor. Participants are critical of this but they also see debt as their only option and are at times thankful for it. Clearly families participate in fringe lending out of necessity. A further complimentary explanation is that debt is in many respects abstract and a long-term concern, whereas shoes and clothing for children are real and immediate. Thus debt brings enjoyment and utility into their lives. This, in part, explains how families can be both critical of, and grateful for, the "assistance" that they receive from fringe lenders. People who are escaping an abusive relationship with WINZ can end up in another abusive relationship (with a finance company) due to their lack of resources, choices and life-restrained situations. <u>The relationship with fringe lenders is acknowledged as exploitative, but it is experienced as more generous and humane than those with WINZ (Hodgetts et al., 2013). Fringe lenders seem to be polite and "helpful" rather than punitive and nasty.</u>

In sum, debt exploitation is woven into our economic system and manifests in an overt form through the production and behaviour of welfare agencies and fringe lenders. Many families now avoid welfare offices to the point of preferring to take on private debt with clothing trucks and finance companies because these organisations treat them, on the surface at least, in a more humane manner. It is important to recognise that these vulnerable families exist in a structurally violent and chaotic landscape of often abusive and disordered services from which they must obtain basic support (Hodgetts et al., 2013). This landscape encompasses government and social services, such as budgeting and free-market "entrepreneurs" who run clothing trucks and finance companies. It is useful to think of everyday life for these families as an "obstacle course" that must be navigated (Boon and Farnsworth, 2011) and which is textured by conditionality and exploitation.

Debt, familial relationships and health

Further aspects of the relational nature of debt are enacted when participants are obliged to take on debt for partners, children and relatives, and to participate in culturally patterned practices and events. In several cases, when intimate relationships have ended, our participants are left responsible for debts that they have taken on for partners and the relatives of partners. Some have acted as guarantors on loans for a relative without realising that on this person's death they would be left to pay the loans. Participants have taken on such loans for others with bad credit on the agreement that those being assisted would make the repayments. However, this does not always happen. Not paying others back for such assistance is traditionally seen as a moral transgression. For families who are living in poverty, this is a fact of life, where relationships under pressure can prove to be chaotic and disposable. Worry about becoming socially isolated or dislocated from important cultural relationships also drives fringe lending. This section explores these intimate relational dynamics of debt as well as the health consequences of debt.

Below we provide three examples of different participants accumulating debts for others that exemplify some of these relational dynamics of personal debt. Amelia took on loans for extended family members, including her ex-partner's mother, in an attempt to ease the burden of her daily life:

> We're completely in debt?!... We're got personal loans from taking out for other people, even having to pick up debts that don't even belong to us like my ex-mother in law passed on so we've had to pick up her debt. Yeah, it's quite hard going... Probably at least $40,000 cos over the years of building up and helping others out...

Amelia's account reflects how easily such a situation can arise in these under-resourced lifeworlds. Such debts are perceived as simply being an inequitable part of life that participants have limited ability to resolve. By proxy they become consolidated into one's own debts. Jade provides an example of why such situations arise out of concern for others rather than from financial incompetence:

> It was because my son's biological family, his biological Nana, at the time she was going through rough stuff, but she really needed money and I was able to get it for her. I said, "That's fine," and I got a couple of grand and she was supposed to make the weekly payments, but that didn't happen.

Here we can see how debt is not just a personal issue for our participants; familial relations are often central to their accumulation of debts. Such relational aspects are not lost on fringe lenders, who work to implicate relatives in the debts of family members through guarantor schemes. Our participants often feel obliged to "support" their family members and end up taking on further debt that they cannot afford to pay off. This produces further indentured servitude to fringe lenders and their investors. For example, Ofa discussed such a debt with a finance company, resulting from her being forced to act as a guarantor in order to protect her children and avoid abuse from her ex-partner:

> Apparently it's $9,000 and something. Not for me. It was my partner from 15 years ago... I don't see why I should have to pay anything

towards that. I signed the contract. I should have thought of that before. But in my situation, I was forced to sign a document, which I had no choice but to. But I was thinking of my kids' safety at the time – and myself as well. So, I've been avoiding him.

Debt is embedded in relationships, and it can provide a means of avoiding harm and abuse for relatives and for meeting one's familial and often culturally patterned obligations. Debt for others can be read as stemming from naïvety. However, it is also an example of helping strategies that occur within communities of limited means, and which can backfire at considerable personal cost. Such debts can also allow participants to care for others and they often seem less hazardous or pressing when meeting the immediate needs of others. Such acts of kindness or responses to coercion are also associated with the disruption of familial relationships when recipients do not reciprocate familial aid (cf. Simmel, 1908/1978).

It is particularly wretched when inequities in society require certain communities to take on exploitative loans in order to continue their culturally patterned relationships and practices. This was apparent for Māori and Pacific Island households. Cultural relations surfaced with reference to annual rituals and unanticipated events that carry obligations to provide contributions to collective events. Again, the first port of call is not the welfare agency but fringe lenders:

> I used to ring around the debt collectors [finance companies] – that's what I call them – debt collectors. I ring them up and I said, "My sister died or my father died, I've got no money, is it alright if I miss this week's payment?" That money stays back and that's the money I need then. Because what it is then, the island style is you've gotta donate money. It's $100.00 per head that you put money in, and then you've gotta have food to take along as well... I'm actually putting myself into more debt [both financial and cultural], because by delaying on that, even though you tell them that, I know I'm gonna be penalised down the line.
>
> (Marina)

These families struggle to ensure the dignity of self and others through contributions to cultural events such as funerals. The alternative to contributing to such events is shame and possibly exclusion. One has to take on debt in order to meet one's obligations as a daughter, son, mother, father, cousin and community member. Such accounts reflect how cultural obligations and mutually supportive practices that are indigenous to particular groups in the Pacific have been morphed through colonialism and the imposition of a European monetary system that quantifies contributions to collective life. These accounts exemplify and extend Simmel's (1908/1979) proposition that money can pervert sociocultural and interpersonal relations, and impoverish community life.

Another relational source of debt comes from ensuring healthcare for others. As a core budgeting practice that is associated with families that have been facing poverty for some time (Zelizer, 1994), participants earmark money, or put it aside and prioritise it over other needs. Money for a child's health is the most precious for our participants. Earmarking funds for this purpose weaves debt into the child–parent relationship in a way that challenges the rationalising and dehumanising functions of monetary exchange. This practice allows participants to maintain a sense of self as good parents who provide for their children at all costs. Debt is simply a means of enacting one's parental obligations. For example, Ofa borrows money to address her daughter's health problems:

> I paid gas last week to get to the hospital – twice, to get there and back the next day... But I don't care, it was for her. I went out of my way to borrow money wherever I can, not even thinking about how I'm gonna pay them back... I've borrowed money for medication, if I needed medication for the kids, or borrowed money to get to the doctors... I just explain myself and ask, "Are you okay to wait till next week? I can't give it back to you till the following week".

Participants report being more likely to go into debt to preserve the health of loved ones over their own health. A fear of debt leads many to neglect their own health. Their limited funds are more likely to go to servicing debts and ensuring the health of their children. Participants such as Ofa express self-justification in taking on such debts as it is simply what needs to be done. Through such practices, debt becomes an object of care, compassion and responsibility towards others.

As well as supporting a view of one's self as being able to take care of one's children despite living in poverty, the strain of such debts can come at a personal cost. A growing body of research points to the mental and physical health consequences of debt (Sweet et al., 2013). The stress and burden of debt are associated with reduced self-worth, and lower physical and mental health (Weare, 2006; Walker, 2011). As a social determinant of health, debt gets under the skin and into the heads of our participants through processes of embodied deprivation (Hodgetts et al., 2007). For example, Yvonne reflected on how debt infiltrates and weighs on her mind: "I just can't concentrate. My mind is all over the place...Thinking about how we are going to do this...It is always money weighs heavily...". The health consequences of the stress, anxiety and depression that are brought on by debt were not lost on participants: "Debt can cause you so many health issues, it's not funny. It really can..." (Lorna).

Participants invoke the consequences of financial stress on personal relationships, particularly between intimate partners. Kim spoke of how stress, anxiety and constant worry owing to her financial situation has become all-consuming to the point of leaving her fatigued, and disrupting her ability to plan for the future and move the family forward. Debt traps Kim in the here and now of poverty:

> The DPB [Domestic Purposes Benefit] only pays the essentials. There is no extras to do hire purchase, but I'd done it and it's unbelievably a struggle. You go to bed worried, you wake up worried, the anxieties go up to the roof. It's shocking. You're waiting for people to knock on your door to repossess something. Then when it comes to the simple stuff like going to see WINZ for food grants you just can't do it because your anxieties gone to the roof because I've gone and put myself through all this financial stress. When it comes to the real stuff [trying to forge a better life for her family], what I should be doing, I can't do it because I just haven't got that energy. I haven't got that stamina to move forward because I've dragged myself backwards.

This extract invokes the emotionally taxing impact of debt that occupies debtors, and reduces their ability to comply with the conditions of welfare support and to respond to poverty. Such constant strain and fatigue are associated by our participants with further interpersonal tensions and disruptions. For example, Eva feels shame and fatigue because of her inability to pay for necessities such as food and power, as well as services, such as the doctor or pharmacy. She has focused on paying off the majority of her debts to clothing trucks and finance companies, but this has come at considerable personal and interpersonal cost:

> It makes me worry and upset and I'm feeling unwell all the time...I feel sick all the time. Struggle, struggle – that's the main thing and inside to me I feel hurt and I feel sad...Sad because of the situation of the life I got now...I know I talk rough to my children

sometimes because of the anger, I got it. Because of the stress, I got it. I love my children and cos sometimes I really go mad and swear to them... And sometimes Joy's [daughter] wanted to talk to me to say something and I say to Joy, "I don't want to talk. When you know it's a lot of things in my head, don't talk. Leave me in peace, otherwise I'll go crazy and I'll end into the hospital again and I don't want to go to the hospital."

Here we see financial stress impacting negatively on a mother's relationship with her children and partner, with references to frequent arguments over money and the strain of long-term hardship. The cumulative need to borrow from fringe lenders, family and friends puts a strain on relationships and leaves such participants feeling unsupported and abandoned.

Over time, debt contributes to social isolation and reduces the size of social networks. Debt leads to families avoiding social visits or having friends over because they lack the food to host others. They also avoid cultural and community events due to their inability to contribute their share. Families can also see a reduction in the quality of their extended family relations as when family members who have loaned money to a household call in the favour:

> It's getting to the point where because I ask so much of my family they think they can just ring me up and say, "can you come here now"? They're bullying me now. It's cos I owe them so much they think they can just ring me up and go, "Oh, can you come to Mangere now, blah, blah, blah. Need a ride, blah, blah, blah?" I go, "Do you know I live in Manurewa and you all live in Mangere? The travelling costs – $20.00 gets me to Mangere and then the car's empty already." They've got that thing against me, you owe me... I think it causes a big problem between me and my husband. I take my frustration out on him and I know that money's a big problem with us, that we don't get enough money. It frustrates me, it gets me pissed off. I get all angry. I've got no one else to take it out on but him.
>
> (Kali)

This extract reflects how the nexus of familial relationships within which such participants reside can be put under pressure and soured by debt. Kali reports being treated like a servant by her siblings and being in conflict as a result with her partner. These processes are not unique to

New Zealand or to this time period. Historical work demonstrates that debt can break up families (Graeber, 2011).

Several participants provided further support for such impacts of debt on relationships. Through such accounts we see how debt can disrupt interpersonal processes such as grieving. Melanie also communicates how debt can function as a trap that imprisons families in servient relationships where they must pay endless tributes (interest) when attempting to service loans:

> It's just causing us more debt cos you're paying crazy amounts of interest. Then that is bad for us. It affects me...My worst thing is, when things get really bad, I end up drinking cos I can't cope anymore. That's making wrong choices because of the pressure of the stress. Trying to work out how things are gonna be able to get better. Then that plays on my whanau [family]...Having all our stuff in the pawn shop and trying think of how we're gonna be able to get that out, that causes arguments as well. It's just a big circle...I'd probably say 100% of my drinking, pretty much, is to numb, to forget about all the rubbish that's going on...I don't sleep at night, cos I'm worrying about it. There ends up being lies to cover up. We wouldn't argue as much, there wouldn't be so much frustration in our house causing arguments. The kids are having to put up with us arguing cos we're constantly worrying about how to get money for this and that and then we'll argue cos my husband'll say, "The kids can't do this." And I'm, "But it's not fair for them to miss out."...I'm always sick. I'm either always drinking to numb myself, or always upset. I cry a lot, so I've probably got some kind of depression from it all and our marriage has had such bad points from all of this that we're probably very lucky to still be together. It's caused that much of an impact on our lives.

Tammy's debt contributes to her substance misuse that is impacting her physical and mental health. This extract also reflects the multiplying impacts of trying to service finance company debt, get one's belongings back from the pawn shop, provide for a family, and deal with constant worries about money, alcohol abuse, a lack of sleep, emotional and physical fatigue, depression, dishonesty, crying and deteriorating familial relations.

Briefly, these accounts reveal how debt money is dangerous, unhealthy money. It is a hazard that leaves families at the mercy of an unmerciful debt industry. The use of debt money is embedded in and reproduces exploitative social relations (Zelizer, 1994) that impact family life and the ability of participants to take part in cultural activities that are of core importance to them.

Conclusion

Punitive and exploitative responses to families in need are justified when dominant group discursive constructs of debtors as frivolous, financially illiterate and require paternalistic micromanagement (Landvogt, 2006; Hodgetts et al., 2013). Corresponding interventions aimed at helping families often focus solely on correcting such perceived personal deficits rather than addressing the structural causes of poverty and debt (Bauman, 2005; Standing, 2011). Panoptic practices, such as forcing families to repeatedly access budgeters, do little to change their circumstances. Such practices cynically re-individualise poverty, debt and "dependency" as personal deficits. The rationalising function of money as a unitary measure or abstraction that is devoid of the complexities of human relations (Zelizer, 1994) also allows for the depoliticising and smoothing-out of the parasitic behaviour of lenders, and its relational and health consequences for families participating in our research. In the process, the consequences of current economic arrangements that benefit the underserving wealthy in profiteering from poverty and debt are obscured (Boyer, 2006). Monetary processes of debt flatten out the relationships between debtors and lenders, and obscure the impact of the actions of the latter on the former (cf. Simmel, 1908/1978).

Present relationships between debtors and lenders are ironic when we consider how neoliberal pundits champion the independence of social actors and deny the importance of interdependence in society (Bourdieu, 1998). We are all to achieve economic and social independence (Standing, 2011). One might ask who the real beneficiaries are in this setup. Further, the interdependence of groups in society is exemplified by the reliance of the underserving wealthy on tribute from the poor. Demanding, crippling tributes morph short-term loans into long-term servitude, as has occurred at different times throughout history (Graeber, 2011). Families in need are subject to exploitation by more affluent members of society. Such relational structures undermine civic participation, democracy and the wellbeing of families. The current monitory conquest of civil society by speculative capital has been linked to societal shifts towards more autocratic and tyrannical forms of government, and social unrest (Graeber, 2011).

A similar situation led to the fall of Rome and is currently undermining our society.

Participant accounts that were compiled for this research reveal the functioning of debt bondage. Small loans are topped up as needs arise to the point where participants become bonded to fringe lenders and can only service the interest (tribute). This is what many financial products are designed to do: render families as servants of speculative capital administered on behalf of creditors (new gentry) through institutions (overseers) that prey on the needs of the poor. Speculative capital works against the poor in unregulated fringe markets that are propped up by the dismantling of welfare states and collective forms of sustenance for families in need (cf. Marx, 1844). The accounts of these families reveal a significant contraction. On the one hand, they know that they are being exploited by fringe lenders. On the other, they are avoiding further abuse from welfare agencies and need the fringe lenders. Debt is a pragmatic response to immediate needs, such as clothing and food, and to gain a sense of belonging in society. It is invoked by our participants as a taken-for-granted means to an end. Debt provides a means of addressing hunger and the need for shelter, but it also alienates families from future income (cf. Marx, 1844). This is why our participants worry about the implications of taking on debt for their futures, while knowing that they need debt to get by.

Debt is not created by the poor; it is cultivated by the underserving wealthy and their desire for high returns on capital investment. Therefore, to address the personal debt issues of these families, we need to address the intergroup inequities of our debt society. This is unlikely to occur in a society where formal documents, such as that from the New Zealand Treasury, quantify the rapid growth in household debt while asserting that "High levels of debt are not necessarily a problem, provided adequate income is available for debt servicing" (Henderson and Scobie, 2009, p. 31). Such statements reflect the institutionalisation of the very neoliberal ideology that takes lives (Cromby and Willis, in press; Walker, 2011, 2012; Hodgetts et al., 2013). As long as tribute is paid, the treasury appears to have no problem with the exploitative practices that are endemic in the fringe lending sector and its implications for the lives of families who are in need.

Something is wrong with a society that places an emphasis on poor people paying their way and not getting something for nothing, while allowing investors to profit from misery, and the horrifying health and relational consequences of debt for families who are in need. Resistance to exploitative and harmful debt practices and corresponding debt servitude have been around for millennia (Graeber, 2011). Internationally, contemporary groups such as Srikedebt.com are challenging the re-emergence of debt slavery. A modern jubilee advocated by such groups that reinstates the ancient practice of forgiving existing debts, along with the regulation of practices of usurial debt by the underserving wealthy, warrants serious consideration. Furthermore, we need to provide systems of welfare support that do not require people to access fringe lenders in order to survive and participate in family, community and cultural life. After all, the speculative practices and debts of the underserving wealthy are forgiven through bailouts for financial institutions. Why are the poor not also afforded such second chances?

Acknowledgement

The Family 100 Project was initiated and funded by the Auckland City Mission.

Notes

1. Neoliberalism has taken an intense form in New Zealand through the emphasis of successive governments on shifting the coordination of economic and social life from the state to private interests. Almost all domains of life have been subordinated to market rationality and ideally opened to competition through deregulation and privatisation. Emphasis is placed on self-reliance and the expansion of market interests through state legislative actions that promote economic liberalisation. This has seen a massive increase in managerialism and bureaucracy in support of private interests and to the detriment of families who are living in poverty.
2. Drawing exercises involved our asking participants to think about and draw the role of money and debt in their lives. They pictured organisations that they interact with and relationships that affect, and are affected by, debt. Such visual exercises increase reflection and engagement on the part of participants in the interview process. They give form to issues that can be difficult for people to discuss in the abstract and enable participants to contribute to the interview agenda by highlighting issues, processes and events that researchers may not have anticipated. In this regard, drawing exercises are similar to photoelicitation exercises and other "breaching experiments" in the ethnomethodological sense (Hodgetts et al., 2011).

References

Bauman, Z. (2005). *Work, Consumerism and the New Poor*. London: McGraw-Hill.
Bell, D. (1976). *The Cultural Contradictions of Capitalism*. New York: Basic Books.
Boon, B. and Farnsworth, J. (2011). Social exclusion and poverty: Translating social capital into accessible resources. *Social Policy & Administration*, 45, 507–524.

Bourdieu, P. (1998). *Action of Résistance: Against the Tyranny of the Market.* New York: Free Press.
Boyer, K. (2006). Reform and resistance: A consideration of space, scale and strategy in legal challenges to welfare reform. *Antipode,* 38, 22–40.
Cromby, J. and Willis, M. (2014). Nudging into subjectification: Governmentality and psychometrics. *Critical Social Policy,* 34(2), 241–259.
Dowler, E. and O'Connor, D. (2012). Rights-based approaches to addressing food poverty and food insecurity in Ireland and UK. *Social Science and Medicine,* 74, 44–51.
Flyvbjerg, B., Landman, T. and Schram, S. (2012). *Real Social Science: Applied Phronesis.* Cambridge: Cambridge University Press.
Graeber, D. (2011). *Debt: The First 5000 Years.* New York: Melville.
Green, K. (2012). *Life on a Low Income.* Bristol: Resolution Foundation.
Henderson, K. and Scobie, G. (2009). *Household Debt in New Zealand,* Working Paper 09/03. Wellington: New Zealand Treasury.
Hodgetts, D., Chamberlain, K. and Groot, S. (2011). Reflections on the visual in community research and practice. In Reavey, Paula (ed.). *Visual Psychologies: Using and Interpreting Images in Qualitative Research.* London: Routledge, Chapter 20.
Hodgetts, D., Chamberlain, K., Groot, S. and Tankel, Y. (2013). Urban poverty, structural violence and welfare provision for 100 families in Auckland. *Urban Studies,* 5, 46–59.
Hodgetts, D., Chamberlain, K. and Radley, A. (2007). Health inequalities and homelessness: Considering material, relational and spatial dimensions. *Journal of Health Psychology,* 12, 709–725.
Landvogt, K. (2006). *Critical Financial Capacity: Developing an Alternative Model.* Australia: Good Shepherd Youth and Family Service.
Marx, K. (1844). Estranged labour. In Lemert, C. (ed.). *Economic and Philosophic Manuscripts of 1844.* Philadelphia: Westview, pp. 32–38.
Simmel, G. (1903/1997). The metropolis and mental life. In Frisby, D. and Featherstone, M. (eds.). *Simmel on Culture.* London: Sage, pp. 174–185.
Simmel, G. (1908/1978). *The Philosophy of Money* (Tom Bottomore and David Frisby trans). London: Routledge.
Standing. G. (2011). Behavioural conditionality: Why the nudges must be stopped – an opinion piece. *The Policy Press,* 19, 27–38.
Sweet, E., Nandi, A., Adam, E. and Mcade, T. (2013). The high price of debt: Household financial debt and its impact on mental and physical health. *Social Science and Medicine,* 91, 94–100.
The Debt Resisters' Operations Manual (2012), retrieved on 18 October 2013. Stikedebt.com.
Walker, C. (2011). "Responsibilizing" a healthy Britain: Personal debt, employment, and welfare. *International Journal of Health Services,* 41, 525–538.
Walker, C. (2012). Personal debt, cognitive delinquency and techniques of governmentality: Neoliberal constructions of financial inadequacies in the UK. *Journal of Community & Applied Social Psychology,* 22, 533–538.
Weare, K. (2006). Globalization and free trade: Undermining human dignity. *Nature, Society, and Thought,* 19, 351–356.
Zelizer, V. (1994). *The Social Meaning of Money.* New York: Basic Books.

2
All Roads Lead to Finance: A Critical Overview of Debt in the USA

Daniel G. Cooper and Bradley D. Olson

Introduction

In the USA, in the aftermath of its Great Recession, much discussion has occurred about household and government debt and their ongoing role in a stagnant economic recovery. The media and the public have largely focused on government, big banks or the financial behaviour of people. In US psychology, often a largely uncritical discipline, there has been little beyond silence. Most debate about causes and consequences is too often framed from an individualistic perspective that focuses on personal behaviour without acknowledging the systemic drivers and the broader political economy of debt. The growing trade of psychologists who shape their own professional product around financial, one-on-one or group therapy represents the same, pitfall-filled lens. This individualistic framing effectively limits policy prescriptions and avoids addressing growing income and wealth inequality – inextricably linked to household debt – which has risen even more sharply following the Great Recession (Kochhar et al., 2011; Stiglitz, 2012). If debt results from problematic personal financial practices as opposed to business practices, why should governments intervene at all? Such individual-blame logic pervades dominant debt narratives, such as the first rallying cry that is often credited with giving a name to the Tea Party movement, when, in 2008, US television financial analyst Rick Santelli decried proposals for federal aid to homeowners as rewarding the "bad behaviour" of "losers" – referring to the US citizens who "made poor home purchase choices" (Etheridge, 2009). This chapter challenges this very narrative by analysing the antecedents and consequences of large household debt.

Our argument is that large household debt is primarily accounted for by market shifts and neoliberal public policies, making it a bigger political economy issue. Underlying the macronature of these financial harms to families – most often people who have lower incomes, and disproportionately people of colour – is human suffering and inequality juxtaposed with corporate profits, and therefore a psychological analysis becomes useful to understand both this harm and how its system is maintained.

Too often, psychological theory and practice, because of the discipline's excessive focus on the behaviours, attitudes and emotions of individual human beings, serves to reproduce narratives of personal responsibility. Psychologists design interventions that attempt to ameliorate the negative emotions and cope with, for example, losing a house to foreclosure, and then work to make that individual try to become more successful and responsible in the way in which they live their lives. Yet psychology truly does have more potential. We believe that psychological research, knowledge and practice can add much to the understanding of debt by situating individual experiences within a broader political economy and articulating how the field of psychology helps to reproduce person-centred narratives. We conclude by offering a psychological theory – based on a critical, liberation-oriented community psychology – that would play a stronger role in mobilising discourses of resistance to financialisation, debt-fuelled economic consumption and, hopefully, the rising inequality in the USA.

Defined as a percentage of disposable income, total household debt in the USA grew from approximately 70% in 1980 to, at its peak, nearly 130% in 2007 (Federal Reserve Bank of St. Louis, 2014). Although household debt has been declining slowly but steadily since 2007, it is still well above historical averages. During that same period (1980–2007), defined as a percentage of gross domestic product (GDP), household debt rose from 45% to, at its peak, nearly 96%. Debt has since eased but it remains at the extraordinarily high rate of 77% in early 2014 (Federal Reserve Bank of St. Louis, 2014). The former figure illustrates the historically unprecedented debt burden that is faced by households, while the latter underscores the extent to which fundamental economic changes are responsible.

One of the most glaring economic shifts is that economic growth has become reliant on debt-fuelled consumption. Simultaneously, over the last 30-plus years, economic growth has largely been due to the expanded role of finance, often pseudomechanisms of trading such as the expansion of derivatives, rather than the authentic production of goods and provision of services. Newman (2009) describes this financialisation of the post-industrial economy as moving away from the production of actual widgets (goods) to the production of debt-related financial "widgets", such as mortgages and other debt-backed products. Financialisation – the increasing reliance on financial "innovation" and new investment-related products, and the increasing influence of global finance – is one of the most important determinants of household debt and a historic transfer of capital from those in struggling economic states to the top income brackets (Stiglitz, 2012).

The Great Recession, as we have covered, saw historical accumulations of household debt. Yet we cannot, as people have assumed, attribute these figures solely, or even primarily, to a sudden and sustained shift in the desire of families to take on greater debt. Several key interrelated macrotrends have led to the historic accumulation. First, the economy has produced decades of income stagnation, partially due to a bias towards flexible labour (e.g. part-time rather than full-time jobs). Second, neoliberal policy regimes have deregulated and accommodated the finance industries, which has facilitated the rise of financialisation. Third, governments have rolled back welfare provision and the social safety net. These trends, as has been discussed extensively elsewhere (see Immergluck, 2009; Newman, 2009; Stiglitz, 2012), are part and parcel of a neoliberal deregulatory turn in the US political economy that has paved the way for the unchecked expansion of debt products. This expansion has proved to be highly profitable for global finance but devastating for households.

To understand the rise of financialisation and indebtedness, it is important to look more closely at the ethos of neoliberal policy. Drawing from others, we define neoliberalism as the simultaneous removal of government regulation, services and welfare provision, and the implementation of liberal market-oriented economic processes (Krippner, 2005; Hackworth, 2007). There has already been robust scholarship on neoliberalism, though it is nonetheless important to acknowledge the ways in which its processes psychologically shape and sustain indebtedness. Psychology, in contrast, can also help to situate personal debt within a broader ecology, illuminating the ways in which debt impacts individuals, families and communities. This latter form of critical liberation-oriented community psychology offers promise in better challenging the neoliberal narrative that is so pernicious in reproducing and sustaining family indebtedness.

The production of debt in the USA

Given the alarmingly high level of income inequality in the wake of the Great Recession, again a product of decades of debt-fuelled consumption and stagnant wages, it cannot be overlooked that the primary hardship has been felt by households of colour. While the overall US poverty rate rose from 11% in 2006 to nearly 14% in 2012 (US Census Historical Poverty Tables), the rates for households of colour were comparatively severe. Between 2005 and 2009, accounting for the boom and bust of the recession, white households on average lost 16% of their wealth, yet Hispanic households lost a whopping 66% and black households 53%. The white-to-Hispanic and white-to-black wealth ratios – 15:1 and 19:1, respectively – were recently at their highest levels in 25 years (Kochhar et al., 2011). As striking as these figures are, these loss estimates often soften the impact because they do not typically account for debt. By some estimates, accounting for debt adds a whole percentage point to the poverty rate (Pressman and Scott, 2009). That is a significant amount. Extending this argument, current government poverty rates, because they ignore debt, are likely to be conservative. Deleveraging – that is, debt reduction – has been slow in the USA. US households in 2013 had deleveraged by 12% since the debt peak in late 2008, but the total household debt in 2013 was still 34% higher than in 2004, before the bubble had fully inflated. Consumers in 2013 had also defaulted on their debts approximately three times as quickly as they did in 2004. Further, as of the end of 2013, there were signs that consumer borrowing had again begun to rise (Federal Reserve Bank of New York, 2013). Banks were increasingly willing to lend, and consumers appeared to be growing more confident in the US economy. But since the recovery, the economy has been anything but robust, and very little has changed in terms of household income distribution. Indeed, this recent uptick could indicate a return to previous debt-driven consumption patterns. We now turn our attention to three key co-occurring, interdependent and interrelated determinants of debt in the USA: stagnant wages, financialisation and the removal of government safety nets.

Stagnant wages

First, stagnant wages over the past several decades have played a major role in the explosion of debt in the USA. According to Economic Policy Institute data, between the years 1959 and 1979, the wages of American workers grew mostly in tandem with productivity. Since 1979, real wages have flattened out and remained stagnant, while the nation's economic productivity has continued to grow steadily during the last 35 years (Palley, 2007). While the hands that guide these economic trends are all but invisible, the psychological impact on the average worker can only be called traumatic, choking out more work with far less compensation.

And there is other evidence. Between 2003 and 2013, compensation of private sector workers (adjusted for inflation) has risen by approximately 2%, while broader national economic growth has risen by nearly 20% (Shierholz and Mishel, 2013). Technological advancements and greater international trade are two factors that are partially responsible for this wage suppression but they do not explain the full picture. The cost of capital has declined steadily since 1980, while at the same time free trade agreements have lowered barriers to trade, which has incentivised new investments in technology and the search for cheaper labour abroad. Meanwhile, US labour has remained relatively fixed in place.

Government policy plays a major role in these capital–labour disparities. Lower interest rates incentivise firms to invest in technological efficiencies and to seek lower labour costs in larger global markets (Giovannoni, 2014). Both developments have reduced the bargaining power of labour and placed downward pressure on wages. Keynsian policies are used to ensure that government plays a strong role in providing jobs, at least partially redistributing income and correcting market failures. The once normative ideas about correcting market failure have been replaced, quite strategically, by the narrative of government failure. Government, quite uncritically, is accepted as being inefficient and corrupt compared with the market. Redistribution has been recast as a barrier to efficient market competition, and labour flexibility (e.g. less secure, short-term, part-time, contract hourly employment) has been embraced by corporations and government alike as a necessary feature of a competitive economy (Peck, 2001; Hackworth, 2007).

If there is any doubt that wage suppression is a central concern, one need only look at the fact that the share of corporate profits going to labour has declined over the past several decades, and the majority of wage increases have gone to the top percent of income earners. For example, from 1980 to 2012, corporations have ballooned the CEO to worker compensation ratio from 38:1 to 273:1 (Mishel, 2013; Giovannoni, 2014). The vast majority of this outsized profit has accrued in the financial industry, the rise of which is inseparable from stagnant wages.

Financialisation

Financialisation, here focusing on the increasing role of finance in the economy, is a second important and interrelated driver of household debt. The finance, insurance and real-estate (FIRE) sectors have grown in importance to the US economy since approximately 1980. Again, as phrased by Newman (2009), financial products such as mortgage-backed securities became the post-industrial widget as the economy transitioned from commodity to finance production. In 1979, FIRE comprised 15.4% of US GDP, which rose to 20.4% by 2005, near the peak of the housing bubble (Palley, 2007). Also in 2005, housing-related production comprised approximately 23% of US GDP (Joint Center for Housing Studies, 2006). During this transition, GDP growth relied heavily on financial transactions, such as home mortgages, that could then be packaged together into securities to be sold to investors and speculators. As real-estate prices escalated, the more profitable these securities became, leading to the creation of greater and more complex securities backed by mortgages. In a healthy economy, households have increasing purchasing power to buy goods, which in turn increases GDP growth. Stagnant wage growth, however, necessitated a different path to economic expansion. This path involved the exchange of investment products in the financial sector backed by household mortgage debt. This rise to prominence of FIRE coincided with policy imperatives that were focused on deregulating the industry to encourage innovation while at the same time actively helping to drive demand for its products. Thus the increase in debt-leveraged transactions was actively driven by policy and financial firm competition rather than a sudden proliferation of consumer attitudes toward debt.

One of the most important factors that explains the rapid rise of financialisation is the systematic deregulation of the industry beginning in the early 1980s. We focus here on housing policy since mortgages are the largest source of household debt, and one of the most clear and consistent examples of neoliberal policy imperatives. The government's rolling back of federal housing regulation facilitated less stringent lending standards and greater competition for profits among lenders. The government also supported the expansion of the secondary mortgage market to encourage new private investment in housing. Prior to 1980, credit rationing ruled the day, with the majority of loans being made by depository institutions that lived or died by the quality of their loans. In the decades since and leading up to the housing crash, automated risk-based pricing helped to generate more loans, which were increasingly packaged as securitised by new players, such as mortgage brokers. This shifted housing away from its actual use to a commodity that anyone could invest in through mortgage-backed securities.

Throughout the 1980s, federal policies sought to deregulate the industry, which unleashed these supposed innovations. Here we provide a few key examples. The 1980 Depository Institutions Deregulation and Monetary Control Act permitted lenders to make higher-cost loans, which would become a hallmark of subprime lending. Similarly, the 1982 Alternative Mortgage Transaction Parity Act overrode states' ability to regulate new alternative, adjustable interest rate loans which would also later become hallmarks of subprime lending. State oversight was crippled because lenders could simply opt out of state regulation in favour of less restrictive federal regulation (Krugman, 2009). President Reagan's Commission on Housing exempted mortgage-backed securities from taxation, and then the Secondary Mortgage Market Enhancement Act of 1984 allowed the private sector to get in on the act of securitising mortgages, all while being exempt from more stringent forms of state regulation. The Tax Reform Act of 1986 provided more tax deductions and increased incentives for homeowners to refinance and use their homes as banks to fund non-home-related expenses. As a result, new and often predatory lending products emerged around home refinance. All of these actions further expanded the role of housing finance in the economy (Green and Wachter, 2007). Deregulation incentivised the home finance industry to originate and sell as many mortgages as possible and greatly expanded the number of non-bank brokers and debt-related products.

In the 1990s and the 2000s, subprime lending expanded, as investor appetite for risky but more profitable mortgage-related securities grew. This demand necessitated expanding credit to new homeowners. Many low-income minority households in urban areas, who were traditionally excluded from prime lending, bore the brunt of the riskiest subprime loans (Rugh and Massey, 2010; Immergluck, 2011). Although traditional banks were regulated by the Community Reinvestment Act, loans made by mortgage brokers, which exclusively sold loans to the secondary market, were not. Such companies were responsible for half of the subprime originations by 2002 (Joint Center for Housing Studies, 2004). This brought about a dual regulatory system in which more capital flowed into higher-risk and higher-cost loans, with more abusive terms and less regulation. As a result, the most vulnerable communities were exposed to a less regulated and more predatory market of subprime mortgage products. There is extensive evidence that many subprime borrowers – by some estimates as many as half – could have qualified for a prime mortgage loan but were instead pushed into higher-cost loans, which were more profitable to investors (Newman, 2009). This was particularly true for African Americans, who were consistently more likely than white borrowers to receive a subprime loan with predatory terms regardless of their creditworthiness (Howell, 2006; Wyly et al., 2006).

Housing commodification illustrates financialisation so well because it contributed so centrally to debt and wealth loss after the recession. However, it is only one part of a larger financialisation puzzle that includes corporate practices, monetary policy and the global interconnectedness of finance. Corporate success is increasingly measured by stock-market performance, and outsized executive pay is often tied to short-term stock prices and financial performance, allowing executives to accumulate larger shares of corporate profits at the expense of worker wages (Stiglitz, 2012). Corporate profits have diverged from nominal GDP in each of the last two recessions, and as of 2013 they are diverging yet again. This indicates that corporate success is not aligned with the growth of the economy and the growth of worker wages. Additionally, federal monetary policy has been highly accommodative in keeping interest rates low over recent decades, which has helped to drive debt-fuelled consumption by households and corporations alike. US Federal Reserve chairman Alan Greenspan famously professed his belief that housing prices would continue rising in perpetuity and thus low interest rates would help to continue the endless rally. Finally, a growing concentration of large financial firms has also ensured that financial trends and investment products, particularly related to housing, are not limited to the USA. Indeed, similar housing finance and investment led to over-leveraging in many other countries. In summary, financialisation is also intertwined with stagnant wages, as profits are increasingly divorced from GDP and accumulated by the top income earners (Palley, 2007; Stiglitz, 2012).

The shrinking safety net

The third central perpetrator of high household debt is the rolling back of federal government welfare provision and the social safety net. Since the 1990s, welfare reform has shifted from providing benefits to citizens, to setting benchmarks and performance standards that are aimed at encouraging recipients to seek work. The 1996 Welfare Reform Act allowed states to limit mothers from receiving additional benefits for new children, limit the time during which a recipient could receive benefits, and add employment requirements to receiving benefits. These reforms have been championed by both the right and the left to reduce welfare rolls, yet empirical studies tell a more nuanced story. One indicates that the Welfare Reform Act accounted for approximately 12% of the decline in welfare use and roughly 7% of employment increases, although it was clear that the Earned Income Tax Credit and a general booming economy played much larger roles (Grogger, 2006). However, the reductions in welfare recipients were also short lived and have declined since the Great Recession. The use of Temporary Assistance to Needy Families has continued to decline since it was enacted as a part of the Welfare Reform Act, even during the recession. Even though more families need assistance, fewer are receiving it. What tends not to be considered in the welfare reform claims is that households have increasingly been turning to debt for everyday living expenses – and not just for consumption, for the safety net itself (Montgomerie, 2011). In 2004, by some estimates, for an average of about four months a year, a third of households used credit cards for basic living expenses (Wheary and Draut, 2005). Poor families have also increased their use of credit cards during periods of unemployment (Sullivan, 2008). Nearly 40% of adults struggled with medical debt and often turned to credit cards even before the Great Recession (Doty et al., 2005). The removal of the safety net is particularly insidious for younger (less government support for higher education) and older Americans (less support for senior medical care) (Montgomerie, 2011). These scenarios, for both groups, lead to greater debt accrual.

The removal of government safety nets, like stagnant income growth and a financialised economy, helps to create another pathway to profits for the increasing number of financial firms that are searching for them. The removal of government intervention and the increase in financial firms and lending products, conventional liberal market theories might argue, is merely an example of markets adapting and innovating in order to connect credit with those who were previously excluded from access. By contrast, David Harvey's (1999) theory of capital predicts that government deregulation and more competition between financial players results only in uneven capital accumulation. Deregulation incentivises more competition between firms for new and greater sources of revenue (from people), which leads to overspeculation, more risk-taking (by firms rather than people) and, finally, overextension. Harvey's model takes on the convention neoliberal assumption that financial products respond to demand. Instead, this view illustrates that market competition necessarily works to secure profits for lending institutions at the expense of the consumer, who is only left with debt and ultimately destroyed wealth. A similar perspective is held by Wyly and colleagues

(2006, 2007), who discuss how capital accumulation necessitates spatial inequality, where low-income and minority households are segmented into separate housing markets. Segregation then facilitates a process whereby firms can repeatedly extract profits from the most vulnerable people and places through destructive yet profitable lending. Thus, after the dust settled after the foreclosure crisis and recession, it was segregated African American neighbourhoods that have borne the brunt of devastating foreclosures, debt and loss of wealth (Rugh and Massey, 2010). Similarly, Stiglitz (2012) notes that a deregulated and financialised economy brings about "rent-seeking", where the affluent create by taking it away from others, rather than from an expansion of wealth for all. Increasingly for Americans, there is no road to stability and prosperity; it is blocked by stagnant wages and a shrinking safety net. Instead, all roads lead to finance.

However, even though households have experienced high debt and loss in the past, no other recession of the last 30 years showed severe contagion effects throughout the economy. The Great Recession was so widespread in its devastation because financial institutions themselves had accumulated so much debt leverage. This has even been acknowledged by former chairman Greenspan (Robb, 2014), one of the biggest proponents of deregulation and liberal economic principles. Given this point, reinforcing the individual-level blame narrative becomes even more important for the power structure to maintain the status quo of building wealth for the few at the expense of the many.

Debt and the ecology of consequences for individuals and communities

To this point we have highlighted the political economy of debt. However, it is important to connect debt-related determinants to the experiences of individuals, and to understand how those experiences ripple throughout families, neighbourhoods and communities over time. Psychology as a discipline is uniquely poised to contribute a nuanced understanding of debt, not by merely focusing on its symptoms but by elaborating on debt ecologies – the ways in which indebtedness shapes the life outcomes of people and places, and how these outcomes reshape policies and practices that are related to debt. We briefly summarise the interconnectedness of different forms of personal and household debt (these terms are used interchangeably, depending on the unit of analysis being referenced, to describe consumer debt). Then we provide a focused summary of how debt impacts the lives of people and places.

Given the rise of the financialised economy and the erosion of government safety nets, it is no surprise that individuals and households have amassed different forms of debt. By a large margin, mortgage debt remains the primary type of US household debt. At the end of 2013, households possessed nearly USD 8 trillion (US dollars) in mortgage debt, accounting for approximately 70% of the US total. Student loan debt comprised nearly 10% – over USD 1 trillion – of the total. And finally, auto loans and credit cards made up 8% and 6% of the total consumer debt balance, respectively (Federal Reserve Bank of New York, 2013). Although these forms of debt differ slightly in their origin and determinants, all derive from the same problematic political economy mechanisms that are critiqued throughout this chapter.

The placement of mortgage-related debt as the primary category is unsurprising given its growing importance to the US economy leading up to the Great Recession. It is well documented that subprime loans – which accounted for 23% of all home loans in 2006 and had such features as adjustable interest rates and balloon payments – were more likely than prime loans to be delinquent or to eventually lead to a foreclosure (Immergluck, 2010). Nationally, the number of 90-day-plus delinquent mortgages reached nearly 10% in 2010. As of 2013 it was less than 5% (New York Federal Reserve Bank, 2013).

As mentioned previously, in the absence of rising real incomes and the continual rolling back of the government safety net, much of the resulting credit card usage, included in the category of "revolving loan debt", is related to necessities such as medical bills or typical living expenses (Montgomerie, 2011). Total revolving debt in the USA increased approximately 1,800% between 1980 and 2008. After falling by 18% between 2008 and 2011, it has been rising slowly but steadily since. Almost 10% of credit card balances were more than 90 days delinquent in 2013 (Federal Reserve Bank of St. Louis, 2014). Included in the revolving loan debt category are payday loans – small-dollar loans that often carry predatory features. The low-income individuals who use these loans – often out of necessity – get locked into a cycle of increasing interest payments that snowballs and becomes unmanageable over time.

Alarmingly, student loan debt in the USA, and specifically delinquency, has been increasing more rapidly than any other form of debt since the Great Recession. In 2004 the average college graduate who finished a degree accumulated roughly USD 19,000 worth of debt, whereas the average 2012 graduate finished with over USD 29,000, an increase of 63%. Approximately 65% of college graduates had some student loan debt upon completion, which had risen to 71% by 2012 (Project on

Student Debt, 2013). As a result, 90-day delinquency on student loans has jumped by over 50% just between 2011 and 2013 (Federal Reserve Bank of New York, 2013). Rising tuition costs have outpaced wages. For-profit universities have grown, the federal government has cut student loans, the job market has weakened and thus all of these factors have conspired to place the younger generations at a large disadvantage.

A recent study nicely summarises the combined financial impact: 35% of all Americans have debt currently assigned to a collection agency, meaning that those payments are at least 180 days delinquent (Ratcliffe et al., 2014). The average delinquency amount is USD 5,000. Although the relationship between debt and income is not insignificant – poorer individuals have more – the effect is not strong, signalling that the problem extends from the poor to the middle class, though the poor will, of course, have a harder time finding their way out of an equivalent amount of debt. Debt-collection incidents are reported to credit-rating agencies, which in turn can limit prime credit prospects, and other life outcomes, such as employment. Much of this delinquent debt was concentrated by place, illustrating the problem's tendency to ripple beyond individuals into their communities.

Debt is associated with poor financial outcomes. Just as importantly, it has health-related consequences. Credit card debt has been linked to anxiety (Drentea, 2000), depression (Zimmerman and Katon, 2005), risky health behaviours (Drentea and Lavrakas, 2000) and lower overall health and wellbeing (Brown et al., 2005). These findings extend beyond credit card debt. Homeowners with mortgage debt report more stress than those without a mortgage. Further, mortgage debt mediates the relationship between stressful experiences and psychological distress (Cairney and Doyle, 2004), and it has also been found to exacerbate other forms of pre-existing mental health difficulty (Jenkins et al., 2008).

Once credit strain becomes so severe that a person experiences a bankruptcy or foreclosure, these negative health consequences are only multiplied. Foreclosures are related to psychological distress, hypertension, depression, anxiety and low self-esteem (Nettleton and Burrows, 2000; Pollack and Lynch, 2009). From the type of ecological lens that community psychology considers, it is important to look at the effects of debt and foreclosures beyond the individual or even the household. We need to extend outwards into the complex ecology of neighbourhoods and communities, and to consider the impact of economic antecedents and psychological consequences. To do this we return to the example of subprime loans and their prevalence in African American communities. Numerous studies, for instance, have illustrated that home purchasers in African American neighbourhoods – traditionally excluded from mainstream mortgage lending in the USA – were significantly more likely to receive a subprime loan than those in white neighbourhoods (Calem et al., 2004; Rugh and Massey, 2010). This was irrespective of creditworthiness, educational attainment or any other personal characteristic (Wyly et al., 2006). Subprime loans eventually foreclose at a rate between 10 and 20 times as great as prime or traditional loans (Immergluck, 2010). Subsequently, concentrated foreclosures have mounted in many urban low-income African American neighbourhoods. Families have been uprooted, and vacant and dilapidated homes have become the norm. The more vacant homes accumulate, the greater the likelihood that crime and disorder will increase. In turn, elevated disorder further reduces home values, neighbourhood investment and, finally, damages psychological and social relationships – building blocks of neighbourhood informal social control and social capital (Sampson, 2012).

Subprime loans illustrate just how the ecology of financialisation works to further disadvantage certain people and certain communities. What begins as a financial product – a subprime loan that is created to extract maximum yield for investors from the most vulnerable people and places – ends up impacting the health and wellbeing of individuals, and in turn sends neighbourhoods and families further on a downward spiral of loss and disinvestment that becomes increasingly difficult to reverse. Saegert et al. (2011) refer to this process as serial asset extraction, as both social and financial assets are stripped from neighbourhoods and are transferred to financial institutions and investors. Over time, disadvantage accumulates and is reproduced over generations, leaving little possibility for upward mobility, wealth creation and wellness. A crucial piece of this ecology is the repeated process of profiting from the disadvantaged.

At the time of writing, a new form of financial industry that profits from disadvantaged neighbourhoods is beginning to emerge. Foreclosures have suppressed home values in many areas to the point where investment has become attractive to private equity firms. Large institutional investors have been actively purchasing distressed properties across the USA, in some cases swiftly driving up real-estate prices (Fields and Uffer, 2014). Rather than selling these homes, many firms are entering into the landlord business. One of the objectives is the creation of a new form of bond to be sold to investors, backed by tenant rental revenue (Shenn, 2013). At the height of the US housing bubble, investment banks created bonds that were backed by mortgages, and later bonds backed by nothing more than bets about the probability that those mortgages would fail. As the Great Recession fades in the rearview mirror and homeownership rates have declined – particularly among African American households (Shapiro et al., 2010) – a new opportunity has emerged for investment firms to profit from disadvantage yet again.

Debt maintenance and reproduction: The role of psychology

In order to maintain a system that takes assets from the many to build wealth for the few, powerful structures are needed to reproduce the narrative that debt is an individual issue that bears only personal responsibility. Here we use psychological theory to discuss the ways in which neoliberal debt narratives are maintained and reproduced. We argue that psychology has a significant role to play by helping to uncover and challenge the systems and actors that successfully focus the blame on individuals rather than a broader political economy. Just as an individual-focused psychology is incomplete in understanding indebtedness, so too is a similarly myopic disciplinary lens. Thus we highlight the ways in which psychology can (1) contribute to theoretical understandings of debt structures and (2) help to mobilise resistance to debt, financialisation and inequality.

The narrative that indebted people and households are "losers" who made poor financial decisions is not supported by the evidence that we have presented. Larger systems have squeezed people into debt for profit and continued economic growth. Yet the personal blame narrative is as pervasive as it is durable. So too is the classic neoliberal narrative – that all would prosper in a laissez-faire economy but for the intervention of government – similarly pervasive and durable. This is no accident because both narratives are driven by the actors who stand to benefit from the current status quo of profit-taking on the backs of the most vulnerable communities. For evidence, one need not look much further than the debates that have taken place in the USA around financial system reform, consumer protections and student loans. In each area there have been intense lobbying efforts to frame any government intervention – aimed at limiting the risk-taking behaviour of financial firms, increasing monitoring of lending practices, and providing affordable access to education – as "job-killing" or "government takeovers". Such rhetoric has proved to be efficacious, as evidenced by the federal government rolling back its involvement in subsidised student loans and allowing loan interest to accrue before students have completed their education. The rise in resulting student loan defaults has been swift.

As a final example of how powerful neoliberal financial narratives are, we acknowledge the recent practice of "inversion". In an ironic turn of events, many of the largest US-based investment banks that were bailed out with taxpayer dollars during the Great Recession have recently accumulated new windfalls by advising corporations how to set up tax shelters in other countries to avoid paying US taxes (Morgenson, 2014). So powerful is the accepted logic of financial profiteering that little noise has been made, let alone any attempt to highlight the hypocrisy of taking public funds to stay afloat and later helping to circumvent the refilling of those same coffers.

This practice is not merely a coincidence. Government investment has the greatest potential to rebuild struggling communities where markets have brought only devastation. But it also represents a challenge to the status quo of repeated profit-taking. Thus powerful corporate and financial sector interests actively work to dismantle it, cut off tax revenue and advance narratives of government failure. The goal is always a renewed push for austerity and deregulation. Such is the case with debates about government debt. Even though financial firms paralysed the economy through their own debt holdings – which required a taxpayer bailout and heavy government spending – narratives quickly shifted to the supposed dangers of government debt. These narratives typically, and erroneously, personify government in order to utilise the same victim-blaming framework that is applied to individuals (i.e. "the government needs to be more responsible and tighten its belt just like responsible people do").

These examples should make clear the degree to which financialisation and neoliberalism permeate dominant narratives about debt in the USA. Resisting and dismantling these pervasive narratives is a critical contribution that the field of psychology is uniquely poised to do. Thus far we have located debt within its broader political economy, but we argue that this structure is psychological in nature as well. What is also true, and what also makes the political economy structure psychological, is that individual actors within government, corporations, financial institutions, lobbying firms and elsewhere guide the human activity that shapes political economy. Political economy is not, in reality, random whims of the invisible hands of the market but the actions of significant human intentionality.

Psychological theories and approaches could be more critically applied to debt maintenance and political economy. We highlight one theory and one framework with strong potential to help to counter neoliberal narratives: (1) attribution theory and (2) critical liberation-oriented community psychology. We begin with attribution theory to explicate how indebtedness is a matter of attribution and misattribution (Ross, 1977). Attribution theory is also strongly related to just-world theories, which help to maintain the idea that debt is a personal issue with personal causes and personal solutions. Whether using just-world theory (Walker, 2012) or blaming the victim, dominant narratives that overemphasise individual processes – which psychology largely uncritically follows – ultimately use some form of attribution theory. Dominant economic structures are maintained by attributional narratives that blame the poor for their debt to continue to maintain profits.

We introduce the idea of the "attributional chameleon" to identify the process by which firms intentionally set up policies, or lobby to loosen regulations, or manipulate finance to project the blame that is associated with their own profiteering practices. Such firms – and the powerful actors within them – can shift seamlessly between blaming the victim (i.e. people are responsible for their financial behaviours) to playing the victim (i.e. government regulations made the firm do it). The attributional chameleon changes in a way that is strategic based on profitable self-interest. An example is the devising of new profit mechanisms that put others in debt, while at the same time lobbying for a rolling back of restrictions and consumer protections. If strategic, the chameleon will adapt and play the victim itself, inviting sympathy, saying that the game is unfair, and that it, not the public, needs protection. Such has often been the case with the largest US banks, whose executives have frequently lamented the supposed persecution of banks in the post-recession era.

The chameleon also benefits from psychologists who seek to fix the poor, because that successfully misattributes the problem to the client, to the real victim of the unjust system. As much as the client might hope to feel better, the psychologist does not help them to understand that the house always had the advantage, and whatever the client did was not likely to lead to positive outcomes. We argue that a major reason that victim-blaming debt narratives can persist is due to the fundamental attribution error. The theory states that people are socialised to apply the fundamental attribution error to other individuals, to see any sort of isolated, individual behaviour as due to the character of the person rather than the larger situation. Attribution theory drives both just world theory and blaming the victim, because it isolates the individual rather than the unjust systems of debt and the powerful actors who shape them. For this individual-level theory to be more useful in this context, it must be applied by scholars, policy-makers and practitioners on a broader scale. It provides a bridge that can connect disparate disciplinary lenses in a critical analysis of political economic systems.

We turn lastly to the need for a critical-liberation psychology that is focused on political economy. Too often, social scientists are too limited by disciplinary framing and miss the complex ecologies within which people live. A limited, individual-focused psychology only serves to perpetuate economic systems that create profit and leave individuals with indebtedness. Although psychologists aren't responsible for creating debt systems, they are nonetheless pawns in the game if their only contribution is to help individuals to function better within broken and unjust systems. Much of the value in psychology is in helping to uncover powerful neoliberal narratives. Being better able to identify the misleading and unjust features of political economy can help to uncover the specific psychological mechanisms that help to maintain it. Too much of psychology, particularly positive psychology, does not recognise the existence of bad actors with bad intentions.

A non-traditional psychology that utilises research, values, ecological theories and action can help to identify and counter financialisation, neoliberalism and debt. Community psychology is an alternative discipline within psychology that has the potential to contribute just this. Community psychology in the USA and elsewhere arose from a common desire to develop theories and research that would illuminate complex transactions between people and the larger systems within which they are embedded. The rise of indebtedness has its own complex ecology that necessitates critical, interdisciplinary examination. The field of psychology could contribute more meaningfully to the issues that are discussed in this book by utilising ecological models that connect individuals to political economy.

Psychology must be able to critique unjust power structures and work collaboratively and appreciatively with others – particularly by educating and empowering those who are most affected by debt – to transform systems that produce and maintain debt. This psychology would counter the attributional chameleon's propagandist manipulations, work towards truth and authenticity, and help to reclaim people as human beings rather than commodities (Fromm, 1956). This psychology would counter the blaming of the oppressed and work, instead, to fix the maladaptive psychologies of the political economy. This psychology would better appreciate multiple perspectives at multiple system levels: the individual, families, community and organisation. Such a psychology would emphasise ethics and humanistic values, and it would appreciate culture, diversity and disenfranchisement. It would also contribute new interdisciplinary understandings of rapidly changing political economies. And, finally, its understandings must be used to educate, organise and empower those who are most affected by indebtedness to insist on economic rights and justice. Such a field needs to appreciate historical context, yet continually change to avoid stagnation and neoliberal co-optation. This is the promise of an economic-focused critical, liberation-oriented community psychology.

Conclusion

This chapter provides an overview of how debt in the USA is produced and maintained by an increasingly neoliberal political economy. Debt, stagnant wages and inequality are all intertwined with a hyperfinancialised economy that constantly seeks new people and places to profit from. This perspective is contrary to the ways in which debt is usually discussed – as an individual problem. The chapter also discusses ways in which psychology could become more relevant in both helping to understand the ecology of debt and helping to resist its expansion. We conclude with five concrete actions that could further this resistance:

- All disciplines must be concerned with indebtedness, and must provide clear theories and research about the ecology of debt, from people to political economy and everything in between. This requires considering the entire psychology and pathology of financial systems, corporations and neoliberalism in general. It necessitates ecological perspectives, and it necessitates expanding inquiry to the global scale rather than focusing only on a national scale, as capital is increasingly mobile.
- More work must be done to uncover the specific mechanisms and approaches that maintain and reproduce indebtedness. We provide some preliminary examples of how psychological theory can be applied to debt narratives and key actors. However, more knowledge is needed about exactly how people accept or resist neoliberal narratives, the role that powerful people and institutions play in manipulating public opinion, and how governments and academies reproduce debt.
- Debt scholarship in general can become more relevant by ensuring that inquiry serves to empower those who are most affected by the

issue to change the system or demand better agreements with, for instance, financial institutions. This critical knowledge must play a more powerful role out in communities, fostering more effective education and organising. Rather than simply uncovering or treating the symptoms of debt, cross-disciplinary work must help individuals to understand its determinants and ways of resisting it.

- More work must be done to mobilise the disparate forms of resistance to debt across different geographies. Organising efforts such as Strike Debt – a popular education initiative aimed at resisting debt and pushing for economic justice – have the potential to educate and liberate those people who are most affected by debt. Given that most individuals, regardless of place, possess some form of debt, there is a massive base of people who could be organised around the issue.
- Finally, critical scholars and activists must work to help to imagine and create new forms of social and economic relations. A potential silver lining in all of the defeating statistics about consumer debt is that young people in the USA have recently begun retreating from the auto loan and mortgage markets (Federal Reserve Bank of New York, 2013). This new generation, if mobilised, could help to create a paradigm shift in housing and transportation usage. A generation that is unwilling or unable to take on massive mortgage and auto debt could pave the way for an expansion or reimagining of social housing (e.g. community land trusts, limited equity cooperatives) and a shift away from automobile dominance.

References

Brown, S., Taylor, K. and Wheatley Price, S. (2005). Debt and distress: Evaluating the psychological cost of credit. *Journal of Economic Psychology*, 26(5), 642–663.

Cairney, J. and Doyle, M. (2004). Home ownership, mortgages and psychological distress. *Housing Studies*, 19(2), 161–174.

Calem, P., Hershaff, J. and Wachter, S. (2004). Neighborhood patterns of subprime lending: Evidence from disparate cities. *Housing Policy Debate*, 15(3), 603–622.

Doty, M., Edwards, J. and Holmgren, A. (2005). *Seeing Red: Americans Driven to Debt by Medical Bills*. The Commonwealth Fund. Issue Brief, August, 2005.

Drentea, P. (2000). Age, debt and anxiety. *Journal of Health and Social Behavior*, 41(4), 437–450.

Drentea, P. and Lavrakas, P. J. (2000). Over the limit: The association among health, race and debt. *Social Science & Medicine*, 50, 517–529.

Etheridge, E. (2009). Rick Santelli: Tea party time. *New York Times*, Opinion Pages, 20 February 2009.

Federal Reserve Bank of New York (2013). *Quarterly Report on Household Debt and Credit*. Federal Reserve Bank of New York Research and Statistics Group,

Microeconomic Studies, retrieved on http://www.newyorkfed.org/research/national_economy/householdcredit/DistrictReport_Q22013.pdf.
Federal Reserve Bank of St. Louis (2014). *Economic Research: Federal Reserve Economic Data*, retrieved on http://research.stlouisfed.org/fred2/graph/?graph_id=136424&category_id=7519.
Fields, D. and Uffer, S. (2014). The financialization of rental housing: A comparative analysis of New York City and Berlin. *Urban Studies*, 31 July 2014, http://usj.sagepub.com/content/early/2014/07/31/0042098014543704.
Fromm, E. (1956). *The Art of Loving*. New York: Harper and Row.
Giovannoni, O. (2014). *What Do We Know About the Labor Share and the Profit Share? Part II: Empirical Studies*. Levy Economics Institute. Working Paper No. 804.
Green, R. and Wachter, S. (2007). The housing finance revolution. *The 31st Economic Policy Symposium: Housing, Housing Finance, and Monetary Policy*. Kansas City: Federal Reserve Bank of Kansas City, retrieved on http://www.kc.frb.org/Publicat/Sympos/2007/PDF/Green_Wachter_0415.pdf.
Grogger, J. (2006). The effects of time limits, the EITC, and other policy changes on welfare use, work, and income among female-headed families. *The Review of Economics and Statistics*, 85(2), 394–408.
Hackworth, J. (2007). *The Neoliberal City*. Cornell: Cornell University Press.
Harvey, D. (1999). *The Limits to Capital*, 2nd edn. London: Verso.
Howell, B. (2006). Exploiting race and space: Concentrated subprime lending as housing discrimination. *California Law Review*, 94(1), 101–147.
Immergluck, D. (2009). *Foreclosed: High Risk Lending, Deregulation, and the Undermining of America's Mortgage Market*. New York: Cornell University Press.
Immergluck, D. (2010). Neighborhoods in the wake of the debacle: Intrametropolitan patterns of foreclosed properties. *Urban Affairs Review*, 46(1), 3–36.
Immergluck, D. (2011). The local wreckage of global capital: The subprime crisis, federal policy and high-foreclosure neighborhoods in the US. *International Journal of Urban and Regional Research*, 35(1), 130–146.
Jenkins, R., Bhugra, D., Bebbington, P., Brugha, T., Farrell, M., Coid, J. and Meltzer, H. (2008). Debt, income and mental disorder in the general population. *Psychological Medicine*, 38, 1485–1493.
Joint Center for Housing Studies (2004). *Credit, Capital, and Communities: The Implications of the Changing Mortgage Banking Industry for Community-Based Organizations*. Boston: Graduate School of Design, Kennedy School of Government, Harvard University.
Joint Center for Housing Studies (2006). *State of the Nation's Housing 2006*. Boston: Graduate School of Design, Kennedy School of Government, Harvard University.
Kochhar, R., Fry, R. and Taylor, P. (2011). *Wealth Gaps Rise to Record Highs Between Whites, Blacks, Hispanics*. Pew Social and Demographic Trends Report, retrieved on http://www.pewsocialtrends.org/2011/07/26/wealth-gaps-rise-to-record-highs-between-whites-blacks-hispanics/.
Krippner, G. (2005). The financialization of the American economy. *Socioeconomic Review*, 3, 173–208.
Krugman, P. (2009). Reagan did it. *New York Times*, 31 May 2009.

Nettleton, S. and Burrows, R. (2000). When a capital investment becomes an emotional loss: The health consequences of the experience of mortgage possession in England. *Housing Studies*, 15(3), 463–479.

Newman, K. (2009). Post-industrial widgets: Capital flows and the production of the urban. *International Journal of Urban and Regional Research*, 33(2), 314–331.

Mishel, L. (2013). The CEO-to-worker compensation ratio in 2012 of 273 was far above that of the late 1990s and 14 times the ratio of 20.1 in 1965. *Economic Policy Institute: Economic Snapshot*, retrieved on September 24, 2013 http://www.epi.org/publication/the-ceo-to-worker-compensation-ratio-in-2012-of-273/.

Montgomerie, J. (2011). *The Age of Insecurity: Indebtedness and the Politics of Abandonment*. Center for Research on Social Change, Working Paper No. 92.

Morgenson, G. (2014). Private equity's free pass. *New York Times*, 26 July 2014.

Palley, T. (2007). *Financialization: What It Is and Why It Matters*. The Levy Economics Institute, Working Paper No. 525.

Peck, J. (2001). Neoliberalizing states: Thin policies/hard outcomes. *Progress in Human Geography*, 253, 445–455.

Pollack, C. E. and Lynch, J. (2009). Health status of people undergoing foreclosure in the Philadelphia region. *American Journal of Public Health*, 99(10), 1833–1839.

Pressman, S. and Scott, R. (2009). Consumer debt and measurement of poverty and inequality in the US. *Review of Social Economy*, 67(2), 127–148.

Project on Student Debt (2013). *Student Debt and the Class of 2012*. The Institute for College Access and Success Research Report, December 2013.

Ratcliffe, C., McKernan, S. M., Theodos, G. and Kalish, E. (2014). *Delinquent Debt in America*. The Urban Institute. Opportunity and Ownership Initiative Brief, 30 July 2014.

Robb, G. (2014). Greenspan says bubbles can't be stopped without crunch. *MarketWatch.com*, 27 July, 2014.

Ross, L. (1977). The intuitive psychologist and his shortcomings: Distortions in the attribution process. In Berkowitz, R. (ed.). *Advances in Experimental Psychology*, vol. 10, 174–214. New York: Academic Press.

Rugh, J. S. and Massey, D. S. (2010). Racial segregation and the American foreclosure crisis. *American Sociological Review*, 75(5), 629–651.

Saegert, S., Fields, D. and Libman, K. (2011). Mortgage foreclosure and health disparities: Serial displacement as asset extraction in African American populations. *Journal of Urban Health: Bulletin of the New York Academy of Medicine*, 88(3), 390–402.

Sampson, R. J. (2012). *Great American City: Chicago and the Enduring Neighborhood Effect*. Chicago: University of Chicago Press.

Shapiro, T. M., Meschede, T. and Sullivan, L. (2010). *The Racial Wealth Gap Increases Fourfold*. Research and policy brief. Waltham, MA: Institute on Assets and Social Policy.

Shenn, J. (2013). Blackston lures investors to home-rental bonds: Credit markets. *Bloomberg News*, 6 November 2013.

Shierholz, H. and Mishel, L. (2013). *A Decade of Flat Wages: The Key Barrier to Shared Prosperity and a Rising Middle Class*. Economic Policy Institute Briefing Paper No. 365.

Stiglitz, J. (2012). *The High Price of Inequality: How Today's Divided Society Endangers Our Future*. New York: Norton.

Sullivan, J. (2008). Borrowing during unemployment: Unsecured debt as a safety net. *Journal of Human Resources*, 43(2), 383–412.
Walker, C. (2012). Personal debt, cognitive delinquency and techniques of governmentality: Neoliberal constructions of financial inadequacy in the UK. *Journal of Community and Applied Social Psychology*, 22, 533–538.
Wheary, J. and Draut, T. (2005). The plastic safety net: The reality behind debt in America, retrieved on http://www.demos.org/publication/plastic-safety-net-reality-behind-debt-america.
Wyly, E. K., Atia, M., Foxcroft, H., Hammel, D. J. and Phillips-Watts, K. (2006). American home: Predatory mortgage capital and neighborhood spaces of race and class exploitation in the United States. *Geografiska Annaler*, 88B(1), 105–132.
Wyly, E., Atia, M., Lee, E. and Mendez, P. (2007). Race, gender, and statistical representation: Predatory mortgage lending and the US community reinvestment movement. *Environment and Planning A*, 39(9), 2139–2166.
Zimmerman, F. and Katon, W. (2005). Socioeconomic status, depression disparities, and financial strain: What lies behind the income-depression relationship. *Health Economics*, 14(12), 1197–1215.

3
The Impact of the Swiss Franc Loans Crisis on Croatian Households

Petra Rodik

Introduction

Between 2000 and 2007 there was a period of extensive expansion in lending to households in Croatia. Due to the deep economic crisis, many households now face problems with the repayment of their significant, barely repayable debt. Among them, the most prominent are those with loans denominated in Swiss francs.[1] The rise in Swiss franc value against the Croatian kuna (HRK),[2] combined with high interest rates, increased the monthly loan payments for these loans by an average of EUR 220 (euros; an average salary in Croatia being EUR 730). In 2011, when the Swiss franc was at its highest value (before the intervention of the Swiss National Bank in September 2011), there were around 100,000 Swiss franc-denominated loans. Most of them – around 75,000 – were long-term housing loans.[3]

The Croatian government has refused to address the problem for two years. In the autumn of 2013 it temporarily fixed interest rates for Swiss franc-indexed housing loans to 3.23, which diminished monthly payments to some extent. In August 2011, bank clients with Swiss franc-denominated loans started an NGO called Franc Association[4] that, together with Croatian Alliance for Consumer Protection, filed a lawsuit against the eight largest Croatian banks.[5] The Swiss franc loans crisis triggered a public debate about the consequences of and responsibility for the debt crisis, which is still ongoing. There are two main positions within this debate. On the one hand, there is a camp that argues that debtors are suffering the consequences of unfair contracts in which all of the risks are transferred to the side of the debtor, while the banks are earning extra profit. Inadequate regulation of the financial sector and the weak oversight of the banks, it holds, are the main sources of the current debt crisis. According to this position, since the crisis has cumulative social and economic consequences which directly or indirectly affect the whole society, the government should take responsibility and protect the citizens by introducing policies that would alleviate the problem. On the other hand, those who subscribe to the neoliberal position argue that the responsibility lies with the individual debtors. For instance, economist Damir Novotny argues that

> It was an individual decision of every citizen. It is true that banks didn't appropriately warn their clients of the fact that the exchange rate could drastically change. But I'm convinced that, for a good part, they were aware of the risks they are taking. It is the same as if you are buying stock shares. Why would the state now jump in to protect the losers?
>
> (Novotny, 2011)

The aim of this chapter is to offer an insight into the sources, the structure and, especially, the consequences of the Swiss franc loans crisis in Croatia. After a brief overview of the socioeconomic factors that led households into debt-repayment problems, the chapter presents both quantitative evidence on the extent of the repayment burden and qualitative evidence on the experience of becoming and being (over)indebted, based on the results of a survey that was conducted in February 2012 among indebted households.

From credit boom to Swiss franc loans crisis

The Croatian post-socialist transition was marked by war and economic crisis. The negative trends in productivity and the labour market, with unemployment reaching 16.1% in 2000, were temporarily stopped in 2001, to be reversed in 2002 (Matković, 2003, pp. 257–258). After 2002, the country experienced a period of economic growth until 2008, when the current crisis started. It developed into an economic depression with no end on the horizon, with an unemployment record of 21.9% in February 2013 and youth unemployment reaching 51.6% in March 2013. With most of industry ruined during the privatisation process, and the agriculture sector characterised by small and dispersed production, Croatian economic growth in the 2000s was a case of unsustainable debt-based growth, which was a common pattern for transition countries (Bakker and Gulde, 2010). Starting in the early 2000s, there was a substantial rise in the financial infrastructure for mass consumption (banking system, credit cards and loans), along with a fast increase in new spaces of mass consumption: shopping malls, online shopping and so on[6] (Burić, 2010). The unsustainable character of the debt-based growth was additionally underlined by the overall climate of short-termism and fast enrichment of the new elite during the 1990s, openly promoted by the ruling elites.[7] The privatisation of previously state-owned enterprises was characterised by clientelism and corruption, the banking sector being no exception.[8] After the initial, mostly untransparent privatisation[9] of state-owned banks and the rise in the number of small private banks, there was a banking sector crisis in 1996–1998.[10] This included the bankruptcy of several banks and extensive bailouts. According to the Croatian National Bank's (CNB's) report, bailouts amounted to more than 27% of GDP (Šonje and Vujčić, 1999, p. 11). Immediately after that crisis, foreign banks (mostly Austrian and Italian) entered the Croatian market in 1999 and 2000. The ownership structure of the banking sector changed completely over two years: in 1998, foreign banks held only 6.7% while in 2000 they held 84–87% of the banking sector (Kraft, 2002, p. 13; Ćetković, 2011).

The CNB has conducted research on the motives of foreign banks entering the Croatian financial market, and this confirmed that the most important were the high interest rates and the expectations of market expansion (Kraft, 2002). Croatian citizens were keen to get more and more consumer goods and new cars. Even more, however – after the decade in which credit was unavailable for most citizens[11] – there was a huge demand for housing loans. Foreign banks recognised this while entering the Croatian market: "At the time of entry, the foreign banks were most interested in financing real estate transactions by households and Croatian exports" (Kraft, 2002, p. 17). They started to invest extensively in construction and the real-estate industry, and simultaneously boosted demand by lowering interest rates for housing loans and loans for housing improvements, and introducing various new revolving and debit card offers, which were commonly used to purchase housing appliances.

Within the trend of growth in overall citizen's debt, the figures for housing loans were especially prominent, contributing to around half of the overall households' debt. From the end of 2000 to the end of 2008, these loans grew by 700% (see Figure 3.1) and the

64 Understanding Institutionalised Suffering

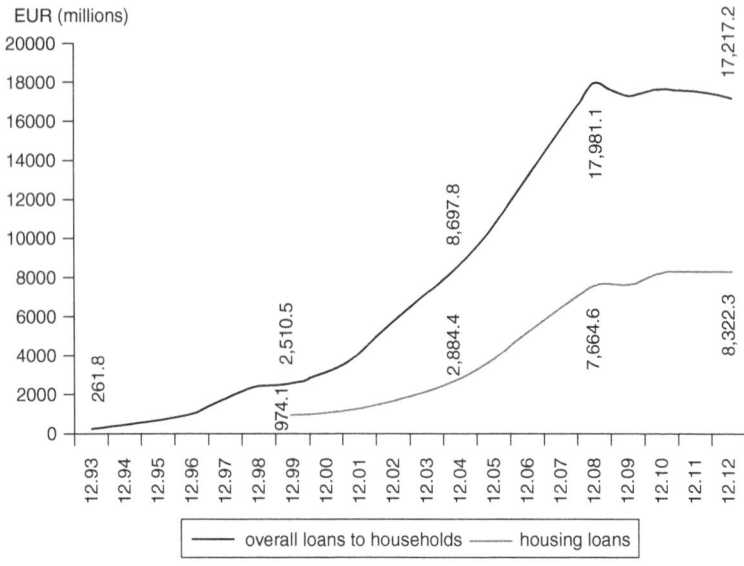

Figure 3.1 Bank loans to households
Source: CNB. Time series D5: Distribution of credit institutions' loans by domestic institutional sectors.

real-estate prices increased continuously from 2000 to 2008. Maruška Vizek's (2009) comparative analysis shows that housing affordability was very low for Croatia.[12] Bulgaria, Croatia and Estonia were countries with the worst housing affordability, and the capitals with the most unaffordable housing prices were Sofia and Zagreb, followed by Madrid, Ljubljana and London (Vizek, 2009, pp. 292–293). Housing purchase was the most important area of lending to households. Within the trend of growth in overall citizen's debt – which started at the level of 15.9% of GDP in 2000 and stabilised at around 40% from 2008 (CNB, 2005, p. 47; 2011, p. 27) – the figures for housing loans were especially prominent, contributing to around half of the overall households' debt.

Given the rising real-estate prices, the most important factor in fighting for new clients was the interest rates. Nevertheless, shortly after their market entrance, in 2002 "the banks feel that interest rates have fallen about as far as possible, so that nothing (not even foreign banks) is likely to make them fall further" (Kraft, 2002, p. 22). But in late 2003/early 2004, the local branches of Austrian-owned banks started to issue loans with the currency clause in Swiss francs with even lower interest rates.

Compared with other loans on offer (the loans in Croatian kunas or denominated in euros), Swiss franc-denominated loans had the lowest interest rate.[13]

An additional factor that influenced the expansion of the cheaper Swiss franc loans was the lack of regulation of interest rate contracts. For that reason, contracts included the variable interest rate clause, without any definition of variable parameters behind the interest rate variation (such as Libor). Most of the contracts had the clause that the interest rate is variable, without any other qualification. For banks, this meant that they could change the interest rate whenever they wanted, only informing the clients of the change.[14] The other important consequence of unregulated interest rate contracting was that the low interest rates were used for aggressive marketing purposes. Banks literally advertised "housing loans on discount", with interest rates below 4%, knowing that they could increase them shortly after the contract was signed.[15] This resulted in rapid Swiss franc loan expansion, characterised by the fact that the banks almost never warned the clients about the extent of the risk behind the combination of the floating Swiss franc exchange rate and the variable interest rate (Figure 3.2).

The CNB recognised that this trend was somewhat worrying. In 2006 it offered warnings about Swiss franc volatility, stating that the worst scenario could be an 18% increase in its value against the Croatian

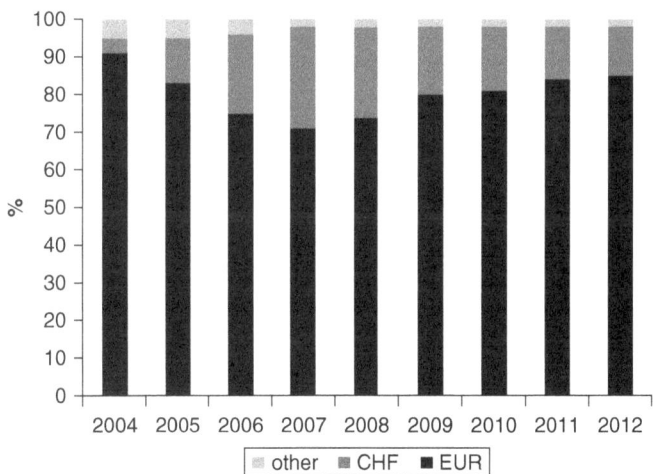

Figure 3.2 The structure of foreign-currency loans to households
Source: Table prepared according to data from the CNB (2009, 2013).

kuna. The warning was published in the CNB's bulletin and the vice governor mentioned it as a problem when addressing the parliament. But even those warnings were dismissed in the media by some finance analysts. In any case, CNB's rather shy warnings were barely noticeable as the media were full of banks' advertisements that suggested cheap Swiss franc loans as the best choice. Although aware of the possible risks, the CNB didn't intervene to stop this development. On the other hand, the average client didn't know much about floating currency risks. In particular, they weren't aware how much higher the risk of the Swiss franc loan was compared with the loan denominated in euros.[16]

Beginning in 2008, Swiss francs started appreciating and the monthly payments for the loans gradually started to rise. The sharp increase in Swiss franc value started in the summer of 2011, and at that point it rose by around 40% in comparison with the time when most of the loans were contracted (2006–2007). On top of that, the banks increased the interest rates several times in 2008–2009. Even after they slightly lowered them in 2010, they were still higher by an average of 1.08 p.p., compared with the starting interest rates.[17] The combined effect of the interest rate and the exchange rate increase produced a rise of monthly instalment payments of about 50%, to even 100% in some cases.[18]

An additional problem arose due to the fact that the principals were also pegged to Swiss francs. The debtors, after years of repayment, now owed the bank more than they received in the first place. This meant that the two "escape plans" – the first being to change the loan currency clause from Swiss francs to euros or Croatian kuna, and the second being to sell the property – were out of the question. If the person from the example in endnote 1 wanted to take a new loan in euros to repay the first one, it would have to be EUR 22,000 more than the original loan (and on top of that they would have to pay all of the refinancing fees). There was a very good chance that this person would not even be creditworthy for the new, more expensive loan. The other option – selling the property – also became impossible. Even if the person could get the original property price – which was not likely as property prices fell after 2008 – it would not cover the increased debt to the bank.

Therefore in 2011 around 100,000 people got stuck with their Swiss franc loans, about 75,000 of them with housing loans. Early 2015 estimates are that there are still around 60,000 Swiss franc-denominated housing loans outstanding. These are available estimates, because the exact number of contracts are not publicly available, as CNB publishes

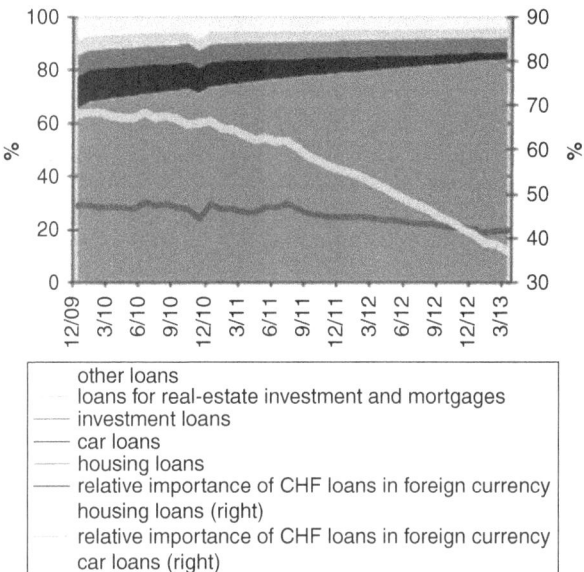

Figure 3.3 Share of different loan types within Swiss franc-denominated loans outstanding
Source: CNB (2013, p. 40).

only the figures on total (gross) loans. Data that are available regarding the structure of the Swiss franc-denominated loans (Figure 3.3) show that the housing loans represent over 80% of Swiss franc-denominated loans outstanding in 2013 and over 40% of the overall housing loans that have been extended to households,[19] while car loans are mostly paid off under the most unfavourable conditions. The amounts that were eventually paid for the cars made the whole purchase a complete nonsense. One of the respondents from our survey said:

> If I knew this, when I was buying my car, I would rather be walking around as pedestrian, along with my whole family, believe me. With 172,000 HRK [cca EUR 23,000] in 7 years I could have had a taxi every day in front of my house and not worry about anything.
> (10472000)[20]

Additionally, Figure 3.3 shows that most of the Swiss franc-denominated debt is composed of loans to households (housing and car loans), while investment-related loans, held by the non-financial enterprises, represent the minor part of Swiss franc-denominated debt. The Swiss franc loans became the source of financial and other social, psychological and health problems for many households, but especially for those having the housing loans, which are of particular importance in many respects. Bourdieu (2005) pointed out that the purchase of the house is both an economic and an affective investment. While buying a house, the household expects to create a permanent material basis for the reproduction of the family as the social unit. In economic terms, there is an expectation that the house will retain its value and that in the long term this can be transferred to the children through inheritance – that is, it is a non-financial form of saving. At the same time,

> what is being tacitly asserted through the creation of a house is the will to create a permanent group, united by stable social relations... It is a collective project for, or wager on, the future of the domestic unit, that is, on its cohesion, its integration or, if one prefers, on its capacity to resist break-up and dispersal. And the very undertaking that consist in choosing a house together, fitting it out, decorating it and, in short, making it a "home" that feels to be truly a "home of one's own"... is a product of affective cohesion which in its turn intensifies and reinforces that cohesion.
> (Bourdieu, 2005, pp. 20–21)

Consequently, repayment difficulties and the fear of losing the family residence through mortgage repossession (see Figure 3.5) cannot be reduced only to its economic dimension; social and psychological consequences also have to be taken into account. The financial loss is at the same time experienced as a failure of a project of making a home and family of one's own.

The impact of the Swiss franc loans crisis on Croatian households

The indebted households study

Franc Association conducted a survey as part of its activities to raise awareness and campaign for policy measures to address the Swiss franc debt problem.[21] This included questions about the banks, the loans, the debt burden, the risk of mortgage repossession, the bank–client interaction and some basic sociodemographics. The open-ended question at the end of the survey aimed to collect short descriptions of the personal experiences of the debtors. The intention was to collect stories that can be published,[22] which was explained in the introduction to that part of the survey, along with rough guidelines about the format. We collected 176 short narratives in response to this question, which gave us an important additional insight into the debtors' motives for taking the loans, their reflections and recollections of the loan contracting process and their experiences of repayment difficulties.

Data collection was conducted in February 2012 using the online survey tool Kwiksurveys. Two methods of survey distribution were used: the link to the survey was sent to the members of Franc Association directly by e-mail and it was distributed via Facebook and other Internet communication channels, including news portals. Of the 1,374 answers,[23] 1321 were eventually analysed, others being removed (blanks, double entries, etc.). This kind of data-collection method influenced the characteristics of the sample. Internet access is not equally distributed, as younger people living in urban areas and with higher incomes are much more likely to have Internet access, whether at home or at work (GfK, 2012).[24] Internet access probably had more impact regarding the age distribution (as our respondents were somewhat younger),than the other two characteristics mentioned. Those who live in rural areas have fewer internet connections per capita, but at the same time they are also less likely to have a loan (Herceg and Šošić, 2011, p. 213). Regarding the income distribution, the most relevant factor is that people in the lowest-income categories were not able to obtain the loan in the first place, although during the period 2005–2007 the banks relaxed their crediting policies (Herceg and Šošić, 2011). Therefore the lowest-income families are under-represented in the population of debtors, and in our sample the debtors tended to be of middle or higher than average income. Compared with the available data on the debtors' population (Herceg and Šošić, 2011, p. 208) our sample had over-represented middle-income categories of debtors, while the highest-income debtors were under-represented. A possible explanation is that they had fewer concerns with the repayment, so they were not motivated to participate in the survey. Having in mind the context of the research and its stated purpose (media awareness campaign), those more burdened by the loan payments wanted to let the public know about the extent of the problem so were more motivated to participate.[25]

The results

Sociodemographics show that the debtors with repayment problems were mostly young families with children, of an average income somewhat above the average. Most of them were 30–39 years old (52.9%, with

70 Understanding Institutionalised Suffering

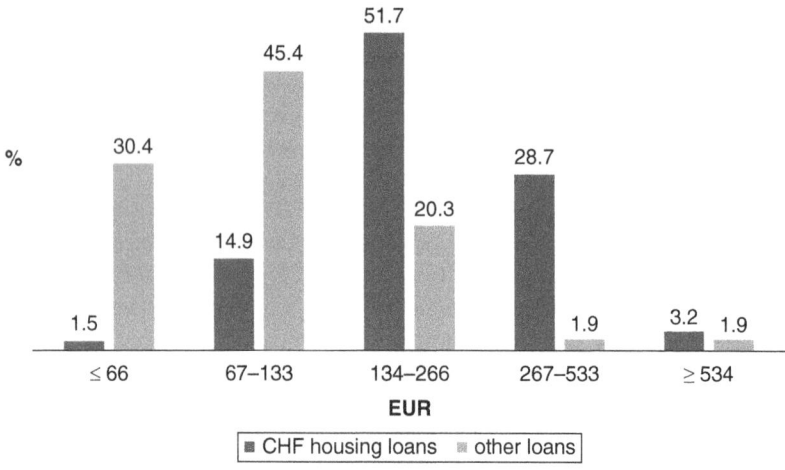

Figure 3.4 Instalment increase
Source: FA study 2012. The category "other types of loans" includes car loans, loans for the refurbishment of real estate and cash loans secured by mortgages – in Swiss francs and in other currencies, and the housing loans in Croatian kunas or denominated in euros.

an additional 28.4% between 40 and 49),[26] more often men (64.85%) than women (35.15%). It seems that men contract loans more often than women,[27] for both cultural and structural reasons – as family breadwinners and because of their higher employment rate and average salary.

The results show that loan instalments significantly decreased the disposable income after loan payments. This was especially the case for families with housing loans,[28] as can be seen from Figure 3.4.

It is not a fact of having a Swiss franc-denominated loan itself but having a housing loan in Swiss francs that is the predictor of having a much increased repayment burden. The increase in instalments for smaller Swiss franc-denominated loans (e.g. car loans) contributed less to the repayment burden. Therefore Figure 3.4 compares the debtors with Swiss franc-denominated housing loans to debtors with all of the other types of loan (see endnote 28), including Swiss franc-denominated loans for other purposes, the difference between groups being significant at 0.01 for both absolute and relative-to income increase.[29]

It should also be mentioned that 34% of respondents experienced, for at least one month, that their instalment was higher than their overall monthly income. However, even the continuous payment of more than 50% of the income creates a huge stress for the families. Bearing in mind that in Croatia the average household spends most of its income on food and energy (CBS, 2013, p. 15, figure G-2), the quality of life of the families with such a loan payment is certainly very low and, for some, at the level of bare survival.

The additional stress for the debtors in arrears comes from the fear of foreclosure and repossession. Croatian statistics on house and flat foreclosures show an increase from 122 foreclosures in 2006 to 2,964 in 2013 (CCE, 2014). Available CCE data do not identify the currency of the loan in default, but CNB's data on bad loans – those in risk of default – show that the share of the bad loans is 2.5 times as high for the Swiss franc-denominated loans compared with those denominated in euros (CNB, 2013, p. 44).

Some 38.4% of respondents with Swiss franc-denominated housing loans estimated that the risk of foreclosure was high or very high (Figure 3.5), and some had already experienced it. As Nettleton and Burrows (2000) have shown, foreclosure is an extremely stressful experience. This is especially so during the period after the termination of the contract, when the family is waiting to be moved out from the property, which is characterised by uncertainty and fear for the future. What adds to this uncertainty and fear is the fact that there is no personal bankruptcy law that could give them a hope of any kind of fresh start.

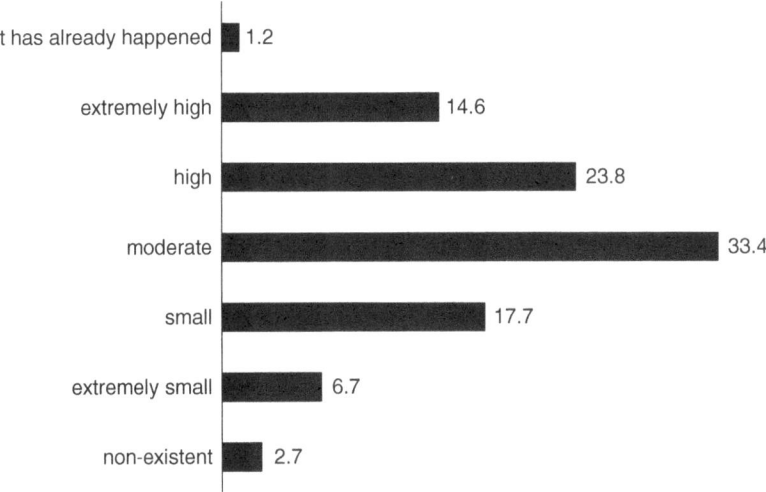

Figure 3.5 The self-assessment of the probability of foreclosure – debtors with Swiss franc-denominated housing loans ($n = 854$)

In Croatia, when the debtor falls into arrears, the bank can choose which means of insurance it will draw on first – usually the first being collecting from the guarantor/co-debtor. As the real-estate market contracted after 2008, banks usually cannot sell the repossessed property for a good price, or they cannot sell it at all for a while. During that time the family stays in the property until it is sold. This means that, by the time they are forced to move out, they are completely exhausted, financially and in every other way, and still in debt. In the case of Swiss franc-denominated loans, the debt after repossession can still be very large. To illustrate this, I will refer once more to the example of the person who took a loan worth EUR 71,000 (see endnote 1). If they faced foreclosure, it is likely that they would be moved out of their home broke and with a debt of around EUR 30,000–40,000. First, the debt increases to about EUR 20,000 more because of the increased principal (some of it being repaid, but not much). Second, these are not mortgage loans (see endnote 3), so the real-estate repossession does not mean that the debt is cleared. In fact, only the selling value that the bank achieves is deducted from the debt. So an additional EUR 10,000–20,000 of the debt would not be covered by the mortgage because the real-estate prices fell. Besides the real-estate market contraction and property price decline, the banks do not have incentives to get the best selling price, because they expect to collect the debt eventually anyway. Third, as Croatia still has no regulation on personal bankruptcy, the individual would eventually be left with a lifelong debt.

The narratives on becoming and being indebted

As respondents structured the narratives in a similar way, the overview of the main themes will follow the narrative logic of the stories. The typical narrative structure was the following: the motive to take out the loan → choosing the bank and the loan → debt problem description → comment. This structure closely resembles Labov's six elements of storytelling: an abstract, orientation, complicating action, evaluation, resolution and coda. Some narratives are fully formed and contain all six elements, while others lack some of the elements. Therefore I chose narrative analysis as an appropriate approach to analysing debtors' accounts. I conducted thematic narrative analysis (Riessman, 2008; Blom and Nygren, 2010), trying to identify the typical themes and patterns in repayment problems.

In their comments, respondents often expressed the sentiment that they had been tricked, that their trust had been misused and that they were not protected by the government; and many of them felt stress, anxiety and hopelessness, and that their situation had become meaningless. The comments vary from personal introspection to complex insights into the causes or the consequences of the Swiss franc debt crisis, and they shed light on the debtors' interpretation of the issue at hand. The narratives also describe the respondents' perceptions of debt-repayment circumstances, and what strategies have been used to cope with repayment problems.

Taking out the loan

While writing about the reasons why they decided to take out the loan, the debtors often mentioned two motives: to end their tenancy status and to secure a permanent home for themselves and their families. The other motives often mentioned were children (childbirth, planning to have children, wanting to create a future for their children, etc.), their good financial situation at that time (permanent job, good salary), their optimistic future perspective, and the fact that they were at a point in their lives when they wanted to "stand on their own feet" and move out of their parents' home. One of the respondents wrote: "Both of us are young, able, with a university degree, employed on a permanent contract, with comparatively good earnings, we decided to take out the loan and head for the adventure of buying our own flat" (10450874).

Following the decision to take out the loan, there was often a long and exhausting period of collecting information and searching for the best option: choosing the bank, reviewing the offers, sometimes facing the fact that their options were completely limited or non-existent,[30] discussing the options with personal banking advisors, filling in the forms and waiting for the evaluation of their creditworthiness (that procedure itself lasting three to four weeks on average). Analysis of their accounts reveals that people's expectations and decisions while choosing the loans were framed by the information that they had gathered, and that most of the information came from two sources: the bank's marketing material and personal banking advisors.

Besides the usual marketing strategies evoking the lifestyle, trust, partnership, care for their clients, flexibility, quick procedure and so on, there were various marketing campaigns focused specifically on selling Swiss franc loans. These advertisements[31] show a comparatively lower interest rate for the Swiss franc loan in comparison with the interest rate of the euro-denominated loan, and very often they rushed people to the banks with the message that it is a limited sale offer.[32] Several respondents explicitly mentioned the banks' advertising, but the most prominent theme was their communication with personal banking advisors (PBAs), which framed their perceptions of what choices were available. Looking back, many expressed the feeling of regret, bitterness or anger for being misled, misinformed or tricked by their PBAs. As there was no regulation regarding information disclosure, the information that clients got from their PBAs was usually limited, it very much depended on the clients' competence in asking the right questions and it also depended on the competence of the PBAs, which varied greatly. In addition, the PBAs had a motive to sell more loans, in the form of a salary bonus based on their sales record. Thus some of them were prone to withholding information about the risks so as to sell more loans. Over 75% of debtors' accounts regarding their reasons for taking a Swiss franc-denominated loan mention PBAs' recommendations. According to the debtors, the most frequent arguments from the PBAs were that it was the best offer and that the Swiss franc was a safe and stable currency. For instance, one account mentioned that "in the bank, they were convincing me that it is better to take out the loan indexed to Swiss franc because franc is STABLE, and with euro 'who knows what will be' with euro, they told" (10619255).

If we recollect Novotny's quote from the introduction, we might ask whether people really knew the risks when deciding to sign a contract. An important characteristic of the phase of choosing the loan is the asymmetry of the information. One of the respondents commented: "Yes, I did sign the loan contract. My friends were buying shares. They wanted to make money, they knew the risks involved. I wanted a family and four walls for my family. I wasn't buying a vacation house and I thought the risks were small. Was it necessary for me to know all about the banking business in order to get a housing loan?" (10469075).

Repayment problems

The situation with the repayment problems was very stressful, both financially and emotionally. The psychological impact was for many aggravated by the fact that the main source of the repayment problems were external factors (the appreciation of the currency and the bank's one-sided increase in the interest rate), which were completely out of their control. Therefore many narratives make reference to the emotional state that people and their families were experiencing. These included an array of negative emotions: fear for the future, anger, a feeling of there being no way out, despair, helplessness, humiliation, a lack of perspective, meaninglessness and pessimism. For example: "every time I remember the fact that my debt is bigger than 5 years ago, I despair" (10451594). Some explicitly mentioned depression and illness as a consequence of the debt problem. For some of them, the financial problems have led to marital issues and divorce, and others have had to turn to their parents for financial help or even to move back with them, which then affected their sense of self-respect as they perceived that they had failed in a life, not being able to create their own families and take care of them. As can be seen from the quote at the beginning of the next section, people felt ashamed and stigmatised.[33]

The main strategies for coping with the financial problems were borrowing from parents and friends, increasing borrowing using revolving credit and credit cards, finding additional jobs and selling personal property (from jewellery to real estate). Some managed to increase their income by doing several jobs, but this strategy was limited by the recession and high unemployment. It is interesting that, contrary to the myth of the irresponsible borrower, the accounts of the people who finally gave up paying the loan show that they did this only when they were faced with a "bare life vs. loan" situation, as in the following case: "The moment when I was left without electricity and water, I stopped paying my loan annuities regularly, so as to pay the electricity and water bills" (10460258).

The typical paths towards repayment problems

The analysis of the sequence of events described in the narratives revealed two main patterns, or "the paths towards repayment problems", depending on whether there was an interference of different life events that triggered/increased the repayment problems. The first pattern included cases in which there were no disruptive life events, but the very fact of instalment increase created the repayment problem. The typical account of this pattern is: "As the troubles with CHF [Swiss francs] started, our revolving and credit card debt was growing. Finally, we had to move out from the apartment. We moved to my parents and let the apartment to tenants" (10451368).

In those cases, sometimes disruptive life events, such as illness, followed and complicated the repayment problems further:

> I pay over 75% of my earning towards the loan, and the rest is covering the bills. My 15-year old car is now gone, so is the occasional additional income, as mobility is crucial to the particular job I'm doing. The everyday life of a 34-year old man looks as if it is the everyday life of a pensioner. My friends/guarantors are helping me with

76 Understanding Institutionalised Suffering

food, and covering unexpected expenses. My personal life is ruined. People are avoiding you knowing they cannot help you. I got ill. The situation where you face the wall, without any choice and where the only goal of your existence is to cover the loan on time, brought me to depression.

(10454822)

The second pattern is the one that is well documented in the literature on overindebtedness (Valins, 2004; EC, 2008; Fondeville et al., 2010): disruptive life events led towards the repayment problems. In this pattern, the same trajectory from the first pattern, the trajectory of financial problems leading to other problems, could be found too. For example, in one case the wife lost her job, then they fell into arrears with the loan repayment, and then, she writes: "My husband finally flipped, he left me, the children, flat and loan, and he ran away" (10468870).

Among the life events that led towards repayment problems, the most common were unemployment or a reduction in income,[34] divorce, illness or childbirth. All of these events have in common that they have led to financial strain, which, combined with the instalment increase, multiplies the loan burden.

Conclusion

While the debate regarding the causes, consequences and responsibility for the Swiss franc loans crisis is still far from being concluded, the data regarding the structure of the Swiss franc loans and the problems that they caused shows that the Swiss franc issue is becoming a housing loans in Swiss franc issue. Not only are all of the other types of loan being repaid, but the number of mortgage repossessions has increased rapidly in the last few years. Homeowners with Swiss franc loans are at very high risk of falling into arrears because of their strained budget. The situation of having a continuous fear of falling into arrears and of possible mortgage repossession is very stressful and may have psychological and health consequences (Nettleton and Burrows, 2000). The narratives of the debtors show that the existential fear for the future is completely justified because any kind of life event that creates further expense or reduces income (divorce, childbirth, unemployment, illness, etc.) may push the household over the cliff towards the abyss of arrears and, eventually, mortgage repossession.

The analysis of personal accounts of the debtors on the one hand and the institutional and socioeconomic background of the introduction and expansion of Swiss franc loans on the other shows that the path towards the current debt crisis was far more complex than the idea of the "irresponsible debtor who gambled" would like to suggest. The banks pursued aggressive market expansion within the context of inadequate regulation and supervision of loan contracts. The citizens, after a decade of war and economic depression, saw the opportunity to achieve their aspirations and life goals by taking on low-interest loans. The banks, wanting to sell as many loans as possible, rarely warned them of the possible risks. Nothing comparable to this debt crisis existed in the collective memory, and people never dreamt of the possibility that a loan could completely ruin their lives. After the crisis created an unexpected shock, the banks used the contract clauses, which are now under judicial review, to transfer all of the costs of the rising exchange rate and increased business costs to the debtor. We can conclude that structural socioeconomic factors (banking policies, real-estate prices) pushed the respondents to take the loans, and institutional and communicational factors in bank–client relations influenced the respondents' decision-making process (i.e. the decisions were made based upon the "expert advice" that was provided by PBAs, bank employees selling high-risk banking products). The external events of exchange rate and interest rate variation combined with various life events that reduced debtors' income (divorce, job loss, etc.) triggered repayment problems.

As only long-term housing loans are left to be repaid, these were given much more attention than the other types of loan. It can be concluded that people perceived housing loans primarily as a means of affective investment (Bourdieu, 2005), an investment in their life goals and long-term security of home ownership for their families. As the external shock of the financial crisis created a financial strain at the level of the household, and all of the hidden risks of Swiss franc loans came to the fore, financial problems led to the other kinds of problem: psychological, health and family issues. Paraphrasing Nettleton and Burrows' (2000) title, we can conclude that affective investment became the source of emotional loss. On a broader scale, all of the social, psychological, health and other costs were socialised, while the profit was secured for a while. As a consequence of such a short-sighted policy, the number of unpayable loans ("bad loans") is rapidly rising, and is also threatening the private profit itself.

Acknowledgements

I should like to thank Karin Doolan, Suzana Kunac, Lana Bosilj, Marijan Crnjak, Nicole Kwiatkowski, Branka Lukačević-Gregić, Tomislav Prpić, Andrea Gerenčer, Mihailo Radosavljević and the editors of this volume.

78 *Understanding Institutionalised Suffering*

I am grateful for their useful feedback and kind help, either with preparing the survey that I conducted in early 2012 as a Franc Association activist, with analysis of the narratives, or with preparing this chapter.

Notes

1. The loans were contracted with a currency clause in Swiss francs, which means that the repayment plan is given in Swiss francs but the payments are made in Croatian kunas. Every instalment is paid in Croatian kunas, according to the exchange rate valid on the day of payment, and the Croatian kuna value of the principal also varies with the exchange rate. For example, someone who obtained a 30-year housing loan worth HRK 530,000 (cca. EUR 71,000) at the time when CHF 1 was equivalent to HRK 4.4, after five years of repayment owed the bank around HRK 700,000 (cca. EUR 93,000; at the exchange rate of CHF 1 = HRK 6.2).
2. In 2007, when the contracting of Swiss franc-denominated loans was in full swing (see Figure 3.2), the Swiss franc reached its lowest value against the Croatian kuna at HRK 4.36, while in mid-2011 it peaked at HRK 7.23. The banks discontinued Swiss franc-denominated loans from their offering by the end of 2008.
3. I use the term "housing loans" to differentiate them from mortgages. In Croatia, housing loans differ from the Anglo-Saxon type of mortgages because they are secured by various other means, on top of the mortgage itself. The typical housing loan issued during the mid-2000s was secured by a mortgage, at least one co-debtor and/or at least one guarantor, plus an insurance policy (health, life or pension insurance) that serves as a form of obligatory savings that banks can use to cover the debt if necessary, or other kinds of savings account.
4. In Croatian, Udruga Franak (www.udrugafranak.hr).
5. The lawsuit is grounded on the Consumer Protection Law and the Law of Obligations. On 4 July 2013 the first-instance court ruled in favour of the clients. The High Court of Commerce decision (16 July 2014) confirmed one of the two claims: it said that the interest rate changes were unlawful, but dismissed claim that the CHF currency clause was contracted in a manner that violated the *Consumer Protection Law*. The case is currently reviewed by the Supreme Court.
6. By 2007 some 1,500,000 m^2 of new retail store space bigger than 1,000 m^2 was built, and the market share of the big supermarket chains jumped from 25% in 2001 to 69% in 2006 (Burić, 2010, p. 108).
7. The first president of Croatia, Franjo Tuđman, promoted a notorious development vision: to create an elite class of 200 rich families.
8. The State Audit Office's (SAO's) final audit report on privatisation states that of 1,556 cases reviewed, only 75 lacked any flaws. Of the total of 1,936 irregularities found, 721 constitute a violation of law and 271 of them are criminal offences (SAO, 2004). The SAO never audited the privatisation of banks, but there are many indices of corruption, some of which have been published by the media. For instance, in 2012 the former prime minister, Ivo Sanader, was sentenced to ten years in prison for taking USD 695,000 in bribes from

Hypo-Alpe-Adria-Bank in 1995 and USD 12.8 million (GBP 8 million (British pounds); EUR 10 million) from the Hungarian oil company MOL in return for securing MOL's takeover of Croatia's state oil company, INA. Supreme Court's final decision, in June 2014, sentenced Sanader to 8.5 years in prison.
9. Kraft points out that

> The Croatian method of bank privatization was unusual. Under the former Yugoslavia, banks had been 'founded' by real sector enterprises. When the socialist system was overhauled in 1989–1990, equity was allocated (for the most part) to these same enterprises, even though they were the banks' debtors. This decision institutionalized an unhealthy cross-ownership in the state-owned banks. After this, the state-owned banks were not the subjects of any direct privatization procedures. Instead, the banks' owners, real sector firms, were privatized. In this way, the banks were privatized in passing.
>
> (Kraft et al., 2002, p. 3)

10. Škreb and Šonje evaluate two banking crises of the 1990s:

> Croatia has, over the past 10 years (since independence), undergone two banking crises: The first... could be called a structural or inherited crisis. The second crisis occurred in banks founded during the transition, because of weak management, including fraud, connected and insider lending, increased competition in the market as the transition period progressed, and inadequate regulation and supervision of the banking industry.
>
> (Škreb and Šonje, 2001, p. 66)

11. During the 1990s, the banks didn't pay much attention to the household sector market. When loans were offered to citizens, the interest rates were extremely high (sometimes over 20%).
12. Vizek compared housing prices in Croatia with those of Austria, Bulgaria, Estonia, Ireland, Poland, Slovenia, Spain and the UK.
13. For the historical reason of high inflation during the 1980s, most of the savings in Croatia are not in Croatian kunas but in euros (previously in Deutsche marks), and the majority of the loans issued in Croatia have the currency clause in euros (see Figure 3.2). The Swiss franc lending boom in Croatia was part of a broader trend of Swiss franc-denominated lending in Eastern Europe. Foreign banks advanced low-yielding Swiss francs to their branches in Eastern European countries, which were then used to fund loans (mostly to households) with low interest rates. For the expansion of Swiss franc-denominated loans, see Galati et al. (2007), Brown et al. (2009), Avdjiev et al. (2012) and Bohle (2013).
14. This was the reason for the ongoing lawsuits against the eight banks, the other being the fact that the banks hadn't warned their clients of the risks of the Swiss franc currency clause.
15. If there had been a regulation that forced banks to connect the interest rate variation to Swiss franc Libor or Euribor for the loans in euros, this could not have happened.
16. CNB defends the HRK–EUR exchange rate, keeping it at 7.3–7.6.

80 *Understanding Institutionalised Suffering*

17. The figure is based on the result of the self-reported figures on the starting and current interest rates (FA, 2012 survey, reported in this chapter).
18. Although 1.08 percentage points does not sound like much of a difference, it actually translates into a greater difference in annuity (monthly instalment). For example, for a 20-year loan worth EUR 100,000, with interest rate of 4%, the annuity is 606 EUR. If the interest rate is increased to 5.08%, it is 665 EUR. The annuity is 59 EUR higher, which is an increase of 9.7%, compared to the payment if interest rate is 4%. In other words, the increase of 1.08 p.p. in interest, translates to an increase of 9.7% in monthly payments. However, in some banks, the interest rate increase was greater than average. In a real example, where the starting interest rate was 3.5 and is now 7.10, the increase in the monthly instalment was 95%.
19. The rest of the housing loans were mostly denominated in euros. Figure 3.2 shows the predominance of euro-denominated loans within the overall loans to households.
20. The numbers after the respondents' quotes refer to the ID code used in the research.
21. My colleagues from Franc Association helped with suggestions for the questionnaire, and I am especially grateful to our economics team: Branka Lukačević-Gregić and Tomislav Prpić.
22. Many of the stories were eventually published in a book, *Crna knjiga* (Black Book), which is available from http://www.scribd.com/doc/117597766/Crna-Knjiga-Udruge-Franak-Web.
23. It is only possible to give a rough estimate of the response rate for the Franc Association members because other respondents who were not members reached the survey via Facebook sharing or news web portals that published the survey invitation. Around 3,000 Franc Association members received an email with the request to take part in a survey. In response to a question about whether they are members, 436 respondents (of 1,321) said that they were Franc Association members. Therefore the response rate among the Franc Association membership can be estimated at around 15%.
24. The debtors who were in the worst financial situation were perhaps excluded from the online survey because they had to cancel their Internet subscription. For comparison, cancelling one's cellphone contract is found to be the most common cost-reduction strategy in other research (Backert et al., 2009, p. 287).
25. Some 33% of respondents were Franc Association members.
26. It is interesting that only 4.5% of them are younger than 30.
27. A similar gender distribution was found in Herceg and Šošić (2011, p. 209), where 69.52% were male and 30.48% female.
28. Most of the respondents had housing loans (73%), but there were also other type of loan (for buying a motor vehicle, general-purpose loan and other). Most of the loans in the sample were denominated in Swiss francs (84%), but there were some in euros (13.4%) and a small number in Croatian kunas (2.6%). Some people were holding more than one loan (14.3% two, 1.1% three or more).
29. As mentioned earlier, average salary in Croatia equals 730 EUR. Category boundaries in the original survey were round numbers, but in Croatian kunas. Here they are recalculated as euros using a rate of EUR 1 = HRK 7.5.

30. For instance, the banks would not allow loans for people on temporary employment contracts. Nevertheless, if a bank had signed an agreement with the firm (public or private), its employees on a non-permanent contract (sometimes this could mean a contract for several years) could obtain a housing loan from that bank, but only from that bank.
31. The analysis of the advertising campaigns from 2004 to 2008 was conducted in the process of preparing evidence for the litigation case against eight banks. It included all of the print and TV advertisements that explicitly or implicitly referred to Swiss franc loans.
32. One of the banks extended the "limited sale offer" seven times in two years so that "the sale" in fact lasted continuously all this time.
33. In fact, one of the reasons for conducting the survey was to collect a pool of personal accounts for the Franc Association's media releases because debtors were rarely willing to speak about their debt problems to the media, especially TV.
34. Since 2008, the lowering of salaries was a common strategy among private sector employers who tried not to dismiss their employees. There are also many cases of people working but not being paid for months.

References

Avdjiev, S., McCauley, R. and McGuire, P. (2012). Rapid credit growth and international credit: Challenges for Asia. *BIS Working Papers* No. 377.

Backert, W., Brock, D., Lechner, G. and Maischatz, K. (2009). Bankruptcy in Germany: Filing rates and the people behind the numbers. In Niemi, J., Ramsay, I. and Whitford, W. C. (eds.). *Consumer Credit, Debt and Bankruptcy: Comparative and International Perspectives*. Oxford, UK: Hart Publishing, 273–288.

Bakker, B. B. and Gulde, A.-M. (2010). The credit boom in the EU new member states: Bad luck or bad policies? *IMF Working Papers*, 1–45.

Blom, B. and Nygren, L. (2010). Analysing written narratives: Considerations on the "code-totality problems". *Nordic Journal of Social Research*, 1, retrieved on https://bells.uib.no/index.php/njsr/article/view/66.

Bohle, D. (2013). Post-socialist housing meets transnational finance: Foreign banks, mortgage lending, and the privatization of welfare in Hungary and Estonia. *Review of International Political Economy*, 4, 1–36.

Bourdieu, P. (2005). *The Social Structures of the Economy*. Cambridge, UK: Polity Press.

Brown, M., Peter, M. and Wehrmuller, S. (2009). Swiss franc lending in Europe. *Aussenwirtschaft: Schweizerische Zeitschrift Für Internationale Wirtschaftsbeziehungen/The Swiss Review of International Economic Relations*, 64(2), 167–181.

Burić, I. (2010). *Nacija zaduženih: Od komunističkog pakla do potrošačkog kapitalizma*. [Nation of indebted: From the communist hell to consumer capitalism]. Zagreb: Naklada Jesenski i Turk.

CBS (2013). *Results of Households Budger Survey 2011*. Zagreb: Croatian Bureau of Statistics.

CCE (2014). *Forclosures by Type and Year, 2006–2013*. Zagreb: Croatian Chamber of Economy. (Unpublished analysis, retrieved on author's request from CCE Business Information Centre.)

Ćetković, P. (2011). Credit growth and instability in Balkan countries: The role of foreign banks. *Research on Money and Finance*, 27, retrieved on December 9, 2012 http://ideas.repec.org/p/rmf/dpaper/27.html.
CNB (2005). Makrobonitetna analiza [Macroprudential analysis] (No. 1). Zagreb: Croatian National Bank.
CNB (2009). *Financijska stabilnost* [Financial stability] (No. 2). Zagreb: Croatian National Bank.
CNB (2011). *Financijska stabilnost* [Financial stability] (No. 7). Zagreb: Croatian National Bank.
CNB (2013). *Financijska stabilnost* [Financial stability] (No. 11). Zagreb: Croatian National Bank.
European Commission (2008). *Towards a Common Operational European Definition of Over-Indebtedness*. European Commission.
Fondeville, N., Özdemir, E. and Ward, T. (2010). *Over-Indebtedness. New Evidence from the EU-SILC Special Module*. Research note 4/2010. European Commission.
Galati, G., Heath, A. and McGuire, P. (2007). Evidence of carry trade activity. *BIS Quarterly Review*, 3, 27–41.
GfK (2012). *Hrvatska kućanstva – prihodi (troškovi) u 2011. godini* [Croatian households – income (expenses) in 2011], retrieved on March 8, 2012 http://www.gfk.hr/public_relations/press/press_articles/009457/index.hr.html, accessed 8 March 2012.
Herceg, I. and Šošić V. (2011). The anatomy of household debt build up in Croatia: Enlisting more creditworthy households or relaxing lending standards? *Comparative Economic Studies*, 53(2) (June), 199–221.
Kraft, E. (2002). Foreign banks in Croatia: Another look. *CNB Working Papers* W – 10, retrieved on August 9, 2013 http://www.hnb.hr/publikac/istrazivanja/w-010.pdf.
Kraft, E., Hofler, R. and Payne, J. (2002). Privatization, foreign bank entry and bank efficiency in Croatia: A Fourier-flexible function stochastic cost frontier analysis. *CNB Working Papers* W – 9, retrieved on August 9, 2013 http://www.hnb.hr/publikac/istrazivanja/w-009.pdf.
Matković, T. (2003). Opseg i oblici zaposlenosti na povetku informacijskog doba [Disappearance of Work? The Scope and Forms of Employment at the Dawn of the Information Age]. *Društvena Istraživanja*, 13(1–2), 241–265.
Nettleton, S. and Burrows, R. (2000). When a capital investment becomes an emotional loss: The health consequences of the experience of mortgage possession in England. *Housing Studies*, 15(3), 463–478.
Novotny, D. (2011). Treba li vlada pomoći dužnicima u Švicarcima [Should the Government help the Swiss franc debtors]. *T-portal*, 2 June 2011, retrieved on April 19, 2012 http://www.tportal.hr/biznis/novaciulaganje/131319/Treba-li-Vlada-pomoci-duznicima-u-svicarcima.html.
Riessman, C. K. (2008). *Narrative Methods for the Social Sciences*. London: Sage.
SAO (2004). *Final Audit Report on Privatisation*. Zagreb: State Audit Office.
Škreb, M. and Šonje, V. (2001). Financial sector restructuring: The Croatian experience. *Financial Transition in Europe and Central Asia: Challenges of the New Decade*. Washington, DC: International Bank for Reconstruction and Development/World Bank.

Šonje, V. and Vujčić, B. (1999). Croatia in the Second Stage of Transition 1994–1999, *CNB Working Papers* W – 10, retrieved on March 4, 2015 http://www.hnb.hr/publikac/istrazivanja/w-010.pdf.

Valins, O. (2004). *When Debt Becomes a Problem: A Literature Study*. Ministry of Social Development, retrieved on March 15, 2013 http://www.familybudgeting.org.nz/documents/when%20debt%20becomes%20a%20problem.pdf.

Vizek, M. (2009). Priuštivost stanovanja u Hrvatskoj i odabranim europskim zemljama [Housing Affordability in Croatia and Selected European Countries]. *Revija za socijalnu politiku*, 16(3), retrieved on August 9, 2013 http://www.rsp.hr/ojs2/index.php/rsp/article/view/809.

# 4
The Consequences of Evictions in Spain

Aïda Ballester, Moisés Carmona, Rubén David Fernández, Ana González, Johanna Jiménez, Elies Martínez, Irene Moulas, Laura Peret and Carolina Viano

Background

That the lived experiences of heavily indebted families are characterised by risk, exclusion and eviction is not a new phenomenon. However the record numbers of such experiences in Spain in recent years is a concern of Spanish citizens (Centro de Investigaciones Sociológicas, 2014). According to the approximate figures from *Consejo General del Poder Judicial* (CGPJ; General Council of the Judiciary), the total number of *ejectments* (i.e. evicting the occupants of a house) in 2012 was around 101,034. Of these, 43,853 corresponded to non-paid mortgages and another 54,718 were applied with regard to verbal leases (including unpaid rent). These relate not only to principal residence evictions but also to commercial and local plots. The intention is not to be alarmist but to present an accurate picture of social reality. According to the *Banco de España* (Bank of Spain), in 2013 about 50,000 family homes were lost due to non-payment of mortgages, of which the vast majority (39,000) were the families' principal residence (Stop Desahucios, 2014). It would be ideal to be able to compare those figures with the same situation before 2008, but these data are not available owing to poor statistical records in Spain (Hernández, 2014, March 28). These figures would be necessary to clarify the role that the financial crash has played in this situation.

Insufficient official figures induce the necessity to take into account the data that the social organisations involved in finding solutions to this problem are managing. The *Plataforma de Afectados por la Hipoteca*

(PAH; Platform of People Affected by Mortgages), which combines many entities and platforms that have been created by citizens in response to this social scourge, estimates that from 2008 until the third quarter of 2012 at least 362,776 evictions occurred in Spain (Colau and Alemany, 2013). While the number of evictions in 2008 was 49,848, in 2011 it reached the alarming figure of 94,825, and thus we can say that the economic crisis has played a determining role in this dwelling drama that is faced in Spain every day. In March of 2014 the newspaper *El País* showed that in 2013 the number of evictions had only decreased by 9.8% compared with 2012. In spite of this "better" number, evictions are still being suffered at an average of 184 a day (Hernández, 2014, 28 March). The numbers can be quite confusing depending on who measures the phenomenon, and this becomes a problem because not collecting quality statistical data could be argued to be a political decision that contributes to making the problem invisible, and thus difficult to address.

In addition, according to UNICEF's report about the impact of the Spanish crisis on children, the number of houses with children in where all adults are unemployed rose from 324,000 in 2007 to 714,000 families in 2010, an increase of 120% in three years (UNICEF España, 2012). The present number of families in poverty is still larger, reaching almost 2.5 million families (Ibáñez and Sust, 2011, October 21) both with and without children, disaggregated data is not available in the *Instituto Nacional de Estadística* (INE; National Statistics Institute). The PAH gathered statistics that show that 82% of evictions are suffered by families with children (La Vaguardia, 2012, June 2). Furthermore, child poverty in Spain in 2012 was 27.2% (UNICEF España, 2012, October 8; Save the Children, 2012). This rate rose to 33.8% in 2013, which means that almost 3 million kids in the country live below the poverty line (Save the Children España, 2014).

These numbers cannot be understood without bearing in mind the Spanish socioeconomic context and the current economic crisis. Adopting a historical perspective, from the second half of the 20th century, Spanish society switched from a prevalence of rented houses to the almost absolute supremacy of housing properties (Aramburu, 2010). The culture of ownership had its beginning in the policies of the dictatorial regime and was consolidated during democracy. The housing sector has become the major source of investment for families and, as a result, has also been its major cause of expenditure.

Thus Spain has become one of the European countries with the highest rate of owner occupation in the UE according to the 2010's Eurostat

(Aramburu, 2010). Added to this property culture in Spanish society, it is important to state that the country had an economy based largely on the construction industry. Purchasing a house has historically been encouraged and recommended as the safest investment that families can make, associating ownership with values such as autonomy, stability and tranquillity (Aramburu, 2010). Very specific public policies were adopted to favour indebtedness, which worked to the detriment of rental agreement housing. In Spain there has been a confusion of the fundamental right to live in a house with the ownership of a house.

The so-called "Housing Bubble", characterised by speculation and limited productive diversification, would end up falling apart with disastrous consequences for Spanish society and especially the middle class, now in decline due to unemployment, lower wages (the interprofessional minimum wage in Spain is EUR 645.30/month), increased taxes, monthly increasing commodity prices (as the electricity bill) and the loss of purchasing power. All of these factors among others have resulted in an increase in income inequality, with Spain being the country in the European Union with the highest inequality (Mars, 2014, March 13).

Financial entities were accomplices in supporting the myths concerning property houses as a safe investment that all pockets could manage – messages that permeated the collective consciousness deeply. Banks facilitated access to mortgages, and colluded with different governments to achieve a favourable legislative framework to the detriment of consumers who were becoming increasingly vulnerable. To illustrate this defencelessness, until July 2014 those involved in a foreclosure process could not counter an unfavourable court resolution on an equal footing with banks. With the current Spanish legislation, a bank can present an appeal if it finds the court decision to be unfavourable, while families cannot appeal when the decision is unfavourable to their interest as debtors. This abusive situation is now under review owing to the positioning of the European Court, which has requested another option for families in personal debt and is compelling banks to negotiate new terms with people in order to avoid evictions (Pérez-Lanzac, 2014, July 17).

All of these factors combined have contributed to the social problem of housing and family debt, which is hitting Spanish citizens hard. The key issues will now be addressed.

Characteristics of the problem and psychosocial impacts

Eviction is the last stage of a process of impoverishment that is suffered by many families in Spain. However, there is a lack of studies of the experience of those affected by eviction, and the resulting consequences for intra- and interpersonal experiences. This hinders a clear analysis of the scope of the problem.

Recently, Ramis-Pujol, in collaboration with Cáritas (a Christian confederation which covers basic needs such as soup kitchens and help to ameliorate social exclusion situations), published a case study on the human reality of evictions. It was found that people who entered into an eviction process, in the same way that happens to those who have suffered a car accident, are often suffering post-traumatic stress and emotional collapse, which obstructs adequate decision-making to find solutions to their situation. Moreover, their emotional state can include fear, sadness, anger and disgust. These relate specifically to the different events during the eviction process. This emotional rollercoaster involves intense emotions that alternate unexpectedly, sometimes resulting in depression and emotional collapse. This can be the greatest obstacle to people during the process and can coexist with the frustration of not having a job, which is the most missed thing that people named throughout the process (Ramis-Pujol, 2013).

The study referred to above describes the attitude of those who are involved in evictions as typical of "Dr Jekyll and Mr Hyde": the doors of banks, previously open, are now closed. The workplace, and even staff, in many cases turn their backs on the person affected by eviction. Meanwhile, the government has not responded by creating a framework to protect those vulnerable, and only after strong citizen pressure they ceded by designing a Royal Law Decree (Ley 1/2013), albeit one that is still ineffective in supporting families involved in eviction.

What we are talking about here is a "learned helplessness" (Seligman, 1972) situation that, together with a hostile environment and system, is causing great pain to those who are affected. Eviction increases the risk of social exclusion and the continuity of the underground economy, which is deeply rooted in Spain. Now that we have reached this point, we consider that measures are needed to promote social inclusion and, at the same time, to promote social cohesion.

As pointed out above, children are no stranger to these situations. As reflected in Save the Children's report on the compliance assessment of the 2012–2015 agenda, named *Muchos anuncios, pocos avances* (Many advertisements, little progress): "experiencing an eviction can have a devastating impact on children's lives and it can seriously affect their fundamental rights to education, health and protection" (Save the Children, 2012, p. 6). The same organisation estimated that 82% of families who suffer evictions have children to take care of. The effects of the economic crisis are devastating and are felt particularly in the quality of life of the children, often condemning them to an increasingly widespread, intense and chronic poverty and social exclusion. It is now a priority to design and implement specific policies for children, to avoid inherited poverty.

The Royal Law Decree that we mentioned above, which was adopted to rectify the "exceptional situations across Spain", is not enough to protect children, and neither does it guarantee that their rights are been respected. We must be aware that some children are being neglected and are unprotected in Spanish society. Our obligation as adult social agents is to attend to and protect them, so that they can experience development without these risks.

The impact on children resulting from the loss of housing, without forgetting the previous gradual impoverishment, is diverse, and it presents in relationship problems with parents, sadness, anger, behavioural changes, maladaptive behaviours, decreased quality of life and increased risk of social exclusion (Defensor del Menor de Andalucía, 2012). Despite this, the government has disconnected from the problem, offering no real solutions. It is not paying enough attention to this social drama, and it leaves outside the system with total impunity or lack of shame those who are being evicted.

Practices that contribute to maintenance

The factors that contribute to the maintenance of this system are many and diverse. First, we believe that the economic crisis is proving to be the perfect excuse to dismantle the welfare state to the benefit of the neoliberal ideological authorities. In this frame, the conservative governments of Europe, and especially of Spain, have found the perfect argument for privatising publics services such as education and healthcare. The increase in taxes has had a very negative effect on the middle and lower classes – the value added tax that is levied on a number of commodities (some of them staple goods, such as electricity bills or babies' nappies) has gone up to 21% – at the same time as work conditions and the rights of workers have worsened. Thus, through the discourse of reducing costs for the State, citizens have assumed the increased costs of services that correspond to their primary needs, with a resulting drop in purchasing power and increasing impoverishment.

In this sense we can talk about structural or systematic violence for two reasons. On the one hand is the serious setback in social rights and the deterioration of the population's quality of life, as people are forced to accept the outrage of a situation in which they are blamed "for having lived beyond their means". Meanwhile, corruption cases come to light with impunity and multiply. On the other hand is the criminalisation of the protests and claims of the citizenship. Even Amnesty International published a report entitled "Spain: the right to protest, threatened", echoing this new and generalised strategy of the government to hide the citizen's discontent (Amnistía Internacional, 2014). Government reaction has been the Citizen Protection Law, which will replace its homologue of 21 February 1992. One change introduced by this new law is the shift from competencies of the judiciary to the executive, which increases its power to impose administrative sanctions. The new law, renamed by some as "the Gag Law", has been approved. This structural violence creates in the population a state of learned defencelessness and fear, which paralyses and inhibits action. In this sense, we can conclude that the political, legislative and institutional answers have been insufficient to tackle the negative effects that the debts have imposed on the citizenship. In fact, they have aggravated the problem.

Second, it is important to refer to the irresponsible management of the major banks, which continue evicting, even when these same institutions have been bailed out by the state. If previously there was an excess of permissiveness when it came to granting credit, now the precautions are so extreme that it is impossible for much of the population to access credit for small and medium enterprises. The resulting lack of liquidity for both families and for many businesses has meant businesses having to close down.

Thus, according to an economic report published by the Economic Department of ESADE, between 2008 and 2012 some 177,336 enterprises have closed down. Bigger companies (the ones with more than 500 employees) have endured the economic crisis (Departamento de Economía de ESADE, 2012). The number of companies with 5,000 or more workers even rose from 2007 to 2011, as indicated by data from the *Directorio Central de Empresas* (*DIRCE*; Central Business Directory), which develops an annual census of enterprises in Spain. By contrast, between the same years, companies with 3–5 workers decreased by 13.7%, those with 6–9 by 17.8%, those with 10–25 by 21.3%, those with 26–49 by 23.5% and those with 50–249 by 14.9%. Thus 2012 became the fifth consecutive year in which the number of firms fell (INE, 2013, August 2), and so the economics of the country progress in a downward spiral with little hope of an exit.

Third is the manipulation of information made available by the politicised mass media, jointly with the lack of official data. We should not forget the deaths that have taken place within households that have been hounded by debt and foreclosures. According to the organisation *Stop Desahucios* (Stop Evictions), integrated into the PAH, 34% of the suicides occurring in Spain during 2012 were causally related to eviction situations, the suicides being close to, and following, the eviction dates. However, these cases do not appear on TV, perhaps to avoid the so-called "contagion effect". However, it is revealing that the INE has for two years delayed the publication of statistics on the subject. This lack of transparency contributes to the disguise of the reality and the paralysis of the citizenship.

Fourth, the concept of homeownership is still held as essential and idealised. This has sociocultural meanings in relation to socioeconomic security, social class and identity (Aramburu, 2010). Property is understood in the collective imagination as a guarantee of financial security for the future and consequently of social inclusion. Along these lines, solid alternatives are not offered since legislation has made renting appear unattractive.

We know that many families affected by the current economic crisis and the lack of protection of their fundamental rights do not go to social services because of feelings of shame and a fear of stigmatisation (Masip, personal interview, 28 July 2014). They perceive social services as "support services for the poor", distant to their social status and their own identity, and not as a civil right. Thus we identified that these cognitive structures and the collective imagination cause a certain reluctance to seek help from social services. The *Consell Econòmic i Social de Barcelona* (CESB; Economic and Social Council of Barcelona) in its report on poverty and social exclusion in Barcelona, states that the economic crisis has raised specific issues, and as "the increase of unemployment and job insecurity have conjured new profiles of poverty" (CESB, 2010, p. 29). The blog *Els Nous Pobres* (The New Poors) is a new platform written by people who were previously at a medium to high sociocultural level and have been moved into economically precarious situations.

Thus, poverty in energy, health and services – such as justice or taxed rates – is being locked behind closed doors, constituting different types of hidden poverty.

One should not underestimate the powerful impact of this reality because it has several consequences in people's daily struggle. The number of Spaniards who are at risk of fuel poverty has increased by 2 million in two years (2010–2012). This is the most prominent conclusion of the second annual benchmark study in Spain, published by the Environmental Sciences Association, which has updated data from 2010 to 2012.

The percentage of households that spend a disproportionate amount of their income to pay electricity and gas bills (taking as reference the definition of the UK, since in the Spanish context there is no such definition, which considers that households in fuel poverty are those that need to spend more than 10% of their income on home heating) rose in 2012 to 16.6% – seven million people (compared with five million in 2010). This number results in families suffering too much cold in winter and being overhot in summer, houses with moisture and mildew, power outage owing to unpaid bills (4 million in 2012: double compared with 2006), less money to attend to other basic needs, and premature deaths in winter: up to 7,200 could have been avoided in 2012 if the problem had been eradicated. The causes of fuel poverty are two parallel issues: citizen's income being reduced by the crisis and the disproportionate price of energy, which since 2007 has increased by 60% (Vidales, 2014, March 27). Furthermore, according to data provided by the Observatorio de Sostenibilidad Español, it is estimated that this kind of poverty is a direct cause of over 2,300 deaths per year – more than car accidents (Tirado, López, Martín and Mediavilla, 2012).

Currently in Spain there is no adequate protection against power outages. The opposite is true in more than half of the member states of the European Union, which protect consumers from outages during the coldest months and have reduced rates for groups that are at risk. In some cases, as in Sweden, the social protection system takes over unpaid invoices. These are some alternatives that could help to change the situation in Spain.

With regard to housing, in his article *El drama de las viviendas vacías* (The drama of the empty house), Pedro Antonio Navarro (2012) raises the option of proposing that people take an appropriate rent according to their economic situation, or that the tenants have the option to file bankruptcy and get rid of their bank debt. Another alternative is "cloud housing"[1], which contemplates using buildings such as business units with a specialised manager and shared services (Farràs, 2013). Payment for use can be made with money or time. At the international level, in countries such as France, the UK, Germany, Sweden, Holland and Denmark, there is a commitment to state intervention to protect the right to housing through planning and management policies. Approaches could include grants and subsidies for homeowners in order to rehabilitate housing for social emergency, the legalisation of the occupation of empty homes (Netherlands), tax incentives for those who rehabilitate vacant housing (UK) or penalties against those who have vacant homes for more than six weeks (Denmark).

Role of community psychology

Alipio Sánchez Vidal (2004) asks us:

> If Community Psychology (CP) seeks human development, its basic ethical stance must be to promote the other through his/her social community. And its core values would be: community, shared power (participation and social justice), interdependence, trusting others and collaborating with them. But such stance and values have a base of generosity and otherness, the erosion of which is the implicit program of modernity and capitalism that wishes to change those values for individual autonomy and self-interest, its cultural foundations. We must then ask ourselves, is community psychology ethically and socially viable in Western societies? (p. 93)

One of the most representative functions of CP is to work with the voices that haven't been heard, working with people, and accessing and using their own resources. To achieve this, CP involves addressing the awareness and empowerment of the community itself.

With the emergence of new social movements in Spain, people have moved from voice to action. The so-called 15-M Movement or *Movimiento de los Indignados* (Indignant Movement, integrated by non-partisan and non-unionists) was an example of the biggest movement of dissatisfaction in Spain in recent times. Thousands of people left their homes to be involved. Neighbourhood assemblies were generated, and currently they are still working on different commissions, trying to stop the loss of rights in different domains. The 15-M has allowed associations and cooperatives which were part of the struggle for greater social justice to achieve greater success and representation. Under the mottos "They don't represent us", "Take the square/park", "Indígnate" and "We are not politicians or bankers' merchandise", they display their dissatisfaction and collective discomfort.

Stéphane Hessel, one of the diplomats who participated in the drafting of the Universal Declaration of Human Rights in 1948, wrote: "Comprometez-vous", encouraging people to step forward, stop complaining and start to act in favour of social justice (Hessel, 2011). After three years, a lot of things have been achieved.

With the headline "The 15-M is infinite because we never have enough freedom and justice", the newspaper *Público* commemorated the 15-M anniversary (Ragucci, 2013, May 14). The work continues because there is an implicit social baseline of shared values where citizens are the ones who generate solutions.

At the same time as 15-M continues to develop, there are people like the members of the PAH who begin to work in favour of those who have been abused by exclusion and debt ("Yes it/you/we can" is their slogan). They have prevented many families from being exposed to the rawness of the street. Their main actions have focused on pointing to the principal actors that are responsible for the evictions (speculative banks which don't negotiate the families' debt) and presenting motions in councils. The next actions were the *escraches*, which had the purpose of reminding individual politicians of their responsibility to change the eviction drama. These controversial actions can be categorised as political pressure, but these civil disobedience actions are felt necessary following the paralysis of the government. The most effective responses were to stop the evictions using the pressure of a lot of anonymous people who appeared in the house that was about to suffer the eviction (they have avoided 1,135 evictions), to provide support with the aim of exonerating families from blame in order to prevent suicides (the opposite of the government suggestion), and to reaccommodate around 1,180 families in empty houses that are the property of rescued banks (Plataforma d'Afectats per la Hipoteca Barcelona, 2014, June 25).

In response of evictions, the most common action is the occupation of apartments that are owned by banks, which is being promoted as a response to the madness of the situation. It is important to point out that, while it doesn't stop the rising number of families and people who have been evicted living in the street since the financial crash, empty houses across the country have increased by 10.8% since 2001, which represents a total of 3.4 million (INE cited in Público, 2013, April 18) houses without renters. Plus, the majority of these empty habitable flats are now property of rescued banks, which are not doing anything with them other than waiting for them to recover their value so that they can resume speculating, instead of promoting social rents, so demanded by people affected by evictions and general society.

The system is saturated. We and many others, as citizens, have duties and rights to participate in important decisions, but at the same time we shouldn't forget that we gave certain decision-making powers to politicians democratically. They are the ones who should be accountable. It is paradoxical to talk about representativeness when in the last national election there were 28.31% abstentions (Ministerio del Interior de España, 2011, 21 November). However, there is a change happening in the never-ending bipartisanship that characterises Spanish politics, in which the ideological colour of the parties has been diluted to become the perpetuation of economic power. Now that people are aware of this phenomenon, it is expected to be reflected in the democratic processes that will take place in 2015.

People are no longer willing to lose their rights in exchange for the wellbeing of the rich. And this change, in our opinion, is a great victory of citizen's efforts in recent years, mediated by organisations working tirelessly on these social concerns.

What has to be the role of CP? In their community, many people find support in situations of poverty. How do we generate actions that promote structural changes in the long term? Utopia is the horizon that can make us move forward. However, to achieve good outcomes, first we have to think, discuss and agree.

The actual panorama is demanding new alternatives, points of view and instruments from our profession. The interrelation between CP, political concerns (with reference to shared values) and the public (understood as common things) is stronger than ever. What we are trying to encourage with this chapter is to identify goals and values to face a global problem.

If we pursue goals that are too idealistic, they may become unreachable and immeasurable. Is this a reason for not having them? Why not believe in the potential of people? There is a certain tendency to think with apathy and with indifference to other citizens, but the fact is that, due to the economic scam, Spanish people have started to meet their neighbours, associate with each other and take action. As professionals, we must maximise this natural trend.

The role of our work: The "Apropa't" ("Get closer") Association

Nowadays there are an increasing number of evictions in Spain, including both individuals and entire families. In fact, Catalonia is by far the region where most cases are recorded. There is no efficient response to this situation from Spain's central government, and the measures that have been developed by the Catalonian government are insufficient to stop the psychosocial effects of the evictions on the families. The serious consequences (psychosocial, psychological and health-related) are turning this phenomenon into a social emergency.

The decrease in psychological wellbeing of those who are suffering the stress and uncertainty of being evicted deserves special attention. In a family the parents tend to feel ashamed of the situation, so their isolation grows and it makes it difficult to access the help of the social protection net. In this context, the psychological and social effects of poverty and social inequality in childhood keep growing. The suicides, even though they have been invisible, also keep growing. Taking all of this into account, we must consider the short-, medium- and long-term repercussions of this new skyline, where the right to have a decent house is being violated. As professionals it is within our sphere to consider what we can do to prevent and relieve the suffering that these situations cause people.

The most interesting and powerful programs can be found into the social network, but as a consequence of the lack of institutional support this net cannot cope with all the growing needs of the population.

The Apropa't project was born while we were studying a master's degree in psychosocial intervention at the University of Barcelona. One of the first pieces of research was to create a proposed intervention based on an analysis of social needs that were not covered in Barcelona. At this point we were wondering what our role could be in the social emergency of evictions. We believe that academic knowledge should have a real impact in the world we are living in. That is why we have decided to take a step forward towards social justice, welfare, and opportunities equality, by starting our psychosocial interventional project, self-managed, to try to help the families who have lived through or are at risk of eviction. In addition, we want other professionals and families to reap benefit from our experience, because from our point of view the academic entities, especially the university, should be involved and should lead regarding social change.

The pilot project Apropa't stands out because up until now all of the projects that have been developed around evictions were focused on legal and social areas, not on the psychological effects that these situations entail. Apropa't has been created based on the participants' specific needs but, because of its flexible methodology and the fact that it is treating a real problem in our community, it will probably be adapted for use in other neighbours.

Apropa't has been developed in Ciutat Meridiana, a neighbourhood on the outskirts of Barcelona. This is a symbolic location because it is at the epicentre of the eviction issue in Spain, popularly called "Villa desahucio" ("Eviction town"). Mestre Morera is a public school with children aged between 3 and 12 years, located at the end of the main street of the neighbourhood – the street which agglutinates the biggest number of evictions in Spain. The school witnesses the weekly eviction of its students. Mestre Morera believes that "if it is possible at school, it has to be possible in the world", and all of the work developed by different actors involved with the kids focuses on this social change through the children's education and taking into account their proposals to improve the neighbourhood. The school, constantly involved in the development of its neighbourhood, opened its doors to our group of professionals from the psychology and social work spheres. We didn't waste the opportunity to intervene to try to ameliorate some of the psychological effects on the children living through eviction process.

Our work is related to the quality of life and the psychological and social wellbeing of the families that have suffered an eviction or are close to one, which is the reason why we decided to work with children. Through therapeutic games we create an atmosphere where they can feel relaxed, and that allows us to work on the recognition and expression of their emotions, their capacity for resilience and their thoughts about the future.

As the eviction situation affects the whole family structure, our work is based not only on the children but also on their parents. Within this context we offer families the creation of a help group where psychoeducative sessions take place and tools such as communication strategies, teaching methods, relaxation workshops, problem-solving workshops and emotion management are provided. Due to our flexible methodology, we focus working in real-life situations on problems that families are already facing, so that they can try to solve difficulties in a different way, and where both parents and kids are taken into account and validated.

These two ways of working were already defined: one focused on the children and the other directed to the parents; it is time to add the third one: we focus on designing and accomplishing activities where both parents and children participate. This is an opportunity to improve communication and spend some time together far from everyday problems, and where we try to make the families' bonds stronger through a range of different activities.

The scholarly community is the other element that supports this project. The communication and collaboration with the school team is useful as an information source and as a link to the families. It also gives us the spaces required to carry out the intervention.

Finally, we use a built-in evaluation system that assesses the project at an initial point, at the halfway point and at the end. Currently we are analysing the quantitative information that we have gathered in relation to resilience, social support and self-concept, although the preliminary results are not yet available. Examining the content of the semistructured interviews that were conducted at the end of the project, the participants' appraisal is favourable, indicating that the time that was spent working with us was useful for them and their children.

As can be seen, we are looking for a solution in a local context, and we want the participation, agreement and implication to keep being part of our identity as professionals and human beings.

Conclusions

Spanish families suffer a crisis when their members of working age remain unemployed and without income, when they are evicted, when the whole situation gets worse due to reduced opportunities of finding a job and settling their debts, when the quality and quantity of food are depleted, when the family environment deteriorates, when they suffer fuel poverty, and when they cannot afford medical treatments that are not covered by the public system. They are also affected by policy decisions to reduce the public budget for social services, education and health.

The psychosocial effects of going through an eviction process affect families' welfare, tearing the social fabric and collective sense, and generating guilt and shame. It is from the citizen base that there has been the greatest response to these problems. Levels of need and social emergency are so extensive that government does not reach to cover even necessities. However, there are associations, cooperatives and informal support networks that are filling the gaps and relieving the discomfort. The state's role has thus been relegated to a distant second place.

The outlook, our mentality and the way in which society operates is changing. Social movements have contributed to the visibility and appreciation of social problems. While systemic violence is spreading, segregation and the undercover poverty phenomena are becoming priorities on people's current agendas despite the ghost of "living beyond our means", a phrase that is endlessly repeated to citizens by politicians since the economic crash.

"The personal is political" was one of the most famous feminist slogans of the 1960s, and certainly it is not easy to discern the line between personal principles and the political in our profession. However, we need to unite strength and values, and begin to conceptualise what is inherent and unavoidably political in our day-to-day job, if unquestioned values emerge. We must clarify our complexes and fears, and our professional ethics will help us move forward.

We also invite readers, whether professionals in CP or not, to reflect on their role in this plot. What world do we want to build for future generations? We have the tools and the capacity, the only thing we have to do is operate the machinery. Because of this, we would like to emphasise our hope for change. The citizen's power, their work and values, provide all of us with encouragement. We must put aside apathetic opinions to focus on people's potential, and teach them to unlearn helplessness and to promote civic mobilisation. We believe in the transformative potential of local communities to make a change despite global issues.

Finally, we would like to end with a hopeful message. Despite the obstacles that we may encounter on the road, it makes sense to keep fighting, keep working and keep believing that any change is possible if we work for it. If we as citizens, and future generations, do not associate, do not cooperate and do not encourage critical thinking, we will remain alone. But while it exists, a sense of community, as long as we value the gains, as long as we locate ourselves within a social world with historical process and we give importance to that which deserves it, not what they told us it should have, there will be a way forward. As an African proverb states, popularised by Eduardo Galeano, "Many little people, in little places, doing little things, can change the world" (n.d.).

Note

1. For more information about this Project, visit this website: http://www.vidamesfacil.com/en/how-does-cloudhousing-work/.

References

Amnistía Internacional (2014). *España: El Derecho a Protestar, Amenazado*. Retrieved on https://doc.es.amnesty.org/

Aramburu, M. (2010). *La resignificació de la tinença de l'habitatge a Catalunya davant la crisi econòmica: una aproximació a través de grups de discussió*. Barcelona: Generalitat de Catalunya.

Centro de Investigaciones Sociológicas (2014). *Tres problemas principales que existen actualmente en España (Multirrespuesta %)*. Retrieved on http://www.cis.es/

Colau, A. and Alemany, A. (2013). *2007–2012: Retrospectiva sobre desahucios y ejecuciones hipotecarias en España, estadísticas oficiales e indicadores*. Retrieved on Plataforma de Afectados por la Hipoteca website: http://afectadosporlahipoteca.com/wp-content/uploads/2013/02/RETROSPECTIVA-SOBRE-DESAHUCIOS-Y-EJECUCIONES-HIPOTECARIAS-EN-ESPA%C3%91A-COLAUALEMANY1.pdf

Consell Econòmic i Social de Barcelona (2010). *Informe sobre pobresa i exclusió social a Barcelona*. Retrieved on http://www.bcn.cat/barcelonainclusiva/blogs/taules/informepobresa_cesb.pdf

Darley, J. M., and Latané, B. (1968). Bystander intervention in emergencies: Diffusion of responsibility. *Journal of Personality and Social Psychology*, 8, 377–383.
Defensor del Menor de Andalucía (2012, December 10). *Incidencia de los desahucios en las personas menores de edad.* Retrieved on http://www.defensordelmenordeandalucia.es/node/2263
Departamento de Economía de ESADE (2012). *ESADE. Informe Económico. Enero 2012, No. 12.* In a Ballabriga, F. C. (ed.). Retrieved on http://itemsweb.esade.edu/biblioteca/archivo/informeeconomicoenero2012.pdf
Els nous pobres (2012, June 8). *Yo también soy una nueva pobre* [Web log message]. Retrieved on http://elsnouspobres.wordpress.com/
Farràs, L. (2013, January 20). Ni inquilino ni propietario: usuario. El "cloud housing" propone el pago por uso como alternativa a la compra o alquiler de un piso. *La Vanguardia*. Retrieved on http://hemeroteca.lavanguardia.com/
Hernández, J. A. (2014, March 28). Home evictions averaged 184 a day in Spain last year. *El País*. Retrieved on http://elpais.com/archivo/
Hessel, S. (2011). *El moviment Hessel.* Barcelona. Ediciones 62, S. A., labutxaca.
Ibáñez, M. J. and Sust, T. (2011, October 21). 1.2.5 millones de familias españolas subsisten en situación de pobreza. *El Periódico*. Retrieved on http://www.elperiodico.com/
Instituto Nacional de Estadística (2013, August 2). *Notas de prensa: Estructura y dinamismo del tejido empresarial en España. Directorio Central de Empresas (DIRCE) a 1 de enero de 2013.* Retrieved on http://www.ine.es/prensa/np794.pdf
La Vanguardia (2 June 2012). El desahucio afecta a 159 familias cada día en España. *La Vanguardia*. Retrieved on http://hemeroteca.lavanguardia.com/
Ley 1/2013, de 14 de mayo, de medidas para reforzar la protección a los deudores hipotecarios, reestructuración de deuda y alquiler social. In *Boletín Oficial del Estado*, 15 May 2013, No. 116, pp. 36373–36398.
Mars, A. (2014, March 13). España sufre el mayor aumento de la brecha social en Europa por la crisis. *El País*. Retrieved on http://elpais.com/archivo/
Ministerio del Interior de España (2011, November 21). *Elecciones Generales 2011. Total Estatal.* Retrieved on http://elecciones.mir.es/resultadosgenerales2011/99CG/DCG99999TO_L1.htm
Navarro, P. A. (2012). El drama de las viviendas vacías. *El Siglo de Europa: Los dossieres*, 971, 32–38. Retrieved on El Siglo de Europa website: http://www.elsiglodeuropa.es/siglo/historico/2012/971/971Dossier.pdf
Pérez-Lanzac, C. (2014, July 17). El tribunal de la UE también considera abusiva la reforma de la ley hipotecaria. *El País*. Retrieved on http://elpais.com/archivo/
Plataforma d'Afectats per la Hipoteca Barcelona (2014, June 25). 1.180 realojos y victoria de ImPAHrables en Barcelona. Retrieved on http://pahbarcelona.org/2014/06/25/impahrables-1180-realojos-conseguidos-y-nueva-victoria-en-barcelona/
Público (2013, April 18). España tiene 3,4 millones de viviendas vacías. *Público*. Retrieved on http://www.publico.es/
Ragucci, F. (2013, May 14). El 15-M es infinito porque nunca se tiene libertad ni justicia suficiente. *Público*. Retrieved on http://www.publico.es/
Ramis-Pujol, J. R. (2013). *Razón económica y realidad humana: Una aproximación multidisciplinar al desahucio hipotecario basada en estudios de caso.* Barcelona: Universitat Ramon Llull y Fundación Innovación, Acción y Conocimiento.

Retrieved on Fundación, Innovación, Acción y Conocimiento website: http://www.fiayc.org/fileserver2/340479920desahucioshipotecarios.estudioscaso.enfoquemultidisciplinar.Ramis.Vinversa.V2.pdf.

Sánchez, A. (2004). Acción social en tiempos de conformismo: Por una ética possible de la intervención comunitaria. In Sánchez, A., Zambrano, A. Y. and Palacín, M. (comp.). *Psicología Comunitaria Europea: Comunidad, poder, ética y valores* (pp. 93–106). Barcelona: Publicacions de la Universitat de Barcelona.

Save the Children (2012). *Muchos anuncios, pocos avances. Informe de evaluación del cumplimiento de la Agenda de Infancia 2012–2015 un año después de las elecciones generales.* Retreived from http://www.savethechildren.es/ver_doc.php?id=152

Save the Children España (2014). *2.826.549 razones. La protección de la infancia frente a la pobreza: un derecho, una obligación y una inversión.* Retrieved on http://www.savethechildren.es/docs/Ficheros/644/INFORME.pdf

Seligman, M. E. P. (1972). Learned helplessness. *Annual Review of Medicine*, 23(1), 407–412.

Stop Desahucios (2014, July 9). Los nuevos datos del INE vuelven a mostrar el fracaso de ley criminal del PP y la vulneración del derecho a la vivienda. Retrieved on Plataforma de Afectados por la Hipoteca website: http://afectadosporlahipoteca.com/2014/07/09/los-nuevos-datos-del-ine-vuelven-a-mostrar-el-fracaso-de-ley-criminal-del-pp-y-la-vulneracion-del-derecho-a-la-vivienda/

Tirado, S., López, J. L., Martín, P., and Mediavilla, L. (2012). *Pobreza energética en España: Potencial de generación de empleo directo de la pobreza derivado de la rehabilitación energética de viviendas.* Madrid: Asociación de Ciencias Ambientales (ACA). Retrieved on Universidad de Zaragoza website: http://catedrazaragozavivienda.unizar.es/Jornada2012/PobrezaEnergetica.pdf

UNICEF España (2012, October 8). 80.000 niños más bajo el umbral de la pobreza en España. Retrieved on http://www.unicef.es/actualidad-documentacion/noticias/80000-ninos-mas-bajo-el-umbral-de-la-pobreza-en-espana.

UNICEF España (2012). *La infancia en España 2012–2013. El impacto de la crisis en los niños.* Madrid: UNICEF España.

Vidales, R. (2014, March 27). La pobreza energética se dispara. *El País.* Retrieved on http://elpais.com/archivo/

5
The Experiences of Individuals in Debt during an Era of Extreme Austerity in Greece

Alexandra Papamichail and Petros Mizamidis

This chapter presents experiences of indebtedness during an era of extreme austerity in Greece. The principal aim is to contribute to debates on the psychosocial determinants of psychological wellbeing by drawing upon a qualitative analysis of the experiences of seven individuals in debt. A secondary aim is to bring to critical appraisal the stigmatisation of individuals in debt and the individualisation of indebtedness, an issue which mainly arises as a consequence of specific socioeconomic structures and arrangements (Turner, 2008).

Introduction

It has long been established that psychological wellbeing is affected by socioeconomic and environmental factors, such as employment, education and perceived financial strain (Herrman et al., 2005). As far as debt is concerned, although there is a large volume of research that illustrates the statistical associations of debt, financial strain and poor mental health (Hintikka et al., 1998; Skapinakis et al., 2006; Jenkins et al., 2009; Madianos et al., 2011), the number of qualitative studies which enable us to capture the meanings that individuals attribute to their experiences with debt, their emotions and the subjective explanations of the relationship between emotional wellbeing and indebtedness is quite small (Nettleton and Burrows, 2001). In Greece in particular, no previous qualitative studies are known to us. Additionally, much psychological research views debt solely as an individualised problem that is attributed to financial incompetence and personal consumerism (Webley and

Nyhus, 2001; Graeber, 2011). In contrast, a growing number of recent studies demonstrate that debt results as a consequence of unexpected life events, drops in income and unemployment (Becker, 1997; Ambrose and Cunningham, 2004; Orton, 2009; Dearden et al., 2010; Marmot, 2010). According to Graeber (2013), in interview provided to Grave and Tincq stated that:

> The ideology of debt is one of the most powerful tools ever created to justify situations of violent inequalities and not only does it make them seem moral, but also it makes them seem as if it is the victim who is to blame.
>
> (Grave et al., 2013)

Indeed, an economic analysis of the increase in personal debt during recent decades shows that debt constitutes a social phenomenon that is closely related to structural inequalities and neoliberal economic policies (Turner, 2008). Due to the fact that debt is closely related to the socioeconomic environment and because of the importance of socioeconomic context in the understanding of psychological functioning (Walker et al., 2012), the next part of this study gives a brief overview of the economic crisis and the transformations that it evoked in Greek society.

The social context: Greece's national debt within the neoliberal agenda

The basic tenets of the neoliberal ideology incorporate a belief in the superiority of the market against any interventions from the state's side, low interest rates, public burden theory of welfare state, downward pressures on wages and a preference for individualism over collectivism (Pratt, 2006). According to this doctrine, society is split between successful and unsuccessful people depending on their financial power (Beresford, 2005). In line with the aforementioned theory, indebtedness is viewed as an individualised problem of lack of responsibility and financial competence. Media coverage as well as politicians' language enhances further the stigmatisation and demonisation of individuals who are in debt. A characteristic example is the statement of the vice president of the Greek government who signed the first memorandum – "we all spend it [the money] together" – in an attempt to explain the high levels of national debt in the country (*Kathimerini*, 2012). Another popular assertion fostered by the media was that "Greeks were living beyond their means" although the household and total private debt in Greece was among the lowest in the Eurozone before the crisis (Eurostat, 2014).

The global financial crisis that started in 2008 affected the vast majority of developed and industrialised countries. In Europe, Greece was particularly affected, and it is now facing the most severe economic recession of its modern history (Diamandouros, 2012). In April 2010 the prime minister, G.A. Papandreou, announced that the country would ask for help from the International Monetary Fund (IMF) due to a dramatic increase in Greece's public debt levels to 144% of its GDP (EUR 320 billion). A memorandum of agreement was signed between Greece, the IMF, the European Union and the European Central Bank, with Greece borrowing EUR 110 billion and EUR 130 billion in May 2010 and February 2012, respectively. This first bailout loan was agreed on May 2010 and it was conditional on the implementation of the neoliberal austerity measures which started in the late 1990s and aimed to restructure the society according to market needs (Garuda, 2000; Karamessini, 2008). In May 2013 the national debt reached a record high of 175.2% of GDP. For a more detailed review of the economic crisis in Greece, see elsewhere (Fraile, 2009; Kouretas and Vlamis, 2010; Arghyrou and Tsoukalas, 2011).

The austerity measures that Greece has adopted include minimising public expenditure, lowering public and private sector wages, reductions of up to 30% in pensions, the elimination of subsidies for energy, education and health, and the cutting of social benefits (Ghellab and Papadakis, 2011). In addition, there have been increases in taxes, both direct and indirect, as well as in electricity bills (Frangos et al., 2012). The social impact of these austerity measures is tremendous. Between 2010 and 2014, Greece lost 25% of its GDP, while individuals lost up to 40% of their income. The percentage of individuals that were living in risk of poverty or social exclusion rose to 33% in 2011 (Smith, 2012), while, according to recent research conducted by the Economics Department of the University of Athens, 44% of the population had an income below the poverty line (i.e. EUR 665 per person). Additionally, 14% of the population were living below the line of extreme poverty. Indicatively, this percentage was 2% in 2009 (*Kathimerini*, 2014). Unemployment reached 27% of the active population, while unemployment among the young rose to 63% in mid-2013 (Eurostat, 2013b). The population's health had deteriorated significantly, especially among vulnerable groups, while there had been an increase in levels of criminal activity (Kentikelenis and Papanicolas, 2011). Indicatively, the Greek division of Doctors of the World argues that the percentage of those asking for medical care from the organisation increased from 3% before the crisis to 30% in 2011 (Kentikelenis and Papanicolas, 2011).

Mortgage and credit card loans

In 2000, household debt in Greece was 20% of its GDP, while in 2010 it reached 65% of its GDP (Cecchetti et al., 2011). The numbers show that since the adoption of the euro and during the decade 2000–2010 there has been a rise in loan formation.

According to a recent survey conducted in Greece in 2012, some 41% of households had bank loans (*Public Issue*, 2013). The vast majority of loans were mortgage loans (25%), while consumer loans constituted 10%. From 2008 to 2012, household loans decreased from 49% to 41%, which was due not only to the emerging difficulty of Greek households to support new loans but also to the strict bank policy on loan formation (Euromonitor International, 2013).

Since the beginning of the crisis in 2008, there have been increased difficulties with loan repayment. The mortgage loan segment is facing severe problems (*Public Issue*, 2013). The percentage of non-performing loans (NPLs) rose from 10% in 2010 to 19% in 2012, while before the crisis it was 4%. According to the Bank of Greece, NPLs in the card lending segment climbed to 31% by the end of 2012 from 20.5% in 2010 (as stated in Euromonitor International, 2013). The percentage of NPLs in the non-card lending segment increased from 15% in 2010 to 24% by the end of 2012, while in June 2013, NPLs reached 30%. According to PricewaterhouseCoopers (PwC), this percentage would rise by up to 40% during 2014, due to the continued economic crisis, high unemployment rates and cuts in wages (PwC, 2014).

From the statistics, some clear conclusions can be drawn. First, it is clear that the number of households that are incapable of repaying their loans, either in the card or non-card lending segment, has dramatically increased during the period of the crisis in comparison to the years before that. Furthermore, taking into consideration the PwC data, this tendency will continue. At this point it is worth mentioning that this incapability of repaying the loans is not due to receiving additional loans, since it becomes clear from the aforementioned data that the number of new household loans has decreased. Second, the similarity in the increase in NPLs in the card and non-card lending segment shows that Greek households in debt are incapable of repaying not only loans that derive from consumer needs but also high-priority loans, such as mortgages.

The issue of debt, its psychological impact and social suffering in the literature

The problem of indebtedness, relative poverty and their impact on human wellbeing has received great attention by both the media and researchers, especially since the beginning of the global financial crisis in 2008 (Bridgesa and Disney, 2010). The growing interest in the literature on the association between "psychological stressors, relative deprivation and psychosocial injuries of structural inequalities" is therefore unsurprising (Elstad, 1998, p. 40). Research has provided strong evidence, according to which, alterations in psychosocial life, for instance self-esteem, sense of control and social status, affect mental and physical health (Wilkinson et al., 1998).

As far as debt is concerned, the vast majority of quantitative studies illustrate a correlation between debt worries, financial strain and negative mental health (Vinokur et al., 1996; Hintikka et al., 1998; Drentea, 2000; Kahn and Fazio, 2005; Skapinakis et al., 2006; Jenkins et al., 2009). Skapinakis et al. (2006), in a psychiatric morbidity survey that recruited 2,406 participants in the UK, demonstrated that debt was correlated with major depression after controlling for employment status, standard of living and psychiatric symptoms, although there was no correlation found with debt and anxiety disorders. Another longitudinal study that recruited 209 families found that worrying about debt repayments was strongly related to depression, both at baseline and at the follow-up (after six months) (Reading and Reynolds, 2001). It should be noted, however, that causal interpretations cannot be drawn, due to the fact that both of the aforementioned studies did not test for psychiatric history before they began.

As far as studies that were conducted in Greece are concerned, a recent survey which took place during the period of economic crisis also showed that financial hardship was associated with major depression, whereas perceived financial strain was correlated with suicidal ideation (Madianos et al., 2011). Another study from the University of Ioannina that was conducted at the beginning of the crisis from June 2009 to January 2010 found a rise in common mental health disorders in individuals who face serious financial difficulties (Skapinakis, 2009). More precisely, those individuals with perceived financial strain were three times as likely to develop mental ill-health in comparison with their counterparts with no financial problems. Economou et al. (2011), in a telephone survey in Greece, observed a 36% increase in attempted suicides in 2011, compared with the data gathered in 2009. In addition, as stated previously, no qualitative research conducted in

106 Understanding Institutionalised Suffering

Greece is known to us. Kempson (1996), in qualitative research with mothers with young children, found that anxiety about debt repayments triggered depression. An interesting qualitative study of mortgage repossession by Nettleton and Burrows (2001), in England, indicated that participants reported stigma, insecurity, anxiety and uncertainty after the repossession of their home. Ethnographic studies illustrate that debt begets psychological burden and social stigmatisation (Williams, 2008; Graeber, 2011).

The aforementioned studies, as well as the plethora of work investigating the impact of indebtedness on individuals, suggest that there is a potential risk for the psychological wellbeing of individuals in debt, especially if one takes into consideration the current economic crisis. However, while the relationship between debt and poor psychological health is established, there is a need for qualitative studies in Greece for the meanings and the experiences of individuals in debt to be captured. Finally, debt as a social phenomenon needs to be addressed not only at an individual level but at a public level, through action against policies that promote increases in consumers' debt and the continuation of structural and income inequalities.

The study

Design

Before the interviews and the pilot interview, an interview plan was constructed that included the main areas of life that are affected by indebtedness. The final interview plan incorporated questions about the effect on mood and mental health, life choices, impact on personal life, social stigma, aetiologies of indebtedness and feelings towards being in debt. The interviews were semistructured and they were conducted in a friendly and relaxed way, owing to the sensitivity of the subject being investigated. Because of the fact that the aim was to capture the experiences from the participants' perspective, a phenomenological approach was adopted (Moustakas, 1994).

Participants

This research constitutes a small-scale case study that recruited a purposeful sample of seven participants (five women and two men) through snowballing. The participants' mean age is $M = 51.7$ years while the age range is 32–68. Three participants came from Thessaloniki (A, B and C), which is the second biggest city in Greece, three from Katerini (D, F and G), a small city close to Thessaloniki, and one from Crete (E). Of the seven participants, four had two children each (A, C, F and G) while the rest had no children. Four participants were married, engaged or with a partner (C, D, F and G), one was a widow (B) and one was divorced (A). Semistructured qualitative interviews were conducted during 2013 in places that were convenient for the participants, while consent was formally obtained from all of them.

Data analysis

The transcripts were translated from Greek to English and they were content analysed. An interpretive approach was adopted in order to capture the meanings and experiences of individuals in debt, and how it affects their lives and their emotional wellbeing (Henning, 2004). Major and minor themes were identified and a codebook was created with lists of themes – for instance, reasons for indebtedness; impact on mood, mental health and emotional wellbeing; social exclusion; and loneliness. The extracts presented below were chosen as those that were most representative of the major themes that derived from the interviews and they reflect the most important aspects of the individuals' experiences of indebtedness.

Findings

Links between indebtedness and the current economic crisis

When asked, all of the participants apart from one (E) reported either directly or indirectly that their difficulty in repaying their debts and their indebtedness was associated with the current economic crisis in Greece, either because their income had dropped or because they had had to borrow money to make ends meet. Four participants (A, B, D and F) also said that the socioeconomic environment affected them negatively, besides their problems with debt, due to worries about the future:

> Of course it is related. At least this is what my job shows. If people do not have money, how are they supposed to come and buy things from my shop? I sell ... and this is luxury today, it is not a basic commodity. If you don't have, I won't have either. We are interdependent. (B)

> It is definitely related! And they have to introduce policies that deal with the non performing loans based on the bad economic situation of households in Greece today. I mean, they are talking about non performing loans today so what? ... when the percentage of non-performing loan is so high you cannot do anything. (A)

and it is not only our debt; this is our main problem, of course, but the whole situation is very bad too, the whole situation gives you a very bad feeling here. Both of my children are unemployed, I see them sad and I want to do something but I cannot. (F)

Reasons for indebtedness

Two of the participants (A and B) were experiencing serious financial problems. One of them was a divorced woman with two children (A) and the other was a widow (B). One male participant (E) did not have problems paying off his debt due to the fact that it was a small amount and he moved to another country to work. Additionally, all of the participants' debt was due to card loans (A, B, C, D and E), mortgage loans (A, C, F and G) or both (A, C and F). Before 2007, none of the participants had experienced problems with debt repayments. Apart from one participant (E), the reasons why participants were in debt were health reasons, mortgage loans, everyday life expenses or due to the fact that their business had shut down:

> That I don't have a job. And of course this is a political issue. You have personal responsibilities when you run your own shop but, if the socioeconomic environment is so adverse, what could you do? (B)

> Suddenly, I found myself alone with two kids that I had to raise with just one salary. My salary was not enough to fulfil the needs we had as a family. I took part in the first strike and we didn't get our salary for two months so I got my first loan. Then my mother got sick and, if we had left her to the national hospital, she would have died. She had cancer, she was in pain, and they could arrange an appointment after three months. All this ended up in money from credit cards and so, afterwards, a loan to cover the credit card loans which had a very high interest. At the beginning of the crisis, one of my children was at the last grade of high school, [he/she] and about to enter university... I had retired due to health reasons earlier that year but in the first memorandum agreement they decided to cut pensions up to 40% for those under 55. So I had a pension of 700 euros to pay my mortgage loan, my card loan and to send money to my child to study. (A)

> Because of the political choices and the economic crisis. Everyday life expenses are a lot, you cannot make ends meet anymore, and taxes are very high. If we were not into crisis... I mean they cut my salary

up to 30% and 40% since then. I would be able to pay it off like before [the crisis]. (D)

These findings are in consensus with the literature presented above concerning the transformations in society and the impact of the neoliberal alternations in the Greek economy on people's lives (Ghellab and Papadakis, 2011; Frangos et al., 2012). In addition, they are in consensus with the literature which supports the idea that debt is not an individualised problem deriving from personal consumerism and a lack of financial competence – at least in the majority of the cases – but is a sociopolitical phenomenon that is related to structural inequalities (Turner, 2008), and a consequence of unexpected life events and drops in income (Becker, 1997; Ambrose and Cunningham, 2004; Dearden et al., 2010; Marmot, 2010).

Nowadays, in the context of Greek society, where the average person has lost 40% of their income, unemployment has reached 27% and social benefits have been cut or have shrunk, it is perhaps unsurprising that the participants in our study face severe economic difficulties in repaying their debts. Sickness of a relative, unemployment, cuts in salary of 30-40% and closed businesses are the reasons why the participants have not been able to repay their debts. These reasons do not belong to the sphere of irresponsible and unethical use of credit to acquire material items; rather, they are the outcome of unforeseen life events and economic and political decisions that widen structural and income inequalities.

Impact on mental health and emotional wellbeing

All of the participants apart from one (E) reported elevated feelings of stress. Stress was attributed to problems of repaying the debt in the current economic environment in the country. Four of the seven participants reported direct and indirect effects of stress on their psychological wellbeing and physical health. Most of the participants (A, B, C and F) were prescribed anti-anxiety sleeping pills so as to be able to manage their stress, while one male participant aged 32 years reported high blood pressure that started after he had been facing difficulties paying his credit card bill. Two participants (A and F) reported depressive feelings while one had suicidal ideation (A):

> Although I used to be a strong person and participate in political and social life..., I reached this point [suicidal thoughts]. What kept me alive was the thought of my youngest child... because [s/he] was

young, I felt [s/he] needed me. The first time, when not even the thought of my children could suppress these thoughts, was when the technician came to shut off gas. I owed 600 euros and if it hadn't been for my neighbour who lent me 600 euros, I would possibly have jumped from the window that day. (A)

I feel stressed or depressed continuously, even without any other reason since then [when the problem of repaying the loans started]... I can't sleep you know... I don't want to steal their money, I don't feel nice about it, but we cannot do it anymore [pay back]. (F)

I am constantly thinking about my debt; all day long, and when I wake up during the night, all night long. I started taking pills to be able to sleep since then [when the debt problem arose] and I visited a psychiatrist for some time. (B)

My stress definitely increased since then. Sometimes, out of the blue, I have a fast heartbeat, but I try to fight it. There hasn't been a day since then that I am not thinking about how I will be able to pay it back. Even my children; it affects us all. My husband is always very anxious and very angry; we feel like there is no way out of here. I wished that all of this were just a bad dream and we woke up one day and everything was just as before [the crisis]. (G)

The link between psychological ill health and debt has long been established by research, and our findings are consistent with the majority of the literature (Hintikka et al., 1998; Drentea, 2000; Kahn and Fazio, 2005; Skapinakis et al., 2006; Jenkins et al., 2009; Orton, 2009). Perhaps the most worrying indication is the rising number of people who face severe debt-repayment problems in Greece, in a period when public funding for physical and mental health has been slashed. For instance, from 2009 to 2011, public hospital cuts reached 26% (OECD, 2013), while state funding for mental health decreased by 20% between 2010 and 2011, and by an additional 55% between 2011 and 2012 (Anagnostopoulos and Soumaki, 2013). These figures alongside our findings raise concerns about the population's health and they support the need for social health policies that will protect the population from health deterioration.

Social isolation and loneliness

Five participants reported that they were feeling socially excluded and that debt was associated with feelings of loneliness, due to the fact that they could not afford to participate in social events:

> It [debt] is related with my relationships, with my friends and my loneliness, and my choices in everyday life...I want to go to the cinema, to the theatre or to an excursion and I cannot. (B)

> I did not like to go out so much before but at least sometimes we would go with my husband for a trip or out for dinner with our friends; now I don't know...I don't remember when it was the last time I went out for a dinner or to the cinema...it makes you feel you are excluded from what is going on out there. (G)

Economic hardship manifests itself not only as a deprivation of material items but also as restricted social mobility and social isolation (Walker et al., 2013). The findings are consistent with the literature concerning the correlation between debt and mental health, since social isolation is usually a major outcome of debt (Drentea and Lavrakas, 2000; Mind, 2008). In their study, Drentea and Lavrakas (2000) showed that indebtedness does not allow individuals to spend on "quality goods" due to their efforts to make cutbacks. The social wellbeing of individuals is therefore negatively affected, since individuals who are making efforts to repay their debts may be overstretching, as the participants of this study stated. In addition, feelings of failure and shame may result in an unwillingness of individuals to open up and discuss their problems, and this further enforces social isolation, which, in its turn, worsens psychological health (Hayes, 2000; Mind, 2004).

Psychological pressure from contact with the banks

Almost all of the participants, apart from one (E), were dissatisfied with their contact with the banks. They were feeling anxious and afraid of the phone calls, while one participant underlined the impersonal nature of these contacts:

> The way that banks work, I mean the pressure and threats that they will take your home or to take your money directly from your pension account they create a situation that leads you to craziness. (A)

> ...and I am always afraid of the phone calls from the banks. (G)

One participant felt that she particularly disliked the fact that her debt was sold to other debt collectors:

> I mean, the phone rings and they call you for a bill you did not pay from another company to which your debt is now transferred, and they use violence in what they are telling you. This is violent. (B)

Previous studies, such as the one conducted by Nettleton and Burrows (2001) in England concerning the experiences of individuals who lost mortgaged houses, also demonstrated that participants felt "hounded" by the debt collectors, and they noted that they strongly disliked the impersonal nature of their contacts with the institutions. Gulliver and Morris (2011) also found that more than a fifth of their participants felt harassed by the lenders. Walker et al. (2012), in a qualitative study of mental health and the UK credit industry, noted that participants felt distressed, threatened and bullied in their contacts with debt collectors. The results underscore the need for legislation and social protection policies that will protect those in debt from lending abuses, especially during a period of severe financial crisis. It should be taken into consideration that these practices are political in nature and stem from the neoliberal ideology of demonising indebtedness. To put it differently, since debt is viewed as an individualised problem that characterises the individual as financially incompetent or even unethical, the adoption of the tactics of relentlessly chasing the indebted for the repayment of debts is justified. Last but not least, these practices can affect mental health negatively since they enhance feelings of anxiety, despair, shame and guilt (Mind, 2004).

Self-worth and self-esteem

The majority of participants felt that being in debt and having difficulty paying it off had a negative impact on their self-esteem:

> I am so angry and I guess other people also feel the same, and I feel low with myself because, after 30 years of working that I gave my soul and myself to my job, I haven't managed to save some money and give at least 500 euros to my children to buy something so they remember me. (A)

> Very bad, first of all I don't feel like a human being anymore. I don't feel I have rights anymore and I cannot even walk free, I feel permanently suppressed. (B)

> ...sometimes I feel I failed and bad with myself and I think if you had chosen this or that today you would not be in this place. (F)

According to the literature, indebtedness is closely related to low self-esteem and shame (Nettleton and Burrows, 2001; Orton, 2009; Walker et al., 2013). The literature indicates that individuals who face financial difficulties regard themselves as "not trying hard" (Blokland, 2007,

p. 43) or as "not smart enough" (Charlesworth, 2000, p. 235). Similar to our results, Parker and Pharaoh (2008) showed that parents had constant feelings of guilt and a sense of failure due to their inability to provide more for their children.

Shame is a common denominator among individuals in debt. According to social psychologists, it leads to feelings of powerlessness and incompetence, and it is associated with depression and suicidal ideation (Walker et al., 2013). Shame attributed to indebtedness is twofold: it causes both social suffering and psychological pain through social exclusion, isolation and low self-esteem while inhibiting personal agency (Hayes, 2000). Shame is socially constructed since it is the outcome of failing to live up to societal expectations, but individually experienced, since societal expectations take the form of personal aspirations. Taking these into consideration, it becomes apparent that there is a need to challenge media and policy discourse as well as the mainstream psychology literature discourse of stereotyping indebtedness as fecklessness, incompetence and irresponsibility (Graeber, 2011; Webley and Nyhus, 2001).

Lack of control over life

The majority of participants reported that they had made a lot of adjustments to make ends meet and they had a lack of control over their lives due to their debts. Only one participant (E) did not feel that his debt affected his choices in life. A lack of control upon their lives was associated with feelings of insecurity and a sense of being exposed:

> It [debt] takes absolute control over your life. It brought my life upside down. And not only my life but my children's lives as well... All of our lives changed completely, we cut off from everything. Everything depends on the debt; I don't get to decide about anything. It is unbelievable how much your life changes... your life changes so much that you cannot stand it anymore... (A)

> I used to live in independence before, but I had to move back with my parents and now I am trying to find a job here to save money from commuting... everything changes you cannot proceed with your life, you cannot proceed to the next level with your relationship, I mean there is no way you could have a family. (D)

> We don't make decisions as free persons anymore... It [debt] is the centre of our lives; everything is scheduled in order to serve it. Even

at the supermarket, I check the prices, in an attempt to save as much money as possible, because I am in debt. (G)

Social stigma

Interestingly, the majority of the participants, apart from one (F), reported that they did not feel that people who are in debt today are stigmatised, due to the fact that everyone owes money somewhere – to utilities, relatives or taxes:

> Before [the crisis] they [people in debt] were marginalised, but not anymore; now they are everywhere. (D)

> Now, people in debt are faced a little bit better than before. Before they were considered to be unities; now it is easier to say "I owe to the bank or the electricity bills or taxes and they may take me to prison". You say it openly far more easily now, because most people owe money either to their relatives or to the banks, so they are in the same situation as you. (B)

> In Greece, I think we reached the point that it [debt] does not affect your social image. There are not a lot of people who are not in debt anymore, so it does not make any difference. (E)

> I feel quite embarrassed, because I am afraid they would say [her name] owes money to the bank but she spends it on going out. Also, it is your psychological and emotional state. It eats you alive. How are you supposed to really enjoy going out, when you are always worried? (F)

Previous qualitative studies found that indebtedness is socially stigmatising (Hayes, 2000; Nettleton and Burrows, 2001) due to the demonisation of people in debt and the sense of failing to live up to societal expectations – similar to shame. However, according to the results of this study, only one participant reported social stigma due to indebtedness while the rest reported that they didn't feel stigmatised. One interpretation of these findings is that the impact of social stigma is less severe for those who live in localities where indebtedness is widespread, as in Greece nowadays.

Discussion

The present study is in consensus with previous studies that have illustrated indebtedness as a consequence of unexpected life events and drops in income (Becker, 1997; Ambrose and Cunningham, 2004; Dearden et al., 2010; Marmot, 2010). In addition, this research is also in consensus with previous studies that have shown that indebtedness is related to elevated stress levels, social isolation, depressive feelings, low self-esteem, shame and lack of control over one's life (Kempson, 1996; Nettleton and Burrows, 2001; Williams, 2008). In contrast with other studies, however, none of the participants, apart from one, reported any social stigma against individuals in debt. The lack of social stigmatisation was attributed to the fact that the majority of households in Greece nowadays are in debt (Nettleton and Burrows, 2001; Ambrose and Cunningham, 2004; Williams, 2008; Graeber, 2011).

Evidence of severe financial hardship was found with two of the seven participants, one of whom was a single mother and the other one a widow at an older age. Both of these participants attributed their indebtedness to the current economic climate in Greece, which is in line with the fact that the vulnerable groups in society are those who are most affected by an economic recession (WHO, 2009). Perhaps the most worrying findings were those referring to the direct impact on health (i.e. high blood pressure in one participant aged 32), suicidal ideation, lack of sleep and constant, long-term stress attributed to financial strain. These findings raise worries about not only the impact of indebtedness on the psychological wellbeing of the population but also with regard to a range of social problems that Greek society may face, particularly in the current economic environment and with the percentage of non-performing loans increasing (*Public Issue*, 2013).

In response to the Greek debt crisis and the austerity measures, several solidarity groups, independent organisations and movements have been formed to help and support people who are in debt in different ways. Some of them are directly related to the support of those in debt by preventing evictions and providing legal counselling, while others are indirectly related by providing health services, psychological and legal support, food or other living essentials, such as the Women's initiative Against Debt and Austerity Measures in Thessaloniki. In most cases they are formed by people of all ages who come from different social and financial backgrounds. The majority of these solidarity groups operate locally but, as they grow, they tend to connect with other groups in order to cover larger areas of Greece, creating a safety network for people who are in debt, which counters the inability of state services to provide what is necessary. The Committee for the Coordination of Action Groups in Attiki (Syntonistiko Syllogikotiton Attikis) is one of these groups. It was created during open meetings between citizens of Attiki – the biggest prefecture in Greece – that have been affected by the crisis. During these meetings a solidarity group was formed that has been trying ever since to prevent evictions and power supply cut-offs of individuals and families in debt. Syntonistiko Syllogikotiton Attikis is a typical example of how solidarity groups act – it consists of smaller groups that operate in the area and come together for actions that need the support of more people. There are other groups and individuals that take a more direct approach and try to fight back within the boundaries of the legal system through massive lawsuits against banks and, in some cases, the government. Through these lawsuits, they try to protect people who are in fear of losing their home due to their debts.

In conclusion, the findings presented above underline the need for large-scale longitudinal studies in Greece that will address the psychological impact of indebtedness on individuals. Additionally, apart from support at the individual level to people who face psychological ill health, there is a need for political action against policies that prolong indebtedness and poverty.

Acknowledgements

We would like to thank Ms Sotiria Gkatziou for her contribution to the initial editing.

References

Ambrose, P. and Cunningham, L. (2004). *The Ever-Increasing Circle: A Pilot Study of Debt as an Impediment to Entering Employment in Brighton and Hastings*. The Health and Social Policy Research Centre, University of Brighton.
Anagnostopoulos, D. C. and Soumaki, E. (2013). The state of child and adolescent psychiatry in Greece during the international financial crisis: A brief report. *European Child and Adolescent Psychiatry*, 22, 131–134.
Arghyrou, M. and Tsoukalas, J. D. (2011). The Greek debt crisis: Likely causes, mechanics and outcomes. *World Economy*, 34(2), 173–191.
Becker, S. (1997). *Responding to Poverty: The Politics of Cash and Care*. Harlow: Longman.
Beresford, P. (2005). Redistributing profit and loss: The new economies of the market and social welfare. *Critical Social Policy*, 25(4), 464–482.
Blokland, T. (2007). You got to remember you live in public housing: Place-making in an American housing project. *Housing, Theory and Society*, 25(1), 31–46.
Bridgesa, S. and Disney, R. (2010). Debt and depression. *Journal of Health Economics*, 29, 388–403.
Cecchetti, S. G., Mohanty, M. S. and Zampolli, F. (2011). The real effects of debt. BIS Working Papers No. 352. Retrieved on November 16, 2013 http://www.bis.org/publ/othp16.pdf.

Charlesworth, S. J. (2000). *A Phenomenology of Working Class Experience.* Cambridge: Cambridge University Press.
Dearden, C., Goode, J., Whitfield, G. and Cox, L. (2010). *Credit and Debt in Low-Income Families.* New York: Joseph Rowntree Foundation.
Diamandouros, N. (2012). Reforming Greece: Sisyphean task or Herculean challenge? Oxford: South East European Studies. Retrieved on November 2, 2012. http://www.sant.ox.ac.uk/seesox/publications/ReformingGreece3.pdf.
Drentea, P. (2000). Age, debt and anxiety. *Journal of Health and Social Behavior*, 41, 437–450.
Drentea, P. and Lavrakas, P. J. (2000). Over the limit: The association among health status, race and debt. *Social Science & Medicine*, 50, 517–529.
Elstad, J. I. (1998). The psycho-social perspective on social inequalities in health. In Bartley, M., Blane, D. and Davey-Smith, G. (eds.). *The Sociology of Health Inequality.* Oxford: Blackwell, pp. 598–618.
Euromonitor International (2013). Country report. Consumer lending in Greece. Retrieved on December 10, 2013. http://www.euromonitor.com/consumer-lending-in-greece/report.
Eurostat (2013b). Unemployment statistics. Retrieved on January 16, 2013. http://epp.eurostat.ec.europa.eu/statistics_explained/index.php/Unemployment_statistics.
Eurostat, (2014). *Private sector debt, non-consolidated.* Retrieved on March 2, 2015 http://ec.europa.eu/eurostat/tgm/table.do?tab=table&plugin=1&language=en&pcode=tipspd10
Economou, M., Madianos, M., Theleritis, C., Peppou, L. E. and Stefanis, C. N. (2011). Increased suicidality amid economic crisis in Greece. *Lancet*, 378, 1459.
Fraile, L. (2009). Lessons from Latin America's neo-liberal experiment: An overview of labour and social policies since the 1980s. *International Labour Review*, 148, 3, 215–233.
Frangos, C. C., Frangos, C. C., Sotiropoulos, I., Orfanos, V., Toudas, K. and Gkika, E. (2012). The effects of the Greek economic crisis on eating habits and psychological attitudes of young people: A sample survey among Greek university students. *Proceedings of the World Congress on Engineering*, 1.
Garuda, G. (2000). The distributional effects of the IMF programs: A cross-country analysis. *World Development*, 28(6), 1031–1051.
Ghellab, Y. and Papadakis, K. (2011). The politics of economic adjustment: State unilateralism or social dialogue? In Somavia, J. (ed.). *The Global Crisis: Causes, Responses and Challenges.* Geneva: ILO, pp. 81–91.
Graeber, D. (2011). *Debt: The First 5000 Years.* New York: Melville House.
Grave, A. (interviewer) Tincq, B. (interviewer) and Graeber, D. (interviewee). (2013). Can debt catalyze a new rebellion? An interview with David Graeber (interview transcript), retrieved on OUISHARE Collaborative Economy website: http://ouishare.net/2013/10/graeber-morality-debt/.
Gulliver, K. and Morris, J. (2011). Living on the edge: Financial exclusion and social housing. Human City.
Hayes, T. (2000). Stigmatizing indebtedness: Implications for labelling theory. *Symbolic Interaction*, 23, 29–46.
Henning, E. (2004). *Finding Your Way in Qualitative Research.* Pretoria: Van Schaik Publishers.

Herrman, H., Saxena, S. and Moodie, R. (2005). *Promoting Mental Health: Concepts, Emerging Evidence, Practice*. Geneva: World Health Organization.

Hintikka, J., Kontula, O., Saarinen, P., Tanskanen, A., Koskela, K. and Viinamaki, H. (1998). Debt and suicidal behaviour in the Finnish general population. *Acta Psychiatrica Scandinavica*, 98, 493–496.

Jenkins, R., Fitch, C., Hurlston, M. and Walker, F. (2009). Recession, debt and mental health: Challenges and solutions. *Mental Health in Family Medicine*, 6, 85–90.

Kahn, J. R. and Fazio, E. M. (2005). Economic status over the life course and racial disparities in health. *The Journals of Gerontology Series B: Psychological Sciences and Social Sciences*, 60, 76–84.

Karamessini, M. (2008). Still a distinctive Southern European employment model. *Industrial Relations Journal*, 39(6), 510–531.

Kathimerini Pangalos stands by we-all-ate-together statement (18 April 2012). *Kathimerini*, retrieved on December 18, 2013 http://www.ekathimerini.com/4dcgi/_w_articles_wsite1_1_18/04/2012_438123.

Kathimerini (4 January 2014). The income for 44% of the population below the poverty line [Κάτω από το όριο της φτώχειας το εισόδημα για το 44% του πληθυσμού]. *Kathimerini*, retrieved on December 18, 2013 http://news.kathimerini.gr/4dcgi/_w_articles_economy_2_04/01/2014_544926.

Kempson, E. (1996). *Life on a Low Income*. New York: Joseph Rowntree Foundation.

Kentikelenis, A. and Papanicolas, I. (2011). Economic crisis, austerity and the Greek public health system. *European Child and Adolescent Psychiatry*, 22, 4–5.

Kouretas, G. P. and Vlamis, P. (2010). The Greek crisis: Causes and implications, *Panoeconomicous*, 57(4), 391–404.

Madianos, M. G., Economou, M., Alexiou, T. and Stefanis, C. (2011). Depression and economic hardship across Greece in 2008 and 2009: Two cross-sectional surveys nationwide. *Soc Psychiatry Psychiatric Epidemiology*, 46, 943–952.

Marmot, M. (2010). Fair society, healthy lives. Strategic review of health inequalities in England post 2010. London: Institute of Health Equity.

Mind (2004). *Not Alone? Isolation and Mental Distress*. London: Mind

Mind (2008). *In the Red: Debt and Mental Health*. London: Mind.

Moustakas, C. (1994). *Phenomenological Research Methods*. London: Sage.

Nettleton, S. and Burrows, R. (2001). Families coping with the experience of mortgage repossession in the "new landscape of precariousness". *Community, Work and Family*, 4, 253–272.

OECD (2013). OECD factbook 2013: Economic, environmental and social statistics. household debt. Retrieved on December 30, 2013. http://www.oecd-ilibrary.org/sites/factbook-2013-en/03/03/02/index.html?itemId=/content/chapter/factbook-2013-28-en.

OECD (2013). OECD health data 2013. Retrieved on August 22, 2013. http://www.oecd.org/health/health-systems/oecdhealthdata.htm.

Orton, M. (2009). Understanding the exercise of agency within structural inequality: The case of personal debt. *Social Policy and Society*, 8(4), 487–498.

Parker, S. and Pharaoh, R. (2008). *Just Coping: A New Perspective on Low-Income Families*. Maidstone: Kent County Council.

Pratt, A. (2006). Neoliberalism and social policy. In Lavalette, M. and Pratt, A. (eds.). *Social Policy, Theories, Concepts and Issues*, 3rd edition. London: Department of Education and Skills, 32–52.
Public Issue (2013). Greek social issues 3–2013: Loans to Greek households, 2012. Retrieved on January 6, 2014. http://www.publicissue.gr/en/1731/loans-2012/.
PwC (2014). European outlook for non-core and non performing loan portfolios issue 4: A growing non core asset market. Retrieved on January 5, 2014. http://www.pwc.co.uk/transaction-services/publications/european-outlook-for-non-core-and-non-performing-loans.jhtml.
Reading, R. and Reynolds, S. (2001). Debt, social disadvantage and maternal depression. *Social Science & Medicine*, 53, 441–453.
Skapinakis, P. (2009). Epidemiology of mental disorders in Greece. 1st national survey of mental health. Paper presented at 21st National Congress of Psychiatry, 5–8 May 2011, Athens. Retrieved on November 2, 2013. http://pskapinakis.posterous.com/panellinia-epidimiologiki-erevna.
Skapinakis, P., Weich, S., Lewis, G., Singleton, N. and Araya, R. (2006). Socioeconomic position and common mental disorders: Longitudinal study in the general population in the UK, *British Journal of Psychiatry*, 189, 109–117.
Smith, H. (2012, February 12). I fear from social explosion: Greeks can't take anymore punishment. *The Guardian*. Retrieved. http://www.theguardian.com/world/2012/feb/12/greece-cant-take-any-more
Turner, G. (2008). *The Credit Crunch*. London: Pluto Press.
Vinokur, A. D., Price, R. H. and Caplan, R. D. (1996). Hard times and hurtful partners: How Financial strain affects depression and relationship satisfaction of unemployed persons and their spouses. *Journal of Personality and Social Psychology*, 71(1), 166–179.
Walker, C., Cunningham, L., Hanna, P. and Ambrose, P. (2013). *Responsible Individuals and Irresponsible Institutions: A Repost into Mental Health and the UK Credit Industry*. Brighton: University of Brighton.
Walker, C., Johnson, K. and Cunningham, L. (eds.) (2012). *Community Psychology and the Socio-Economics of Mental Distress: International Perspectives*. London: Palgrave Macmillan.
Walker, R., Kyomuhendo, G. B., Chase, E., Choudhry, S., Gubrium, E. R., Nicola, J. Y., Lodemel, I., Mathew, L., Mwiine, A., Pellissery, S., and Ming, Y. (2013). Poverty in global perspective: Is shame common denominator? *Journal of Social Policy*, 42, 215–233.
Webley, P. and Nyhus, E. K. (2001). Life-cycle and dispositional routes into problem debt. *British Journal of Psychology*, 92, 423–446.
World Health Organization (2009). *Financial Crisis and Global Health: Report of a High-Level Consultation*. Geneva: World Health Organization.
Williams, B. (2008). The precipice of debt. In Collins, J., di Leonardo, M. and Williams, B. (eds.). *New Landscapes of Inequality: Neoliberalism and the Erosion of Democracy in America*. Santa Fe: School for Advanced Research Press, 65–90.
Wilkinson, R. G., Kawachi, I. and Kennedy, B. (1998). Mortality, the social environment, crime and violence. *Sociology of Health and Illness*, 20(5), 578–597.

Part II

The Public Face of the Debt Industry: Discourse and Wellbeing

6
Debt Dynamics in the UK and Beyond: How Propaganda Impedes Effective Political Action

Mark Burton[1]

Debt is a scourge of families but, strangely enough, it is not a problem for governments or banks. Yet the contrasting nature of these different kinds of debt is little understood. In this chapter I will examine the contrast between dominant accounts of debt, credit and money in the system today and the underlying realities. I will conceptualise this mismatch in terms of ideology and propaganda. Finally, I will use this understanding to set out some priorities and resources for the fight-back.

Propaganda about debt

In 1980 I was lucky enough to spend a year at the University of New South Wales (UNSW). The Thatcher government had just come to power in the UK and the unprecedented deindustrialisation of the country was in full swing. One of the lecturers at the UNSW was Alex Carey. He was a political activist, particularly concerned at the time with Australia's recent support for the US invasion of Vietnam and the propaganda that surrounded it. Alex had been working for years on what was one of the first social psychologies that I encountered which was really critical and societal. It was on the role of propaganda in the defeat of the socialist movement in the USA in the first half of the 20th century. Some of his most important articles are collected in his posthumous book, *Taking the Risk out of Democracy* (Carey, 1997). As he says,

> a rapid expansion of democratic franchise over the last hundred years created an unprecedented concern on the part of people who controlled resources. Corrupting the electorate rather than opposing the

extension of franchise became the strategy of businesses for protecting themselves from the public. And the method for this corruption was the use of techniques for manipulating public opinion – that is, propaganda.

(Carey, 1997, p. 134)

Alex's use of the term "propaganda" was refreshingly direct. I had become used to the more theorised language of "ideology", and indeed ideology does convey a wider, not always deliberate, and pervasive domination of the very tools that we use to understand the world around us. But propaganda as a description pointed the finger at the culprits in positions of power who consciously mislead the people, "taking the risk (to their interests) out of democracy". Alex had spent a year at MIT with Chomsky, and his understanding of propaganda both influenced and was influenced by the work of Herman and Chomsky. In a reflective article on their model, Herman sums up the web-like propaganda system:

What is the propaganda model and how does it work? The crucial structural factors derive from the fact that the dominant media are firmly imbedded [sic] in the market system. They are profit-seeking businesses, owned by very wealthy people (or other companies); they are funded largely by advertisers who are also profit-seeking entities, and who want their ads to appear in a supportive selling environment. The media are also dependent on government and major business firms as information sources, and both efficiency and political considerations, and frequently overlapping interests, cause a certain degree of solidarity to prevail among the government, major media, and other corporate businesses.

(Herman, 1996, p. 116)

More recently a similar analysis (CRESC, 2009) has been made of official policy prescriptions for reform of the UK banking and finance sector, documenting the closure of debate and the obstruction of necessary reform through the interrelated interests, membership between government, media, academia and the finance sector (Bowman et al., 2013). This is tantamount to "the near monopoly of speaking parts by elite finance insiders and their political hostages" (CRESC, 2009, p. 16) which has led to the recycling of prescriptions that originated in the financial sector itself in supposedly independent inquiries, commissioned by government

As Connors and Mitchell point out, Macroeconomics concepts, such as real GDP, inflation and unemployment rate, the budget deficit, and the interest rate make headlines on a daily basis...with frequent recourse to complex terms that are not well understood by the majority of media commentators or the public. Consequently, the public discourse reflects significant errors that render it almost impossible for participants to make informed assessments of macroeconomic developments independent of the politics involved...Problems in communicating the complexities of economic concepts and evidence are amplified by the ideological assumptions that dominate the public debate. Economics as an academic discipline and profession has come to be defined by a set of beliefs that are associated with the dominant free market paradigm. The consequence of this is a narrow debate that excludes the lessons of history and alternative economic paradigms that offer realistic insights into current economic conditions and related policy options.

Conservative think-tanks and media outlets produce an array of "research" or "policy" reports such that the public understanding has become straitjacketed by orthodox concepts and conclusions that, in themselves, are erroneous, but also lead to policy outcomes that undermine prosperity and subvert public purpose. The willingness to tolerate mass unemployment, rising income inequality and poverty is a manifestation of this syndrome.

(Connors and Mitchell, 2013, p. 2)

In what follows it is important to hold on to the idea that much of what we hear about money, debt and credit, as with other aspects of the economic system, is indeed propaganda (see also Häring, 2013). It is also, as Ann Pettifor (2014) points out, supported by a general lack of interest and understanding among professional economists about the banking system and its role in generating credit and debt.

So let's look at the story that we are being told about debt. This is the one told by the current Tory-Liberal UK government, but it is hardly challenged by the Labour Party. The same story is told throughout Europe, broadly that the country, or the government, is in debt, so there is no money, or only limited money, now available for things such as mitigation of climate change, social and health services, public housing and libraries. So we the people, our households, have to tighten our belts, take real cuts in wages, and watch as many of the social gains of the post 1939–1945 war social settlement are reversed. For a discussion of the way the "austerity story" is framed and the weaknesses of alternative narratives, see Afoko and Vockins (2013).

> Let me turn now to the forecasts for government borrowing and debt. When this government came to office, the deficit was 11 per cent of GDP. That was the highest level in our peacetime history. One pound in every four was being borrowed... The second step we take today to entrench Britain's commitment to sound public finances is this. We will cap overall welfare spending.
>
> (George Osborne, Chancellor of the Exchequer, UK Government Finance Minister, Autumn Budget Statement, 5 December 2013)

> The next Labour government will have less money to spend.
> (Ed Miliband, leader of the UK Labour Party and Opposition, Newham Dockside speech, 6 June 2013)

Debt, credit and the money system

The official story is curious because the figures tell an entirely different tale. Figure 6.1 shows levels of UK government debt as a percentage of GDP over the last 110 years. Today's levels are nothing exceptional,

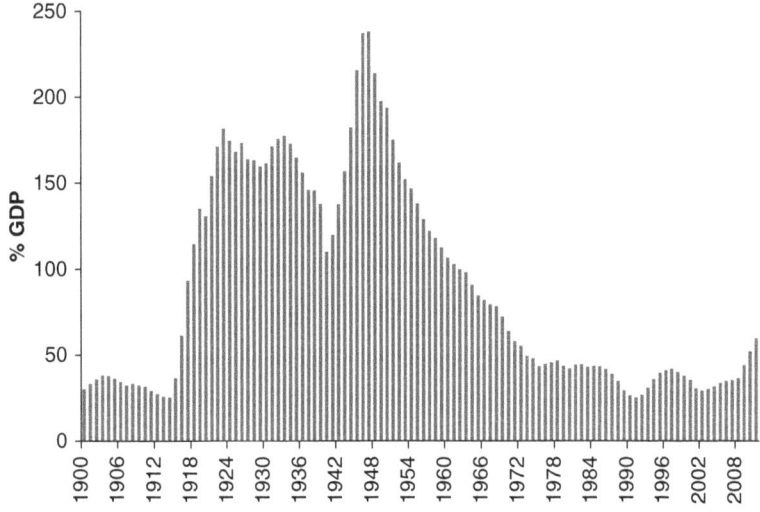

Figure 6.1 UK government debt as a percentage of GDP over the last 110 years

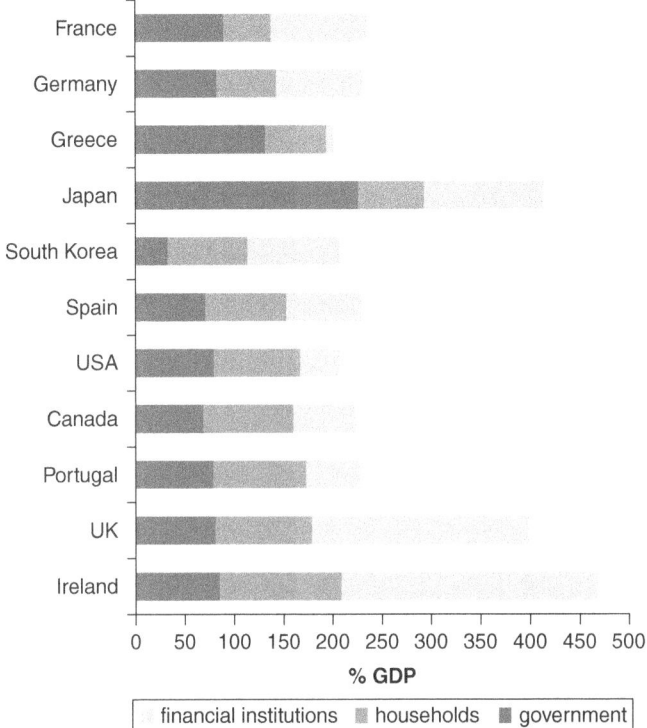

Figure 6.2 Composition of debt, by category, for selected countries, expressed as a percentage of GDP

so how can Osborne talk of the "highest level in our peacetime history"?

Figure 6.2 and Table 6.1 show comparisons of debt in 11 richer countries, as well as Eurozone countries with major economic problems, by type of debt: government, household and financial institutions.

A number of conclusions can be drawn from these data. First, the pattern of debt varies considerably among these countries. Second, high levels of government debt are to be found in countries with relatively "successful" economies (Germany and France) as well as in countries that have been hit by severe economic crises (Greece and Ireland). Third, in the majority of these countries, and this includes the UK, the level of household debt is higher than that of government debt. Finally, in 5 of the 11 countries (including the UK) the level of debt owed by the private financial institutions is greater than that owed by government.

Table 6.1 Composition of debt, by category, for selected countries, expressed as a percentage of GDP

Country	Government debt: rank	Government as percentage of GDP	Government as percentage of total debt	Household debt: rank	Households as percentage of GDP	Household debt as percentage of total	Financial institutions debt: rank	Financial institutions as percentage of GDP	Financial institutions as percentage of total debt	Totals as percentage of GDP
Ireland	8	85	12.8	11	124	18.7	11	259	39.1	663
UK	6	81	16.0	10	98	19.3	10	219	43.2	507
Portugal	4	79	22.2	9	94	26.4	3	55	15.4	356
Canada	2	69	25.0	8	91	33.0	4	63	22.8	276
USA	5	80	28.7	7	87	31.2	2	40	14.3	279
Spain	3	71	19.6	6	82	22.6	5	76	20.9	363
South Korea	1	33	10.5	5	81	25.8	7	93	29.6	314
Japan	11	226	44.1	4	67	13.1	9	120	23.4	512
Greece	10	132	49.4	3	62	23.2	1	7	2.6	267
Germany	7	83	29.9	2	60	21.6	6	87	31.3	278
France	9	90	26.0	1	48	13.9	8	97	28.0	346

Source: Data are for quarter 2, 2011 (MGI, 2012).

Add to this the historical picture of rising household debt over recent decades (as outlined throughout this book; see specifically chapters 1, 2 and 10) and the severity of this crisis of household indebtedness becomes clear.

But there is a further dimension to the question of government debt: government debt is not a problem by its very nature. To understand this assertion it is necessary to set out the nature of money in the modern world and the manner of its creation.

Money is created socially, through the actions of bankers. This happens through the creation of credit. So when a bank lends money, it is not dipping into a deposit placed by a saver or investor but generating that money anew. In the first half of the 20th century, this ability was brought under government control through a set of regulatory mechanisms that were enacted by legislation. Since the early 1980s, these regulations have been loosened and abandoned with the result that central banks are no longer subject to government (and hence democratically decided) policy, and private banks and financial institutions are not controlled by either central banks or governments in any meaningful way. This is still the case after the financial crash that started in 2007. The deregulation of financial markets through the 1986 "Big Bang" in the City of London, and the Gramm-Leach-Bliley Financial Services Modernization Act of 1999 in the USA, meant that the creation of private credit in retail banking acted as a feeder (CRESC, 2009) for the complex, Ponzi-like schemes of the wholesale and investment banking sector. Indeed, it is this relationship between household debt as feedstock to the accumulation of profit by the financial sector (now literally bankrolled by government) that lies at the heart of the everyday personal tragedies that are the reality of the credit boom. These "financial instruments" that packaged debt took the role of spurious substitute for risk assessment and management, precipitating the entire system into a state whereby debt default by poor borrowers (the subprime mortgage debtors) detonated the near collapse of the whole system. However, governments also can, and do, create money (Lawn, 2010; Pettifor, 2014). They did this to the tune of billions of pounds with bank bailouts and the policy of quantitative easing, which came not come from taxation but from the creation of new money (Werner, 2012; Pettifor, 2014) as credits to the accounts of private banks. In neither the public nor the private case does the money so created have any physical basis: there is no constraint on the creation of money – its supply is truly elastic. And this facility, properly used, would ensure that there needs to be no shortage of money for public expenditure. There is no reason why health and social services cannot be properly funded. There is no reason why higher education for all should not be free. There is no reason why massive investment in green infrastructure cannot ensure the total decarbonisation of our energy systems (New Economics Foundation, 2008; Werner, 2012; Centre for Alternative Technology, 2013; Green New Deal Group, 2013). However, the private creation of money has created major problems. When private money is created through the lending activities of banks (e.g. by loans to businesses, credit card and mortgage advances to you and me), they exact a high cost for this service by charging rates of interest that are way above their need to cover their administrative costs for the service. The reason is twofold. First, the banks are private entities that make a profit. Second, the system of privately generated credit has itself been subject to a secondary process of commodification where loans are packaged and sold on, again to enable the extraction of profit. The only way such continued accumulation of profit can be sustained is through the conversion of land (the resources of the ecosystem) to commodities, and through the exploitation of workers. It is this that drives the constant expansion of capitalism, to new markets, new labour forces, new extraction of primary resources, new commodities, new desires and new needs. This has inescapable consequences for human life, and indeed human survival (Meadows et al., 2005; Rockström et al., 2009; Anderson and Bows, 2010; Lietaer et al., 2012):

> Today humanity uses the equivalent of 1.5 planets to provide the resources we use and absorb our waste. This means it now takes the Earth one year and four months to regenerate what we use in a year.
>
> Moderate UN scenarios suggest that if current population and consumption trends continue, by the mid 2030s we will need the equivalent of two Earths to support us. And of course, we only have one.
>
> Turning resources into waste faster than waste can be turned back into resources puts us in global ecological overshoot, depleting the very resources on which human life and biodiversity depend.
> (Global Footprint Network, 2012)

So we can contrast this private creation of money, as credit, for private profit, for endless capital accumulation, with what could be, and at times has been, the government creation of money to meet social and ecological goals – to secure for all of us the conditions for the maintenance and reproduction of livelihood.

The government creation of money has to be done responsibly (Connors and Mitchell, 2013). Failure to do so will create problems in society and the economy. For example, too much liquidity would lead to inflation. Or too much money in private pockets can lead, in a deindustrialised, deruralised and globalised economy such as that of the UK, to high levels of imports and a loss of sovereignty as the economy becomes dependent on overseas sources. That has indeed happened through the expansion of privately created credit and a reduction in local production. But a government can mount control measures to prevent this (Lawn, 2010). Taxation is the most obvious of these, but there is also the control of interest rates, the system of tariffs and duties for trade, and the role of legislation. For example, a government could simply ban the use of motor cars that fell below a certain level of fuel efficiency. It could ban particularly damaging food imports, such as those that are dependent on habitat destruction – just as governments from time to time ban certain food imports on the basis of public health concerns. It could initiate a system of tradeable caps on hydrocarbon-based energy usage (Davey, 2012). Rather than the ideological use of "austerity" to justify the transfer of public and household resources to corporate players, truly democratic governments could take command of the economy for social and ecological benefit, in a kind of updated version of the British Left's Alternative Economic Strategy of the 1970s (Rowthorn, 1981).

So let's recap, by way of a contrast between the official propaganda and the facts of the situation, as shown in Table 6.2.

Table 6.2 Government debt: propaganda and reality

Propaganda	Reality
There isn't enough money.	Money is a social creation and it can be made as needed to meet social need.
Governments have been profligate with their money.	It is never a problem when governments create credit.
There is a huge debt mountain.	In most countries this debt mountain is largely owed by private households and non-government financial corporations, banks.
We can't afford to put the environment first.	It is the high price of private credit that is leading to the orgy of ecosystem destruction. If we don't put the environment first we put ourselves last.
Households get into debt through their own mismanagement of money.	The financial system has encouraged the creation of consumer credit to generate profit.

Social psychology of debt: Obfuscation and identity

So what are the really-social psychological (Burton and Kagan, 2009) dimensions of this? I suggest that they can be understood in terms of two main processes, both of them ideological. First, as already suggested, there is obfuscation that has elements that are deliberate (propagandistic) and casual ("ideological ignorance", the unknowing reproduction of ruling ideology (Burton, in press) through the neglect of significant elements – typically those dynamic structural aspects of the system that constructs everyday experience). Second, the system creates many false wants. It does this through the technologies of advertising and marketing, but also at a deeper level as it destroys alternative, cultural and associative bases for identity, so that identity becomes bound up with what we have: the sad situation whereby people buy mass-produced items to assert their individual identity. In both cases a really social psychology can unmask this, while helping to suggest ways of resisting, including the construction of alternatives to that social reality. Curiously, this has not been a strong focus for social psychology, despite its knowledge of the methods of the advertising industry. Only a few critical texts have covered the problems of consumerist false wants and identity, and these have emerged from the fringes of the discipline (e.g. Packard, 1977; James, 2008). Nevertheless, thinkers and activists from other disciplines and traditions have examined these questions (e.g. Illich, 1973; Mies and Bennholdt-Thomsen, 1999; Assadourian, 2010; O'Neill et al., 2010; Fatheuer, 2011; Lanza, 2012; Latouche, 2012b). Together, their work, and that of the movements that they belong to, present an alternative philosophy for a prosperity that is genuine (Burton and Steady State Manchester, 2012) and frugal (Latouche, 2012a) – for a world where people can thrive without harming the planet.

But the consequence of these two social psychological processes – obfuscation by propaganda and ideology, and the foisting on us of a false understanding of human need – means that political action is shackled, which is I believe the intention of the propaganda. In the first place, the dominance of the spurious story about debt means that all but the most marginal anti-system voices are co-opted into a political and policy debate on false premises, one that accepts that there is no money, that governments have overspent, that deficits are bad, and that the welfare of people and planet will have to wait for the "economy to improve"; and meanwhile public wealth transfers to corporate hands, not just via bank bailouts and Quantitative Easing (in the UK) but via the medicines of privatisation and welfare cuts prescribed to deal with the alleged deficit problem. So opposition politicians end up asking for less austerity rather than for a completely different paradigm (for a forensic social psychological analysis of the Miliband speech referred to earlier, see Crompton, 2013), and there is an almost complete lack of credible policy alternatives that could galvanise a popular movement and form the basis for an alternative government's programme. In the second place, there is also an almost complete absence of vision as to what an alternative to the eviscerated everyday culture of retail-based meaning could look like. Where hesistant steps are taken in this direction – for example, in the UK by the centre-left Compass group – they tend to be hampered by a tendency to fall back to the language of the received model. Compass (see http://www.compassonline.org.uk/) has made a valuable contribution to helping the centre left reject the neoliberal, market-is-god approach. It has done this through a series of thoughtful and well-researched publications and polemics, as well as through effective networking. But it seems torn between the idea of a better yesterday – back to neo-Keynesian management of an otherwise malign system – and the difficult task of constructing something for the future, a better, green and caring socialism resting on a one-planet economy and a radical re-evaluation of what prosperity really means.

The fight-back

It remains then to suggest some priorities in the struggle against both the obscuring of the reality of credit and debt, and debt-fuelled hyperconsumerism.

At the political and policy level, citizens first need to reclaim the democratic control of the State and its central bank, as well as campaign for strong regulation of the priorities and practices of the private banks. This can only be done through building an alliance for change that unites the interests and perspectives of environmentalists, social justice campaigners, trade unionists and so on, or else the resistance of the system will not be overcome. In doing this, it is vital to avoid being sidetracked by limited reforms. So, for example, the creation of more competition in the banking sector will do some, limited good, especially if that competition comes from mutual, cooperative and locally focused operations (Lewis and Conaty, 2012). However, if the overall functioning of the banking system is unchanged, then the problems will persist. That is the current situation where, for example, there has not been significant "deleveraging" or reduction of the very high levels of debt carried by the banks.

Second, there is a need to promote policies for a post-growth, steady-state economy that does not rely on endless accumulation in the forlorn hope of redistributing the crumbs from the table at which the beneficiaries of this system sit. This is important for ecological, social and economic wellbeing. My own activist work in Manchester is orientated towards this goal (Burton and Steady State Manchester, 2012).

At the level of ideology, the priority is to construct alternative images of possibility for the society and world that we want to live in. This is the enormous gap in critical, anti-system narratives that tend to try and fight on the terrain of the neoliberal consensus. What is needed are convincing pictures of how all our lives could be more fulfilling without being defined by the retail consumerist model. Any such approach has to get to the root of identity and culture, and in this it can learn from a variety of subaltern movements and cultures from oppositional youth subcultures and transition town groups in the cities of the capitalist core countries, to movements in the global South that are reclaiming and reworking elements of their, often indigenous, cultural heritage. This is not just a matter of telling better stories or painting better pictures, though. This alternative "imaginary" needs to connect to people's lives, and particularly to the huge "reserve army of activism" – that section of the population that does from time to time try to get involved in struggles against the system, but whose enthusiasm is typically squandered by political and social movements. (Where are the hundreds of thousands who marched against the Iraq War now?) This is another area where social psychological understanding can be helpful if it is used in a critically selective way (Burton et al., 2013).

In articulating any alternative, care should be taken to resist the temptations of workerist/moralist discourse that tends to reproduce the official ideology. Left politicians and activists on the whole share a rhetoric that appeals to the moral superiority of "hard-working families" (marginalising unemployed and disabled people), and "more jobs" (despite the structural tendencies that are absolutely drying up the supply of jobs, and rendering the majority of jobs precarious and repetitive (Braverman, 1974; Gorz, 2010)). Instead, it is necessary to present a truly anti-productivist ethic that is at once ecological and feminist, and that values culture above economy (Williams, 1982; Shiva, 1988).

Conclusion

This chapter is deliberately polemical: its subject matter requires a polemical treatment. That is to say, the social and economic realities and the way in which they are obscured by propaganda and ideology cannot be either understood nor dealt with in the absence of an ethical and political analysis and action stance. In a short chapter like this it is only possible to introduce the issues and suggest what in a traditional social psychological text would be "directions for further research", but here are "directions for scholarly activism".

Note

1. Scholar-activist, Manchester. Visiting professor, Manchester Metropolitan University.

References

Afoko, C. and Vockins, D. (2013). *Framing the Economy: The Austerity Story*. London: New Economics Foundation, retrieved on http://www.neweconomics.org/publications/entry/framing-the-economy-the-austerity-story.

Anderson, K. and Bows, A. (2010). Beyond "dangerous" climate change: Emission scenarios for a new world. *Philosophical Transactions of the Royal Society A: Mathematical, Physical and Engineering Sciences*, 369(1934), 20–44, doi:10.1098/rsta.2010.0290.

Assadourian, E. (2010). The rise and fall of consumer cultures. In *State of the World 2010: Transforming Cultures*. Washington, DC: Worldwatch Institute. Retrieved. http://blogs.worldwatch.org/transformingcultures/wp-content/uploads/2009/04/Chapter-1.pdf.

Bowman, A., Froud, J., Johal, S., Moran, M. and Williams, K. (2013). *Business Elites and Undemocracy in Britain: A Work in Progress* (No. 125) (p. 30). Manchester: Centre for Research on Socio-Cultural Change, University of Manchester. Retrieved. http://www.cresc.ac.uk/publications/business-elites-and-undemocracy-in-britain-a-work-in-progress.

Braverman, H. (1974). *Labor and Monopoly Capital: The Degradation of Work in the Twentieth Century*. New York: Monthly Review Press.

Burton, M. (in press). Social reproduction. In *Encyclopedia of Critical Psychology*. New York and London: Springer, 1802–1804. Retrieved. http://www.springerreference.com/docs/html/chapterdbid/304917.html.

Burton, M. and Kagan, C. (2009). Towards a really social psychology: Liberation psychology beyond Latin America. In Montero, M. and Sonn, C. (eds.). *The Psychology of Liberation. Theory and Application*. New York: Springer, 51–73. Retrieved. http://dx.doi.org/10.1007/978-0-387-85784-8_3.

Burton, M., Kagan, K. and Duckett, P. (2013). Making the psychological political – challenges for community psychology (Vol. 4, 50–63). Presented at the 2nd International Conference of Community Psychology 2008, Lisbon: Global Journal of Community Psychology Practice. Retrieved. http://www.gjcpp.org/en/resource.php?issue=9&resource=91.

Burton, M. and Steady State Manchester (2012). *In Place of Growth: Practical Steps to a Manchester Where People Thrive without Harming the Planet* (Vol. 1).

Manchester: Steady State Manchester. Retrieved. http://steadystatemanchester.files.wordpress.com/2012/11/inplaceofgrowth_ipog_-content_final.pdf.

Carey, A. (1997). *Taking the Risk Out of Democracy: Corporate Propaganda versus Freedom and Liberty* (A. Lowrey ed.). Champaign, Illinois: University of Illinois Press.

Centre for Alternative Technology (2013). *Zero Carbon Britain: Rethinking the Future*. Wales: Centre for Alternative Technology Publications. Retrieved. http://zerocarbonbritain.com/.

Connors, L. and Mitchell, W. (2013). *Framing Modern Monetary Theory*. Working paper No. 13–06. Newcastle, NSW: Centre of Full Employment and Equity. Retrieved. http://e1.newcastle.edu.au/coffee/publications/wp2.cfm?id=174.

CRESC (2009). *An Alternative Report on UK Banking Reform*. Manchester: Centre for Research in Socio Cultural Change, University of Manchester. Retrieved. http://www.cresc.ac.uk/sites/default/files/Alternative%20report%20on%20banking%20V2.pdf.

Crompton, T. (2013). *A Values Analysis of Ed Miliband's Newham Dockside Speech*. London: Compass. Retrieved. http://www.compassonline.org.uk/publications/crompton/.

Davey, B. (Ed.). (2012). *Sharing for Survival*. Dublin: FEASTA.

Fatheuer, T. (2011). *Buen Vivir a Brief Introduction to Latin America's New Concepts for the Good Life and the Rights of Nature*. Berlin: Heinrich Böll Foundation. Retrieved. http://montreal2012.wordpress.com/2011/10/19/buen-vivir-a-brief-introduction-to-latin-america%E2%80%99s-new-concepts-for-the-g-ood-life-and-the-rights-of-nature/.

Global Footprint Network (2012). *United Kingdom Factsheet* (p. 1). Oakland, CA: Global Footprint Network. Retrieved. http://www.footprintnetwork.org/images/trends/2012/pdf/2012_unitedkingdom.pdf.

Gorz, A. (2010). *Critique of Economic Reason*. London: Verso.

Green New Deal Group (2013). *A National Plan for the UK – From Austerity to the Green New Deal*. New Weather Institute and Green New Deal Group. Retrieved. http://www.greennewdealgroup.org/wp-content/uploads/2013/09/Green-New-Deal-5th-Anniversary.pdf.

Häring, N. (2013). The veil of deception over money: How central bankers and textbooks distort the nature of banking and central banking. *Real-World Economics Review*, (62), 2–18.

Herman, E. (1996). The propaganda model revisited. *Monthly Review*, 48(3), 115–128.

Illich, I. (1973). *Tools for Conviviality*. London: Calder and Boyars.

James, O. (2008). *Affluenza*. London: Vermilion.

Lanza, M. (2012). *Buen Vivir: An Introduction from a Women's Rights Perspective in Bolivia* (No. 2). Toronto: The Association for Women's Rights in Development (AWID). Retrieved. awid.org/content/download/138877/1543706/file/FPTTEC_LivingWell%20March%20ENG.pdf.

Latouche, S. (2012a). *La sociedad de la abundancia frugal: Contrasentidos y controversias del decrecimiento*. Barcelona: Icaria.

Latouche, S. (2012b). *Salir de la sociedad de consumo: Voces y vías del decrecimiento* (first Spanish edition). Barcelona: Ocataedro.

Lawn, P. (2010). Facilitating the transition to a steady-state economy: Some macroeconomic fundamentals. *Ecological Economics*, 69(5), 931–936. doi:10.1016/j.ecolecon.2009.12.013.

Lewis, M. and Conaty, P. (2012). *The Resilience Imperative: Cooperative Transitions to a Steady-State Economy*. Gabriola Island, BC: New Society Publishers.

Lietaer, B., Arnsperger, A., Goerner, C. and Brunnhuber, S. (2012). *Money and Sustainability: The Missing Link; A Report from the Club of Rome – EU Chapter to Finance Watch and the World Business Academy*. Axminster: Triarchy Press with The Club of Rome.

Meadows, D. H., Randers, J. and Meadows, D. L. (2005). *Limits to Growth: The 30-Year Update*. London: Earthscan.

MGI (2012). *Debt and Deleveraging: Uneven Progress on the Path to Growth*. McKinsey Global Institute. Retrieved. http://www.gfmag.com/tools/global-database/economic-data/11855-total-debt-to-gdp.html#axzz2nXdeyxjg.

Mies, M. and Bennholdt-Thomsen, V. (1999). *The Subsistence Perspective: Beyond the Globalized Economy*. London: Zed Books.

New Economics Foundation (2008). *A Green New Deal. Joined-Up Policies to Solve the Triple Crunch of the Credit Crisis, Climate Change and High Oil Prices: The First Report of the Green New Deal Group*. London.

O'Neill, D., Dietz, R. and Jones, N. (Eds.). (2010). *Enough Is Enough: Ideas for a Sustainable Economy in a World of Finite Resources. The Report of the Steady State Economy Conference*. Leeds: Center for the Advancement of the Steady State Economy and Economic Justice for All.

Packard, V. (1977). *The Hidden Persuaders*. Harmondsworth: Penguin Press.

Pettifor, A. (2014). *Just Money: How Society Can Break the Despotic Power of Finance*. London: Prime Economics. Retrieved. http://www.primeeconomics.org/?wpsc-product=just-money-how-society-can-break-the-despotic-power-of-finance.

Rockström, J., Steffen, W., Noone, K., Persson, Å., Chapin, F. S., Lambin, E. F. and Foley, J. A. (2009). A safe operating space for humanity. *Nature*, 461(7263), 472–475. doi:10.1038/461472a.

Rowthorn, B. (1981). The politics of the alternative economic strategy. *Marxism Today*, (January), 4–10. Retrieved. www.amielandmelburn.org.uk/collections/mt/pdf/81_01_04.pdf.

Shiva, V. (1988). *Staying Alive: Women, Ecology, and Development*. London: Zed Books.

Werner, R. (2012). *Time for Green Quantitative Easing: How to Generate Green, Sustainable Growth at No Cost* (Vol. 3, Issue 1). Southampton: University of Southampton, Centre for Banking, Finance and Sustainable Development.

Williams, R. (1982). *Socialism and Ecology*. London: SERA.

7
The Social Construction of "Indebted Man": Economic Crisis, Discursive Violence and the Role of Mass Media in Italy

Adriano Zamperini and Marialuisa Menegatto

Introduction

It is well known that since the fall of 2008, the world has entered into the deepest recession since the 1930s. The origin of this recession was a financial crisis that began in the USA in the summer of 2007, and which spread rapidly in Europe and across the rest of the world. The main cause was to be found in the collapse of the financial market as a result of colossal debts that were accumulated by major European and US banks, and the consequent institutionalised fraud and financial manipulation. In fact, the "bank bailouts" were implemented on the instruction and support of governments and the political class, which took place through the transfer by lending of the largest amount of money in recorded history, and at the same time created an insurmountable public debt (e.g. Chossudovsky and Marshall, 2010; Gallino, 2013).

In Europe, the European Commission, with the European Central Bank and the IMF, has convinced some European governments to adopt the belief that the crisis of public balances depends on the excessive generosity of the states in the preceding years. Therefore states have decided to start a severe policy of austerity, including Italy. In fact from 2010 onwards, the Berlusconi and Monti governments have produced their own narrative, claiming the excess of expenditure on social protection as the primary cause of the growth of public debt and the crisis. In addition, Italy, through a parliament decision of 18 April 2012, introduced in the constitution the provision that the books must balance. Many economists, Keynesian in particular, do not agree with this further restriction on public spending because it will have perverse effects in terms of a recession. The Nobel Prize winner Paul Krugman (2012) believes that the inclusion in the constitution that the accounts must balance will lead to the dissolution of the welfare state, and that austerity actually serves only to maintain inequalities, without scientific evidence necessary for this kind of measure.

However, the consequences of this kind of "austerity therapy" have until today been mass unemployment, factories closing down, the collapse of state social programmes and the impoverishment of millions of people; public services have been disrupted or privatised, and livelihoods destroyed. At the time of writing (January 2014) the National Institute for Statistics (www.istat.it) has announced in provisional statistics that the rate of unemployment in Italy has reached a new record level of 12.9%, which is 1.1% more than January 2013, and the highest level since 1977. The press release speaks of "the largest haemorrhage of jobs since the crisis". A central node remains the youth unemployment rate of 15–24-year-olds: there are 42.4% out of work, which is 4% more than January 2013, and the number of young people looking for a job is 690,000. From this dramatic data the figure emerges of the "discouraged generation": 1,790,000 people who have given up even looking for a job.

This chapter will begin by reviewing recent research on the meaning of the economic crisis as a concept also by examining some of the international studies. We will examine the public sense of the crisis in Italy through the analysis of major mainstream media. In particular, the role of social communication will be analysed from a theoretical perspective by articulating the crisis and the subjective condition of social unrest. Actually the concept of "crisis" presents a lot of facets: its constituent elements coexist in conflict because they are characterised differently, consequently arousing different points of view and debates; the meaning of crisis is of a contextual nature, so it is tied to a particular historical and cultural range; finally, the crisis is a relevant dimension because it imposes pressure on the members of a community, who cannot avoid facing the changes that it involves.

Understanding the discursive production of the crisis represents the first step in analysing the subjective condition of the citizens who do not react to existential difficulties simply in function of what happens, but mainly in function of the meaning of what happens. In democratic systems, hegemony about meaning becomes strategically important in imposing economic and political policies and directing people to a change of lifestyle – a change that in times of economic crisis also involves "governing emotions".

Crisis: What does it mean?

Beyond the statistical data, this economic crisis is an event. For instance, during natural and environmental disasters, crisis management is a practice to set in motion a series of strategies to cope with the situation of the crisis. In medical usage it refers to a particular stage in the development of a disease which is decisive for the life expectancy – identified as the critical moment in which the disease determines whether the patient will die or recover. However, as Reinhart Koselleck argues, crisis is not only an event; it is also a concept that often indicates insecurity, misfortune, reference to an unknown future, a sort of "cataract of the event", dominated by uncertainty, underlining the double value: on one side it is a conviction, but on the other side it can be an occasion that transforms us (1988, 2002). Although he has written at length about how the concept has varied across time and space, even today the situation has not changed. In fact, after the Great Credit Crash in 2008, the usage of "crisis" is awash in the field of mass and social communication of reported concepts of the economic crisis. To confirm this it is enough to open a newspaper, turn on the TV or quickly consult news on the Internet to realise how the crisis came about. At the most general political level, a global or international crisis, a crisis of nation state, a crisis of European integration may be found. At the economic level a crisis is also mentioned in terms of fiscal crisis, a financial crisis, a crisis of capitalism and a sovereign debt crisis. Crisis tendencies are also located in social assets and human relationships, such as crises of families and crises of confidence. The list goes on.

The history of the concept of crisis is certainly long and tortuous. For the purposes of our analysis, it seems appropriate to dwell on the meaning that is given in the context of the political and psychological sciences. In these contexts the meaning of the crisis indicates a "carrying out", a process leading to a decision. Thus it indicates those moments when a decision was needed but had not been taken yet. Borrowing the meanings from theology and medicine, the use of "crisis" in the social and psychological sciences always calls into play some decisive alternatives of vital importance, in which the just and the unjust, salvation or damnation, are opposed, or rather it enables the re-establishing of wellbeing. Therefore the concept of crisis transmitted a sense of necessity, on the one hand for decision-making and on the other the inevitability of action, an action forced by the same concept of crisis in a situation in which the agents could only choose between alternatives in direct contradiction with each other.

Today the concept of crisis is certainly inflated, especially thanks to the easy use of the word by the mass media. Although over time the concept has become wide-ranging in the lexicon of contemporary life, gaining the status of a key word, it has never managed to free itself from a certain ambivalence of its semantic complexity. For example, at the level of common sense the crisis is sometimes used as an equivalent of psychological subjective disorders; at other times, especially for the mass media, to talk about crises is to talk about international conflicts, such as the Middle East crisis. Especially, but not only, in the socioeconomic sphere the old capacity of the concept to put clear and sharp alternatives has failed, giving space to the uncertainty of arbitrary alternatives. So the concept of crisis needs conceptual links to be better explained. For this the use that is made of the concept is important.

Exploring economic crisis

The global crisis has created serious consequences for the social structures of European countries (Chossudovsky and Marshall, 2010), changing the relationship between citizens and between generations. In the face of economic and financial crisis, scholars' research has focused mainly on the following fields in order to gain a broader perspective of the phenomenon.

An approach came from studies in economic social psychology that aimed to understand the functioning of individuals' behaviour related to various economic phenomena (Roland-Lévy, 1998). In a prospective analysis of the theoretic framework of social representation (Moscovici, 1961/1976, 2001), part of these studies specifically focuses on verifying how individuals perceive and understand the crisis and, in addition, investigating the social representations within different social groups. For example, a study with French citizens (Roland-Lévy et al., 2010) shows that laypeople seem to focus on unemployment when they think about the crisis and differ in their notions of the crisis depending on whether they are afraid or unafraid of its consequences. The people who are most afraid of the crisis are those who have a full-time job which they are afraid of losing, while the unemployed or partially unemployed are only somewhat afraid of the crisis because they perceive their situation as already being bad and feeling that it couldn't get any worse.

They practise the use of credit differently. The full-time employed tend to trust the bank but they don't ask for credit; the unemployed have little or no trust in the banks but need them to borrow money to face everyday expenses. In the same field, Gangl et al. (2012) investigated Austrian experts' and laypeople's social representations of the financial and economic crisis. The results indicated that unemployment is a variable that is central to the social representation of the crisis, in particular for maintaining current confidence. By contrast, regarding the cause of the economic crisis, experts blamed the media, and laypeople blamed the managers, but both blamed the politicians. With respect to the banks, they evaluated them as neutral.

A field research approach in international political and social sciences in particular has focused on the representation of the economic crisis as a traumatic event for people. In fact, especially in the period 2008–2009, the media, and institutional players such as think tanks, have represented the crisis as a trauma or a shock, due to a natural, massive and unexpected disaster such as a "tsunami" or "earthquake" (Brasset and Clarke, 2010). The scholars, through an analysis of the media discourse, argue that a traumatic narrative in terms of fear and shame had a central role in shaping citizens as traumatised financial subjects, and politicians as keen to distance themselves from responsibility. Therefore it is already known that trauma has occupied an ever more important position in the mainstream discourse for mediating major crisis events and catastrophes.

There is substantial literature that states that the consequences of environmental disaster for people include post-traumatic stress disorder, anxiety disorders, depression (Rubonis and Bickman, 1991; Freedy and Hobfoll, 1995; Yule, 1999; Fassin, 2008; Fassin and Rechtman, 2009), and the disaster produced by "traumatic finance" (Pupavac, 2001; Brasset and Vaughan-Williams, 2012) can be associated with a series of negative emotions such as fear, shame, guilt and anger. This situation becomes still more serious for people's wellbeing when the "traumatic situation" persists for a long time (Yehuda and McFarlane, 1995), thus having a negative impact on the quality of life as measured by severe health determinants.

The economic crisis, given its persistence, is expected to produce adverse health consequences according to a World Health Organization report (WHO, 2011). In fact, research has consistently demonstrated that economic crisis is negatively associated with mental health (Solantaus et al., 2004; Stuckler et al., 2009; Uutela, 2010; Giotakos et al., 2011; Zivin et al., 2011). As the WHO report states, it is demonstrated that the main health outcomes are an increase in depression and anxiety; a rise in the use of tobacco, alcohol and drugs; a general neglect of overall health; and, in addiction, the production of secondary mental health effects, such as an increase in suicide and alcohol death rates. The principal social determinants are the increase in unemployment, the deterioration of safety nets for social protection, the erosion of savings and pension funds, and the reduction in health and social spending programmes.

The effects of unemployment and job loss on human relationships

The impact of the current economic crisis on the labour market had the result of changing significantly the processes between the economic system and society at large, thereby redesigning human relationships. The progressive increase in the number of companies that are closed as a consequence of accumulated debts or failures has contributed to lifting the number of unemployed so that, especially in Italy, the labour market is incapable of generating enough jobs to provide full-time wage employment for all workers. Thus one of the major consequences is the increase in flexibility in non-standard employment relations (Goldthorpe, 1984; Casey, 1991; Green et al., 1993; Kalleberg, 2000). This new type of job is a form of atypical employment (Córdova, 1986; Delsen, 1995; De Grip et al., 1997) and it includes part-time work, temporary contracts, short-term and contingent work, independent contracting and precarious employment. These types of employment are not new, but in the present economic crisis the experiences of employment are more and more uncertain. Compared with the past, the loss of a job is no longer seen as something transitory or short term that affects only certain segments of the population, but rather as a constant, structural, frequent, daily phenomenon (Sennet, 1998). Moreover, it spreads over numerous employment sectors (companies, industries, professions, etc.) and is of varying social composition (youth, women, managers, professionals, workers of high-level specialisation or education). For many employees or the unemployed, this change in working life which we have witnessed from the fall of 2008 has caused a feeling of insecurity concerning the nature of one's own existence and job (Stuckler et al., 2011; Chang et al., 2013; Gili et al., 2013).

In this context, job insecurity has emerged as an important aspect, in particular for employees who have economic responsibility for their family or think that they will have serious difficulties in finding a new job. To work is an activity through which people can obtain an income to face the different needs of survival, their lifestyle, taking care of themselves and their family. At the economic level, precariousness and job loss create damage by reducing the power of purchase, and endangering the supply of primary goods such as food, a house, clothing and so on. At the social level, a job enables someone to build a sustainable social and professional identity to establish meaningful relationships, giving the individual a sense of belonging.

Losing a job, and the acquired social status, can make someone experience feelings of shame, worthlessness, inferiority, guilt, apathy and stigmatisation (Scambler, 2004; Zamperini, 2010) with the risk of social exclusion, disadvantage and social isolation.

Moral debt

In the scenario of the current economic crisis, and especially from 2010, European governments, international institutions, analysts and also the media started to speak of the great crisis of the public – namely, a sovereign debt crisis. This statement that governments have spent a lot of money on social protection relegates to the background the banking crisis and the crisis of the entire financial system, and it exerts a powerful hold over citizens. Behind this rhetoric lies a system that is intended to defraud many people – for example, by pushing them to take out a mortgage which it was already known they would not be able to repay, by using false or no information, through inadequate regulation, indiscriminate use of alternative loan products and a lack of accountability in the industry (Nguyen and Pontell, 2010; see also Financial Crisis Inquiry Commission, 2011; Permanent Subcommittee on Investigations of United State Senate, 2011). This type of fraud, also known as "white-collar crime" (Rosoff et al., 2010), was committed at various institutional levels by a long chain of social actors such as brokers, business executives and underwriters, who lied with the aim of maximising purchases of mortgages and reaping sumptuous rewards. To identify these illegal activities is difficult, so the amount is underestimated (Black, 2008). The growth of the broker system has drastically complicated and fragmented the loan origination process, thus reducing accountability between the actors involved (brokers, lenders, appraisers, etc.), and the lack of government standards has not allowed an oversight of mortgage brokers. In addition, studies have found consistent evidence that white-collar criminals explain their actions as legal and ordinary occupations activities, a manner to redefine criminal act to alleviate or eliminate culpability (Coleman, 2002; Shover and Hunter, 2010). As Zuboff (2009) argues, this economic crisis derives from a business model that distances and dehumanises citizens and is compounded by a widespread abrogation of individual moral judgement. Zuboff evokes the "banality of evil" during the Holocaust events to indicate the indifference to suffering, repudiation of responsibility, conflicts of interest and systemic absence of individual moral judgement that produced an administrative economic massacre of such proportion that it constitutes an economic crime against humanity. In fact, Gallino (2013) noted that the total number of people who had the task of monitoring, controlling and designing the economic and financial systems around the world are in their tens of thousands while the victims of the crisis are tens of millions.

The rhetoric of the sovereign debt crisis suggests that the crisis was unexpected and depended on the excessive generosity of states in the preceding years. This plays a fundamental role in the media discourse in spreading and sustaining this representation of the crisis and related emotions. Watson (2009) argues that media discourse, particularly in the UK, nurtured and mobilised a sense of angst and social panic in people. This allowed the government to justify incredibly large interventions in recapitalising banks. This "emotional" strategy can justify particular interventions in the context of environmental disaster, and government decisions in favour of the banks looked credible in the eyes of the citizen. In addition, because risk is omnipresent in a state of crisis, European governments decided to cut from balances a relevant part of the welfare state, expenses for education and pensions, and other elements for a dignified life, causing discontent, frustration and anger, but also guilt.

Recently, Chryssochoou et al. (2013) explored the effects of the major economic crisis in Greece's population when everyday events contributed to a changing and threatening sociopolitical environment. Their results show a series of emotions that denoted a negative psychological state in relation to the crisis, such as fear, frustration, sadness, stress, disappointment, guilt, humiliation and helplessness. In addition, emotions play an important role in predicting reactions to the crisis, from collective violent practices to individual solutions and depression. Anger is confirmed as a predictor of political participation and collective action, whereas fear and frustration are major predictors of depression. As can be seen, the results of this study clearly summarise the consequences in emotional terms of the European strategy. In particular, guilt is shown to be an effective strategy in governing people to a point of obedience where they do not oppose political decisions, thus taking responsibility for the crisis (Kiersey, 2011).

The social construction of "bad conscience"

As we have already written, it seems that the sovereign debt crisis is the origin and the core of the current economic crisis, while the cause is in the result and the consequence of the failure of US banks and the transnational financial system.

In this scenario the subjective production of the crisis acquires a major role since in order to persuade individuals, it is necessary to attempt to elaborate, to spread and to make the image of the "indebted man" (Lazzarato, 2011).

The literature on attributional processes at the societal level (Hewstone, 1989) shows how the interpretation of historical, political and economic events mediates the event and the response given by the people. Thus cognitive attitudes, emotional reaction and behaviour in coping with a negative event are mediated by casual attributions and attributions of responsibility that people develop in a certain sociocultural environment. For instance, in a study that focused on the cause of poverty in the UK conducted by Furnham (1982), it emerged that voters for the Conservative Party attributed greater importance to individual explanations compared with voters for the Labour Party. These different points of view have affected decisions regarding welfare and job actions in different directions. These studies (see also Furnham and Bond, 1986) also show that similar differences at the level of individual attribution should be understood on the basis of the various forms of social representation that characterise a given society.

From this perspective, debt can be considered as a technique to remind citizens of their responsibility, that contributes to the construction of a "bad conscience" and to a sense of guilt that are the subjective conditions that are necessary to maintain the collective promise of redemption that the debt incurred by the state implicitly contains (Lazzarato, 2011). Thus states, governments and media must make great efforts to make the European population feel guilty for a debt that they never incurred and for mistakes that they never committed. The "memory of the debt" on which technical governments base themselves feeds on laws, texts and words that circulate continuously through social communication, trying to place itself as a hegemonic representation of the crisis. At this juncture, we believe that it is no exaggeration to speak of "discursive violence". As Maurizio Lazzarato (2011) suggests, tax is central from the subjective point of view because it is based on the expiation of guilt that is represented by the debt. And when the debt is public, the guilt is expiated not individually but collectively though the tax that acts as a vector that is capable of transforming every human being into indebted citizens. The required sacrifice consists not only of the payment of taxes but also of the willingness to give up certain rights that are represented as too expensive and no longer economically bearable, such as the dismantling of the health and social services of the welfare state or the acceptance of low wages and precarious employment contracts.

The political use of guilt to govern "indebted man" requires a focus on guilt and a subjective sense of inadequacy. The psychological literature on guilt (see Taylor, 1985) stressed that the emotional state of guilt arises when the individual considers their own inadequate and wrong behaviour. The sense of guilt is usually attributed to the belief of having caused harm to someone and/or having transgressed some moral and legal imperative. A primary component of a sense of guilt is the negative evaluation of the action committed by the offender. A second component is the assumption of responsibility (Zamperini, 1998). Finally, the third component is the sharing of norms and values in relation to which we feel guilty, so as to damage the moral self-image of the individual (Miceli and Castelfranchi, 1995). The feeling of guilt is accompanied by a corrective action that is a sort of reparation for the mistake that was made. If we don't see any possibility of repair, guilt can be transformed into another feeling of inadequacy: shame.

Ultimately an indebted citizen feels guilty for being wrong. They are asked to take responsibility for what they have (or have not) done, and within a moral framework that obliges all citizens to take charge of collective debt through payment of tax or renunciation of services.

The research

On the basis of this social diagnosis of indebted man, the objective of this research is to empirically analyse whether and how the media have actually taken on this societal function. The theoretical orientation that guided this societal function is that of a "concrete" and "critical" social psychology – a concrete social psychology in the sense that it assumes an ecological perspective that is capable of including the material conditions of human existence within a specific society, as is the case in Italy. It is a critical social psychology in the sense that it assumes a perspective of emancipation (critical emancipatory psychology, cf. Maiers, 1991) that seeks to make citizens aware of the psychosocial processes that they experience.

Method: Data and instrument

We analysed the content of newspaper articles related to public debt issues that appeared in the three high-circulation Italian newspapers: *Il Corriere della Sera*, *La Repubblica* and *La Stampa*. These were chosen because they are recognised as the pre-eminent newspapers in Italy which set the media agenda (FIEG Report, 2013). On the whole, during 2011 they reach a print circulation of 568,266,947 copies, while the digital circulation during 2012 was based on a total of 2,921,062 web users and 19,667 page views. *La Stampa* is owned by a large industrial group, *Il Corriere della Sera* has a moderate liberal approach and *La Repubblica* has an orientation towards social democracy. In terms of economic position, although they have some differences, the three can be considered mainstream media. Using the database on their Internet section, we searched for economic crisis-related articles. Our data-collection period was from January 2011 to December 2013, and we looked for the following words in the headline and the text article: "economic crisis", "debt", "austerity" and "sacrifice". The research rendered 922 articles that represented the final sample for our study. Table 7.1 shows the number of articles per year of the corpus.

We included in the analysis those articles that met any of four inclusion criteria: (1) articles that discuss societal or policy implications; (2) personal human interest articles related to a discussion of policy or societal implication; (3) stories about the economic crisis in Italy (e.g. we excluded those from the other European countries, such as the Greek and Spanish crises); and (4) stories about people committing suicide because of economic debts.

The articles were analysed with ATLAS.ti (a qualitative analysis tool). The first step was developed using the method of "open coding" (Strauss and Corbin, 1998). Here we selected portions of text (quotations) to which we assigned codes (codes) – that is, verbal labels that identify

Table 7.1 Number of articles per year of the corpus

Newspaper	Year			Total
	2011	2012	2013	
Il Corriere della Sera	211	174	125	510
La Repubblica	75	81	57	213
La Stampa	61	88	50	199
Total	347	343	232	922

conceptual themes emerging from the text. The next step involved "axial coding", which consists of the identification of the relationships between the codes. Subsequently the codes were aggregated into broader theoretical dimensions called "families of codes" (codes families), or rather higher-order categories that allow the codes to connect with each other to a higher level of extraction. In this way they are created as the main thematic areas from which it was possible to analyse and understand the different connections.

Results

Representation of the event
Economic crisis as a catastrophic event
What is discussed in the Italian media of the economic crisis includes the use of a metaphorical framework. It states that the situation that we are living in in Italy is a massive disaster. In fact the representation of the economic crisis is compared to a natural disaster, a catastrophe (the content expressed in this quote recurs in 63 fragments). The following quotation illustrates this point: "The epicenter of the earthquake", "the perfect storm", "a tsunami", "the image of a river that suddenly starts to flow in the opposite direction: is disquieting".

As indicated in these quotations, a recurring theme of the Italian media discourse is that of the catastrophic event, as suggested by the US study of Brasset and Clarke (2010). In addition, the media reported the range of gravity – in fact the event is of enormous proportions in terms of: "A very dangerous situation", "certainly it is a very difficult situation", "the severity of the emergency", "a terrible crisis", "difficult moment", "an abyss", "a dramatic moment".

This catastrophe is not limited merely to a particular area of Italy, involving only a portion or a specific part, but it is spread across the country and involves all of the citizens inside the national boundaries. In this case we see a generalisation of the disaster: "We are faced with a national emergency", "the country is on the brink of the abyss", "our country suffers from all the economic, financial and social European problems".

In general the economic crisis framework relies heavily on an appeal to emergency due to a catastrophic event that struck right across Italy with no exceptions. This message is important in terms of the assumption of responsibility by everybody. In this scenario of collective responsibility, not all countries have the same responsibility, and

Italy is considered to be among the countries that are most responsible. Although there is general agreement about the fact that the global crisis that erupted in the USA with the bankruptcy of Lehman Brothers has had financial sources, the importance of this fact does not seem to be fully understood and communicated. In the case of the public debt crisis in the euro area, there has been a renewed emphasis on a tighter fiscal policy, relegating to the background the mechanisms of financial speculation. However, the implementation of harsh austerity measures (involving cuts to pensions and public spending), as well as the privatisation of public services, imposed by the European Union and the European Central Bank as part of their efforts to address the Italian sovereign debt crisis, has led not only to job losses and impoverishment but also to widespread social unrest in the country.

Italy becomes a seriously ill "patient"

The second framework that emerges is that when the media report the consequences of the disaster they describe Italy in medical terms (16 fragments). The consequence of the disaster is to have reduced the country to a "seriously ill patient" that needs care, because it is at the point of death: "A heart attack patient in intensive care, try to prevent the next attack", "an artificial respirator will not make the patient healthier", "a patient who needs Monti's care", "seriously ill", "a patient that otherwise will die", "a death spiral".

Note the use of medical language in the quotations that reflect the social representation of "economic crisis as disease". This is a condition that conveys the idea of a serious problem that forces you to get to work and gives to certain members of the community (experts) the "power to heal". The experts (economists) are seen to be a new form of authority based on rational scientific knowledge. In the sick role, the patient is essentially a passive receiver of expert knowledge that the doctor-economist uses to diagnose and treat.

High level of risk

From a theoretical point of view the media discourse frames risk as a negative phenomenon that can lead to further negative consequences, such as a derailment or a crash and, on the medical plane, the risk represents a "contagion" coming from Greece. Italy (not the government or the political system) is construed as being responsible for the failure of the economic system. The word "risk" recurs in 273 fragments: "Italy threatens to stain itself with the responsibility of making the European economy negative", "the risk of derailing", "it is risking the future of the country", "the risk of Greece contagion", "risk of default", "risk of social conflicts".

In the following extracts the conception of risk emerges as something measurable in terms of loss. The certainty of the loss is used as an argument to support the existence of austerity: the loss of the welfare state, wellbeing, richness or savings, and places of employment for young people. This type of loss will lead to poverty and forms of social exclusion, even to death. Once again the collective character is stressed because the category "Italian" is always stated. This alarm prepares the emotional climate so as to be suitable for the call for a moral commitment: "The risk of losing the welfare, to which we were comfortably accustomed", "the well-being accumulated through generations is at risk", "three Italians out of ten risk poverty", "poverty and social exclusion risk", "the risk of youth unemployment", "the risk of dying because of austerity", "we put at risk the richness conquered", "the Italians' savings are at risk".

As can be seen from the example mentioned above, risk is calculated on the basis of loss and death for the whole country, and the logical connection or the main goal is that: "We had to prevent and contain the systemic risk".

The sphere of debt

The measure of Italian debt

As we have mentioned above, from the perspective of attributional processes, a central role in the context of the economic crisis is the use of debt to spread the construction of a sense of guilt. Through the analysis of the media discourse, we found that the lexical category of "debt" recurs in 323 fragments of the 922 articles.

By using the construct of "debt" to describe the economic crisis, the newspapers create a discursive context in which they stressed, similarly for the category of "catastrophic event", the collective characteristic of this type of debt, that it is often expressed as "Italian", "our" or "public" and "sovereign". Related to this category, in addition to the collective value, the media also mentioned the measure of gravity. For example, they reported: "A heavy public debt", "to heal public debt", "the Italians' public debt is very large", "unsustainable combination of huge debt and low and negative growth", "the mountain of public debt", "abnormal weight of public debt", "maxi Italian debt".

Here it is interesting to note that there is a particular dramatisation of the debt which obscures the real Italian situation. Although Italy has the second-highest sovereign debt in the euro area, it does not feature among the countries that have excessive private debt. Its firms owe somewhat less than the euro area average and Italian household debt is especially low.

Whose guilt is it?

The media discourse indicates the cause of the debt to the Italian people. The word "guilt" is presented in 80 quotations of 922 texts: "The fault is of the Italians, who in the past have not given enough weight to the situation", "the state will collapse and it is our fault", "we Italians had for too long a way of life in which we spent more than we could afford", "the guilty society".

It is significant that such an argumentative line adopts the Italians' guilt as the cause of the "catastrophic event", underlining the negative hallmark that confirms the primary component of the sense of guilt in the negative evaluation of the action committed by the offender but without ever specifying what kind of errors they committed, or even how or when they were committed.

A call for a collective sense of responsibility

Responsibility is a fundamental concept that is related to risk theory, the feeling of guilt and the handling of economic crisis. One prevalent idea in sociology (Giddens, 1991; Beck, 1999) is that people are becoming increasingly responsible for managing their life, and, for Dean (1999), responsibility is part of the strategies that are exercised by governing authorities.

Through our data the word "responsibility" recurs in 459 quotations of 922 texts, showing that media discourse emphasises the individual, families, households and communities taking responsibility for their own debt. Here are some examples: "Everyone is called to assume their responsibility", "national responsibility", "President Napolitano asks to everybody the maximum effort of responsibility", "we are taking great responsibility supporting the government", "we must not forget our own responsibility", "greater responsibility in common", "you will find some forms of cooperation and shared responsibility", "if we have a sense of responsibility it will save the country", "collective responsibility to respond to the emergency".

Sacrifice as a fiscal measure

The attribution of guilt regarding the economic crisis and the sovereign debt crisis is clearly directed at "Italians citizens", so as a consequence they are called to take some responsibility. In this framework, "sacrifice" is the privileged social representation through which the collective is persuaded to pay the price in the form of a direct payment or waiver of rights and it becomes part of the moral media discourse.

The word "sacrifice" recurs in 835 fragments of the 922 articles, showing that it is widely shared. Given its high frequency we have separated the word "sacrifice", placing it in the following different subcategories. The results show that "sacrifice" is a fiscal manoeuvre.

"Fiscal sacrifice" recurs in 124 fragments of the 835 quotations: "The measure of the sacrifices is approved", "the season of sacrifice", "the sacrifices imposed by this maneuver", "it is an important maneuver in term of sacrifices", "the policy of sacrifices promoted by the government".

"Collective sacrifice" recurs in 188 fragments of the 835 quotations: "At the top, the Chigi Palace will discuss the debt problem, everyone realizes that a drastic operation is needed to bring it down otherwise the sacrifices made so far will not be served and Italy will not regain credit at international level", "an immense sacrifice is what the government asks the country to make".

"Citizenship sacrifice" recurs in 354 fragments of the 835 quotations, which shows that a large part of the population are called to make a sacrifice as the following quotations demonstrate:

Italians: "The plurality of sacrifices we ask to Italians. We want them to be seen in the context of a reawakening of the Italian economy", "what we are asking of Italians is great sacrifice".

Citizens: "Our citizens have understood that the sacrifices and reforms were made for the good of the country", "the crisis, the government asks for sacrifices from all citizens", "the sacrifices imposed on citizens', the decree imposes sacrifices on citizens", "at a time of crisis in which the citizens are asked for enormous sacrifices".

Pensioners: "Somehow the retirees and pensioners have the merit of having made sacrifices necessary to help the public accounts".

Doctors and patients: "Ready to face the sacrifices that are required of us: doctors and patients".

Workers: "The sacrifices, only we have to make, only the self-employed and employees", "all the burden and sacrifices of the crisis on workers and the lower classes".

Generational sacrifice: "Support for the policy of sacrifice is not popular but you have to make them for the future of our children".

Families: "In the last year families have faced many sacrifices", "the sacrifices of millions of Italian families", "for 22% of Italian households it will be a difficult autumn of many sacrifices".

Conclusion

Thompson (1987) states that ideology operates through the mobilisation of discourse. So the processes of ideology, as a means of mobilisation of meaning, are also the means of mobilisation of consciousness. Obviously the conscience of individual citizens is not merely a passive container that simply repeats the others' words as if they were its own. Contemporary democracies are places of opinions where citizens have points of views and ideas regarding a variety of social problems, and these opinions are of vital importance for governments, especially in times of crisis. The huge investment put into the field for surveys of attitudes and opinions shows how it is important, both for those who want to sell goods and for those in power, to understand what citizens think (cf. Billig, 1991).

In order to govern, every society develops disciplinary methods (Foucault, 2008), not only of a repressive type but also at the level of regulation and organisation, and through a flexible and light-measured way, seek to build an environment that encourages and solicits the individual to react in one way rather than another. Thus, in such scenarios, to be disciplined becomes the right way of thinking. Discipline and will are two categories that are tied to the individual.

For example, risk is currently placed at the base of the human condition (Beck, 1986), therefore it is necessary to determine the weight that we have to assign to the pros and cons. An exercise to ponder is what is required at the moment of choice, in order to clarify gains and losses, usefulness or uselessness; and the imperative is to identify the rational way to do it. In addition, the assumption of risk – how to cope with it – necessarily implies the responsibility of the actor (Zamperini, 1998). Consequently, risk summons up a moral imperative of action and tends to diminish that of abstention. Here, risk and income are opposed. Around this theme, two major forms of human existence go in different directions: on the one hand, those individuals who accept the risk, claim it and accept their condition as beings devoted to risk; on the other, those who reject it, avoid it and try to defend themselves from it. On the one hand the brave, on the other the fearful and our culture, past and recent, tends to celebrate the first rather than the second: the hunter, the warrior, the pioneer, the entrepreneur or inventor, the scientist – in short, those who make investments and not those who are supported such as by inheritance. As Ewald and Kessler (2000) indicated, such a counterposition is not the same as that between "riskphobic" and "riskphiliac". In fact, the "riskphobic" is not necessarily regarded negatively. Thanks to this, we can avoid an excessive exposure to risk while protecting the others. The distinction between "riskphobic" and "riskphiliac" refers to a second choice criterion: that of more or less prudent risk management. Although our culture certainly does not skimp on encouraging risk – the courage of the daring – at the same time it regards recklessness with suspicion, even condemning it. In economic reality, we are so ready to praise an entrepreneur but we look at a speculator with suspicion.

However, during this economic global crisis, society doesn't limit itself to encouraging individuals through a call for a sense of responsibility; it also imposes a sense of conscience. This is based on the image of "indebted man", now governed by guilt for having demanded too much and experiencing the shame of not being capable of the sacrificial rite of reparation (to pay taxes and to give up services in order to settle the public debt) that, in our opinion, authoritarianism suggests. In the case that we have analysed, it emerges in the form of discursive violence enacted through social communication. Serge Moscovici (1989) argues that social psychology should try to study the "thinking society", to underline the necessity to move from the "discovery" of the individual's mental structures to collective factors such as the language. In our case, the study of the language of the mass media, aimed at identifying themes that establish the public performance of the economic crisis, has highlighted the subordination of the person to the debt, as a new threatening totem in front of which one prostrates oneself and for which to sacrifice oneself. Medical and religious metaphors coagulate to argue that the human being is responsible for the condition into which they fell. The language operates as a mantra to remind the individuals of their sins, prescribing the saviour in the form of the payment of taxes.

Through such communication it is expected that the citizen becomes aware of the errors made, they feel a sense of guilt and they start along the path of expiation. However, that doesn't automatically mean that individuals have to submit to this belief. Conversely, they can develop alternative interpretative repertoires by organising groups of speakers to express different configurations of discourse and different opinions with respect to the mainstream communication. For example, in research carried out by Galli et al. (2010) involving three Italian social groups (bank clerks, university students from the faculty of economics and shopkeepers), the different groups of participants, although sharing the typical themes communicated by the media, gave different importance and different meanings to the themes in the representation of the crisis. For bank clerks the crisis was unemployment; for shopkeepers it was a lack of money; and for students it was a political and economic problem that generates poverty and social exclusion.

Nevertheless, the attempt to define the public image of indebted man allows us to understand how, in addition to the violence of expropriation of resources and rights, there is also a discursive violence that affects attitudes and reasoning – a structural violence and a symbolic violence synergistically allied to pushing individuals to honour a debt that will never be fully settled and only variously modulated. From this argument comes the beginning of a new genealogy of modern slavery: the indebted man.

Acknowledgements

This research was supported by a grant from the Coop School of Montelupo – National Institute of Training for Consumer Cooperatives, Florence, Italy. We would like to thank Enrico Parsi and his colleagues of the Coop School of Monetelupo for their invaluable comments on earlier drafts of this chapter.

References

Beck, U. (1986). *Risikogesellschaft: Auf dem Weg in eine andere Moderne.* Frankfurt am Main: Suhrkamp Verlag.
Beck, U. (1999). *World Risk Society.* London: Polity Press.
Billig, M. (1991). *Ideology and Opinion: Studies in Rhetorical Psychology.* London: Sage.
Black, W. K. (2008). *Why Greenspan's & Busch's Regulatory Failures Allowed a "Criminogenic Environment",* paper presented at the Levy Institute's Minsky Conference. New York: Annandale-on-Hudson.
Brassett, J. and Clarke, C. (2010). Performing the sub-prime crisis: Trauma, fear, and shame as governmentalities of the financial subject. Garnet working paper No. 77/10. Warwick: University of Warwick.
Brasset, J. and Vaughan-Williams, N. (2012). Governing traumatic events. *Alternatives: Globals, Local, Political,* 37, 183–187.
Casey, B. (1991). Survey evidence on trends in "non-standard" employment. In Pollert, A. (ed.). *Farewell to Flexibility?* Oxford: Blackwell, 179–199.
Chang, S. S., Stuckler, D., Yip, P. and Gunnel, D. (2013). Impact of 2008 global economic crisis on suicide: Time trend study in 54 countries. *BMJ,* 347, f5239.
Chossudovsky, M. and Marshall, A. G. (eds.) (2010). *The Global Economic Crisis: The Great Depression of the XXI Century.* Montreal: Global Research Publisher, Center for Research on Globalization.
Coleman, J. W. (2002). *The Criminal Elite: The Sociology of White-Collar Crime.* New York: St. Martin's.
Córdova, E. (1986). From full-time employment to atypical employment: A major shift in the evolution of labour relations? *International Labour Review,* 125, 641–657.

Chryssochoou, X., Papastamou, S. and Prodromitis, G. (2013). Facing the economic crisis in Greece: The effect of grievances, real and perceived vulnerability, and emotions towards the crisis on reactions to austerity measure. *Journal of Social Science Education*, 12, 41–49.
Dean, M. (1999). Risk, calculable and incalculable. In Lupton, D. (ed.). *Risk and Sociocultural Theory: New Direction and Perspectives*. Cambridge: Cambridge University Press, 131–159.
De Grip, A., Hoevenberg, J. and Willems, E. (1997). Atypical employment in the European Union. *International Labour Review*, 136, 49–71.
Delsen, L. (1995). *Atypical Employment: An International Perspective-Causes. Consequences and Policy*. Groningen: Wolters-Noordhoff.
Ewald, F. and Kessler, D. (2000). Les Noces du risque et de la politique. *Le Débat*, 109, 55–99.
Fassin, D. (2008). The humanitarian politics of testimony: Subjectification through trauma in the Israeli-Palestinian conflict. *Cultural Anthropology*, 23, 531–558.
Fassin, D. and Rechtman, R. (2009). *The Empire of Trauma: An Inquiry into the Condition of Victimhood*. Princeton and Oxford: Princeton University Press.
Federazione Italiana Editori Giornali (FIEG) (2013). La stampa in Italia. www.fieg.it.
Financial Crisis Inquiry Commission (FCIC) (2011). *The Financial Crisis Inquiry Report*. Washington, DC: Official Government Edition.
Foucault, M. (2008). *The Birth of Biopolitics*. New York: Palgrave Macmillan.
Freedy, J. and Hobfoll, S. E. (eds.) (1995). *Traumatic stress: From theory to practice*. New York: Springer.
Furnham. A. (1982). Why are the poor always with us? Explanations for poverty in Britain. *British Journal of Social Psychology*, 21, 311–322.
Furnham, A. and Bond, M. H. (1986). Hong Kong Chinese explanations for wealth. *Journal of Economic Psychology*, 7, 447–460.
Galli, I., Markova, I., Bouriche, B., Fasanelli, R., Geka, M., Iacob, L. and Iacob, G. (2010). La représentation sociale de la crise économique dans quatre pays européens. *Les Cahiers Internationaux de Psychologie Sociale*, 87, 585–620.
Gallino, L. (2013). *Il colpo si stato di banche e governi*. Torino: Einaudi.
Gangl, K., Kastlunger, B., Kirchler, E. and Voracek, M. (2012). Confidence in the economy in times of crisis: Social representation of experts and laypeople. *The Journal of Socio-Economics*, 41, 603–614.
Giddens, A. (1991). *Modernity and Self Identity: Self and Society in the Late Modern Age*. Cambridge, UK: Polity Press.
Gili, M., Roca, M., Basu, S., McKee, M. and Stuckler, D. (2013). The mental health risks of economic crisis in Spain: Evidence from primary care center, 2006 and 2010. *European Journal of Public Health*, 23, 103–108.
Giotakos, O., Karabelas, D. and Kafkas, A. (2011). Financial crisis and mental health in Greece: Findings from the association between financial and mental health factors. *Psychiatriki*, 22, 109–119.
Goldthorpe, H. J. (ed.) (1984). *Order and Conflict in Contemporary Capitalism: Studies in the Political Economy of Western European Nations*. Oxford: Oxford University Press.
Green, F., Krahn, H. and Sung, J. (1993). Non-Standard Work in Canada and the United Kingdom. *International Journal of Manpower*, 14, 17–86.

Hewstone, M. (1989). *Casual Attribution: From Cognitive Processes to Collective Beliefs*. Oxford: Blackwell.
Kalleberg, A. L. (2000). Nonstandard employment relations: Part-time, temporary and contract work. *Annual Reviews of Sociology*, 26, 341–365.
Kiersey, N. J. (2011). Everyday neoliberism and the subjectivity of crisis. Post-political control in an era of financial turmoil. *Journal of Critical Globalisation Studies*, 4, 23–44.
Koselleck, R. (1988). *Critique and Crisis: Enlightenment and the Pathogenesis of Modern Society*. Oxford: Berg.
Koselleck, R. (2002). *The Practice of Conceptual History: Timing History, Spacing Concepts*. Stanford, CA: Stanford University Press.
Krugman, P. (2012). *End This Depression Now*. New York, London: Norton and Company.
Lazzarato, M. (2011). *La fabrique de l'homme endetté. Essai sur la condition néolibérale*. Paris: Amsterdam.
Maiers, W. (1991). Critical psychology: Historical background and task. In Tolman, C.W. and Maiers, W. (eds.). *Critical Psychology: Contributions to an Historical Science of the Subject*. Cambridge: Cambridge University Press.
Miceli, M. and Castelfranchi, C. (1995). *Le difese della mente. Profili cognitivi*. Roma: La Nuova Italia Scientifica.
Moscovici, S. (1961/1976). *La psychoanalyse, son image et son public*. Paris: Presse Universitaire de France.
Moscovici, S. (1989). Precondition for explanation in social representations. *European Journal of Social Psychology*, 19, 407–430.
Moscovici, S. (2001). Why a theory of social representations? In Deaux, K. and Philogène, G. (eds.). *Representations of the Social: Bridging Theoretical Traditions*. Oxford: Blackwell.
Nguyen, T. H. and Pontell, H. N. (2010). Mortgage origination fraud and the global economic crisis. A criminological analysis. *Criminology & Public Policy*, 9, 591–612.
Permanent Subcommittee on Investigations (2011). *Wall Street and the Financial Crisis: Anatomy of a Financial Collapse*. Washington, DC: United States Senate.
Pupavac, V. (2001). Therapeutic governance: Psycho-social intervention and trauma risk management. *Disasters*, 25, 358–372.
Roland-Lévy, C. (1998). Psychologie économique de la consommation et de l'endettement. In Roland-Lévy, C. and Adair, P. (eds.). *Psychologie Economique: Théories et Applications*. Paris: Economica, 299–317.
Roland-Lévy, C., Pappalardo Boumelki, F. E. and Guillet, E. (2010). Representation of the financial crisis: Effect on social representations of savings and credit. *The Journal of Socio-Economics*, 39, 142–149.
Rosoff, S. M., Pontell, H. N. and Tillman R. (2010). *Profit without Honor: White-Collar Crime and the Looting of America*, 5th edition. New York: Prentice Hall.
Rubonis, A. V. and Bickman, L. (1991). Psychological impairment in the wake of disaster: The disaster-psychopathology relationship. *Psychological Bulletin*, 109, 384–399.
Scambler, G. (2004). Re-framing stigma: Felt and enacted stigma and challenges to the sociology of chronic and disabling conditions. *Social Theory and Health*, 2, 29–46.
Sennet, R. (1998). *The Corrosion of Character*. New York: Norton and Company.

Shover, N. and Hunter, W. (2010). Blue-collar, white-collar: Crimes and mistake. In Bernasco, W. (ed.). *Offenders on Offending: Learning about Crime from Criminals*. Cullompton: Willan, 205–227.
Solantaus, T., Leinonen, J. and Punamäki, R. L. (2004). Children's mental health in times of economic recession: Replication and extension of the family economic stress model in Finland. *Developmental Psychology*, 40, 412–429.
Strauss, J. and Corbin, A. (1998). Grounded theory methodology: An overview. In Denzin, N. K. and Lincoln, Y. S. (eds.). *Strategies of Qualitative Inquiring*. Thousand Oaks, CA: Sage, 158–183.
Stuckler, D., Basu, S., Suhrcke, M., Coutts, A. and McKee, M. (2009). The public health effects of economic crisis and alternative policy responses in Europe: An empirical analysis. *The Lancet*, 374, 315–323.
Stuckler, D., Basu, S., Suhrcke, M., Coutts, A. and McKee, M. (2011). Effects of the 2008 Recession on health: A first look at European data. *The Lancet*, 378, 124–125.
Taylor, G. (1985). *Pride, Shame, and Guilt: Emotions of Self-Assessment?* Oxford: Oxford University Press.
Thompson, J. B. (1987). Language and ideology: A framework for analysis. *The Sociological Review*, 35, 516–536.
Uutela, A. (2010). Economic crisis and mental health. *Current Opinion in Psychiatry*, 23, 127–130.
Yehuda, R. and McFarlane, A. (1995). Conflict between current knowledge about post-traumatic stress disorder and its original conceptual basis. *American Journal of Psychiatry*, 152, 1705–1713.
Yule, W. (1999). *Post Traumatic Stress Disorders: Concept and Therapy*. New York: Wiley.
Watson, M. (2009). Headlong into the Polanyian dilemma: The impact of middle-class moral panic on the British government's response to the sub-prime crisis. *British Journal of Politics and International Relations*, 11, 422–437.
World Health Organization, Regional Office for Europe (2011). *Impact of Economic Crisis on Mental Health*. Copenhagen: WHO.
Zamperini, A. (1998). *Psicologia sociale della responsabilità*. Torino: Utet.
Zamperini, A. (2010). *L'ostracismo. Essere esclusi, respinti e ignorati*. Torino: Einaudi.
Zivin, K., Paczkowski, M. and Galea, S. (2011). Economic downturns and population mental health: Research findings, gaps, challenges and priorities. *Psychological Medicine: A Journal of Research in Psychiatry and the Allied Sciences*, 41, 1343–1348.
Zuboff, S. (2009). Wall street's crime against humanity. *Bloomberg Businessweek*, 20 March 2009.

8
Chasing Happiness through Personal Debt: An Example of Neoliberal Influence in Norwegian Society

Salman Türken, Erik Carlquist and Henry Allen

Introduction

This chapter investigates a Norwegian TV show called *Luksusfellen* (The Luxury Trap). Each episode follows an individual or a couple who are having problems with personal debt. Like many others of its ilk, it presents a variety of indebted individuals whom the hosts try to help out of their predicament. What this particular show provides is an acute example of how debt, and implicitly the debt industry, is articulated in a public arena. It also enables an analysis of how various discourses around debt are both constructed and reproduced. This analytic frame is with particular reference to sociocultural dimensions and how often complex personal circumstances are presented as simplistic financial ones. Debt, and the debtor–creditor relationship, functions in a social capacity as much as it does a financial one. Understanding how the social conditions, specifically the various discourses, around debt are constructed is of significant importance as these attempt to smuggle in various moral and political assumptions, which contribute to legitimating and reproducing the currently hegemonic neoliberal ideology.

We begin with an overview of some recent literature on debt as a sociocultural phenomenon, and outline our theoretical framework based on a Foucauldian understanding of neoliberal governmentality. We then present a discourse analysis of *Luksusfellen* and discuss its implications for the subjectivity of debtors participating in the show and the audience, arguing that such debt TV programmes function as technologies of governmentality.

Understanding debt as a social phenomenon

Debt as a political and sociological phenomenon, beyond being merely a financial condition, has seen increasing interest, especially since the 2008 financial crisis in which "toxic" debt is broadly understood to be a fundamental cause. By analysing cultural products, such as debt TV shows such as *Luksusfellen*, we gain a better understanding of how debt exists as a social and political phenomenon (Atwood, 2008; Graeber; 2011; Lazzarato, 2012; Ross, 2013).

To begin, Atwood (2008) paints a comprehensive picture of what these programmes entail, which is worth reproducing in full:

> We seem to be entering a period in which debt has passed through its most recent harmless and fashionable period, and is reverting to being sinful. There are even debt TV shows, which have a familiar religious-revival ring to them. There are accounts of shopaholic binges during which you don't know what came over you and everything was a blur, with tearful confessions by those who've spent themselves into quivering insomniatic jellies of hopeless indebtedness, and have resorted to lying, cheating, stealing, and kiting cheques between bank accounts as a result. There are testimonials by families and loved ones whose lives have been destroyed by the debtor's harmful behavior. There are compassionate but severe admonitions by the television host, who here plays the part of priest or revivalist. There's a moment of seeing the light, followed by repentance and a promise never to do it again. There's a penance imposed – *snip, snip* go the scissors on the credit cards – followed by a strict curb-on-spending regimen; and finally, if all goes well, the debts are paid down, the sins are forgiven, absolution is granted, and a new day dawns, in which sadder but more solvent man you rise the morrow morn.
>
> (Atwood, 2008, pp. 41–42)

What Atwood suggests, in line with Graeber (2011), is that there is a significant religious dimension to how debt as a concept is discussed in contemporary Western culture, and that this dimension to the discourse has a long history. Both Atwood and Graeber consider that essentially we are born into a debt to God for our life, and we spend our lives trying to pay it back but only really ever make the interest. The individualising tendency of this religious dimension occurs in parallel with our principal concern regarding neoliberal ideology. In this ideology, the individual is positioned as being the principal agent of responsibility in their life while society more broadly, and the debt industry specifically, is not of significance. In this way debt is a social condition couched in religious/moral language and discourse that ultimately creates subjectivity through a particular power relation. Particularly interesting in assessing *Luksusfellen* is how the concept of debt and the relative indebtedness of individuals are discussed and constructed, both explicitly and implicitly.

Moreover, Graeber's (2011) arguments regarding debt take into account not merely financial debt but a variety of obligations that people owe to one another. This is important because it shows how debt as a social relation is rooted in how individuals interact with each other, and do so in a variety of very different human societies. A sense of obligation, and more specifically debts, forms social bonds between people. According to Graeber, debt relations are fundamentally social relations and are therefore also relations of power: someone owes, and someone is owed. Lazzarato (2012) takes this further to suggest that contemporary subjectivity, and by extension the contemporary social order, is in large part determined by these debt relations.[1] This is especially important for contemporary Western society where money and debt are reified and treated as though they exist independently of and alongside "social relations", with finance being treated as mere calculation. Graeber argues that debt is fundamentally, and has been throughout millennia of various human civilisations, a social relationship – from the slave trade, to medieval blood feuds to the financial crisis today. In all of these circumstances there are people in positions of power who are owed something by those who are then subjugated or exploited in some way through being indebted.

Within this social dimension to debt, specifically financial debt, has also always been an additional religious aspect. This concerns the way in which debt and sin are related – that being in debt is somehow sinful or, as Atwood puts it more starkly, "financial debt as a metaphor for sin" (Atwood, 2008, p. 47). It is not only in the language used in the discussion of debt but also in the overbearing moral dimension to attitudes towards both debt and debtors that it is somehow sinful. Graeber suggests that in the major religions, Christianity specifically, people owe a "life debt" to the saviour – their whole lives being repayment for the ultimate sacrifice of the son of God. These religious aspects, as Atwood argues, can be witnessed in how this kind of TV show operates to position the protagonist as a sinner who needs saving from themselves, and the experts who will help them to "see the light".

This is a crucial part of seeing further that debt, and money more broadly, is a social relation that requires tacit agreement among those involved. This agreement is implicit and is also how ideology functions (Billig, 1999). In this way, there is a shared understanding among people about particular social concepts and the relationships that may underpin the concept themselves. This is particularly the case in what debt, and being indebted, means for people, and how this is either reinforced or undermined by particular social and political conditions. In this way, contemporary technologies of governmentality such as the TV show reinforce and reproduce these narratives and discourses with the result that a particular social and political order is upheld. In addition, a power relation between the debt industry and the majority of citizens of Western democracies is instituted. Both middle and working classes are engaged in a debt economy in order to fulfil particular visions of "the good life" through acts of consumption, in which their often unrealisable dream is to be relieved from the burden of these debts. The fact that it often goes without question that it is people as individuals who are held entirely responsible for their relative indebtedness is part of the way in which this ideology functions.

Going further, Lazzarato (2012, p. 24) discusses debt in terms of its being the social condition of our time, and suggests that it is fundamentally a power relation: "Debt is finance from the point of view of the debtors who have to repay it. Interest is finance from the point of view of creditors, security-holders who guarantee they benefit from debt." For Lazzarato, debt, and the creditor–debtor relationship, has become the lynch-pin for contemporary neoliberal capitalism. This is made apparent in both how universal these relationships have become, being recognizable to all, and how the debt crisis has consumed normal politics – collective decision-making is very much about how we managed the debt, both in terms of national and personal debt. This is particularly the case when seeing the rise and the popularity of "austerity" as a political manifesto (Blyth, 2013).

Following from the arguments of Graeber and Atwood about the social nature and deeply moral dimensions of debt is the importance of debt to contemporary subjectivity. This is vital in considering how debt TV shows such as *Luksusfellen* function as technologies of governmentality. Foucault argues that citizens are governed in ways that produce, and reproduce, forms of subjectivity that make them more easily governable. This is achieved through various "technologies of governmentality" – that is, strategies and techniques that both knowingly and unknowingly conform to and articulate this "governmentality". Individualisation of the social and responsibilisation of the individual are two major technologies of neoliberal governmentality, as Rose (1999) elaborates, and which we argue apply to programmes such as *Luksusfellen*. These shows position both the subject and the audience through the (re)production of particular discourses, and these discourses function to govern and discipline subjects, especially with regard to morality, sin and guilt. As our close reading will show, these are ways in which subjects are understood and understand themselves in terms of the debtor–creditor relationship and how the debt industry is, or more likely is not, taken into consideration.

In short, individual debtors, those participating in TV shows and often the audiences too are constructed through a variety of discourses around debt which contain implicit power relations. The language of debt is linked to its history as a social institution, to religious dimensions, and to how individuals today are understood as citizens. In order to be part of society, all individuals are scrutinised as debtors:

> The logic of debt now structures and conditions the process of individualization, a constant for social policies. Each individual is a particular case which must be studied carefully, because, as with a loan application, it is the debtor's future plans, his style of life, his "solvency" that guarantees reimbursement of the social debt he owes.
>
> (Lazzarato, 2012, p. 131)

What this demonstrates is that debt's historical roots in religious discourse, as discussed by Graeber and Atwood, are bound to contemporary subjectivity and how indebted individuals are both financially in debt but also suffer from the associated social pressures. It is the social dimension of debt, the more abstract form, that we are concerned with here, and how these particular discourses are reproduced in debt TV shows. The abovementioned literature suggests that debt has a heritage of being far more than just a financial condition, and that debt today strongly shapes the social identities and relations of contemporary citizens of most Western nations. Despite the fact that Norway is more insulated from global economic pressures, due to the lack of national debt, the significant sovereign wealth from oil revenues and the strong, well-functioning welfare system, the presence of personal debt in people's lives is still significant and most importantly normalised.

Individualisation and neoliberal governmentality

So far this chapter has discussed how debt can be understood in social and cultural terms, and what part this plays in the functioning of the debt industry. Now we will connect this notion of "debt subjectivity" with broader social theory, and then move to consider the context of Norway and the empirical example of Luksusfellen.

As well as living in increasingly indebted societies, we also live in increasingly individualised societies (Beck, 1992; Bauman, 2001). Beck states:

> In the individualized society, the individual must therefore learn, on pain of permanent disadvantage, to conceive of himself or herself as the center of action, as the planning office with respect to his/her own biography, abilities, orientations, relationship and so on... As a consequence the floodgates are opened wide for the subjectivization and individualization of risks and contradictions produced by institutions and society.
>
> (Beck, 1992, pp. 135–136)

Such processes of individualisation have been fuelled by strong global developments towards neoliberalism in recent decades, shaping both political-economic practices and "common sense" (Bourdieu, 1998; Harvey, 2005). In contemporary societies, individual selfhood is continually produced through the discourses and practices of neoliberalism (Rose, 1999). Our arguments in this chapter draw heavily upon Foucault's (2008) understanding of neoliberal governmentality. Neoliberal governmentality as "conduct of conduct" refers to the ways in which neoliberalism works by installing in society a concept of the human subject as autonomous, rational, individualised, self-directing and decision-making agents who understand themselves in terms of human capital. The individualistic subject of the Enlightenment which came to fore in the early stages of capitalism has been refashioned as an entrepreneur. Neoliberalism encourages individuals to become self-entrepreneurs and demands a stronger degree of self-determination by pushing subjects toward engaging individually in the solution of the social problems of life – for example, illness, unemployment, education, poverty – which have been seen as more collective concerns, and have more recently been the very essence of the welfare state (Ferge, 1997; Foucault, 2008). In doing so, neoliberalism replaces more overtly coercive disciplinary mechanisms on society and fabricates the subject as someone who is autonomous yet governable, engaged in self-monitoring and self-disciplining. The self-understanding of the individual is repeatedly constructed through an internalised discourse as being the master of their own existence, compulsively leading the subject to engage in endeavours of self-improvement and self-critique. Ultimately, these rational ("individual") subjects therefore becomes the only sites of blame for their own misery. Such Foucauldian perspectives resonate well with Beck's theorisations of the individualisation of risk.

Workings of neoliberalism are particularly strengthened by the psy-complex, which contributes to further individualisation of the social through various discourses and helps to preserve the status quo, namely neoliberal governance (Rose, 1999). The psy-complex refers to all institutions relating to human sciences, particularly psychology and its affiliates, which diffuse in society a certain type of psychological expertise – the heterogeneous knowledges, forms of authority and practical techniques that make it possible for individuals to construe and conduct themselves in certain ways. Rose's claim is that "the psy disciplines and psy expertise have had a key role in constructing 'governable subjects'... making it possible to govern human beings in ways that are compatible with the principles of liberalism and democracy", shaping the private selves in contemporary societies (1999, p. vii). He further states:

> However constrained by external or internal factors, the modern self is institutionally required to construct a life through the exercise of choice from among alternatives. Every aspect of life, like every commodity, is imbued with a self-referential meaning; every choice we make is an emblem of our identity, a mark of our individuality, each is a message to ourselves and others as to the sort of person we are, each casts a glow back, illuminating the self of he or she who consumes.
> (Rose, 1999, p. 231)

The psy-complex contributes to spreading the values of autonomy and self-realisation. As can be read from the quote above, conduct of conduct is achieved through personal labour to assemble a way of life within the sphere of consumption. Self-realisation is thus imagined to be achieved by becoming a consumer. Indeed, globally, the contemporary way of living is characterised by consumerism (Miles, 1998). We are increasingly exposed to the mantra "To have is to be", and living in consumer societies, "the very essence of being" is equated with "having; that if one has nothing, one is nothing", as Fromm asserted earlier (1978, p. 25).

Thus consumerism and debt also provide an illustration of how a particular form of governmentality functions through the reproduction of particular discourses around debt, and in so doing it produces particular individualised subjects. *Luksusfellen*, as we will show, contributes to this process and is emblematic of it.

Debt in Norwegian society

Although Norway remains one of the most successful welfare states with prominent social democratic values, Norwegian society has been increasingly influenced by neoliberal policy. This happened with the introduction of New Public Management in the 1980s, with increased privatisation, deregulation of markets and incorporation into the global market economy. Citizens of the welfare state have increasingly been constructed as consumers (Nafstad et al., 2007) who, to a large degree, depend financially on debt. There is also a widespread discourse of materialism in Norwegian society, especially among the youth, who not only establish relationships and bond with peers through activities such as shopping (Brusdal and Lavik, 2008) but also understand happiness, to some extent, in terms of material possessions (Türken et al., submitted). Moreover, the debt economy is sustained not only by financial institutions (e.g. banks and credit card companies) that provide less restricted consumer loans than before, but also by state regulation and deregulation that encourage young people to become debtors (e.g. education loans, mortgage regulations). As mentioned earlier, in this respect subjectivity, and to a degree citizenship, is bound together with being in debt – in order to own property, a car and so forth one needs to take on debt. Citizens are thus influenced and shaped into agents who keep the debt economy in place.

Debt, then, has arguably become part and parcel not only of the financial structure of Norwegian society but of the lived experience of its inhabitants. Some 83% of households are in debt: the average debt for a Norwegian household (not including students) increased from NOK 626,000 (Norwegian krone) in 2004 to NOK 104,800 (approximately EUR 135,000) in 2011(Statistics Norway, 2013). In 2011, 209,222 out of a total of 250,456 students were receiving education loans from the state (Lånekassen, 2013). Additionally, the percentage of households reporting to have consumer debt, as opposed to mortgages and education loans, increased from 12% in 2007 to 20% in 2011. Credit card usage involving following-month payment, as opposed to debit cards, increased from 41% in 2007 to 65% in 2011 (Lavik and Tufte, 2011).

Such numbers imply that in Norwegian society most citizens, including students, have been structurally transformed into debtors.

Luksusfellen

The TV show (*Luksusfellen*) is introduced on its website with the following words:

> "To get into the luxury trap" has become a common phrase used for individuals whose overconsumption of clothes, travel, electronics and other consumer goods is funded through borrowed money... When the money is used on everything but bills and the down-payment of credit cards, and the debt increases to such a height that one cannot see a way of out of the problems, Luksusfellen experts come to help.
>
> (authors' translation)

Luksusfellen is a popular show in Norway that is aired by the commercial channel TV3. Currently in its tenth season, it has an average audience of approximately 250,000 (e-mail communication with TV3), which is considerable given the Norwegian population of roughly 5 million.

Drawing upon Foucauldian understandings of governmentality and discourse, we will outline ways in which individual debtors are constructed by the programme as certain kinds of subjects. We will also discuss how the psy-complex through the involvement of expert psychologists and economists in the programme contributes to constructing the neoliberal subject and the enforcement of neoliberal governance. In doing so we will discuss the extent to which the psy-complex may sustain the debt industries by placing demands on individuals (debtors) and neglecting the social factors that constrain their choices, thus stigmatising those who fail to measure up to the moral imperatives of the dominant discourses.

Method and analysis

Foucauldian discourse analysis

Subjectivity cannot develop independently of culture. Each society or culture contains diverse discourses that have implications for subjectivity. Connolly (1998, p. 14) asserts that as "discourses tend to define how the social world is ordered and organized, then it is inevitable that discourses will reach into the very hearts of individuals and come to influence and shape their sense of identity". A Foucauldian understanding thus maintains that discourses create certain ways of being that, when negotiated and taken up by individuals, have implications for their subjectivity and experience (Hook, 2001; Willig, 2008). Discourse analysis can be utilised to provide knowledge of how particular understandings of the self and the world are diffused in society. It also offers the possibility of questioning and challenging those understandings, as discourses function ideologically and present an oppressive version of the world, defining what is normal and what is deviant (Parker, 2005). The ways in which we make sense of our world enable us to become particular kinds of subject. A discursive framework then affords us the view of, in our case, debtors as practising how to be a certain kind of person or "do identity" by negotiating meanings that are embedded in the various discourses that they face, in this case through *Luksusfellen*.

We start our analysis by presenting the typical script of *Luksusfellen*, showing how the programme develops in each episode. We have chosen the most recent complete season (the eighth) for our analysis. Then we investigate how debt is constructed in *Luksusfellen* and analyse interactions between the debtors and experts. We do this by analysing the discourses that the experts and the debtors draw upon and by discussing what subject positions are enabled by those discourses. Our argument is that these shows provide an example of a technology of governmentality that supports the debt industry in Norway through the normalisation of debt and the disciplining of subjects (audiences and participants) into being financially literate, or at least knowing how to be financially literate and feeling guilty about not living up to this.

The script

The eighth season consists of 14 episodes. Each episode (about 45 minutes) begins with a presentation of the debtor by means of a montage, including scenes from their daily life, and interviews of the participant and a close friend or relative. The montage, including voiceovers by the participant and the narrator, serves to associate the participant with a financial problem and a particular consumption or spending style. A short presentation of the two experts – a financial advisor and a psychologist, follows. Thereafter the experts arrive at the home of the participant, and are greeted by the participant and the close friend or relative. Usually one of the experts stays in the home with the participant, while the other expert typically goes out (e.g. for a walk, to a café) with the accompanying person. The participant is then invited to describe their financial situation, including an estimate of the amount and composition of their debt. Other people, sometimes the accompanying person, are often portrayed as being negatively affected by the financial situation and its management. The participant and the accompanying person are then left alone, and sometimes their emotional reactions to the situation are shown. After having assessed the financial situation, the experts return, often with a message that the debt is even larger than the participant initially thought. The expert confronts the participant about practical consequences and moral concerns. The participant is then presented with an authorisation that temporarily transfers the management of their finances to the expert, which the participant then signs. Again, the participant appears to be left alone and often displays troubled emotions. Usually a commercial break takes place at this stage.[2]

After the break the experts present a magnetic blackboard, categorising the monthly expenses of the participant by use of NOK 1,000 and NOK 500 notes which are fixed to the board under headings such as "food" and "transportation". This exercise is conducted in the home of the participant. Typically, participants show surprise at the level and composition of their consumption. Other illustrations with "pedagogic" aims are then shown – for example, the experts slicing and eating a cake with no pieces being left for the participant. The experts then present possible methods to improve the financial situation and alleviate the debt, such as quitting smoking or selling a car. The solutions sometimes require a considerable life change on behalf of the participant, such as taking on an extra part-time job. In some episodes the participant is asked to make telephone calls to, or participate in meetings with, creditors to negotiate, say, down-payment plans or postponements. In other episodes, experts engage in off-screen negotiations on behalf of the participant. In the third section of the programme, the participant is portrayed as moving into in a new phase of better managing their debt. A revised blackboard budget is presented, the participant allocating bank notes according to the instructions of the experts.

The final phase of the episode invariably involves the experts returning to visit the participant after about a month. During this follow-up the participant and experts co-narrate a story of progress and typically display smiling faces. The experts return the signed authorisation to the participant. They then present the participant with a corporate-sponsored gift of around NOK 20,000 – for example, grocery coupons or a month's supply of fuel for driving to work.

Overall, a typical episode of *Luksusfellen* involves a debtor and usually a significant other, two experts (often an economist and a psychologist), the debt problem, the creditors and a solution.

Constructing debt

In *Luksusfellen*, debt is hardly ever posited as a shared problem requiring a structural or collective solution. It is rather framed as a result of the individual's irresponsibility, as a result of a lack of thinking or reflection on the part of the individual debtor, or as a lack of financial literacy. Any contextual explanation is left out. Any construction of debt provided in the programme posits it as the individual's own problem, to be resolved by the individual themselves. Such construction of debt functions in a reductionist way and conceals the structural elements or mechanisms of the current economic system, thus masking many important dimensions of the debt industry that we intend to draw out here.

Occasionally the debtor, and the viewers of the show, are reminded by the experts that the consumer debts that most debtors struggle to pay back have a "horrendous interest rate" (e.g. 15%). While this fact is openly shared with us, the show or the experts never question why actors/creditors in the financial sector should demand such interest rates. On the contrary, this high interest rate is taken for granted and the individual debtor is instead encouraged by the experts to shape up and "take control" over their debt situation.

Additionally, the creditors in *Luksusfellen* are portrayed not only as innocent but also as good actors within the financial sector. The audience is reminded that the debtor is, also figuratively speaking, in debt to the creditors who could by their legal right seek legal action, although mostly they don't. As the psychologist in Episode 7 informs us, the debtors are "dependent on creditors' patience and kindness". In this way, the TV show can be said to function to normalise the debt industry and its practices while debt is constructed as solely an individual's problem.

From failed subjecthood to entrepreneurial subject

In each episode we are introduced to a debtor who is constructed as a failed individual. This person is morally condemned by the experts for not living up to the standards that are expected of normal citizens in contemporary society. The failed subject, in different episodes of the show, is described as an individual who "spends too much", has an issue with "impulse control", is "struggling", is "partying too much", is "in need of personal transformation" or needs to engage in "self-development".

In Episode 14, for instance, we are introduced to debtor M. We are told that M had been partying and spending a lot of money. He has six different credit cards to afford his lifestyle and now has a debt of about EUR 50,000 which he has been struggling to pay back. His friend portrays him as "a good guy", yet "as failing with [the management of] money". The narrator contributes: "He has to tidy up his life now if he is ever going to have a normal future". Thus, right from the beginning of the show, as in each episode, the debtor is constructed as a failed individual and as lacking financial literacy to manage his life.

The narrator and the experts in the TV show implicitly construct an ideal/competent subject of contemporary society. This subject is posited as someone who is rational, responsible for their own life choices and autonomous, implying a certain isolation from (significant) others or society in managing life – and crucially being able to manage their debt. The debtors in *Luksusfellen* are constructed as failing when compared with this standard. Accordingly, the programme operates to position the debtors as sinners who need to be saved from themselves, and the experts are depicted as those who will help them to "see the light", as Atwood (2008) suggests. The construction of the debtor as a sinner justifies the intervention by the experts in order to transform the subject into an entrepreneur who, according to Foucault (2008), then understands themselves in terms of human capital and thus develops into a competent citizen/subject/debtor.

Discourses of rationality, responsibility and entrepreneurship

The most frequent discourses we encounter throughout *Luksusfellen* are those of rationality and individual responsibility employed by the experts. The debtors are constructed as sinners because apparently they do not act rationally and they take responsibility for their choices. Accordingly they are disciplined by the experts:

> *Expert, economist:* "You say you don't have an overview...to get 6 credit cards in the space of a year, that's insane..."
> *Debtor:* "I don't know what I was thinking."
> *Expert, economist:* "No, I don't think you have thought at all."
> ...
> *Expert, psychologist:* "You are fooling yourself."
> ...
> *Expert, psychologist:* "We cannot make your debt disappear."
> *Debtor:* "No, I don't expect that either."
> *Expert, psychologist:* "Yes, it is you who after all has to fix this. But we will of course help you get there."
> *Debtor:* "Thank you."

In this dialogue between the experts and the debtor in Episode 14, we witness the disciplining dimension. First the debtor is portrayed as failing to "think at all", drawing on a discourse of rationality. No one with the slightest capacity to think (rationally) would behave the way he did to get himself into this mess, as the expert puts it. Furthermore, he is given full responsibility to solve the problem. We witness that he is indeed disciplined as he accepts his fault and takes full responsibility. Later in the show the debtor admits that he "needs to reflect" upon and fix things; after all, he "is in control". Such a discourse of individual responsibility places the burden on the shoulders of the individual debtor while limiting any possibility of considering the complex ways in which debt can become a problem in peoples' lives. This results in an ignorance of social and structural mechanisms of society that make being in debt (the behaviour) possible for individuals.

In each episode of *Luksusfellen*, the proposed solution to the debt problem is that the debtors become entrepreneurs of themselves. The debtors are constructed as having the potential to change and to become better versions of themselves. Experts here function to influence the debtors to "internalise" the problem and thereby seek solutions within. Each debtor in each episode is taught several techniques to become the better version of themselves in order to increase their financial literacy and manage their debt. The disciplined individual thus feels the need to refashion and develop themselves. The debtors seem to accept the construction of themselves by the experts as "self-made", and they are willing to increase their value and capacity by drawing upon a discourse of lifelong learning, which is argued to preserve neoliberal governance (Olssen, 2006). No debtor, regardless of age, gender or ethnicity, in any episode shows resistance to this construction. They all, either implicitly or explicitly, accept that they need to change, while debt as a social or a structural phenomenon remains unquestioned.

For instance, talking about the options for debtor M in Episode 14, as mentioned above, to get out of the dire situation that he is in, the experts make the point that he needs to make better use of his abilities:

> *Expert, psychologist:* "I think all people feel good about themselves if they can make use of all of themselves [their full capacity]."
> *Expert, economist:* "It is going to be tough... he needs to do everything in his power to increase his income."

The first quotation implies that the debtor has apparently not done enough to make use of his full potential and, as such, can be blamed for his debt problem. Employing a discourse on the inner life of the individual, the psychologist represents the psy-complex, implying that the subject who develops himself to become a competent debtor would also feel good about himself. The only conceivable solution to the debt problem then lies within the individual debtor. The economist supplements the psychologist's advice: the solution is "doing everything in his [debtor's] power" to increase income – for instance, getting an extra job – as was the case in the episode analysed above.

In a repetitive manner, each episode shows us a debtor, characterised as a sinner, who is constructed as the person who is solely responsible for their debt problem, while the systemic and structural mechanisms that make such behaviour (indebtedness) possible for individuals are taken for granted and kept out of discussion. The debtor in Episode 7 is a good example. The narrator informs us:

"[He] has [NOK] 1.5 million in debt because he has for a long time been struggling with impulse control. The experts through several exercises have tried to help him change his behavior..."

Here, again, the debt problem is attributed to the internal or psychological characteristics of the debtor. This construction is arguably enabled by a discourse of individualism which also permeates psy-expertise. Understanding such a complex problem as debt only in terms of individuals' inner characteristics is reductionist and may often lead to the fundamental attribution error in which the contextual factors that influence subjects' behaviour are ignored, a common bias in Western societies that is well established by social psychological research (e.g. Markus and Kitayama, 1991). Indeed, recent mainstream psychological research tends to construe overindebtedness mainly in terms of individual's irresponsibility, financial incompetence and/or inability to delay gratification (Walker, 2012). Such individualising/psychologising constructions of the problem also limit the solutions to the potential changes that the debtor can make of their own accord:

Debtor: "I must try this. It is going to be tough but I have to try."
...
Debtor: "There is plenty of stuff I have to sort out on my own... I have got to do this. I have started doing it."
Expert, psychologist: "So, you take responsibility?"
Debtor: "Yes, I do."
...
Expert, psychologist: "What you need from now on is better structure, predictability and routines."

Later on, while talking to the camera, the psychologist informs us: "It is totally decisive that [he] gets the right habits and changes his behavior." What is proposed as a solution to the debt problem here is "work on the self by the self" (Rose, 1999). This discourse of individualism not only enables a subject position of a guilty debtor but also limits the responsibility for the solution of the problem as residing within the boundaries of the individual. Thus a self-developing entrepreneurial subject is enabled by this discourse, which functions in ways that are consistent with neoliberal governmentality. It seems that the debtor understands themselves and what they can and should do through the particular position of this subjecthood of guilt and repentance.

Expert roles, lack of resistance and disciplined subjectivities

The narrator of the programme informs the audience in each episode that the experts "are eager to increase people's knowledge about the economy" and "have for a long time been helping individuals in dire situations ... They wish to provide people with simple tools so that they can better manage their economy in everyday life." The experts are portrayed as knowledgeable individuals who play their role as "priests or revivalists" (Atwood, 2008) and only want to help debtors to increase their financial literacy.

However, in their help to the debtors as exemplified in both of our examples above, the experts contribute to individualisation of the debt problem which is principally a social and structural, as well as a political, problem. The psy-knowledge deployed by the experts thus functions to conceal the workings of the debt economy. Individualisation of the debt problem and responsibilisation of the individual debtors thus normalise the debt economy in a particular way.

Discourse analysis opens up an understanding of individuals as active agents who engage in and negotiate with, but who can also potentially resist, the dominant discourses and subject positions that they enable (Willig, 2008). Our analysis, however, reveals that in *Luksusfellen* there is limited resistance by the debtors to the dominant discourse of individual responsibility which the experts consistently draw upon in their disciplining of these "failed subjects". The debtors in each episode are portrayed as completely "obeying" the experts and they appear to internalise the subjectivity that is offered to them. They are constructed as accepting the position of the failed and struggling subject who, with the help of the experts, can improve themselves to become a competent, financially literate, morally responsible individual. The words of one of the debtors are illustrative of the success of *Luksusfellen* in disciplining, and of the degree of subjectification which is achieved by the show:

> What I appreciate most is that they [experts] "kicked me in the ass" and lifted me up to finally tidy up [my economy] and sort of provided me with a good instrument to get in control of things. I am sure I will manage myself... I am positive about the future...
>
> (debtor in Episode 14)

Given the dominant underlying assumption of individualism that permeates all of the subject positions offered to the debtors, *Luksusfellen* is suggested to contribute to: (1) individualisation of the social and (2) responsibilisation of the individual, both of which are mechanisms of neoliberalism (Rose, 1999). As an example of neoliberal influence, the programme achieves and promotes "multiple responsibilization of individuals" for their own actions and risk, which implies that responsibilities for risk minimisation (getting rid of the debt in the case of our debtors) become a feature of the choices that are made by individual debtors as consumers (Dean, 1999). Such interpretation resonates with Beck's (1992) discussion of the individualisation of risk in contemporary societies, revealing especially the expert discourses which demand that individuals control the risky futures that they are headed towards as morally failing indebted individuals.

Similarly, Lazzarato (2012, p. 46) considers the debt relationship as a way in which capitalism reaches into the future in order to address the risk of not knowing what the future will hold: "The effects of the power of debt on subjectivity (guilt and responsibility) allow capitalism to bridge the gap between present and future." In this way the social dimensions of debt and the subjectivity of debtors are fundamentally connected to the way in which the economic system functions – there are structural elements in how individuals behave with regard to the debtor–creditor relationship.

Concluding remarks

Our point in this chapter is not to advocate one form of financial understanding over another but to indicate how the various demands on individuals (debtors) that are made by neoliberal discourses and the psy-complex neglect the social and structural factors that constrain and influence individuals' choices, and thus potentially stigmatise those who fail to measure up to the moral imperative of the dominant discourses. Indeed, in each episode of *Luksusfellen* we are introduced to a failed subject who is condemned morally, or punished, for the life choices that they have made. This again reflects the moral dimensions of guilt and sin as discussed by Graeber (2011) and Atwood (2008). The subject, with the help of experts, is disciplined through several exercises to become a morally acceptable individual – namely, an obedient and responsible subject who develops themselves to be able to pay their debt. In addition, the audience is simultaneously disciplined through engaging with the narrative of sin and redemption. The audience is shown how one should be indebted, what is the correct way to take on debt and what is not.

The episodes powerfully convey the normative message of transitioning from inadequacy to success by means of moral judgement by experts, emotional displays, scenes of punishment, confession, insight and change. If the rational autonomous individual takes responsibility to refashion themselves, learn new ways of being, engage in self-improvement and fulfil expectations of financial literacy, there will be no hindrance on their way to success. The individual is constituted as "the master of her life" (Bauman, 2001) who is thus obliged to "work on the self" to accomplish life (Rose, 1999).

Underlying the two major subject positions – the failed and the self-improving – among participants is the fundamental assumption of individualism: none of the positions offered allows for collectivity or group identity. The entire narrative is focused on the individual's personal (ir)responsibility, (un)awareness and (un)willingness to change. These are powerful ways in which to frame the future selves of debtors, and also viewers of the TV show by extension, setting up a constraining binary (positive self/negative self) and impressing on the debtors, and the viewers, their personal responsibility to manage life on their own or be consigned to endless struggle and disadvantage.

Overall, as exemplified by the discourses employed in *Luksusfellen*, neoliberalism, by strengthening individualism, provides social control, and legitimates and reproduces the existing social structural mechanisms with all of their inequalities, In shows like these, the social and structural components of the debt industry remain taken for granted and hidden, but through detailed analysis we can draw attention to them.

Notes

1. Ross (2013) also develops this line of argument to suggest that, in fact, in the USA at least but increasingly in Western Europe, we are living in "creditocracies" where credit, and therefore debt, has become omnipresent.

2. Although, as Williams (1974) suggested, advertisements form part of the media text by becoming part of the flow of images and information, we have chosen to concentrate on the actual show due to space. We recognise this possible extension.

References

Atwood, M. (2008). *Payback: Debt and the Shadow Side of Wealth*. London: Bloomsbury.
Bauman, Z. (2001). *The Individualized Society*. Cambridge: Polity Press.
Beck, U. (1992). *Risk Society: Towards a New Modernity*. London: Sage.
Billig, M. (1999). Commodity fetishism and repression: Reflections on Marx, Freud and the psychology of consumer capitalism. *Theory & Psychology*, 9(3), 313–329.
Blyth, M. (2013). *Austerity: The History of a Dangerous Idea*. New York: Oxford University Press.
Bourdieu, P. (1998). *Acts of Resistance: Against the New Myths of Our Time*. Oxford: Blackwell.
Brusdal, R. and Lavik, R. (2008). Just shopping?: A closer look at youth and shopping in Norway. *Young: Nordic Journal of Youth Research*, 16, 393–408.
Connolly, P. (1998). *Racism, Gendered Identities and Young Children*. London. Routledge.
Dean, M. (1999). *Governmentality: Power and Rule in Modern Society*. London: Sage.
Ferge, Z. (1997). The changed welfare paradigm: The individualization of the social. *Social Policy & Administration, 31*(1), 20–44.
Foucault, M. (2008). *The Birth of Biopolitics. Lectures at the Collège de France 1978–1979*. New York: Palgrave Macmillan.
Fromm, E. (1978). *To Have or to Be?* Harmondsworth: Penguin Press.
Graeber, D. (2011). *Debt: The First 5000 Years*. New York: Melville House.
Harvey, D. (2005). *A Brief History of Neoliberalism*. Oxford: Oxford University Press.
Hook, D. (2001). Discourse, knowledge, materiality, history. Foucault and discourse analysis. *Theory & Psychology*, 11(4), 521–547.
Lånekassen (2013). Historisk oversikt [Historical overview]. Retrieved on August 10. http://lanekassen.no/nb-NO/Toppmeny/Om_Lanekassen/Statistikk/Stipend-og-lan-samlet-statistikk/Stipend-og-lan-siden-1947/Historisk-oversikt/.
Lavik, R. and Tufte, P.A. (2011). Husholdningenes økonomiske situasjon 2011. Betalingsproblemer i etterkant av finanskrisen. Prosjektnotat nr. 12–2011 [Households' economic situation 2011. Payment problems in the aftermath of the financial crises. Project notes 12–2011]. Oslo: Statens institutt for forbruksforskning.
Lazzarato, M. (2012). *The Making of the Indebted Man*. Los Angeles: Semiotext(e). http://lanekassen.no/nb-NO/Toppmeny/Om_Lanekassen/Statistikk/Stipend-og-lan-samlet-statistikk/Stipend-og-lan-siden-1947/Historisk-oversikt/
Markus, H. R. and Kitayama, S. (1991). Culture and the self: Implications for cognition, emotion, and motivation. *Psychological Review*, 98(2), 224–253.
Miles, S. (1998). *Consumerism as a Way of Life*. London: Sage.

Nafstad, H. E., Blakar, R. M., Carlquist, E., Phelps, J. M. and Rand-Hendriksen, K. (2007). Ideology and power: The influence of current neo-liberalism in society. *Journal of Community & Applied Social Psychology*, 17, 131–327.
Olssen, M. (2006). Understanding the mechanisms of neoliberal control: Lifelong learning, flexibility and knowledge capitalism. *International Journal of Lifelong Education*, 25(3), 213–230.
Parker, I. (2005). *Qualitative Psychology. Introducing Radical Research*. Glasgow, GB: Open University Press.
Rose, N. (1999). *Governing the Soul. The Shaping of the Private Self*, 2nd edition. London: Free Association Books.
Ross, A. (2013). *Creditocracy and the Case for Debt Refusal*. London: OR Books.
Statistics Norway (2013). Husholda sine inntekter og formue [Households' income and assets]. Retrieved on August 10. http://www.ssb.no/inntekt-og-forbruk/statistikker/ifformue.
Türken, S., Nafstad, H. E. and Blakar, R. M. (submitted). Youth's future orientation and well-being: Materialism and concerns with education and career among Turkish and Norwegian youth. Young: Nordic Journal of Youth Research.
Walker, C. (2012). Personal debt, cognitive delinquency and techniques of governmentality: Neoliberal constructions of financial inadequacy in the UK. *Journal of Community and Applied Social Psychology*, 22, 533–538.
Williams, R. (1974). *Television: Technology and Cultural Form*. London: Fontana.
Willig, C. (2008). *Introducing Qualitative Research in Psychology*. Glasgow, UK: Open University Press.

9

"Financial Capability" Considered from a Community Psychology-Informed Process in the North East of England

Jacqui Lovell and Jacqui Akhurst

Introduction

This chapter introduces the concept of "financial capability" as the basis of proposed interventions by the financial sector. After contextualising the development of the concept in the current climate of financial austerity in the UK, a measurement tool that was developed for a community-based project will be considered. This will describe the community psychology process that was used to co-modify a financial capability questionnaire using dialogical approaches, with diverse people who have experienced social and economic exclusion and mental distress in the North East of England. The results of the process lead to a considered critique of the ideas that are embedded in the construct. Fundamental questions are asked about the value of the concept, in the context of experiences of the effects of extreme poverty. What becomes clear is that governmental and financial services' attention needs rather to be focused on people's fair access to appropriate educational and other services, and the dramatic inhibition of widespread practices of extortionate lending, which is currently underwritten by legitimate financial providers.

Financial rhetoric at the global level

In a recent publication by the World Bank it is noted that there are a number of driving forces that are shaping the practices on which the rhetoric of financial and credit services are based (Ledgerwood,

2013). Housed at the World Bank, the Consultative Group to Assist the Poor (CGAP) has a global network of members, which includes over 30 development agencies, private foundations (many of them banks) and national governments "that share a common vision of improving the lives of *poor* people with better access to finance" (CGAP, 2012; added emphasis).

Describing itself as an "independent" organisation, CGAP is located within the World Bank and works towards a world in which everyone has access to the financial services, which we are assured are needed, to improve the lives of people living in poverty. These corporate-run and managed organisations open up markets for "products" on a global basis through the language of "development", with the intended remit of "educating and empowering" people from economically deprived communities to develop financial literacy and/or capabilities that are purported to sustain and improve their economic outcomes. Within CGAP's annual report (2012), successful projects are highlighted. These focus on improvements in income and "nutritional intake", alongside such facts as families working 28% more hours on non-programme activities and the transfer of assets taking place over time between these newly acquired "consumers" and financial service "providers". The focus is on the "development" of financial literacy and capability in an otherwise, or so we are told, financially excluded population, described as people who live in poverty.

It is pertinent to recognise that "while the market for more affluent and business clients becomes saturated, providing the world's poorest with access to financial products is an unmatched growth opportunity" (Fioreti, 2013). Indeed, large conglomerates have joined forces to ensure that the people who are living in the countries of this "unmatched growth opportunity" are sufficiently "educated" and "developed" to avail themselves of these "services". The rhetoric for this is located within development programmes that aim to achieve progress in relation to the financial literacy and capability of people who are categorised as currently living in poverty. The majority of these people reside within the southern hemisphere and those countries experiencing marked economic growth, notably Brazil and China, among others in Asia, Africa, Latin America and Eastern Europe (Chaia et al., 2009). The Financial Access Initiative described in the paper "Half the world is unbanked" notes that "if policymakers are to realise their ambitions to spur the creation of *new markets* and expand access to the under-served, then the analysis of data related to initiatives at a global level are *needed*" (Chaia et al., 2009, p. 10). This serves to highlight just whose "access" the initiative is in favour of – not "access" in social inclusion terms of people to "services", but in economic terms of potential "new markets" for policy-makers. Initiatives now abound globally to meet this identified "need", including the Corporation for Enterprise Development (CFED), a national not-for-profit organisation that is supported by a range of corporate banks and funders in the USA. Of nearly 100 applicants to CFED's Behavioural Economic Technical Assistance Project funding round in 2014 almost half (44) focused on financial education and counselling. In the UK such initiatives were, until recently (2013), supported by the Financial Services Authority (FSA) – for example, commissioning a survey of financial capability upon which to base its Financial Capability in the UK: Delivering Change programme (FSA, 2006a, 2006b).

So what are financial literacy and capability, and what is the difference between these concepts? According to the OECD, financial literacy is defined as

> knowledge and understanding of financial concepts and risks, and the skills, motivation and confidence to apply such knowledge and understanding in order to make effective decisions across a range of financial contexts, to improve the financial well-being of individuals and society, and to enable participation in economic life.
>
> (Atkinson and Messy, 2012)

Financial literacy is thus conceived in a decontextualised way, defined as knowledge and skills, which presumably could be taught, in the same way that actual literacy is taught. The implication is that without financial literacy, people will not be enabled to "participate" in economic life and will fail to make "effective decisions". One wonders by whose standards these decisions are judged to be "effective" and for whom or what the "well-being" is aimed – that of the individual or the society? It is also notable that "financial contexts" are important enough to warrant inclusion in this definition but others such as the "social context" are not.

In contrast, financial capability asserts that people will develop context-specific knowledge and skills as a basis for making decisions and taking action with confidence and competence (Rabbior, 2005). In the UK it is defined as

> a broad concept, encompassing people's knowledge and skills to understand their own financial circumstances, along with the motivation to take action. Financially capable consumers plan ahead,

find and use information, know when to seek advice and can understand and act on this advice, leading to greater participation in the financial services market.

(HM Treasury, 2007)

The concept is also said to incorporate the impact that decisions have on individuals' and families' sense of security, standards of living and social contexts, supposedly moving beyond knowledge acquisition to the consequences of behaviours. The wider ramifications for communities are also noted, and are purported to contribute to the type of "social inclusion" that is associated with economic stability, moving beyond knowledge to include the types of so-called responsible and informed behaviours that are favoured by neoliberal governments.

Financial capability and rhetoric at the UK level

Following a consultative process and a commissioned medium-scale survey conducted in the Bristol area in the UK, the FSA (2006b) identified five key areas of financial capability:

- being able to manage money;
- keeping track of finances;
- planning ahead;
- choosing financial products;
- staying informed about financial matters.

However, while it proposes that these key areas each need attention, scrutiny of the data in the baseline survey (2006b) hides some interesting features, where "financial capability" does not appear to correlate with income level:

- people who struggle to "make ends meet" include many who are earning an average or even an above-average income;
- groups such as single parents, those living in social housing, the unemployed and people without current bank accounts all perform better than average when "keeping track" of their finances, and women outperform men;
- people at all income levels are not careful at "planning ahead", yet there were many examples of people with very low incomes who do plan ahead.

These findings therefore imply that financial capability does not correlate with economic or social circumstances, or possibly other forms of literacy. This raises questions about the term "capability", and readers are left with many questions about what influences its development. For example, if there is evidence of people on limited incomes or in difficult situations being able to keep careful track of their finances, whereas people who seem otherwise to be making economic progress struggle with debt, is the concept individually related (with associated educational implications)? We suggest that it may be a smokescreen to cover up systemic problems by locating the problem as one of individual responsibility.

In 2006 the FSA developed a seven-point programme that was aimed at improving the financial capability of people in the UK. Following the Thoresen Review of Generic Financial Advice, the FSA implemented its Pathfinder programme, which offered "free, impartial information and guidance on money matters". The stated intention was that over time this would "not only benefit them [people] directly, but also enable them to exert a stronger influence in the retail markets, creating more effective and efficient markets and reducing the need for regulatory intervention" (de Meza et al., 2008, Foreword).

No mention was made of what the "regulatory intervention" refers to and why this should be reduced. However, given that this was developed just prior to the financial crisis and the scandal of mis-sold "services" and "products" by the majority of financial providers in the UK, it is concerning that financial capability was being linked to practices that exploited consumers. More worrying is the suggestion that "Many behavioural economists take the view that the best response is not informing consumers of the problem or trying to change them but institutional design and regulation that recognises the psychology" (de Meza, et al., 2008, p. 3). From our perspective as community psychologists it is difficult to imagine how "not" informing people of a problem is helpful to them in being able to solve it. In addition, there is clear arrogance involved in assuming that people are unaware of the financial problems that are facing them and that in such situations they would then look to financial advisors within large corporations to increase their awareness of the problems.

Indeed, in their paper de Meza et al. (2008) highlight a number of points, including the belief that financial advice does not increase income, that financial education does not change behaviours or significantly increase financial capabilities in the people who receive it, and that "intrinsic psychological attitudes" are implicated in relation to someone's behaviour. The latter could be interpreted as having pejorative biopsychological implications, and the former are simply common sense and have face validity considering the reality of the everyday experiences of people who live in poverty. It is very difficult to change one's behaviour and, for example, commence with saving when one has no disposable income to save.

Financial capability as a concept is therefore not focused on the essential need to alleviate poverty or to improve people's life circumstances. The sentiments of the FSA's documents appear to be characteristic of the individualising and blaming rhetoric which has proliferated in recent years in relation to people living in poverty. As Dorey (2010) notes,

> Non-state actors might be able to provide services and support to the poor and socially marginalised, but it is not yet clear how this, in itself, will reduce the gulf between the rich and poor, particularly as David Cameron's Conservatives are highly unlikely to make a serious effort at curbing pay at the top, regardless of their occasional denunciation of bankers' bonuses (p. 191).

In addition to this, all of the evidence reviewed by de Meza et al. (2008) was from the USA because the "evidence base", we are told, does not exist in the UK. While this may be true, in some fields of enquiry there is a growing body of evidence (as shown by Walker et al., 2012a, 2012b, 2012c). However, the authors state that "there is no particular reason to think the effect on UK consumers would be different..." (de Meza et al., 2008, p. 11). This contradicts the asserted relevance of context and contravenes research practice in that research from one population should not be extrapolated, overinterpreted and then applied to another population, with generalisations drawn between them in support of the arguments that are being proffered by the researcher. MacCoun (1998) notes that this is not an altogether uncommon practice when stating that "biased assimilation is an established phenomenon with troubling implications for efforts to ground contemporary policy debates in empirical analysis" (p. 267). The ecological validity of the two populations and any bias in the sampling based upon the voluntary involvement of the participants are also ignored by such practices. Although the UK does have some similarities to the USA, it is not clear whether these translate across psychological and economic "behaviours" and other important political, cultural and community practices.

Many of the above points are also made in a later substantive review by Kamleitner et al. (2012). They note the importance of social and cultural factors in the use of credit, and the dearth of studies that elucidate these in detail. They note the importance of "assessing the meanings and connotations associated with credit" (p. 21). Their findings support the assertion that financial capability is not associated with levels of income, citing some studies that "report no difference in disposable income between credit users and non-users" (p. 4), as well as a Canadian study that showed that credit use increased with income level, whereas savings decreased. They also note that "individuals with higher incomes find it less important to teach thrift to their children". Such research provides further evidence that counters the contentions of the FSA that a focus on developing financial capability might alleviate problems with debt that are encountered by those on lower incomes.

Finally, de Meza et al (2008) in their conclusions acknowledge the "lack of direct evidence that the National Strategy for Financial Capability will substantially improve long-term financial decision making". Rather, they note that "the indirect evidence from behavioural economics is that low financial capability is more to do with psychology than with knowledge" (p. 4). This "psychology" is defined as "intrinsic psychological attributes", the meaning of which, as applied by the FSA, is "deep seated behavioural biases", which they describe as "widespread". The FSA has thus decided on an approach to direct people towards actions that it considers to be "norms", such as saving and the use of active interventions through counsellors and advice services, as opposed to passive information or education. So it appears that funding would be channelled towards financial advice services and "directed" saving, as opposed to the alleviation of poverty through economic policies and provision.

These decisions appear to be in direct opposition to the results of the British Household Panel Survey, which was also conducted by the FSA, in which the

> findings suggest that the large differences in financial capability between the more educated and the less educated is related to differences in income levels associated with education attained rather than the level of education itself. This has important implications, as it suggests that raising general education levels will not directly improve financial capability itself, and will only do so through an income effect.
>
> (Taylor, 2009, p. 51)

So it would appear that education is the answer, though not quite in the way in which the FSA would have us believe. More effective education needs to be aimed at achieving a higher income per se, rather than education towards financial capability, which looks to increase savings and the purchase of financial "products". More recently, with the demise of the FSA and more attention rather being directed towards some regulation of certain aspects of financial practices in the banking sector, the discourses around financial capability appear to have moved to the background (at a time when surely these would appear to have had more relevance).

Economic austerity and its effects in the UK

It is within this culture of "behavioural" economic and financial rhetoric, which is aimed at those people who are living in increasingly higher levels of deprivation, that the current UK government aims to significantly reduce public expenditure by GBP 63.4 billion by 2015, which when protected services such as the NHS, pensions and growth are taken into account equates to cuts of GBP 75.2 billion (Duffy, 2013). The Centre for Welfare Reform on behalf of the Campaign for a Fair Society outlined the changes in real terms in relation to spending on a range of services across the UK. Some 50% of cuts impact on two main areas – that is, benefits and local government – both of which make up only 26.8% of central government expenditure yet compose fully 60% of local government's spending, paying for social care for both adults and children (Duffy, 2013).

The UK austerity cuts are thus targeting those people and their families who already live in poverty. No effort has been made to understand the cumulative effects of cuts on minority groups, especially those with the greatest level of need, with women across all groups, but especially from black and ethnic-minority groups, being most adversely affected. This is due to the high levels of care for which women are responsible in relation to older people, young people, children and families, and the low level of wages that they receive, in what is all too often part-time unskilled employment or no paid employment (Liberty, 2011). Calls for a cumulative impact assessment of the cuts on people in relation to social care, benefits, housing and tax increases have been ignored (Duffy, 2013).

In addition, cuts are being felt to other services, such as legal aid, which are impacting upon people's access to support and social justice. This results in people on reduced incomes being financially unable to enact their employment, asylum/immigration, human, political and economic rights: "As such the removal of areas such as immigration, family, employment, welfare and debt law will effectively reduce access to public law remedies for those unable to pay" (Liberty, 2011, p. 8). None of the aforementioned impacts appear to have been noted by the government. To add insult to injury, it seems that people who live in poverty are now to be "advised" about how to take action at the level of the individual in order to counter and prevail against the "austerity measures" to which they have been subjected and over which they have, to date, had no control. This brings us to the picture from the perspective of people who live in poverty.

Poverty at a personal level

People who live in poverty are bearing a financial burden which is estimated to be five times as great – for disabled people this amounts to nine times as great, and for disabled people with multiple and profound impairments (2% of the population) it is thought to be 19 times as great – as that borne by the general population (Duffy, 2013). The Special Interest Group of Municipal Authorities (SIGOMA) outside London calculated the impact on localities of the cuts to public spending. The North East of England has the highest cuts in spending per person, amounting to a GBP 146 reduction in 2012, and this is predicted to be GBP 305 per person excluding welfare cuts (GBP 665 with welfare cuts) by 2017–2018 (SIGOMA, 2013). Meanwhile the problem of personal debt is growing (European Parliament Directorate General for Internal Policies, 2010), with borrowing across Europe standing at EUR 9.08 trillion in 2011 and those with financial acumen recognising that many people are unable to manage without it (Benn, 2012).

There is a growing body of research that highlights the continuation of personal debt for the foreseeable future (Harvey, 2010; Gregg and Machin, 2012; Kelly and Pearce, 2012, Walker et al., 2012a, 2012b). Average household debt in the UK in 2014 was GBP 54,197, with the average debt per adult being GBP 6,016, which is significantly higher than the figure of GBP 3,185 given in 2012. In 2012 and 2013, respectively, 8,500 and 7,015 new debt problems were being presented daily to one national service provider (Creditaction, 2012, 2014). Among people who are classed as "low wage earners" with incomes below GBP 9,500, two-thirds have problems with debt (Department of Trade and Industry, 2006).

Despite a work and pensions secretary articulating that "work is the best route out of poverty" (McCarron and Purcell, 2013, p. 6), the

Joseph Rowntree Foundation (Aldridge et al., 2012) found that 60% of households who were living in poverty were actually in employment. In addition, there were simply not enough jobs to go round with up to 45 unemployed people in one region of the UK per advertised position available, while six of the worst ten places to find employment were in the north (Adzuna, 2011).

This situation was compounded for women in particular as the European Women's Lobby asserts that "cutbacks in care and health services may lead to the reprivatisation of care and a return to traditional gender roles, as they transfer the responsibility for care from the society to households, i.e. women" (Elomaki, 2012, p. 12). According to Elomaki this could happen to women with caring responsibilities through a number of processes.

- People who provide care might be forced to leave or reduce their paid employment to take over the care roles that are no longer supported as a result of cuts to services and rising care costs.
- Services that enhance the equal division of care being reduced, such as paternity leave. Child and family benefit being reduced, so economic independence is compromised and poverty heightened.
- Lone mothers and female single pensioners losing the most when benefits and services are cut.
- Violence Against Women services being reduced and the financial crisis being used as the reason for not maintaining, increasing and improving what are often already inadequate services.

This is supported by the Local Government Association, which describes the roll-out of the replacement for diverse benefits through the proposals related to Universal Credit as creating greater incentives for one partner to work but weaker incentives for both partners to work (Wilson et al., 2013). Again, this would widen the gender divide because women, typically in lower-paid positions, would be economically forced into relinquishing paid employment in favour of their often, though not always, higher-paid male partners. Indeed, the

> majority of the impacts of reforms affecting housing costs for households out of work are unlikely to be met through claimants finding work or moving home. And at more plausible estimates, at least four out of every five households are likely to need further assistance – with cumulative financial impacts in excess of £1 billion per year (p. 41)

People from black and ethnic-minority groups, and minority groups within minority groups, are also greatly affected, such as people seeking asylum and those who have been granted refugee status (Crossley and Fletcher, 2013), plus people with long-term health needs (Wilson et al., 2013) and disabled people. It therefore becomes clear that the problem is not financial capability per se but the effects of the austerity measures on reducing the income and opportunities for generating income through employment for many thousands of people, leading to countless households being ever more dependent on credit because they are unable to cope. This then has a multiplicity of diverse impacts, including the dramatic rise in people who need to access food banks in 2013–2014 (Trussell Trust, 2014).

Income inequality and the impact on health and wellbeing

A recent report by the British Academy (2014) notes: "socioeconomic factors that have the largest impact on health – 40% of all influences" (p. 2). Pickett (2014) highlights the "paradox at the heart of understanding population health and health inequalities in rich, developed societies" (p. 23). Although comparisons between rich, developed societies' income and spending on healthcare are not associated with improvements in the health of the population, income discrepancies between the wealthy and the poor appear to be a predictor of health within societies. Pickett suggests that this indicates the "importance of relative social status for health" (p. 23).

Similarly, Nazroo (2014) states: "much, if not all, of ethnic inequalities in health are the product of economic inequalities". The evidence is now clear "that morbidity and mortality within all ethnic groups... is strongly patterned by socioeconomic position" (p. 96). Nazroo continues that additional aspects of social inequality, such as racism, discrimination and living in an area of high deprivation, also have an impact, subjecting those who experience multiple levels of discrimination and economic hardship to even greater levels of inequality.

Despite these findings, the social, political, historical and psychological aspects related to the inequality that is experienced by people at the bottom of the social hierarchy are seldom the focus of policy documents to improve financial conditions for the poorest and programmes of intervention. Rather, decisions are made by government during top-down processes, which are utilised to ensure their "development" (often through individually focused means such as the "financial capability" initiatives). It is clear that structural solutions would be better suited to the issues that are highlighted here.

The importance of context and a dialogical approach

In direct contrast with the government-driven approaches described above, Jovchelovitch (2007) has developed a social psychological approach to knowledge that attempts to overcome its dehumanisation. She does so by analysing the emotional and relational aspects of knowledge, which are essential to the formation of knowledge and the context within which it is located. Such an approach aims to "retrieve its connection between knowledge and the personal, interpersonal and socio-cultural worlds in which it is produced" (p. 2).

At the heart of this approach is the analysis of "representation", including the means by which someone or something is represented at the individual, interpersonal and sociocultural levels. Jovchelovitch (2007) aims to "retrieve the dialogical view of representation, reaffirm its symbolic and social character and connect its dynamic to different forms of knowing" (p. 3). Representation thus includes analysing who did this, how the representation came into being, how it was done, why it happened, what the purpose was and, importantly, what it achieved.

What follows is an account of a Community Psychology-based consultation process that is related to "financial capability" that aims to illustrate a process based on the ideas introduced above. The questionnaire used as the basis for this work was developed in 2008–2009 within an academic environment for a project where we wanted to use it as a before-and-after measure to evaluate a community-based educational intervention, which was planned and designed to improve financial capability. As such the items reflected the lived experience of mainly white, middle-class, relatively financially secure, employed people. Therefore critiquing it from the point of view of people from diverse groups and communities was thought to be a useful starting point in developing the tool's ecological validity and usefulness. As an organising framework the narrative below draws on Jovchelovitch's (2007) theory of knowledge in context, using the "who, how, why and what for" representations. In answering these questions, the answers reflect the social and cultural worlds in which representations are created and sustained.

Who did this?

The people who took part in the consideration of the questionnaire were from diverse communities who had experienced stigmatisation, social exclusion, poverty and the resulting mental distress that these foster.

The discussions occurred within a community organisation with a social inclusion focus, whose members were all people who had experienced multiple layers of discrimination in relation to their country of origin, race, culture, religion, age, disability, sexuality and/or gender and immigration status or lack of this.

Added to this are the economic circumstances of members, all of whom live in some degree of poverty, many of whom are attempting to survive on incomes that are well below the required level, in relation to their social situations as disabled people; single people; single, cohabiting and/or married parents; older and younger people; people seeking asylum; and those granted refuge. Ten people took part in the group discussions.

How was this done?

The process of representation and production of knowledge was achieved by sharing knowledge about our lived experiences at a personal, interpersonal, group and community level, and the suitability and workability of the questionnaire to fit with these realities.

The financial capability tool was used as starting point. It was divided into sections in line with the FSA (2006b) identification of the five aspects of financial capability needing to be present in order to assess all aspects of financial inclusion and capacity: being able to manage money, keeping track of finances, planning ahead, choosing financial products and staying informed about financial matters. Each section had six questions, and five potential answers were given for each. Each question and the given answers were discussed in turn both interpersonally and collectively. The discussion and dialogue focused on a range of issues, mostly in relation to the "fit" between the questions being asked and the person's individual and, at times, shared lived experience.

The consultation process was facilitated through an informal, dialogical, informative, facilitative and at times spontaneous and humorous process in which knowledge was both shared and received by the people participating.

Why was this done?

The purpose of the discussions was to modify the questionnaire in relation to its value as a tool for capturing knowledge from diverse people who were drawn from shared social contexts. The driving force behind this process, it has to be admitted, was not a bottom-up one but our desire to pilot and adapt the tool for use with people whose economic circumstances were such that they faced financial exclusion. The intention was to make changes and improvements to the tool to increase its ecological validity so that it could potentially map changes over time in relation to someone's financial capability. This was done with a view to piloting the tool with the members of the community organisation in which this process took place.

What did it achieve? What learning took place and what knowledge was gained?

Freire (1970) reminds us that there is no teaching without learning, and that this is a two-way process. The learning that took place was not a linear hierarchical process but a shared experience: with new knowledge being gained, previously acquired knowledge being shared and for some simultaneously contested, and it is to be hoped ultimately updated as a result.

What follows are a number of insights and observations that are drawn directly from this experience by one of us. They don't represent the experience of all who took part, so we don't claim to present here a definitive narrative of the process which took place but merely our account of it. The findings are first arranged by considering the five categories of the financial capability tool, and these reflections are then followed by more substantive discussion of the evolving process.

Section 1: Making ends meet

Questions in this section focused on juggling your finances, temptations to buy consumer goods, strategies when food shopping, mobile phone payments, being paid (for employment) and household appliances needing repair/replacing.

Group discussions centred on the need to use clear and culturally benign language, potential answers that did not reflect lived experience, the limitations of the options given, the lack of an open option (to allow for further learning, which could then be shared by respondents with those administering it), the lack of community networks in answers given (which could be drawn on in times of need), and the individualised nature of the options given, which without exception focused on the "I" and not the "we". As the people taking part in this process were predominantly from countries in the southern hemisphere, the recognition that communities often rally to support each other was a reality in their experience.

Some examples of responses to how people "make ends meet" are:

"I eat cheap food so I keep my food bill down using own brands and reduced items."
"I forget about it because I know I can't afford it."
"I have a monthly sim card but not a mobile phone contract."
"I use a mobile phone provider with free calls to the same network."
"I would go to a local drop-in and get some free food."
"I never ring 0845 numbers from my mobile but look landline numbers up on the Internet through sites like www.saynoto0870."
"I take my clothes to a friend's to wash."
"I put an advert in freecycle via the Internet."
"I ask my landlord to fix it as they provide the washing machine."
"I borrow the money from a friend and then pay them back with no interest."

Particularly interesting is the inclusion of items that were suggested, which evidence the realism, ingenuity and resourcefulness of the people taking part in the process.

Section 2: Keeping track

Questions in this section focused on knowing how much cash you have available, bank and credit card statements, frequency of checking account balances, risking an overdraft, spare money and money in reserve.

The majority of these questions were not applicable to people seeking asylum in the group since there has recently been a move on behalf of the government to exclude people in this group from having bank accounts. However, some of the people who took part have been in the UK for some time and therefore did. All, however, did not resonate with the concept of an overdraft, something that they are excluded from in relation to their lack of credit history.

The concept of "spare money" and "money in reserve" was also alien to the people taking part, although it did add to the humour of the experience for all concerned. All were aware of exactly how much cash they had in their purses/pockets and in their bank accounts if they had one, and they attributed this fact to not having sufficient funds.

Section 3: Planning ahead; Section 4: Choosing products; Section 5: Staying informed

These sections are discussed together as they were largely reported to be irrelevant to the people who took part: planning ahead would involve a degree of financial and political freedom, which for all simply was not the case.

Suggestions were made for word changes such as from "wage" to "benefits", to align them closer to the lived experience of the people taking part, but the major change was in the addition of an open-ended answer with space for qualitative input to the process for people completing the questionnaire. The "staying informed" section was also redundant for this group since it included financial "products" that were of little use to them. The discussions about future planning led to moves towards action, prompted by the group discussions, as noted below.

"Conscientization", dialogical pedagogy and a bottom up approach

As discussions in the group unfolded, the overall purpose of the tool and the broader concepts embedded in the proposed project became the target of discussions, including a certain amount of scepticism in relation to what if anything this tool would measure and why anyone or any organisation would want to use it anyway. The process became a "concientization" and co-modification process, which was informed by Freire's (1970) concept and praxis and Martin-Baro's (1996) focus on the transformative, bottom-up process of facilitating social change in order to frame the description and outcomes of the dialogical learning process undertaken and the production of knowledge that resulted from it.

The praxis of conscientization as proposed by Freire (1970) in his seminal work *Pedagogy of the Oppressed* is similar to the framework that was proposed by Jovchelovitch (2007), with the dialogical approach being central to both. Freire (1970) demonstrates the importance of dialogue to the learning process. Conscientization is practised, it is hoped, as a reciprocal experience. Inherent within conscientization is the process of changing people's relation with their surrounding environment in the transformative relationships that they have with other people. Within the conscientization process the political, the historic, the psychological and the economic are important elements of both the answers to the questions raised and the contextualisation of this dialogical process. These are utilised together with the personal and interpersonal lived experience of the person, but essentially what is needed is a willingness to begin at the bottom and to look up together from there (Martin-Baro, 1996).

Martin-Baro's (1996) refocusing of perspective in psychology, in which he advocates for the whole of psychology to be turned on its head and to begin with the experiences of diverse people from the bottom up, highlights the need for psychology to be directly influenced by the lived experiences of the most socially excluded people as a matter of priority: "we are proposing that the task of the psychologist must be to achieve the de-alienation of groups of persons by helping them attain a critical understanding of themselves and their reality" (p. 41). Added to this is the imperative that the concern of the social scientist should be not so much to measure the world as to change it.

Political awareness

All who took part in the discussions about the questionnaire appeared to increase their awareness of the political context in the UK and globally, within which the focus of attention had shifted to issues that are connected with the economy, financial crises, the upcoming and planned elections in the UK, and the behaviour of those in positions of power in relation to the financial solvency or otherwise of the UK, and globally.

Some people contributed situational experiences from their countries of origin in relation to financial corruption and the misappropriation of funds which were intended to support the needs of the people. Some highlighted the social situations of conflict, war and crisis that are promulgated by world powers, in order that the people's gaze was not directed towards the looting and pillaging of both the people and the land, in the pursuit of the acquisition of wealth through the supposedly "free" market economy. Reference was also made to the appropriation and selling of natural resources, such as those incorporated into mobile phones and computer equipment, and those used by large industries such as oil and gas for profit. Other issues were raised, including people sold into slavery as a result of poverty and debt, with education being seen as a means to combat and overcome poverty. Comparisons were drawn and similarities noted between the histories and practices both past and present, of similar practices in the UK and those of countries in both the northern and southern hemispheres.

Far from lacking political insight into the financial implications of what was happening around the world and in relation to their own contexts, the people undertaking this dialogue were well informed, articulate and had well-developed opinions, thoughts and feelings based upon their lived experiences. In addition, other discussions that they had with members of their peer group, and education and learning that they had conducted either independently or within both informal and formal settings, were cited as contexts within which awareness had been raised.

It is worth noting that for people seeking asylum the option to engage in informal and formal learning has now been removed by immigration legislation because, until very recently, this was allowed up to but not including university education (Coram Children's Legal Centre, 2013). This will impact on people's ability to integrate into the communities and cultures in which they find themselves in the UK and may exert further pressure in relation to the real need to navigate the various institutions and systems that exist in the country to support its citizens. Given the level of administration contained within institutional systems, for people who have little or no understanding of these institutions to be able to prevail without any form of education, apart from English for Speakers of Other Languages, this becomes exceptionally challenging. This has even greater importance in light of the government's agenda of integration (albeit couched within an anti-extremism agenda).

Although women's and men's experiences were thought to be more similar than they were different, it was noted by some that the position of parents, both male and female, with care responsibilities was very difficult financially. This was especially so for people seeking asylum with child dependents, given the small amounts upon which families are meant to live: approximately GBP 35 per week, per person for all food, clothing, health and travel needs.

The exclusion of people seeking asylum from employment is a historically recent imposition in the UK following the events of 9/11, preventing their take-up of paid employment (O'Neill, 2010). This has been thought to have had a negative impact both mentally and in terms of physical health. Parents discussed feelings of being under pressure because they could not provide for their families, and they often felt that their physical and mental health had deteriorated as a result of the stress of the asylum process. Other reasons included the change in diet due to restrictions on where money on cards, given in lieu of payments through the asylum system, could be spent and a lack of physical activity due to unemployment and no income for leisure activities, such as cycling, swimming and going to the gym.

It was also thought that single people were economically worse off owing to a number of factors. These included having less income, having to pay more for housing in relative terms than married/cohabiting couples, not being able to pool resources, and the lack of social support for young and mature males due to societal priorities and services geared towards women and children.

Women, however, were aware that the existing services to provide for the needs of women and children were chronically underfunded and resourced, and oversubscribed. Where services were open to all, the women expressed discomfort about attending those services to get supplies, such as food banks and drop-ins (for clothing, shoes, electrical and household goods), if there was a predominantly male presence as they did not always feel safe and often felt ashamed that they were having to attend these places at all.

The evolving process of discussion in the group

As the process unfolded, people became more vocal about the "industry" of financial literacy, advice, guidance and capability, and the organisations that deliver it. The majority of the people involved would look to independent organisations such as the Citizens Advice Bureau in the first instance and would be wary of accepting advice from organisations that are likely to make a profit on any "financial product" that was sold.

However, it should be added that some people who took part had used high street lenders and shops that convert consumer goods into cash out of necessity rather than preference. No one had knowledge of credit unions, a situation that we chose to address together. We are now communicating with our local credit union to help it to understand the particular needs of people who experience multiple layers of social exclusion. This is in order to strive for changes in the sometimes stringent rules applied by credit unions prior to agreeing to lend money and to extend the timeframes over which the money is paid back. Their current period of a year does not work well when budgets are as tight as they are for the people with whom we live and work. It seems that the situation will only get worse if those in positions of power fail to fully appreciate the impact of the policies that they enact at a governmental level on those people further down the social and economic hierarchy.

In conclusion

Following the in-depth deconstruction and critique of the tool, as described above, our decision was not to use it at all. Financial institutions appear to be asking people to make increasingly sophisticated decisions about managing their money, and it is reported that individual credit card debts, for example, run to billions in many developed countries. People have been, and are continually, encouraged, through marketing and advertising, to want more and more material goods, often beyond their current financial income. Many thus become indebted to both banks and other commercial institutions, and the interest charged upon these ongoing and often increasing debts leads to increased corporate profit margins. It is therefore in the interests of such organisations to keep people in debt, but much of the rhetoric is to locate difficulties with managing this as an individual's responsibility (e.g. FSA, 2006a) rather than seeing it as a product of very problematic broader national and international practices.

The community-based enquiries and discussions that are described above illustrate the disconnect between such concepts and the lives of people who have experienced multiple levels of exclusion. While the work around the concept of financial capability has been resourced to the tune of GBP 35 million – GBP 40 million per year since 2004, it appears that this could better have been invested in ways that are more meaningful to those who are most in need.

At the end of the project we were thus left feeling very uncomfortable about the entrenched middle-class attitudes that are embedded in concepts such as "financial capability" and educational schemes related to it. Such well-meaning "community" projects clearly target particular groups of people and may be perceived as patronising. It is necessary to use more participatory methodology from the outset. Furthermore, the project highlighted the dominant worldviews that are espoused in the broader field, with particular discourses related to socioeconomic class, without empathy for or understanding of the experiences of people who are on limited incomes. The experiences on this project highlight the failures of an individualised mode of trying to address personal debt, and the need for widespread systemic attention to be focused instead on curbing the excesses related to the whole debt industry and the vested interests embedded in governmental neglect of these.

References

Adzuna (2011). The best and worst cities to find a job in the UK. Retrieved on January 19, 2014 http://www.adzuna.co.uk/blog/2011/08/17/the-best-and-worst-cities-to-find-a-job-in-the-uk/.

Aldridge, H., Kenway, P., MacInnes, T. and Parekh, A. (2012). *Monitoring Poverty and Social Exclusion.* Joseph Rowntree Foundation. Retrieved on January 18, 2014 http://www.jrf.org.uk/publications/monitoring-poverty-2012.

Atkinson, A. and Messy, F. (2012). *Measuring Financial Literacy: Results of the Organisation for Economic Co-operation and Development (OECD)/International Network on Financial Education (INFE) Pilot Study*. OECD working papers on finance, insurance and private pensions No. 15, OECD Publishing.

Bartley, M. (2006). *Capability and Resilience: Beating the Odds*. London: UCL.

Benn, D. (2012). *European Consumer Debt Now a Structural Feature, International Investment*. Retrieved on January 21, 2014. http://www.ifaonline.co.uk/international-investment/news/2180440/european-consumer-debt-structural-feature.

British Academy (2014). *If You Could Do One Thing*. Executive summary. Retrieved on January 31, 2014. http://www.britac.ac.uk/policy/Health_Inequalities.cfm.

Chaia, A., Dalal, A., Goland, T., Gonzalez, M. J., Morduch, J. and Schiff, R. (2009). *Half the World Is Unbanked*. [Electronic version] Retrieved on January 31, 2014. http://www.microfinancegateway.org/gm/document-1.9.40671/25.pdf.

Consultative Group to Assist the Poor (CGAP) (2012). *Annual Report*. Retrieved on January 31, 2014. http://www.cgap.org/publications.

Coram Children's Legal Centre (2013). *Growing Up in a Hostile Environment: The Rights of Undocumented Migrant Children in the UK*. Retrieved on January 31, 2014. http://www.childrenslegalcentre.com/index.php?page=hostile_environment.

Creditaction (2012). *Debt Facts and Figures – Compiled October 2012*. Retrieved on February 2, 2014. http://creditaction.org.ukdebt-statistics/.

Creditaction (2014). *Debt Facts and Figures – Compiled January 2014*. Retrieved on January 26. http://themoneycharity.org.uk/debt-statistics/.

Crossley, S. and Fletcher, G. (2013). *Written Out of the Picture: The Role of Local Services in Tackling Poverty amongst Asylum Seekers and Refugees*. Retrieved on January 31, 2014. http://www.poverty.ac.uk/sites/default/files/attachments/NEP001%20Report%20Web%201.pdf.

Department of Trade and Industry (2006). *Tackling Over-Indebtedness – Annual Report*. Retrieved on September 23, 2009. http://www.berr.gov.uk/files/file33134.pdf.

de Meza, D., Irlenbusch, B. and Reyniers, D. (2008). *Financial Capability: A Behavioural Economics Perspective*. [Electronic version] London: Financial Services Authority. https://www.fca.org.uk/static/fca/documents/research/fsa-crpr69.pdf.

Dorey, P. (2010). A poverty of imagination: Blaming the poor for inequality. *The Political Quarterly*, 81(3), 333–343.

Dorey, P. (2011). *British Conservatism: The Politics and Philosophy of Inequality*. London I. B. Tauris.

Duffy, S. (2013). *A Fair Society? How the Cuts Target Disabled People*. Retrieved on January 16, 2014. http://www.centreforwelfarereform.org/library/by-az/a-fair-society1.html.

Elomaki, A. (2012). *The Price of Austerity – the Impact on Women's Rights and Gender Equality in Europe*. Brussels: European Women's Lobby.

European Parliament Directorate General for Internal Policies. (2010). *Household Indebtedness in the EU. European Parliament*. Retrieved on May 4 2011 http://www.europarl.europa.eu/document/activities/cont/201103/20110324ATT16330/20110324ATT16330EN.pdf

Financial Services Authority (2006a). *Financial Capability in the UK: Establishing a Baseline*. Retrieved on January 6, 2014. http://www.fsa.gov.uk/pubs/other/fincap_baseline.pdf.

Financial Services Authority (2006b). *Financial Capability in the UK: Delivering Change*. Retrieved on January 6, 2014. http://www.fsa.gov.uk/pubs/other/fincap_delivering.pdf.

Fioreti, J. (2013). *Big Banks See Rich Opportunities in World's Poorest*. Retrieved on January 17, 2014. http://www.reuters.com/article/2013/12/09/us-financial-inclusion-idUSBRE9B80IS20131209.

Freire, P. (1970). *Pedagogy of the Oppressed*. Harmondsworth: Penguin Press

Gregg, P. and Machin, S. (2012). *What a Drag: The Chilling Impact of Unemployment on Real Wages*. London: Resolution Foundation.

Harvey, D. (2010). *The Enigma of Capital and the Crises of Capitalism*. Profile Books.

Her Majesty's Treasury (2007). *Financial Capability: The Government's Long Term Approach*. [Electronic version] http://webarchive.nationalarchives.gov.uk/+/http:/www.hm-treasury.gov.uk/d/fincap_150107.pdf

Her Majesty's Treasury (2008). *Thoresen Review of Generic Financial Advice: Final Report*. Retrieved on March 1, 2014. [Electronic version] http://webarchive.nationalarchives.gov.uk/+/http:/www.hm-treasury.gov.uk/media/8/3/thoresenreview_final.pdf

Holzmann, R., Mulaj, F. and Perotti, V. (2013). *Financial Capability in Low and Middle-Income Countries: Measurement and Evaluation*. A Report on the World Bank's Research Program and the Knowledge from the Russia Financial Literacy and Education Trust Fund. Retrieved on March 1, 2014. [Electronic version] http://www.microfinancegateway.org/library/financial-capability-low-and-middle-income-countries-measurement-and-evaluation

Jovchelovitch, S. (2007). *Knowledge in Context: Representations, Community and Culture*. London: Routledge.

Kamleitner, B., Hoelzl, E. and Kirchler, E. (2012). Credit use: Psychological perspectives on a multifaceted phenomenon. *International Journal of Psychology*, 47(1), 1–27.

Kelly, G. and Pearce, N. (2012). After the coalition: What's left? *Public Policy Research*, 19(2), 92–101.

Ledgerwood, J. (2013). The New Microfinance Handbook: A Financial Market System Perspective (Eds) Ledgerwood, J., Earne, J., & Nelson, C. Retrieved on January 27 2014 https://openknowledge.worldbank.org/bitstream/handle/10986/12272/9780821389270.pdf

Liberty (2011). *Liberty's Response to the Ministry of Justice Proposals for the Reform of Legal Aid*. Retrieved on January 7, 2014. http://www.liberty-human-rights.org.uk/pdfs/policy11/response-to-ministry-of-justice-consultation-on-legal-aid.pdf.

Lilico, A. (2010). *Household Indebtedness in the EU, European Parliament*. Retrieved on January 24, 2014. http://www.europarl.europa.eu/document/activities/cont/201103/20110324ATT16330/20110324ATT16330EN.pdf.

Martin-Baro, I. (1996). *Writings for Liberation Psychology*. Cambridge, MA: Harvard University Press.

MacCoun, R. J. (1998). Biases in the interpretation and use of research results. *Annual Review of Psychology*, 49, 259–287.

McCarron, A. and Purcell, L. (2013). *The Blame Game Must Stop: Challenging the Stigmatisation of People Experiencing Poverty*. Retrieved on January 24, 2013. http://www.church-poverty.org.uk/stigma.

Nazroo, J. R. (2014). Ethnic inequalities in health addressing a significant gap in current evidence and policy (pp. 91–101) in The British Academy (2014) *"If you could do one thing..." Nine Local Actions to Reduce Health Inequalities*. Retrieved on January 31, 2014. http://www.britac.ac.uk/policy/Health_Inequalities.cfm.

O'Neill, M. (2010). *Asylum, Migration and Community*. Bristol: Policy Press.

Pickett, K. (2014). Addressing health inequalities through greater social equality at a local level: Implement a living wage policy (pp. 22–31) in The British Academy (2014) *"If you could do one thing..." Nine Local Actions to Reduce Health Inequalities*. Retrieved on January 31, 2014. http://www.britac.ac.uk/policy/Health_Inequalities.cfm.

Rabbior, G. (2005). *Why Financial Capability Matters*. Retrieved on January 31, 2014. http://www.fcac-acfc.gc.ca/Eng/resources/researchSurveys/Pages/WhyFinan-Pourquoi.aspx.

Special Interest Group of Municipal Authorities (SIGOMA) (2013). *A fair future or a growing divide?* – SIGOMA figures pre-autumn statement. Retrieved on January 6, 2014. http://www.sigoma.gov.uk/Docs/sigomareports/A%20Fair%20Future%20or%20a%20Growing%20Divide_SIGOMA%20Updated%20Figures.pdf.

Taylor, M. (2009). *The Impact of Life Events on Financial Capability: Evidence from the BHPS* (British Household Panel Survey). Retrieved on January 7, 2014. http://www.fsa.gov.uk/static/pubs/consumer-research/crpr79.pdf.

Trussell Trust (2014). Latest foodbank figures top 900,000. Retrieved on August 18, 2014. http://www.trusselltrust.org/foodbank-figures-top-900000.

Walker, C., Cunningham, L., Hanna, P. and Ambrose, P. (2012a). *Responsible Individuals and Irresponsible Institutions: A Report into Mental Health and the UK Credit Industry*. Brighton: University of Brighton.

Walker, C. (2012b). Personal debt and cognitive delinquency: Neoliberal constructions of financial inadequacy in the UK. *Journal of Community and Applied Social Psychology*, 22, 533–538.

Walker, C. (2012c). *Neoliberal Ideology and Personal Debt in the UK. In Community Psychology and the Socio-Economics of Mental Distress: International Perspectives*. London: Palgrave Macmillan.

Wilson, T., Morgan, G., Rahman, A. and Vaid, L (2013). *The Local Impacts of Welfare Reform: An Assessment of Cumulative Impacts and Mitigations*. A report commissioned from the Centre for Economic and Social Inclusion by the Local Government Association. Retrieved on January 13, 2014. http://www.cesi.org.uk/sites/default/files/publications/The%20local%20impacts%20of%20welfare%20reform%20version%207.pdf.

10
The Indebted Individual: Dominant Discourses and Alternative Understandings of Personal Debt in the UK

Paul Hanna, Liz Cunningham and Carl Walker

Introduction

The individualisation of debt

During Europe's Middle Ages, individuals who found themselves in debt that they were unable to repay were incarcerated together in large single cells until their families paid their debt. Conditions for these "debt prisoners" were often very poor, with disease, starvation, abuse from other prisoners and death frequently being reported (Hutter and Power, 2000). Throughout this regime it was clear that society placed responsibility for borrowing and incapacity to repay debts firmly on that of the individual. During the 13th century, King Edward I realised the potential of the credit industry, regulating it and establishing an institution called the Exchequer of the Jewry in an attempt to control, promote and profit (via tax) from lending practices in the UK (Koyama, 2010a, 2010b). Despite the promotion and regulation of the credit industry by governments, throughout history the individuals who have borrowed have been responsible for this practice, with stiff punishment being meted out to those who were incapable of repaying. Indeed, the practice of debtors being placed in debtors' prisons was not something that disappeared following the Middle Ages. Rather, such practices were the focus of campaigns for financial reform in the 17th century by the Levellers, and by the novelist Charles Dickens in the 19th century. However, the practice continued until the Debtors Act of 1869, which all but abolished imprisonment due to debt (Rajak, 2008). Worryingly, though, there are reports of some courts in the state of Ohio in the USA reconstituting the imprisonment of debtors, primarily for state fines, such as parking tickets (ACLU, 2014).

From such a historical positioning, debt, particularly the inability to service an individual debt, has largely been understood from a rational, individualistic perspective. Most economists see logical positivism as a guiding tenet, with the idea that we are essentially rational, independent economic actors. This is not only prevalent in the behavioural economics literature but also widely shared in society (Lewis, 2010). Montgomerie (2007) suggests that mainstream accounts from policymakers and economists highlight the fact that they tend to see individuals as rational actors who respond to changing economic conditions. This was a point highlighted by the 1971 Crowther Committee, which concluded that users of consumer credit should be "treated as adults, who are fully capable of managing their own financial affairs, and not to restrict their freedom of access to it in order to protect the relatively small minority who get into difficulties" (Richards et al., 2008, p. 502). Indeed, within the field of psychology there is an abundance of research that seeks to highlight what it is about individuals who find themselves unable to service their debt that makes them dysfunctional (e.g. Amar et al., 2011; Wanga et al., 2011). For example, Webley and Nyhus (2001) argue that absent-mindedness, external locus of control and poor money-management techniques are all psychological factors that are associated with debt.

As a result of such "economic rationalism", financial education has become the prominent solution that is circulating in public and political rhetoric. Recent policy conjecture focuses on strategic priorities to address the issue of problem debt, and education appears to be the key approach. There is a desire to "increase levels of financial capability and awareness" (Department for Work and Pensions, 2006, p. 11), thereby "improving people's ability to take control of their own finances through the National Strategy for financial capability pilot projects" (Department for Work and Pensions, 2005, p. 9). There is also an aspiration to "increase levels of financial capability and awareness, so that more individuals can take control of their finances, and participate effectively in the credit markets" (Department for Work and Pensions, 2004, p. 5) and a need to address "those lacking essential financial skills, including the ability to budget sensibly, [who] may over-commit themselves by taking on excessive debts" (Department for Work and Pensions, 2007, p. 6). Such commitments have seen initiatives such as embedding financial capacity training into the GSCE maths curriculum from

2008 (Department of Trade and Industry, 2006), and the government's drive to offer financial competency training to those who are most marginalised through the Now Let's Talk Money campaign (Department for Business Enterprise and Regulatory Reform, 2007).

However, alternative fields of psychology have addressed issues of individual responsibility from a rather different position. For example, rather than looking for individual "attributes", a number of contemporary scholars have argued that a particular version of "subjectivity" is dominant in contemporary Western society (Rose, 1989, 1998, 2001; Heyes, 2007). They suggest that dominant individualistic norms mean that people are increasingly coming to understand themselves and their life stories in terms of outcomes of their own deliberate and rational choices (Gill, 2008; Layton, 2010). Therefore, rather than looking to possible economic conditions to understand personal debt, individuals who are struggling with money are presented as "knowing" financial subjects rather than the objects of problematic economic processes that exist at the national and international level. Thus within this "economic rationalism" the autonomous subject should be able to cope with any conditions that it faces. If this is not the case due to a range of potential factors (e.g. a drop in real-term wages) then it is simply understood as individual incompetence (Walkerdine, 2002). For Gill (2008) it is hard to overestimate just how prevalent this individualised "subject" has become in understanding society.

Building the case for an alternative way of thinking

While such an approach to understanding debt may have remained dominant throughout UK history, it isn't without its challenges. Research has suggested that consumers are very clearly not rational decision-makers (Watson, 2003). Although there is evidence that credit use results from the weighing of pros and cons against each other (Kamleitner et al., 2012), research has consistently shown that future benefits and costs of credit are discounted compared with their valuation in the present, that consumers are characterised by intertemporal discounting and myopia as major drivers of borrowing (Kamleitner et al., 2012). Increasing an individual's credit limit leads to more spending and greater credit use, and low levels of information search are commonly reported. This is perhaps not surprising since American borrowers who searched were no more likely to borrow in favourable conditions than those who did not. Kamleitner et al.'s review of the literature also showed that consumers' understanding of APR is limited with a denial of risk being frequent. Research has shown that individuals are unable to correctly value their income and in fact use credit limits as a signal of their future earnings potential (Soman and Cheema, 2002). It has been shown that people tend to underestimate their own likelihood of experiencing an unfavourable event (Editorial, 2008), and that they often exhibit an inability to process user-unfriendly features of disclosure forms (Stark and Cholpin, 2010). It also seems to be the case that people tend to underestimate the future burden of a loan and overestimate their capacity to adapt to future circumstances (Hoelzl et al., 2009). Therefore, in understanding personal debt, it appears that an alternative theoretical approach to the one offered by positivistic mainstream psychology and "economic rationalism" is needed. An approach that provides an account of the "indebted individual" as being positioned within a multifarious social system might offer a more complex understanding. For this we turn to the work of Michel Foucault.

Foucault argued through the "technologies of knowledge" and "technologies of power" that individuals are constructed and positioned as particular types of "subject" (Foucault, 1972). This positioning constrains the array of behaviours, experiences and "feelings" that each individual can engage with. Practices are formed in relation to the individual and legitimate "ways of being" are constructed. For example, the discourses that are inherent in psychology and the criminal justice system utilise "technologies of knowledge" to position certain sexual behaviours as "illegitimate", thus labelling the individual "deviant" (Foucault, 1990). Subsequently, this limits the credibility and rights of that individual, often silencing their voice. Foucault also suggests that "knowledges" shift over time and that these dominant understandings enable and constrain individuals through what is "acceptable" or "unacceptable", "normal" or "abnormal", "good" or "bad". Furthermore, in his studies of biopower, he presents an account in which "technologies of power" control and construct the individual through the discursive regimes (Bevir, 1999). It is through "technologies of power" that a modernist discourse masks the power relations that dominate individuals through an account of individual freedom, in this instance in relation to rational choice and debt. Therefore it is through the relationship between power and knowledge that certain ways of being are made possible and normalised, particular "truths" accepted, subjectivities offered and "pictures of the self" (Heyes, 2007) promoted. Thus financial competency, rational choice and fiscal acumen can all be understood as disciplinary technologies that formulate and constrain the subjectivity of the "indebted individual".

With the possibility of "seeing debt differently" being highlighted, what follows in this chapter draws on interview data to explore the dominant discourses in individuals' accounts of debt. The analysis offered first aims to highlight the extent to which the dominant individualised account of debt circulates in a range of stakeholder understandings of being in debt. The chapter then moves on to highlight how an alternative understanding is possible and present in such accounts while also exposing how this alternative struggles to find a voice in a world that is dominated by neoliberal individualism. First, however, attention turns to a brief account of our participants, method and analytic framework.

Methodology

Participants and method

Between February 2010 and December 2011, 53 semistructured interviews were carried out with a range of stakeholders in the mainstream UK credit industry.[1] These included:

- 11 debt counsellors/advisors from the community and voluntary sector (including the Citizen's Advice Bureaux, the Consumer Credit Counselling Service and Money Advice and Community Support);
- 17 debt clients who were recruited from the aforementioned advice agencies who had sought help for a range of debt-related issues and included first-time clients and those who had previously experienced overindebtedness; a number of the workers from high street banks and debt-collection companies also related experiences of being debt clients;
- 17 employees and former employees who were recruited from the finance sector, including nine from a range of UK high street banks (and from five separate banks, two of the bank workers had since moved on to other occupations); these stakeholders were recruited from towns and cities across East and West Sussex; we interviewed representatives from the Lending Standards Board, the Centre for Responsible Credit and the British Banking Association; we also interviewed a professional bailiff, a worker and a manager from a local credit union, an employee from the Illegal Money Lending Team in Birmingham and an employee from the Personal Finance Education Group, a leading finance education charity.
- 8 workers from five different debt collection organisations, most of which were from the collection sections of high street UK banks.

The purpose of this recruitment portfolio was to bring together a range of stakeholder experiences in order to build a picture of the practices of lending, collecting and advice over recent years in the mainstream commercial credit sector (e.g. overdrafts, banks loans, credit cards) (Kamleitner et al., 2012). Legal doorstep lending, payday lending and illegal loan-shark activity were not the focus of this project.

Data analysis

Epistemologically, this chapter adopts a critical realist approach. This will allow the research to give material practices "an ontological status that is independent of, but in relation with, discursive practices" (Sims-Schouten et al., 2007, p. 102). A multilevel discourse analysis will be used to interrogate the interview data, drawing on aspects of both Foucauldian Discourse Analysis (FDA) and Discursive Psychology (DP) (Potter and Wetherell, 1995). FDA will be drawn on to examine subject positions, discourses and links to broader power structures and how discourses can justify oppressive structures (Parker, 1994; Parker, 1999). In addition, concepts of DP, such as, blame attribution, action justification and ideological dilemmas (Billig, 1991; Billig, 2001), will also be employed. Further, this multilevel discourse analysis will identify and give status to the extradiscursive – for example, materiality. The multilevel analysis will allow the research to offer an in-depth understanding of "the action orientation of participants' talk; the ways-of-being produced through locally used discourses; and the orientation of participants' talk to any embodied, material or institutional factors identified" (Sims-Schouten et al., 2007, p. 119). This eclectic approach will allow the analysis to fully explore the complex network of psychological and sociological issues that surround the UK credit industry.

Analysis

The individualisation of debt choice and responsibility

> I think you know if someone wants to get themselves into debt problems so from me I mean I will see students who max out their overdrafts.
>
> (Kyla, bank manager)
>
> Some people don't even care if they are, if they get kind of defaulted on their accounts and they are 22, 23 years old you know they don't bother about it, they don't think it is going to affect them.
>
> (John, debt collector)

Working in the post office for a couple of years, it's, it's very... agitating to be standing there giving out literally thousands of pounds a month to people who don't work, who don't do anything and then they just go out and get more loans and continually screw the system.

(Carl, bank worker)

The above extracts make it clear the extent to which the dominant understanding of the individual as being responsible for their choices permeates these individuals' accounts. In the first extract, Kyla draws on a discourse of choice to position the indebted individual as a rational subject who actively pursues a "want" – that is, to "get themselves into debt problems". It is through the explicit positioning of the indebted individual as agentic that the bank is implicitly constructed as the passive victim within this relationship. The first person "I" is exploited to strengthen the construction of this relationship via the suggestion of first-hand experience. The perpetrator of this relationship is also made explicit through reference to "students" and thus drawing on the taken-for-granted assumption that it is certain "types" of individual who choose to actively pursue unsustainable levels of credit.

This notion of the young student, or in John's account the "22, 23 year olds" featured prominently throughout the corpus of data and, as we can see from the above extracts, serves a particular function. That function can be understood as a form of "cognitive delinquency" in which immaturity in decision-making skills and feelings of responsibility are central (Walker, 2011). While this could be understood entirely at the individual level, we could also draw on Wacquant (2009) to suggest that it is actually serving a social function in its ability to sustain the debt industry via a glossing-over of the problematic elements of such a system (e.g. lending practices). It is through a discourse of choice and responsibility that this position is maintained in all three accounts. For example, in the second extract the indebted individual is firmly positioned as the young, carefree and irresponsible individual who engages problematically with the neutral system that is the bank.

The third extract draws on a discourse of choice and responsibility but, rather than offering this through notions of the "youth of today", choice and responsibility function through understandings of the unemployed via the rhetoric of the "deserving" and "undeserving" poor that is reminiscent of the English Poor Laws in the 18th century (Rose, 1971). Constructing the indebted individual in this way overcomes challenges to a corrupt system while also positioning the "other" as those "who don't work, who don't do anything" and "continually screw the system" and thus deserve to be in such a situation (Kaika, 2012). Presenting the "other" as the agent of their debt helps to reinforce the position of the bank as the victim and enables a situation in which an appeal is made to the police such a situation. It is through this appeal that not only is the indebted individual positioned as entirely agentic and thus responsible, but also implicitly the employed "citizen" is suffering from the actions of this "other". Furthermore, this final extract couples such a construction with the dominant understanding of spending beyond your means through the use of "literally thousands of pounds". It is this concept of feckless consumption and excessive lifestyles that the following section will explore in more detail.

Lifestyle

> for lots of people they are stuck in this mind-set of maintaining a lifestyle.
> (Elizabeth, debt counsellor/advisor, p. 7)

> The reason for increasing debt is I think amongst a lot of people it is a desire to maintain a lifestyle which is comparable with everybody else and in some instances well in all instances there are people who don't earn as much money but still want the consumer goods that they see their, see other people having, the flat screen TVs and the nice car and the holidays and that sort of thing and they will go into debt to achieve those things.
> (Paul, bank worker, p. 1)

In the two extracts presented above, the maintenance of a consumerist lifestyle is presented as the problematic "mind-set" or "desire" of the indebted individual. The first extract presents a more sympathetic and perhaps critical angle on this consumerist lifestyle through an understanding in which the individual is "stuck", thus rendering the indebted individual disempowered and potentially exonerating some of the blame for their debt status. However, the lexical positioning of "maintaining a lifestyle" returns agency to the indebted individual and brings to the forefront notions of choice and responsibility. These concepts of lifestyle maintenance as a choice is further developed in the second extract. For example, "consumer goods", such as "flat screen TVs", "holidays" and a "nice car", are offered up as objects of consumption, and are positioned as objects of excess that are desired by the undeserving poor and yet are a right only of "everybody else".

Through this construction the indebted individual is positioned not only as inferior to those "others" but also as an individual who succumbs to greed and desire. These highly individualised "traits" function to place blame and responsibility on the abnormal "other" and silence any challenge to the credit industry and more broadly the consumerist "picture of the self" that currently dominates contemporary subjectivities (e.g. Heyes, 2007). Thus through the utility of the discourses of individual responsibility and of feckless consumers, fallacious interpretations of indebted subjectivities are both protected and reproduced (Wacquant, 2009) – a position that is reproduced through mainstream psychological focus on concepts such as "locus of control" (Pinto et al., 2004) and "delay of gratification" (Wood, 1998).

Education and the uneducated "other"

> Help children, young people have all the confidence skills and knowledge that they need in financial matters, to fully take part in society.
> (Gemma, financial education, p. 1)

> You know and a lot of them blame the banks for that but at the end of the day I think a lot of it is down to you know the school systems and things like that. I mean when at school do you ever have a lesson on dealing with debt or personal finances or anything that really is gonna be a driving force to your future happiness.
> (David, debt collector, p. 5)

As with the above section, Gemma opens her account with the explicit construction of the indebted subject. Young people are the target of such a construction with the individual competencies of "skills and knowledge" being identified as potential solutions. Not only is such an understanding firmly located within the broader constructions that are explored in the sections above, but also such an account implicitly positions the indebted individual as uneducated and incompetent when considering financial decision-making. Such an account resonates with recent policy with a focus on "those lacking essential financial skills, including the ability to budget sensibly, [who] may over-commit themselves by taking on excessive debts" (Department for Business Enterprise and Regulatory Reform, 2007, p. 4). With education constituting the primary focus of potential solutions, the systemic issues are silenced in favour of an individualised account that draws on a rational choice discourse which can be understood as positioning the indebted individual as not only responsible for their situation but also uneducated and incompetent. Moreover, financial capability (and thus engagement with credit) is situated as an essential part of modern living with the incompetent "other" being considered dysfunctional and unable to "fully take part in society".

In the second extract, David draws on a more systematic approach to understanding debt and indebted individuals. Rather than explicitly presenting the indebted individual as "uneducated", the "schooling system" is explicitly positioned as the target for blame. By rendering the individuals as non-agentic, this goes some way towards positioning the indebted individual in a different light from the account offered by Gemma, yet the notion of education still functions to mobilise a rational choice discourse and to implicitly construct the issues on individual terms. Thus the nihilism of the poor is taught as part of an ideological oppression that is maintained by a focus on personal debt management (Moreira, 2003). In addition, the uneducated and incompetent "other" is reinforced through such an understanding that enables an "othering" and the construction of "us" and "them". Finally, the extract draws on the contemporary consumerist "picture of the self" (Heyes, 2007) in which happiness is achievable via an individual's consumption patterns and money management, once again positioning the indebted "other" as uneducated and as a symbolic non-member of contemporary society and its legitimatised ways of being.

Summarising a focus on the individual

The above analysis has demonstrated the ways in which an individualised understanding of overindebtedness circulates centrally through the participants' research accounts. Drawing on notions of choice and responsibility, stakeholders offer accounts that position the indebted individual as being responsible for their situation through lifestyle choice or poor money-management skills. This, rather unsurprisingly, leads on to financial education being offered up as the primary solution to the problem. Such a solution serves to reinforce the individualistic understanding of overindebtedness and also goes some way towards rendering the "other" as both uneducated and socially dysfunctional. However, when turning to existing research that explores more social impacts of indebtedness, it has been suggested that most people in the problem debt group use it to pay for everyday essentials of living, which make framing the problem as one of financial incapability problematic (Walker et al., 2012). Orton (2010) notes that there is a persistent finding that low income holds back people's ability to move beyond indebtedness, even with careful budgeting.

Perhaps for this reason it has been suggested that the effect of financial knowledge on the persistence and level of debt is equivocal (Kamleitner et al., 2012). Erturk et al. (2007) argue that although boosting financial literacy may be a worthwhile objective, improved literacy does not in its own right secure positive economic outcomes for people of indebted households. Ben-Galim and Lanning (2010) suggest that it is unlikely that financial planning could change things for a significant number of low-income families in problem debt and that the literature suggests that low-income families tend to do better than wealthier families when budgeting. Mandell and Klein (2009) found that individuals who had undertaken a financial literacy course were no better in their financial literacy and financial decision making than those that had not taken the course. They noted that these results were not unique, a point that Watson (2003, p. 736) further elaborates on, commenting: "one has to wonder whether education alone will be enough".

It may be the case that recent efforts to improve adult and child financial literacy, debt awareness and money management (Dearden et al., 2010) do have some merit. However, Harper (2003) questions such an individual explanation, suggesting that the focus on people who have no control over world economic resources as opposed to governments and transnational corporations that do is inherently problematic. Of course, in the above analysis the discourses employed constructions of debt and positioning of the actors involved, and the subsequent solutions proposed are by no means a surprise from a Foucauldian perspective given the history from which such understandings emerge. Yet what is surprising is the ways in which these discourses were actively challenged throughout the interviews, offering examples of what Foucault termed "resistance", while also highlighting how such resistance is both difficult and often problematic. It is the complexity of the relationship between dominant discourses and counterdiscourses that the following sections of the analysis focus on to highlight the ways in which these play out in the participants' speech and the implications of this.

Grappling with alternative understandings: Wrestling the discursive economy

Choice and responsibility: Problematic sales practices

> There was this culture of if you have got a credit card, got three credit cards, got five credit cards, we will give him another one cos we can get some debt on that and earn some interest out of him as well.
>
> (Paul, bank worker, p. 8)

At the end of the day, it's the same as any other retail industry, it's all sales, and you've got to sell haven't you? You make money by selling. So, you've got to incentivise people in some way, shape or form to sell and they do in every industry across the board.

(Carl, bank worker, p. 3)

The above extracts present an account of choice and responsibility that is in stark contrast with that explored in above. The first extract employs the term "culture" to draw on an alternative construction of the credit industry and indebtedness in which the "culture" or "community" of those in the industry are positioned as the ones that act in feckless ways. Financial gain is presented as the motivation for such practices of lending via the benefits of the indebted individual to the banking system. No longer is the individual positioned as central to this relationship; rather, an alternative in which the indebted individual is largely silenced and disempowered is offered. In addition, individual responsibility on the part of the individual lender is also largely absolved via the position of the "culture".

The second extract draws on a capitalist/consumerist discourse that enables a similar construction to that highlighted above. However, in this extract the discourse is employed to achieve a very different outcome. Here, profit, consumption and sales are used to position the "industry", or in Paul's words the "culture", as the basis for such exchange. Individuals within such a system are largely rendered powerless, with the sales person being victim to a system of sales and the indebted individual passive in the process of being sold to. Use of the rhetorical question "You have got to sell, haven't you?" functions as a disclaimer and further discredits the possibility of responsibility and blame on the part of the individual bank worker. Finally, a rational choice discourse functions by reference to the use of "incentives". However, while earlier in the analysis such a discourse enabled blame and responsibility to be located with the indebted individual, here it works to further support the position of a debt system being responsible while the creditor is rendered passive to the demands of their working role, and the indebted individual is merely the outcome of the systemic processes.

Throughout this section the construction of debt as the discursive object is distinctly different from that presented above; while still functioning through understandings of rational choice, consumerism and responsibility, the subjects in this section are positioned in binary to those that were examined previously. From this it is possible to view people as victims of a financial system that depends on them to go deeply into debt in order for the debt system to function and generate income as a result of indebtedness (Ritzer, 1995). Yet while this may be the case, such understandings struggle against the dominant understandings, as will be highlighted below.

[Ir]responsible lifestyles

> I think from seeing people's accounts sort of day-to-day what they're using, like what they're using their accounts for, my personal opinion is people are living beyond their actual means. So they've got, like you'll see it all like on people's accounts they're going shopping every day, like they've got direct debts for like Sky, mobile, like three or four mobile phones, just yeah, ridiculous things that like they then, they don't, they can actually live without to be honest...So like around Christmas time there was a big push on that and like we were doing like 0% credit cards and things, sort of just to looking at it and how much money they will save people.
>
> (Julie, bank worker, p. 2)

> I think now and certainly the last six to twelve months, if not a bit more, a lot of it is unemployment and people basically using credit cards to essentially live on.
>
> (Harry, bailiff)

The first account from Julie draws on exactly the same construction as that exposed previously in this chapter. Rational choice and responsibility function through the suggestion that people are active in their indebtedness and "are living beyond their actual means". While this position is offered up only as a "personal opinion", Julie draws on her experience as a personal witness to strengthen this position and to reinforce the notion of the feckless or irresponsible consumer. Here "Sky" TV and not just one mobile but "three or four phones" are offered up as practices above and beyond what is deemed essential. The suggestion that such an account of consumer goods as essential is "ridiculous" enables choice and responsibility to be placed firmly on the shoulders of the indebted individual while silencing any critique of the banking system and perhaps the consumerist society more generally.

While this account functions in a perfectly sensible manner, when we look a little further into the interview, what becomes apparent is the extent to which contradictions in accounts of responsibility come to the fore. For example, while consumer responsibility and living beyond ones means are presented as the reasons for overindebtedness, later on in the interview we see an account of the banking practices which explicitly contradict this. While this may not be conscious in Julie's mind, an alternative understanding of indebtedness is presented which functions through a different discursive position that locates irresponsibility within the system and its "push" on "0% credit cards" around the Christmas period when individuals are at their most stretched. While such an account of debt is incompatible with the individualistic discourse that was offered earlier in the interview, reference to "saving money" goes some way to negotiate such a gulf in positions.

Drawn from a separate interview, the second extract gives voice to a position that was largely silenced throughout the dataset despite having equal, if not more support, from social theory and research (Ford, 1991; Ritzer, 1995; Tutton, 2009). In this account the use of credit is not presented as an irresponsible and feckless practice. Rather, the use of credit here is offered up as a means for individuals' to live with the most basic of essentials rather than a living beyond their means. While such a position has received extensive support academically (Wacquant, 2009; Walker, 2011; Walker et al., 2012; Walker, 2013), throughout the dataset it was clear to see that it is largely marginalised in people's accounts, with the irresponsible consumer maintaining its stronghold on people's understandings. Furthermore, this silencing of an alternative understanding not only places responsibility and blame on the shoulders of the individual but also functions to exonerate the banks' lending practices from blame, and the broader social and political arena is rendered irrelevant.

Education and the uneducated "other"...

> We've got financial advisors, mortgage advisors, people like that who are in debt themselves and they are giving advice to other people.
> (Victoria, debt counsellor/advisor, p. 11)

> I don't think banks deliberately get people to borrow money they can't pay back...The fact that you can increase the limit on someone's credit card, without having any conversations with them about it, clearly a computer based assessment is done...that sort of thing shouldn't be allowed without having an informative conversation with the customer so they don't sleep walk into these debt situations, which is happening so often...but people need to take more responsibility for their own actions, saying it needs to be more regulated is

fine but then people should take responsibility for their own actions as well.

(Harriet, bank worker, pp. 4–10)

As highlighted above, education functions to strengthen the position of the rational choice model and helps to reinforce the individual as the central agent in the process of becoming indebted. In the first extract we see an alternative to the position of "education as solution" through the first-hand account of financial advisors being individuals who are also in problem debt. While such an account may offer something of an insight into the situation as it stands in the UK from the perspective of someone experiencing it first hand, it was not common to hear of such alternative constructions within our data.

When we turn our attention to the second extract it becomes a little clearer why this might be the case. Throughout the account the participant is battling with a dominant understanding of debt as an individual's "fault" and the marginalised position of the irresponsible banking system – for example, the suggestion that "I don't think banks deliberately get people to borrow money they can't pay back." Such a statement is largely unsurprising when considering the extent to which the individual as responsible circulates as the dominant understanding throughout our data. However, through the suggestion that "you can increase the limit on someone's credit card, without having any conversations with them about it", an alternative is attempted which appears more in line with research, such as that of Richards and colleagues (2008), that suggests that 88% of successful credit card applicants were not requested to show any proof of their income.

Here the statement is in direct opposition to the opening remark and positions the banking systems as responsible. Such a position is enhanced through the personal reflection on the ways in which such practices are considered to be problematic or wrong in the eyes of the participant. In addition, not only are the banks implicit in this account of responsibility but also the indebted individual is explicitly exonerated from such responsibility through an account in which banks need to do more to prevent people from "sleep walk[ing] into these debt situations". While this account is suggested to be "happening so often" it appears to represent an understanding that largely struggles to find its place in the discourse of our participants. Furthermore, within the account offered here it is clear to see how difficult it is to maintain such a position, with the default position of the individual as responsible rising to prominence by the end of the extract with the suggestion that "people need to take more responsibility for their own actions", and thus we return to the notion of better financial education despite the lack of evidence for money management being the cause (see also Ben-Galim and Lanning, 2010).

Conclusion

This chapter set out to offer a brief account of the way in which personal debt is currently understood in the public sphere. It was suggested at this stage that personal debt is seen as exactly that: a problem with the person. Such an understanding appears to dominate policy and research that explores the social problem of "indebted individuals". Following this account an alternative was briefly suggested to highlight the ways in which "personal" debt can be understood on a more "social" level, despite the dominance of individualised ways of thinking in contemporary Western society. Attention then turned to the analysis of interview data with a range of stakeholders within the debt industry. This started by exposing the strength of the dominant individualised discourses that are circulating in relation to understandings of debt and indebtedness. The second half of the analysis unpacked the alternative discourses that individuals drew on in their understandings of debt in order to highlight the contradictory and problematic "nature" of debt talk. Throughout this section of the analysis, moments of resistance were highlighted to show how debt is, and indeed can be, understood differently. This perspective builds on the well-established work of Ambrose and Cunningham (2004), which suggests that financial and emotional vulnerability, stemming from unpredictable life changes, are often the cause of personal debt. Throughout the analysis such an understanding appeared to be difficult to establish and maintain in the participants' accounts due to the power of the dominant discourses. However, it is suggested here that such alternative understandings need to be given more "voice" if academics, policy-makers and the public are to make sustained attempts at "seeing debt differently" in order to offer a genuine and empathetic attempt at tacking individual overindebtedness. Such a position could be achieved via the reformation of banking policies, "educational" initiatives, financial counterdiscourses and, more generally, through an alternative to the individualisation that is proliferated in much of the mainstream psychological research in the field.

Note

1. Pseudonyms are used throughout this chapter.

References

ACLU (2014). American Civil Liberties Union. Retrieved on April 23, 2014. http://www.acluohio.org/the-outskirts-of-hope.

Amar, M., Ariely, D., Ayal, S., Cryder, C. E., Rick, S. I. (2011). Winning the battle but losing the war: The psychology of debt management. *Journal of Marketing Research*, 48, 38–50.

Ambrose, P. and Cunningham, L. (2004). *The Ever-Increasing Circle: A Pilot Study of Debt as an Impediment to Entering Employment in Brighton and Hastings*. The Health and Social Policy Research Centre, University of Brighton.

Ben-Galim, D. and Lanning, T. (2010). *Strength against the Shocks. Low Income Families and Debt*. London, UK: Institute for Public Policy Research.

Bevir, M. (1999). Foucault and critique: Deploying agency against autonomy. *Political Theory*, 27, 65–84.

Billig, M. (1991). *Ideology and Opinions: Studies in Rhetorical Psychology*. London: Sage.

Billig, M. (2001). Discursive, Rhetorical and Ideological Messages. *Discourse Theory and Practice: A Reader*. M. Wetherell, S. Taylor and S. J. Yates. London: Sage.

Dearden, C., Goode, J., Whitfield, G. and Cox, L. (2010). *Credit and Debt in Low-Income Families*. York, UK: Joseph Rowntree Foundation.

Editorial (2008). Behavioral economics and decision making: Applying insights from psychology to understand how people make economic decisions. *Journal of Economic Psychology*, 29, 613–618.

Erturk, I., Froud, J., Johal, S., Leaver, A. and Williams, K. (2007). The democratization of finance? Promises, outcomes and conditions. *Review of International Political Economy*, 14(4), 553–575.

Ford, J. (1991). *Consuming Credit: Debt & Poverty in the UK*. London: CPAG.

Foucault, M. (1972). *The Archaeology of Knowledge*. London: Tavistock.

Foucault, M. (1990). *The Will to Knowledge: The History of Sexuality*, (Vol. 1) (R. Hurley, trans.). London: Penguin Press.

Gill, R. (2008). Culture and subjectivity in neoliberal and postfeminist times. *Subjectivity*, 25, 432–445.

Harper, D. (2003). Poverty and discourse. In Carr, S. and Tod Sloan, S. (eds.). *Poverty and Psychology: From Global Perspective to Local Practice*. United States: Springer, 185–203.

Heyes, C. (2007). *Self-transformations: Foucault, Ethics, and Normalized Bodies*. Oxford: Oxford University Press.

Hoelzl, E., Pollai, M. & Kamleitner, B. (2009). Experience, prediction and recollection of loan burden. *Journal of Economic Psychology*, 30(3), 446–454.

Hutter, B. M. and Power, M. (2000). *Risk Management and Business Regulation. Mastering Risk: Financial Times Mastering Series*, 1. J. Pickford. London: Pearson Education.

Industry, D. o. T. a. (2006). *Tackling Over-Indebtedness – Annual Report*. Department of Trade and Industry.

Kaika, M. (2012). The economic crisis seen from the everyday: Europe's nouveau poor and the global affective implications of a 'local'debt crisis. *City*, 16(4), 422–430.

Kamleitner, B., Hoelzl, E. and Kirchler, E. (2012). Credit use: Psychological perspectives on a multifaceted phenomenon. *International Journal of Psychology*, 47(1), 1–27.

Koyama, M. (2010a). Evading the taint of usury: The usury prohibition as a barrier to entry. *Explorations in Economic History*, 47(4), 420–442.
Koyama, M. (2010b). The political economy of expulsion: The regulation of Jewish moneylending in medieval England. *Constitutional Political Economy*, 32(4), 374–406.
Layton, L. (2010). Irrational exuberance: Neoliberal subjectivity and the perversion of truth. *Subjectivity*, 3, 303–322.
Lewis, A. (2010). The credit crunch: Ideological, psychological and epistemological perspectives. *The Journal of Socio-Economics*, 39, 127–131.
Mandell, L. and Klein, L. (2009). The impact of financial literacy education on subsequent financial behaviour. *Journal of Financial Counselling and Planning*, 20(1), 15–24.
Montgomerie, J. (2007). *Financialization and Consumption: An Alternative Account of Rising Consumer Debt Levels in Anglo-America*. CRESC Working paper series. Retrieved. https://www.escholar.manchester.ac.uk/api/datastream ?publicationPid=uk-ac-man-scw:181191&datastreamId=FULL-TEXT.PDF.
Moreira, V. (2003). Poverty and psychopathology. In Carr, S. and Tod Sloan, S. (eds.). *Poverty and Psychology: From Global Perspective to Local Practice*. United States: Springer, 69–86.
Orton, M. (2010). *The Long-Term Impact of Debt Advice on Low Income Households: The 3 Year Report*. Warwick Institute for Employment Research.
Parker, I. (1994). Reflexive research and the grounding of analysis: Social psychology and the psy-complex. *Journal of Community and Applied Social Psychology*, 4, 239–252.
Parker, I. (1999). *Critical Textwork: An Introduction to Varieties of Discourse and Analysis*. Maidenhead, UK: Buckingham Open University Press.
Pensions, D. f. W. a. (2004). *Tackling Overindebtedness Action Plan 2004*.
Pensions, D. f. W. a. (2005). *Tackling Over-indebtedness Annual Report 2005*.
Pensions, D. f. W. a. (2006). *Tackling Over-indebtedness Annual Report 2006*.
Pensions, D. f. W. a. (2007). *Tackling Over-indebtedness Annual Report 2007*.
Pinto, M. B., Mansfield, P. M. and Parente, D. H. (2004). Relationship of credit attitude and debt to self-esteem and locus of control in college-age consumers. *Psychological Reports*, 94, 1405–1418.
Potter, J. and Wetherell, M. (1995). *Discourse Analysis. Rethinking Methods in Psychology*. J. Smith, R. Harré and R. Van Langenhove. London: Sage.
Rajak, H. (2008). The culture of bankruptcy. In Omar, P. (ed.). *International Insolvency Law: Themes and Perspectives*. Aldershot: Ashgate, 536.
Reform, D. f. B. E. R. (2007). *Tackling over Indebtedness – Annual Report 2007*.
Richards, M., Palmer, P. and Bogdanova, M. (2008). Irresponsible lending? A case study of a UK credit industry reform initiative. *Journal of Business Ethics*, 81, 499–512.
Ritzer, G. (1995). *Expressing America: A Critique of the Global Credit Card Society*. Newbury Park, California: Pine Forge Press.
Rose, M. (1971). *The English Poor Law 1780–1930*. Newton Abbot, UK: David and Charles.
Rose, N. (1989). *Governing the Soul*. London: Routledge.
Rose, N. (1998). *Inventing Our Selves: Psychology, Power, and Personhood*. Cambridge: Cambridge University Press.
Rose, N. (2001). The politics of life itself. *Theory, Culture and Society*, 18, 1–30.

Sims-Schouten, W., Riley, S. C. E. and Willig, C. (2007). Critical realism in discourse analysis: A presentation of a systematic method of analysis using women's talk of motherhood, childcare and female employment as an example. *Theory & Psychology*, 17, 101–124.

Soman, D. and Cheema, A. (2002). The effect of credit on spending decisions: The role of the credit limit and credibility. *Marketing Science*, 21(1), 32–53.

Stark, D. and Cholpin, J. (2010). A cognitive and social psychological analysis of disclosure laws and call for mortgage counselling to prevent predatory lending. *Psychology, Public Policy and Law*, 16(1), 85–131.

Tutton, P. (2009). A decade of debt: Lessons for the future. *Poverty*, 132, 14–17.

Wacquant, L. (2009). *Punishing the Poor: The Neoliberal Government of Social Insecurity.* Durham: Duke University Press.

Walker, C. (2011). "Responsibilizing" a healthy Britain: Personal debt, employment, and welfare. *International Journal of Health Services*, 41(3), 525–538.

Walker, C. (2013). Manufacturing the right way to be in debt: Can psychologists explore the UK debt industry? *The Australian Community Psychologist*, 25(1), 49–59.

Walker, C., Hanna, P., Cunningham, L. and Ambrose, P. (2012). *Responsible Individuals and Irresponsible Institutions.* University of Brighton.

Walkerdine, V. (2002). Introduction. In Walkerdine, V. (ed.). *Challenging Subjects: Critical Psychology for a New Millennium.* Basingstoke: Palgrave Macmillan.

Wang, L., Lu, W. and Malhotra, N. (2011). Demographics, attitude, personality and credit card features correlate with credit card debt: A view from China. *Journal of Economic Psychology*, 32(1), 179–193.

Watson, J. (2003). The relationship of materialism to spending tendencies, saving, and debt. *Journal of Economic Psychology*, 24(6), 723–739.

Webley, P. and Nyhus, E. (2001). Life-cycle and dispositional routes into problem debt. *British Journal of Psychology*, 92, 423–446.

Wood, M. (1998). Socio-economic status, delay of gratification, and impulse buying. *Journal of Economic Psychology*, 19(3), 295–320.

Part III

Political Histories of Personal Debt: Managed Decline, the Debt Industry and Wellbeing

11
Online Peer-to-Peer Lending as a New Profit Industry and Debt Trap

Ceylan Cizmeli and Mert Demir

The recent financial crisis in the USA has resulted in increased unemployment rates, falling home values and growing household debt. Among the main drivers behind this meltdown are easy to obtain mortgages, student loans and credit cards, which constitute the largest portion of household debt in the USA (Dwyer et al., 2012). Federal student loan volume has increased approximately 833% in the last two decades and consumers now carry more unsecured credit card debt than ever before (Draut, 2005). As of 2010, there were at least six credit cards in circulation for every American family and approximately 80% of households who had credit cards owed more than USD 10,000 in unsecured credit card debt (Woolsey and Schulz, 2009). The role of traditional lenders (e.g. banks) in this trend is of prime concern. The aggressive use of lending practices by these institutions has resulted in an increase of 30% in unsecured credit card debt between 2001 and 2008 (Lawless et al., 2008). Subsequently, credit card debt has become more and more expensive over time, as indicated by the increase in fees that are charged by credit card companies to approximately USD 15 billion in 2009 (White House, 2009).

Despite the vast amount of research, the evidence regarding the implications of debt is not clearcut, making it hard to label it as "problematic" for all. Not all debt is problematic because the risk of overindebtedness varies according to several factors, including sociodemographic background and economic conditions (Schicks, 2014). Debt is socially patterned, affecting marginalised and under-represented groups more than others (Fitch et al., 2007). Among the groups that are most disproportionately affected by overindebtedness are those on a low income and the unemployed (Drentea and Reynolds, 2012). Previous research indicates that personal debt, unemployment and financial crisis are among the key risk factors for mental health problems: individuals in debt are twice as likely to think about suicide after controlling for sociodemographic, economic, social and lifestyle factors (Meltzer et al., 2011). Given its socially patterned nature and severe consequences on mental health, overindebtedness is clearly a social, political and economic problem which requires a holistic approach with concerted efforts by multiple actors.

How successful have we been in correctly identifying and addressing these wide-ranging problems behind overindebtedness? Sadly we are far from success: the massive increase in the number of people with debt problems, especially in the last quinquennial period, is still widely attributed to individual rather than broader, systemic failures. The role that the prevailing consumption-oriented, debt-driven economic models and the agents that – by means of a range of financial tools – sustain these models play in the current household debt explosion has not received as much attention as the role that individual factors play. Failure to identify the primary cause of overindebtedness leads to further problems in addressing it. Consumers who can't pay off their debt due to outrageously high interest rates, fees and penalties resort to debt-settlement services to find at least temporary relief. Unfortunately the vast majority of the options available to those who desperately seek help in reducing their debt have been either manipulated or indirectly controlled by the very lenders from whom consumers seek relief (Witte, 2010). For example, non-profit credit counselling offers "debt management plans" to people with excessive credit card debt. The "non-profit" status of these credit counsellors disguises the fact that many of them are funded by the credit card companies (Kane, 2009). While the majority of these plans on the surface seem to provide struggling consumers with a life-jacket, in reality they give banks one more chance to squeeze money from non-paying consumers (Witte, 2010). These plans roughly work as follows. "Qualified" customers are required to pay the principal debt plus a lower interest rate and a service fee to the counsellor. Unlike in the original loan agreement, the plan's funds are deducted directly from customers' checking accounts, reducing risks and making them perhaps easier to deal with for both the counsellors and the ultimate collectors – credit card banks. Due to such stringent qualification requirements, many individuals do not even qualify for such debt management in the first place, and only 25% of those who qualify successfully complete their plans (Hunt, 2005). This also means that credit card banks get another chance to collect 25% of their otherwise uncollectable debt through these plans, putting the remaining 75% in further distress without providing any sight of relief at all. Given these circumstances, these debt-relief programmes serve to minimise losses for creditors rather than solve the debt problems of borrowers.

Overall, traditional debt-management techniques do not appear to be viable options for many consumers. Consequently, troubled borrowers turn to alternative ways of getting out of their debt spiral. For many of them, online peer-to-peer (P2P) lending with its favourable interest terms and easier-to-obtain loans stands out. However, online P2P lending is far from a perfect solution. As we will argue in this chapter, P2P lending is a false flag solution to the problem of overindebtedness because it is actually guided by the same neoliberal policies that contribute to the development as well as the sustainment of problematic debt industries. Today, public welfare has been replaced by self-care, which, in turn, has forced the working classes to fund their private welfare through private debt. Neoliberal public laws and policies have facilitated the financialisation of the economy, broken the power of organised labour and resulted in an exponential increase in debt. These laws and policies make heavy use of the refashioned concept of "individual responsibility" and describe the borrowers in this financialised economy as "risk-taking entrepreneurs". The working classes, who are faced with restructured labour markets, wage pressures and shrinking welfare, have no choice but to pay for their basic needs through debt. In this context, debt is no longer a private choice but a structural imperative which has become an instrument of control and discipline by neoliberalism (Mahmud, 2012). Apart from a few advantages (e.g. lower rates and easier access), P2P lending is ultimately a product of the same neoliberal policies and serves to keep consumers within the walls of that very system. The concept of the private loan in P2P is not new. The P2P lending system is based on the microcredit principles which date back to ancient times. What distinguishes P2P lending from its traditional counterparts is that it provides a "new platform of loan transactions that bypasses traditional intermediaries by directly connecting borrowers and lenders" (Yum et al., 2012). In particular, with the help of technological advances, loan deals are conducted online through P2P lending platforms. In this respect they trump traditional lenders by allowing borrowers and lenders to connect directly to each other without needing to first connect with an intermediary (e.g. a bank or credit union). Accordingly, unlike traditional loans where the decision of loan origination is centralised in intermediaries, such as banks, the decision process is decentralised in online P2P platforms and taken by actors who are directly involved in the process (e.g. borrowers, lenders and lending platforms) (Bachmann et al., 2011).

Online P2P lending platforms are classified into two groups: for-profit (commercial) and not-for-profit (non-commercial) (Ashta and Assadi, 2009). The former are usually limited to national markets and lenders have the intention of making profits, whereas the latter operate globally and lenders have the intention of "donating" small loans to undeveloped countries (Bachmann et al., 2011). This chapter will focus on online P2P lending for profit where lenders expect to receive reasonable compensation for the risk that they are willing to take.

P2P lending is growing at a fast pace worldwide and in the USA in particular. The two primary P2P lending platforms currently operating in the USA are Lending Club and Prosper.com (Brill, 2010). The monthly loan volume of these two leading social lending networks has exceeded USD 50 million with a more than 100% annual growth rate in 2012 (Renton, 2012). Subsequently, P2P lending has become a rapidly emerging financial services product that competes with traditional banking services. The main driving factors behind its success and fast growth are the convenience of online transactions as well as the considerably lower rates and higher returns that P2P loans offer to borrowers and lenders, respectively. Internet technology that P2P lending relies on not only allows for a more efficient aggregation of consumer loan portfolios but also significantly reduces operating costs.

Despite its advantages, P2P lending involves certain risks as well. First, it is not immune to the risks that traditional lending is subject to, such as lending fraud, identity theft and money laundering. These risks may be even greater given the anonymity and ubiquity of the Internet (Chaffee and Rapp, 2011). There are also other types of risk that pertain to online transactions, such as consumer privacy and data-protection violations. Moreover, in online P2P lending, information asymmetry between lenders and borrowers is a major concern. Lenders seek reliable and credible information to assess the true quality of a borrower. Borrowers, however, are rather heterogeneous in the way in which they practise self-disclosure as transparency might be seen as a double-edged-sword. On the one hand, disclosure works as an effective signalling mechanism through which a high-quality borrower demonstrates their ability to repay a loan and, thereby, distinguish themselves from their otherwise similar, low-quality counterparts. Exercising greater transparency and diligence mitigates adverse selection problems (Akerlof, 1970) and helps good-quality borrowers to receive fairer rates for their good credit, which otherwise would not have been possible due to lack of information to separate the two groups. On the other hand, greater transparency could lead to a comparative disadvantage for low-quality borrowers as higher disclosure reveals their strengths as well as their weaknesses. Overall, such differences create disparities in the amount of information that is disclosed by each borrower and they are mainly driven by divergence in the expected benefits from disclosure. In between these two parties stand social lending platforms that aim to create a more efficient information environment as they are required to act as responsible counterparties by accurately assessing a borrower's ability to repay a loan.

In order to achieve a more efficient information environment, P2P lending platforms employ some mechanisms: They either work with an external, third-party information provider to verify self-disclosed information from borrowers, or ask borrowers to provide additional information that is necessary to help estimate their creditworthiness. This includes hard as well as soft information (Petersen and Rajan, 2002). While the former is verifiable, quantifiable, and easy to transmit, such as a borrower's credit score or debt-to-income ratio, the latter is harder to verify or quantify such as group membership and demographics including gender, race, and education. Soft information is of particular importance in this context as it has its pros and cons: On the one hand, relying on hard and soft information together in these markets facilitates effective screening of borrowers, especially those of lower quality, and helps lenders more accurately predict loan defaults (Iyer et al., 2009). On the other hand, empirical evidence suggests that soft information may also work as a negative determinant in P2P lending resulting in racial and gender discrimination (i.e. the socially patterned nature of P2P lending). For instance, African-Americans are less likely to be funded and more likely to have higher interest rates when they are funded (Pope and Sydnor, 2008; Herzenstein et al., 2010).

Before weighing the advantages and disadvantages, there is a more crucial question that we need to answer about P2P lending: Are the benefits from it (e.g. providing struggling borrowers with a way out of the debt spiral) actually as good as anticipated? Our answer to this question is no. In the absence of a robust regulatory structure, the benefits of P2P lending come with risks for borrowers, lenders, lending platforms and society at large. The problem of overindebtedness necessitates a revolutionary change in our understanding. Neoliberal policies consider overindebtedness as the product of individual failure and therefore focus on moving individuals from "financial difficulty" to "financial capability" status using means of governmentality (Walker, 2011). These mostly emphasise individuals' ability to manage their money, keep track of their finances, plan ahead, choose financial products and stay informed about financial matters (FSA, 2009). We argue that solutions that are guided by neoliberal policies only contribute to the growth of the problem of overindebtedness by putting individuals into the lion's den. It is important to realise that the exponential increase in overindebtedness is not the product of individual failure but of social, political and economic governance practices that are driven by free-market strategies in employment, credit and housing markets.

Putting online P2P lending under the microscope

Stakeholders

As the online P2P lending industry is emerging and evolving, players in the market are also changing considerably as some go out of business and other new players find their way to this new market. In the current environment there are five main groups of stakeholders involved in the online P2P lending system: electronic lending platforms, borrowers, lenders, regulators and groups formed by lenders and/or borrowers.

Electronic lending platforms The recent credit crunch in financial markets and increasing demand for personal loans have induced alternative cost-effective service providers, such as P2P lending platforms, to replace traditional financial institutions (banks, credit unions, etc.) between those who are seeking loans and those who are looking for valuable investment opportunities. A number of online trading platforms such as Lending Club and Prosper have emerged during this period. Placing themselves between borrowers and lenders, these providers facilitate the matching of these two parties and administer loan deals.

While the information flow is controlled by these electronic platforms, trades on them are conducted with "fictitious" or "screen" names (Berger and Gleisner, 2008). However, lenders still have access to the necessary financial and demographic information about borrowers, such as their credit scores, borrowing histories, race, gender and location (Ceyhan et al., 2011). Lenders incorporate all of this information into their decision-making processes to draw inferences regarding a borrower's creditworthiness (Iyer et al., 2009). Lenders from these platforms come from different walks of life, but borrowers are more likely to be those who cannot get a loan from traditional financial institutions.

Trades are made through online auctions. Specifically, once borrowers indicate their willingness to participate, they go through a multistage process. They provide information about their creditworthiness and this is assessed by the lending platform. Then they are either accepted into the system and provided with a credit score to be shared on their platform profile, or they are refused. Those who are allowed to post a loan then state the amount of money they need along with the maximum interest rate they are willing to accept. Lenders, on the other hand, search for loans based on the information provided on the platform about potential borrowers and submit their minimum interest rate along with the amount of money that they wish to finance. All listings on a platform have predetermined due dates by which time they have to be filled (as successful) or they are discarded (as unsuccessful). P2P lending usually works in an "all-or-nothing" way for borrowers. A bid is considered successful only if the amount requested by the borrower is received from lenders and proceeds for further matching. These platforms also help borrowers and lenders to interact with each other before agreeing a loan. This online social interactive feature gives borrowers the chance to "polish" or promote the purpose of the loan and communicate it to their potential lenders. Borrowers can share all necessary information explaining how they would like to use the money, as well as answer lenders' questions about the loan. Among the successful bids, those with the lowest interest rates are identified by the lending platform and the funds are transferred to the borrower. After that, borrowers make monthly payments until the loan is paid, which usually takes three to five years. In the case of multiple lenders (discussed in detail under "Lenders", below), repayments are distributed among them. Monitoring duties regarding the collection of money and repayments are mostly performed by the lending platform.

Similar to traditional financial intermediaries, P2P platforms earn money from the loans that they originate. However, what distinguishes P2P lending platforms from their traditional counterparts is the costs involved in each. P2P platforms eliminate the middleman in traditional lending and thereby can offer higher returns for lenders and charge lower interest rates to borrowers. By replacing the traditional intermediaries between borrowers and lenders with online systems, P2P platforms achieve significant reductions in their overhead costs that help them to improve significantly over their retail bank counterparts in the rates that they charge as well as that they offer to their customers. The Securities and Exchange Commission (SEC) is currently the principal regulator of the P2P platforms in the USA. Unfortunately it focuses on lender protection and is not required to ensure that borrowers are treated fairly. Although borrowers have the benefit of consumer protection laws, the absence of a single federal regulator focused on P2P lending from both a lender and borrower standpoint raises concerns that the existing regulatory structure may not adequately protect borrowers on P2P platforms (Manbeck and Hu, 2014).

Borrowers The main driver of this emerging trend of person-to-person or social lending is the borrowers. P2P lending provides major "benefits" to them. Through these platforms, borrowers can receive a lower interest rate on a P2P loan than they would receive from retail banks. Among other benefits of online lending is its convenience to borrowers, the relative confidentiality and the anonymity of their identity (Chaffee and Rapp, 2012). In the case of an online transaction, individuals save on the effort and avoid the burden of visiting a bank for a loan, sharing their financial and personal information (in particular their identity) and then being rejected because of their unsatisfactory credit history.

P2P lending also provides an alternative venue for those who would not have otherwise received approved for a loan from a traditional bank because of their low credit score, past unpaid loans or defaults. However, unlike bank loans, P2P loans are unsecured – there is no collateral such as real estate or any other asset, nor are they backed by a formal guarantee (e.g. Federal Deposit Insurance Cooperation). Therefore they pose a higher risk for lenders. To alleviate lenders' concerns about this risk, P2P lending platforms carry out certain prescreenings in the form of a credit history check that will also help to determine the interest rate of a loan. After considerably high default rates in the first few years, one of the two leading P2P platforms, Prosper, has revised its underwriting standards. Now it allows borrowers with a minimum credit score of 640 while Lending Club requires 660, meaning that the system serves only good, reliable borrowers who have good credit scores with no history of default on a loan in the past (i.e. an economically patterned form of P2P lending). In other words, services offered by P2P lending are not all-inclusive and accessible to everyone; they are limited to buyers and borrowers who have relatively good profiles. Ironically, individuals who are denied a P2P loan are usually those who are desperately in need of help. This implies that P2P lending does not prevent or ease the increasing debt burden but further promotes overindebtedness by limiting the horizon within which the economically vulnerable pursue strategies of economic survival and security.

Lenders P2P lending has offered several advantages to lenders who are searching for profitable investment opportunities, especially over other traditional techniques. Unlike borrowers, lenders are usually not charged but are paid for their investments in P2P lending. It is worth keeping in mind that P2P lending is also not risk-free, meaning that individuals can gain as well as lose some or all of their money in the case of a borrower default. Following up on the default risk discussion before, lenders are not without alternatives on a P2P platform. They can find a way to mitigate some of these risks with some planning on their own. The most common strategy that they use on P2P platforms is portfolio diversification. Instead of concentrating all of the risk in a single loan, they can invest in a variety of loans across different risk characteristics to build a diversified portfolio that will spread their default risk. If one borrower defaults there is still a chance that a lender will gain from their other investments.

Regulators The P2P lending marketplace offers numerous benefits which also come with a number of risks. A sound regulatory structure is needed to mitigate potential risks that are inherent in P2P lending (Chaffee and Rapp, 2012). While a consensus has been emerging regarding the need to fill the regulatory gap in the online P2P lending marketplace, it is not clear what the most effective legal structure would be to control this new and evolving industry (Chaffee and Rapp, 2012). This stems mostly from the regulatory confusion over deciding on what actions to take as it is highly unclear what the implications of a regulatory regime would be in such a dynamic and new industry. Prosper and Lending Club work in a similar fashion to banks: once an agreement is reached between the borrower and the lender(s), a designated bank originates a loan to the borrower and then the lenders are issued with promissory notes by the bank, the payments on which are contingent upon the repayment of the underlying loan. Involvement of a bank in this model means that these loans are considered to be a type of security and that they require regulatory oversight in accordance with the securities law. The SEC regulates P2P lending platforms in the USA but it is still up to each state to allow trading on these platforms.

Groups The two prominent types of network that are observed in the online lending marketplace are "groups" and "friendship networks" (Lin et al., 2009). These facilitate the transfer of information and resources from members to external parties, providing significant cost advantages regarding information-gathering for P2P networks as well as for lenders in assessing the creditworthiness of a borrower. A group membership or friendship provides significant benefits to borrowers, including a higher probability of attracting funds and lower interest rates payable on loans (Berger and Gleisner, 2009; Greiner and Wang, 2009). These groups can also help third-party outsiders such as potential investors (lenders) to mitigate the information asymmetry between themselves and borrowers. Moreover, given a verifiable and credible network, such memberships can also serve as a source of soft information about borrowers that could broaden their investor bases and increase the chances of their raising the funds that they need (Petersen and Rajan, 1994; Herrero-Lopez, 2009).

Questioning the P2P lending system

Following up on the comprehensive analysis of P2P lending that we offered above, we argue that although at first glance P2P lending looks like an attractive solution for many debtors, it actually contributes to the sustainment of the problematic debt industries in three ways:

1. P2P lending creates a new profit industry with multiple shareholders based on personal debts, and it contributes to the socially/economically patterned nature of the problem of overindebtedness.

P2P lending platforms bring together lenders and borrowers. Each stakeholder who is involved in this platform has the expectation of making a profit/gain. For instance, regardless of their motivation (financial gain or charity), lenders expect and make profit out of "peer" debt, whereas lending platforms make profit out of the relationship between lenders and borrowers. To fulfil the high-profit/gain expectations and to mitigate default risk, P2P lending platforms have evolved to employ highly selective criteria to select high-quality borrowers who do not typically represent the group that is most disproportionately affected by overindebtedness. The latter are the ones who are marginalised – for example, on a low income and/or unemployed (Conroy and O'Leary, 2005). Although P2P lending has become popular owing to its expanded focus to serve such marginal groups, lending platforms treat these people as an important source of profit. Even though these groups are "lucky enough" to secure a loan through P2P, they tend to receive significantly higher loan rates, which is a major contributor to loan default rates. This leads to an increased burden on already-troubled borrowers and broadens the pool of unpaid lenders. In this respect, P2P lending does not resolve the overindebtedness problem but instead exploits it for the same profit objective and contributes to the sustainment of a problematic debt industry.

2. P2P lending promotes the ideology that personal debt is a result of individual failure.

In P2P lending, investments by lenders are not guaranteed or insured by any governmental agency or third party. It is the lender's own risk and responsibility if the borrower does not repay their loans. Risks in P2P lending are shared among many investors through a reverse-auction process. Each lender invests a small amount in multiple loans and thereby shares the risk of a particular loan with other lenders in the system. Unlike in traditional lending, P2P lenders may learn about borrowers' credit quality before they invest in a loan as a result of greater transparency on both sides. It is the responsibility of lenders to decide whom to approve for a loan. This means that in the case of a loan default the lender will be considered as not having made a good decision and it being their "individual failure".

3. P2P lending is likely to add new members to the pool of individuals with personal debt while retaining already existing members by providing short-term, profit-oriented solutions.

Lenders in P2P loans use multiple sources, such as their own savings or bank credit, to invest in P2P lending. This suggests that not only borrowers who may not pay their loans back but also lenders who are not able to get their repayments from borrowers are at risk from physical and mental health problems (Drentea and Reynolds, 2012). Borrowers, who may be able to temporarily reduce the debt they owe to traditional financial intermediaries, are now driven into a new debt trap, with an increased vulnerability to chronic stress and its associated physical and mental health problems. Given that the potential borrowers in the applicant pool of P2P lending are more likely to come from marginalised and under-represented groups that would otherwise be rejected by traditional financial intermediaries, they are more likely to be doubly victimised when they get loans but cannot pay them back (Drentea and Reynolds, 2012). P2P lenders usually have their own compensation schemes in place to protect themselves in the event of a borrower default, but those schemes offer far from complete protection. When Prosper was established in the presence of restructured labour markets, stagnating wages, shrinking welfare, and neoliberal calls for security through the financial market and not the state, it aimed to offer services with lower interest rates to those who were disproportionately affected by the problem of debt. However, after it had experienced high rates of loan defaults, it revised its lending system and imposed more stringent eligibility criteria. Thus there is a tradeoff in P2P lending: P2P platforms may accept borrowers with low credit scores to the system, which means giving another chance to troubled borrowers, but it will also increase the default risk. Alternatively they can define certain eligibility requirements such as a minimum Fair Isaac Corporation (FICO) credit score (the standard US metric for measuring a borrower's creditworthiness) of 640, which will invite high-quality borrowers to the system but will also fail to attract potential investors due to lower returns resulting from lower risk. This lack of interest from lenders works to elevate interest rates, which will eventually harm borrowers and increase defaults.

How can we disrupt the debt cycle?

The debt cycle starts with missed payments on a loan, followed by penalties which are on top of any accruing interest, causing the overall debt to grow further. When missed payments occur, individuals who are already juggling their finances experience pressure from creditors and may be vulnerable to personal and financial breakdown. If lenders and borrowers agree on unrealistic repayment arrangements, this may result in legal proceedings in the form of a court setting a repayment schedule or an enforcement order (Fitch et al., 2007). Given that this whole spiral is also influenced by the factors surrounding individuals, disrupting the debt cycle is not easy. It requires a complete shift in our understanding of debt and debt management. Instead of focusing on moving individuals from financial difficulty to financial capability status, the long-term (as opposed to short-term) implications of policies, rules and regulations should be evaluated for sustainable solutions to the problem of overindebtedness.

First it is necessary and of great importance to redefine overindebtedness. Conventional definitions consider it to be individuals' inability to meet their household's commitments. This is an extremely reductionist and simplistic approach to the problem of overindebtedness and does not capture the complex nature of the problem. Overindebtedness should be redefined in the social, political and economic context in which it occurs.

Second, consumer protection should come high on the agenda of legislators. Rules pertaining to credit-granting should be tightened up by legislators so that credit institutions may not engage in unduly aggressive credit marketing. A legal framework that includes codes of conduct for lending institutions is necessary to prevent inconsiderate or even predatory lending. In addition to this, enhanced disclosure requirements should be imposed by credit legislation to provide more information to individuals so as to improve their decision-making. Full disclosure may prevent the aggressive use of so-called "hidden fees" by traditional credit institutions.

As argued by Klafft (2008), P2P lending networks have similarities with traditional banks regarding their challenges. Due to their similarities to the banking system and considering their fast growth rate, P2P platforms should be regulated more effectively to assure their integrity, improve their transparency and prevent them from going out of control and possibly collapsing. This would affect a substantial number of people, have serious consequences on the debt spiral and further restrain the overall lending conditions in the market. Similarities between the two systems bring to mind a regulatory approach that is similar to those for banks to regulate P2P platforms (Chaffee and Rapp, 2012). Such regulation will (1) clearly inform lenders and borrowers of the requirements to enter the system in advance and (2) break the debt spiral as well as prevent it from being a system-wide problem for all stakeholders who are involved in P2P lending.

Third, debt restructuring is essential for long-term solutions. To this end, an inclusive and comprehensive debt restructuring act is needed that will (1) give every individual who is heavily indebted the chance to solve their financial problems, (2) balance the contradictory interests of creditors and debtors and (3) make credit less readily available to reduce the prevalence of overindebtedness. To prevent social and financial exclusion, the act should also enable overindebted individuals to take an active part in their debt resolution. Moreover, non-profit organisations should be allowed to lend money in the form of "social credits" to individuals who are otherwise unable to obtain loans on reasonable terms and help them to restructure their finances. Since this option is very vulnerable to misuse, due consideration should be given to the formulation and enforcement of legal rules and regulations for this type of lending system.

Fourth, consumers' income and their ability to pay off debt should be re-evaluated to better reflect their individual income. In the early days of its inception, Prosper had relatively lax entry requirements that invited low- as well as high-risk borrowers to the system. This eventually led to higher default rates and a wane in investors' initial positive impression about P2P lending as an alternative channel for low-cost yet high-return investment. In the end, those investors who had taken a safe bet and invested in low-risk loans mostly got their money back, while others who tied themselves to higher-risk borrowers incurred significant loses. Accordingly, Prosper has revised its credit underwriting criteria. These revisions include stricter disclosure requirements regarding relevant financial information, as well as increased minimum credit quality. Results immediately appeared on a variety of measures, such as return on investment and percentage of delinquent loans. Although Prosper responded to this initial shock and revised its policies, a more structured regulatory approach is necessary to address systematic problems, especially in a fast-growing market such as P2P lending. Portfolio diversification is still the most effective strategy to mitigate loan-specific risk in P2P. While it is essential for lenders to spread their portfolio by investing in multiple loans across the range of high and low risk, the lack of necessary regulatory oversight, transparency and sufficient data makes investors as well as regulators concerned about risks such as lending fraud, identity theft and money laundering that these newly emerging online platforms are subject to. In this respect, greater transparency as well as credible and reliable information flow must be assured to establish a more effective information environment that will better serve investors in the long term. This could be achieved through regulatory involvement and oversight of the P2P marketplace.

A contracts act which specifically prevents the enforcement of oppressive contract conditions on debtors – regardless of the type of lending and the lending medium – is also needed. For instance, when a debtor makes a credit agreement which is out of proportion to their financial capacity, a creditor's unfair claims can be adjusted. This may discourage creditors from engaging in inconsiderate lending, which may then reduce the number of overindebted individuals.

In conclusion, the P2P lending system in the USA is a product of neoliberal policies that have led to the current problematic debt industry. P2P lending contributes to this industry by (1) creating a new profit area with multiple shareholders based on personal debts, (2) promoting the ideology that personal debt is a result of individual failure and (3) adding new members to the pool of individuals with personal debt while retaining the existing ones. In this respect, P2P lending does nothing more than pour old wine into a new bottle. Disrupting the debt cycle requires more radical and concerted efforts to restructure social, political and economic policies. This could not be achieved by a P2P lending platform that is rooted in the same neoliberal policies that are responsible for the problem of overindebtedness.

References

Akerlof, G. A. (1970). The market for "lemons": Quality uncertainty and the market mechanism. *The Quarterly Journal of Economics*, 84(3), 488–500.

Ashta, A. and Assadi, D. (2009). An analysis of European online microlending websites. *EMN 6th Annual Conference*, 33, 4–28. Milan: Fundación

Nantik Lum. Retrieved. http://www.european-microfinance.org/data/file/microlendingwebsites.doc.
Bachmann, A., Becker, A., Buerckner, D., Hilker, M., Kock, F., Lehmann, M. and Tiburtius, P. (2011). Online peer-to-peer lending – a literature review. *Journal of Internet Banking and Commerce*, 16(2), 1–18.
Berger, S. C. and Gleisner, F. (2008). Emergence of financial intermediaries on electronic markets: The case of online P2P lending. Retrieved. http://www.uni-graz.at/socialpolitik/papers/Gleisner.pdf.
Berger S. C. and Gleisner, F. (2009). Emergence of financial intermediaries on electronic markets: The case of online P2P lending. *Business Research*, 2(1), 39–65.
Brill, A. (2010). *Peer-to-Peer lending: Innovative Access to Credit and the Consequences of Dodd-Frank*. Washington Legal Foundation Backgrounder, Forthcoming. Available at SSRN. http://ssrn.com/abstract=2235661.
Ceyhan, S., Shi, X. and Leskovec, J. (2011). Dynamics of bidding in a P2P lending service: Effects of herding and predicting loan success. *Proceedings of the 20th International Conference on World Wide Web*, 547–556. ISBN: 978-1-4503-0632-4 doi:10.1145/1963405.196348.
Chaffee, E. C. and Rapp, G. C. (2012). Regulating online peer-to-peer lending in the aftermath of Dodd-Frank: In search of an evolving regulatory regime for an evolving industry. *Washington and Lee Law Review*, Forthcoming, University of Toledo Legal Studies Research Paper No 2012-2004. Retrieved SSRN. http://ssrn.com/abstract=1959884.
Conroy, P. and O'Leary, H. (2005). *Do the Poor Pay More? A Study of Lone Parents and Debt*. Dublin: OPEN – One Parent Exchange and Network.
Draut, T. (2005). *Strapped: Why America's 20 and 30-Something's Can't Get Ahead*. New York: Doubleday.
Drentea, P. and Reynolds, J. R. (2012). Neither a borrower nor a lender be: The relative importance of debt and SES for mental health among older adults. *Journal of Aging and Health*, 24(4), 673–695.
Dwyer, R. E., McCloud, L. and Hodson, R. (2012). Debt and graduation from American Universities. *Social Forces*, 90(4), 1133–1155.
Financial Services Authority (2009). *The impact of life events on financial capability: Evidence from the BHPS*. Prepared for the Financial Services Authority. Retrieved. http://www.fsa.gov.uk/pubs/consumer-research/crpr79.pdf.
Fitch, C., Simpson, A., Collard, S. and Teasdale, M. (2007). Mental health and debt: Challenges for knowledge, practice and identity. *Journal of Psychiatric and Mental Health Nursing*, 14(2), 128–133.
Greiner, M. E. and Wang, H. (2009). The role of social capital in people-to-people lending market places. *ICIS 2009 Proceedings*, 29.
Herrero-Lopez, S. (2009). Social interactions in P2P lending. *Proceedings of the 3rd Workshop on Social Network Mining and Analysis, Article No. 3*. ISBN: 978-1-60558-676-2. doi:10.1145/1731011.1731014.
Herzenstein, M., Dholakia, U. M. and Andrews, R. (2010). Strategic herding behavior in peer-to-peer loan auctions. Retrieved SSRN. http://ssrn.com/abstract=1596899.
Hunt, R. M. (2005). Whither consumer credit counseling? *Business Review*, 9, 13.
Iyer, R., Khwaja, A. I., Luttmer, E. F. P. and Shue, K. (2009). Screening peers softly: Inferring the quality of small borrowers. *NBER Working Paper* No 15242.
Kane, M. (2009). Ties run deep between subprime lenders and financial literary groups. *The Washington Independent*, November 12.

Klafft, M. (2008). Online peer-to-peer lending: A lenders' perspective. *Proceedings of the International Conference on E-Learning, E-Business, Enterprise Information Systems, and E-Government.* Retrieved SSRN. http://ssrn.com/abstract=1352352.

Lawless, R. M., Littwin, A. K., Porter, K. M., Pottow, J. A. E., Thorne, D. K. and Warren, E. (2008). Did bankruptcy reform fail? An empirical study of consumer debtors. *The American Bankruptcy Law Journal,* 82(3), 349–350.

Lin, M., Prabhala, N. R. and Viswanathan, S. (2009). Social networks as signalling mechanisms: Evidence from online peer-to-peer lending. Retrieved on May 20, 2014. http://pages.stern.nyu.edu/~bakos/wise/papers/wise2009-p09_paper.pdf.

Mahmud, T. (2012). Debt, discipline and the 99%: Neoliberal political economy and the working classes. (June 1, 2012). *Kentucky Law Journal, Forthcoming; Seattle University School of Law Research Paper No. 12–26.* Retrieved SSRN. http://ssrn.com/abstract=2072595.

Manbeck, P. and Hu, S. (2014). The regulation of peer-to-peer lending: A summary of the principal issues. Chapman and Cutler LLP. Retrieved on July 31. http://www.aba.com/Tools/Offers/Documents/Chapman_Regulation_of_Peer-to-Peer_Lending_0414.pdf.

Meltzer, H., Bebbington, P., Brugha, T., Jenkins, R., McManus, S. and Dennis, M. S. (2011). Personal debt and suicidal ideation. *Psychological Medicine,* 41(4), 771–778.

Petersen, M. A. and Rajan, R. G. (1994). The effect of credit market competition on lending relationships. *Quarterly Journal of Economics,* 110(2), 407–414.

Petersen, M. A. and Rajan, R. G. (2002). Does distance still matter? The information revolution in small business lending. *Journal of Finance,* 57, 2533–2570.

Pope, D. G. and Sydnor, J. R. (2008). What's in a picture? Evidence of discrimination from Prosper.com. Retrieved SSRN. http://ssrn.com/abstract=1220902.

Renton, P. (2012). Peer to peer lending crosses $1 billion in loans issued. *Techcrunch.* Retrieved on February 25, 2014. http://techcrunch.com/2012/05/29/peer-to-peer-lending-crosses-1-billion-in-loans-issued/.

Schicks, J. (2014). Over-indebtedness in Microfinance – an empirical analysis of related factors on the borrower level. *World Development,* 54, 301–324.

Walker, C. (2011). Personal debt, cognitive delinquency and techniques of governmentality: Neoliberal constructions of financial inadequacy in the UK. *Journal of Community and Applied Social Psychology,* 22, 533–538.

White House (2009). *Press Release, Office of the Press Secretary of the White House, Fact Sheet: Reforms to Protect American Credit Card Holders.* Retrieved. http://www.whitehouse.gov/the_press_office/Fact-Sheet-Reforms-to-Protect-American-Credit-Card-Holders.

Witte, D. S. (2010). The bear hug that is crushing debt-burdened Americans: Why overzealous regulation of the debt-settlement industry ultimately harms the consumers it means to protect. *The Texas Review of Law & Politics,* 14, 277–298.

Woolsey, B. and Schulz, M. (2009). Credit card statistics, industry facts, debt statistics, creditcards.com. Retrieved. http://www.creditcards.com/credit-card-news/credit-card-industry-facts-personal-debt-statistics-1276.php.

Yum, H., Lee, B. and Chae, M. (2012). From the wisdom of crowds to my own judgment in microfinance through online peer-to-peer lending platforms. *Electronic Commerce Research and Applications,* 11(5), 469–483.

12
Thinking about the Personal Debt Industry: Voices from Puerto Rico

Dolores S. Miranda Gierbolini and Ida de Jesús Collazo

Personal debt is not a theme that you would find among most psychology research in Puerto Rico. It is typically problematised as a personal deficit which psychologists may contribute to help overcome. Yet it can also be conceptualised as part of the modernisation of capitalism. This approach suggests that modern capitalism, with its particular model of democracy, is dependent on a political economy of personal debt. What's more, such debt is part of the price of inequality (Stiglitz, 2013) that is the product of this political economy.

Countries around the globe have been engaged in public debt and currently strive to survive the worldwide economic crisis of capitalism. This has been the situation for members of the G20, such as the USA, which are facing economic crisis in times of globalisation and neoliberalism. This situation has contributed to increased social inequality and reduced democracy (Giroux, 2008; Stiglitz, 2013).

This chapter will present an overview of the social-historical context of Puerto Rico as a colony of the USA, a general view of personal debt in Puerto Rico, its impact, the debt industry which sustains it and the various resources to overcome it. It will close by addressing the problem from a broader social inequality perspective and suggest alternatives that families and communities could engage in as a means to build a better world.

Social historical background

Wandering around the different corners of the planet has made us realise that Puerto Rico is barely known by our colleagues in different countries. Some recognise us as part of the USA, while others consider us to be part of Latin America or the Caribbean. The truth is that the island is part of all three, and they all contribute to the various identities that are shared by Puerto Ricans. It is a *mestiza* composite which has diverse subjectivities and world visions. Yet there is an objective context which links us directly to the common ground shared with the USA in terms of economic development, which merits explanation as we inquire into personal debt.

In 1493, Puerto Rico, also known as Borikén, where part of the Taino nation was established, was invaded and conquered by Spain. The Spanish settled on the island and established a colonial relationship until it was occupied by the USA in 1898. Currently, Puerto Rico is a territory and colony of the USA. Although as of 1952 we were declared a commonwealth, our constitution is subject to that of the USA. We have a shared history of colonialism and African slavery with Latin America and the Caribbean.

During the second half of the 20th century, our government was concentrating on the implementation of modernisation via industrialisation, a political – economic model known as Operation Bootstrap. This was an effort to modernise the country, within a capitalist perspective, and was dependent on the USA and the influx of foreign investment evolving within the circuit of US capital and its manufacturing sector. This operation was elaborated as a great social experiment that was referred to as the "Pacific Revolution" (Rivera Medina and Ramirez, 1985). As such it had a chance to develop its own economic model subject to US economy and politics. This context created and sustained the conditions for dependency at multiple levels. It enhanced the US world vision, while underestimating and denigrating the world vision of Puerto Ricans. Our culture was considered premodern and pseudofeudal. The working relations were predominantly agricultural, where the owner of the land dominated the life of the land croppers. In this sense, any reference to the Puerto Rican perspective was considered and construed as retrograde and an obstacle to progress. Historically we were considered lazy because of our relaxed, relational and romantic way of life – one that contrasted with modern capitalism. The population predominantly lived in poor conditions.

It is important to note that, historically, there have been pro-independence efforts utilising a range of tactics, including both political and armed. The independence movement was criminalised through legislation that was referred to as *Ley de la mordaza* or the "Gag Law" (Acosta Lespier, 1987). This created a social imaginary of fear towards pro-independence organisations. The law made it a crime to promote, advocate, counsel or preach – voluntarily or knowingly – the need or desire to overthrow or paralyse the insular government (local Puerto Rican government) by force or violence. It also prohibited printing, publishing, editing, selling and exhibiting information; organising or helping any organisation, group or assembly of persons who encouraged any intention to overthrow, paralyse or destroy the insular government as a political tactic and struggle of pro-independence. Throughout the 1950s a combination of laws and repression was enough to criminalise the independence movement and reduce significantly the organisations and leaders that supported it. The Gag Law was a copy of the Smith Act within the USA, which was applied to Puerto Rico. This act, officially known as the Alien Registration Act of 1940, criminalised advocating the overthrow of the US government. All adult foreigners who were residents of the USA had to register with the government. It was abolished in 1957 when the US Supreme Court declared it unconstitutional.

Furthermore, schooling was instrumental for the Americanisation of the Puerto Ricans (Negrón de Montilla, 1977). Under the Spanish government, the schooling of Puerto Ricans was not a system of public education as we know today; rather, it was implemented through the power of the Catholic Church (Osuna, 1949). Very few (mostly from the upper class) went to school. Under US occupation a more robust system of free public school was implemented. Public schools provided a context in which religious education was not allowed, thus opening a valve for the weakening of the Catholic Church's control over the population. Moreover, during its first decades, teaching was in English and served as a civilising mission.

As was established earlier, Operation Bootstrap became the main economic and political project in Puerto Rico in the second half of the 20th century. Its glorious years, from the point of view of modernisation and economic indicators, were from 1950 to the mid-1970s. Its decline, as economic indicators show, began thereafter when structural problems with the development path emerged. Meanwhile it contributed to the relief of poverty, while at the same time preparing the population for modern times and for a partnership under the imperial wing of the USA. There were, however, social problems that accompanied such fast-track modernisation, such as the growth of urban slums to accommodate the mass of rural workers who were moving in search of opportunities to improve their lives.

As the 21st century approached, Puerto Rico was impacted by neoliberal policies, through both the USA and local government strategies. The neoliberal vision which springs from 18th-century classical economics postulates government intervention in the economy as the main culprit of capitalism's cyclical crises. Should there be no intervention in the sense of regulation to the private sector, the crises would automatically find adjustments towards equilibrium. History does not validate such a conclusion. The neoliberal objective of minimising the role of government translates itself into policies which are highly restrictive, particularly those affecting government employment and expenditures in social programmes. In the case of Puerto Rico the effects of the restrictive nature of neoliberal policies on the population in general and the workers in particular were somehow ameliorated by the federal government's social assistance programmes and appropriations for infrastructure. Despite this there has been a recent increase in the percentage of individuals under the poverty line from 44.6% in 2000 to 45.1% in 2012 (US Census Bureau). This increase significantly underestimates the differential effects on households that are headed by women.

Federal government transfers to Puerto Rico over USD 13 billion each year (Caribbean Business, 2013). Most federal programmes extend to Puerto Rico and with them their economic and political interests. The federal government controls customs, immigration, interstate trade and the licensing of radio and TV stations. It regulates financial institutions, telecommunications, and air and maritime carriers (Caribbean Business, 2013). Puerto Rico has its own social assistance programmes but most of these depend on federal funds.

A special report of the Comisión Económica para América Latina (CEPAL) in 2005 concluded that the economic relations between Puerto Rico and the USA could be analysed from a cost–benefit perspective. These benefits include emigration as an escape valve. We are US citizens, and this valve reduces unemployment tensions; we share the US currency, and we qualify for most federal transfer payments which serve as social shock absorbers. The USA has also contributed labour legislation, which has promoted better salaries and labour conditions. Poverty overall has been reduced and society modernised. However, entering the 21st century, things have taken a different turn. As of March 2012, Puerto Rico's public debt was USD 69,275 billion and exceeded the country's gross national product (Marxuach, 2012). During the years 2006–2011, Puerto Rico has experienced the contraction of its economy. Its growth was 0.4% in 2012 and 0.6% in 2013. The official unemployment rate has remained well above 15% and a major concern is the striking reality of a 39% labour force participation rate (Marxuach, 2012). The remaining 61% fall into different categories, such as housewives, students, disabled, retired and those at voluntary leisure, among others.

Public debt

There is a general understanding which considers debt, both at the national and personal level, as a result of irresponsible behaviour. It is an attribute that refers to irresponsible spending while maintaining a standard of living when income has significantly been reduced. This is the image that is projected by the media (McChesney, 2004). Caraballo considers that the problem is due to a culture of consumption where buying has a psychological reward. He suggests that it's a compulsion that is out of control (Delgado Castro, 2013). Although this perception may have some empirical support, it is also true that the economic crisis which we face goes beyond plain personal irresponsibility. Fostering a consumption culture has been the main strategic target of capitalism. At the local level, government expenditure may be, in part, the result of vote-catching projects but it is expenditure financed by public debt. However, it must be stressed that public debt is also a profit-generating business with a very strong institutional infrastructure and endorsed by the main economies of the world. What constitutes public debt for governments globally translates into private profit for a group of corporations.

Yet the social responsibility of delivering services and social investment on behalf of government has its economic toll, especially in the form of corporate welfare (Bandow, 2012). The limitation of government's capacity to comply with social responsibilities such as social services, education and health is due to the complicated interrelationship between capital and state, as mentioned earlier.

In the case of Puerto Rico, since the 1970s, public debt has become the instrument to manage government's structural deficits, while facilitating projects for political purposes. This practice, which has been generating debt at an increasing rate, is so entrenched in the government that it has been very close to declaring an incapacity to absorb even its payroll. This year, for example, we are expected to pay USD 900 million due to the current debt of 2013. While local government has increased our public debt, the population has been struck with increases in utility bills and taxes, even though Puerto Ricans have not witnessed significant public works in recent years.

Alameda has suggested that, at the local level, this is due to political party responses to populism (Cortes, 2013). As an example, in the face of the economic crisis it is quite popular for governments to boost the economy through infrastructure works. This was the US Keynesian government's strategy during the Great Depression. In this recent recession, Puerto Rico benefited from the economic investment that President Obama made to address the economic crisis through the American

Recovery and Reconstruction Act. Alameda affirms that the funds that we received were spent on education and the police (Cortes, 2013). We suggest that this was a strategy which did not result in boosting the economy because it was not invested in economic development projects.

Acosta has stated that the local economic situation has worsened due to changes in US Congress which have approved legislation regarding the taxation of companies which have invested in foreign countries (Cortes, 2013). In the case of Puerto Rico it has meant the elimination of Section 936 of the Federal Internal Revenue Code, which excused the companies from paying taxes locally, and at the federal level, as an economic incentive for the reinvestment of profits in the territories of the USA. Current legislation treats Puerto Rico as a foreign country, so the money repatriated to the USA incurs 15% in taxes (Cortes, 2013) and hence reduces the incentive to invest here. This possible effect on the incentive to invest is due to the fact that Puerto Rico's development strategy has fully depended on tax exemptions for US corporations. Since we are required to abide by local and federal labour laws and protections, our salaries and taxes compare unfavourably with other countries. Even with total local exemption of taxes, the other costs that are related to making business in Puerto Rico seem to be disadvantageous. Local government has bet on these types of incentive to boost the economy, but it seems to go nowhere. Therefore the economy has taken a turn for the worse.

The government at the local level has insisted on downsizing government and eliminating thousands of jobs. It has increased income tax for the middle class and applied an 8% sales tax. Unemployment has increased and this has impoverished the middle class. In 2009 the Puerto Rican legislature approved a plan to eliminate 20,000 public employees' jobs in the middle of the worst recession since the 1930s. This is the most aggressive response of the government to the economic crisis. Furthermore, as a result of this austerity measure, an estimated 800,000 people have migrated to the USA in the last decade.

Personal impact

The rise in various taxes and the cost of living has become quite noticeable in the resulting increase in corporate and personal bankruptcies (Velazquez, 2013). As of May 2013, individual bankruptcy had increased by 73% compared with the previous year. Quiñones confirms that the US Bureau of Labor Statistics revealed that employment has fallen by

36,900 (Velázquez, 2013). In 2014, 5,454 families filed for bankruptcy. The high unemployment rates and the relatively high cost of living have been identified as two of the main reasons why more people have lost their fear of bankruptcy processes and filed for bankruptcy. Previously they were fearful because filing for bankruptcy meant losing status – people are judged as failures, and particularly men. However, filing for bankruptcy gives them a chance to start at zero and to restructure their lives (Velázquez, 2013). Nevertheless, Quiñones (Velazquez, 2013) considers that filing for bankruptcy is considered to be the last option. People want to pay their debts but they cannot comply due to the significant increase in cost of living, as well the reduced income of unemployment compensation. Filing for bankruptcy does not mean that they are exempt from paying for child support, income tax debts and student loans.

Although the cost of living has risen, income has fallen and bankruptcy has increased, people are doing their best to meet their responsibilities. Knowing this, there has been a boost in the debt industry – in particular, enterprises which are geared towards providing services to those who are in debt. The banks provide alternatives for those who meet the requirements of capacity to pay and are "honestly" in debt due to the shifts in the economy. Alternatives include debt consolidation and personal loans. Others include debt-management agencies, which negotiate with creditors to reduce interest and charges. There are credit-counselling agencies which provide guidance and counselling to avoid future problems. In each case, responsibility is placed on the individual.

The government has legislated policies which, to a certain extent, intend to provide protection to those who are in debt. These are mitigating remedies:

Law 184 (2012) of Compulsory Mediation This has the intention of providing the individual with basic protection if there is a risk of eviction from their residence. This will not cover situations in which the debt is with the Internal Revenue. It should protect the individual from unfair eviction from their homes or foreclosure. This law obligates a mediation process to help those who are on the brink of losing their home to engage with the financing entity and reach a satisfying agreement. The financing entity has to present all of the options.

Law 195 (2011) to Protect the Main Home This is referred to as the secure home law. It aims to protect the owners from embargo, sentencing or eviction when there is an order to pay all debts. Again, it does not apply if there are tax debts or debts with a construction company, or when the mortgage is on protected property.

No appraisal of the results of these laws is available owing to their recent approval.

An alternative perspective

Globalisation for the upper 1% of the population means tax avoidance and influence in politics. Indebted countries lose their sovereignty to their creditors as they succumb to the will of the financial markets (Stiglitz, 2013). If the country does not comply with what the financial markets want, the latter threaten to downgrade the ratings, to pull out their money and to raise interest rates (Stiglitz, 2013). We have witnessed how these threats are usually effective. In the case of Puerto Rico, the four-year period from January 2009 to January 2013 saw the neoliberal policies of the government directly justified by the warnings of Standard and Poor's and Moody's: 17,000 government employees were dismissed, early retirement options were put in place, the public university's tuition rates were significantly increased, and there were budget cuts for all agencies concerned with direct services to the population, among others. The debt arguments centre on taxation and government contraction to reduce spending levels as solutions. They ignore the problems of unemployment levels and growing inequality (Stiglitz, 2013). Downsizing government, instead of investing in good education and technologies to increase skills in labour and to protect the environment, increases inequality. Nevertheless, the sovereign debt discourse avoids the issue of the considerable increase in inequality, placing the emphasis at the personal level (Stiglitz, 2013). However, the real emphasis from an economic perspective should be placed on seriously addressing and reducing inequality. Furthermore, Stiglitz (2013) states that

> one of the ways of the top of making money is by taking advantage of their market and political power to favor themselves, to increase their income at the expense of the rest. They are experts in rent seeking: making markets less transparent, taking advantage of asymmetries of information selling securities that they had design to fail, but knowing that the buyers did not know, taking excess risks with government holding a lifeline, bailing them out and assuming the losses, getting money from the Federal Reserve. The most egregious has been the ability of those in the financial sector to take advantage of the poor and uniformed, as they made enormous amounts of money by

preying upon these groups with predatory lending and abusive credit card practices. (p. 43)

He affirms that an efficient government with a sense of social justice would prohibit these practices. He states that government did not put an end to them in 2007 when it became clear what was happening. The reason was that the financial sector had invested heavily in lobbying and campaign contributions, and the investment paid off. Zizek (2012) agrees, suggesting that the state has a tendency to support the elite – economically and politically. The formal bourgeoisie are a waged bourgeoisie which demand high salaries, claiming that they have high productivity. This is also the case for the CEOs in both public and private corporations. There is downsizing in order to sustain these salaries, while there are salary cuts for those in the lower social echelon in the production line in order to retain their jobs.

Higher education, paradoxically, has contributed to personal debt. The cost of higher education has increased, particularly at the graduate level. Middle- and lower-class students at all levels draw on students loans. Once they start their higher education, they become easy prey for the banks. This is part of a government shift in its vision of what education represents for the individual versus society. Through neoliberal policies there has been a shift of financing to the student and the family. What's more, due to the economic crisis, students at times live on their student loans, credit cards and part-time jobs.

In the case of psychology graduate studies, Novotney (2013) reports that the American Psychological Association's last survey of doctoral students reveals that the debt among psychology graduate students varies from USD 30,000 to USD 120,000. Ghoroury et al. (2012) found that among 364 graduate students whom they interviewed, 70% expressed considerable financial debt as being among the stressors which interfered with their optimal functioning. Novotney (2013) suggests that these, among other concerns, do not end as the students graduate. As an example, she states that they make large payments every month and realise that they will continue to pay until they die. This is further aggravated by the reality of the reduction in employment creation which characterises the technological era of capitalism. Facing this reality is depressing.

Personal debt and mental health

Personal debt is associated with specific common mental disorders (Meltzer et al., 2013). In UK research, Meltzer et al. (2013) found that there was a relation between debt and common specific disorders which included generalised anxiety disorder, depression, obsessive-compulsive disorder, phobia, panic disorder, mixed anxiety and depressive disorder. Those engaged in addictive behaviour showed an increased likelihood of indebtedness. Common mental disorders were not related to specific types of debt. Yet there is an increased likelihood of debt among some sociodemographic and socioeconomic groups: 16–34 year olds, women, unmarried adults, unemployed people and those in rented accommodation. Although this emphasises the individual's mental health, it appears to show the importance of social economic phenomena that surround personal debt.

Fitch, Hamilton, Bassett and Davey (2011) reviewed 50 articles that relate debt with mental health. Finally, nine studies were analysed in which two associated indebtedness with poor mental health. These studies cannot confirm a causal relationship between debt and mental illness. Specific responses such as anger, frustration, sadness and anxiety can be associated with indebtedness, but these are not to be considered abnormal reactions to such a situation. People look forward to paying their debts. Yet debt may have a chain of complications as a result of events which evolve around it. Consider the aggressiveness of the creditors and their collecting efforts. Interpersonal and family relationships are at times lacerated, but they can be reconciled by facing the situation together, or developing support from other family members and friends.

No study in Puerto Rico has collected data that relates to the personal and psychological impact of debt. In our social community workshop we have come across situations that are attributed to personal debt. It could be said that in the past six years there have been youth suicide attempts due to the impact of personal debt on families which have lost the job of the main provider, lost their home and changed their everyday life. The number of homeless families has increased. In a population that was estimated at 3,808,610 between 2000 and 2008, the count of homeless was around 3,445 in 2011.

Emigration has increased with the increase in unemployment and personal debts. Most Puerto Rican migrants go to the USA. Some face language barriers and the other stressors that migration presents. Migration also has a psychological burden on the families who are left behind. Young professionals are among the groups that are now migrating. This is conceptually approached as a loss (brain drain). When in 2009 the government made 20,000 people unemployed, the mainstream discourse became a call for psychotherapy. At that time, organised psychologists in the Puerto Rico Psychology Association, the Social Community

Workshop and various psychology departments, denounced the problem as major structural and institutional violence. An attempt was made to shift the discussion towards social inequality and how the government measures were exacerbating the situation.

Is there any hope?

As we entered the 21st century, hopes on behalf of the state and the corporate world were placed on neoliberalism and globalisation. The promises of success of this economic paradigm have not been kept. On the contrary, the world has to live with uncertainty (Bauman, 2003) which means no stable and secure jobs, and no government protection. This discourse has contributed to a loss of trust and generalised hopelessness. It has produced the fourth world described by Beck (2000), the abandoned (Povinelli, 2011) and the dispossessed (Butler and Althanasiou, 2013). The question we raise is whether these populations, in alliance with civic society, can rebuild trust and hope, and create a social project for a better world.

At the local level in Puerto Rico we have lived the *sumud*, a Palestinian concept which refers to enduring and resisting. We have been able to value our family and gregariousness or collective sense and put together efforts to face adversity. In that process, strength is built and enhanced. Families have taken in homeless children and redefined the extended family, which has been lost in modernity. A potent subterranean economy in the area of services such as home repairs, housecleaning, childcare, elderly care and food preparation has grown. It remains to be seen if a new promising sociology of the family emerges. We have no doubt that the new extended family contributes to rescue cooperation, collectivism and solidarity as priority values, contrary to the competitive individual. The challenge is to learn to live with diversity and not fall into a reactionary attitude that glorifies the past.

We have some experience of where families and the community stand by each other and engage in developing sources of income through social/economic projects. They are oriented by cooperation, networking, citizen participation and sustainable development. As in other countries, we have community socioeconomic proposals which face their problems and are promising. Since the 1980s there have been community movements that are geared towards breaking with the dependency on government and the USA. The developments have been slow but have increased with the economic crisis of the 21st century. While we still direct efforts and claims to government, we are also trying to develop by returning to the land and sea, rescuing traditional trades, producing food and developing small businesses within a collectivist framework. As a result, we are engaged in building on direct democracy, collectivist enterprises, alliances with communities and social sectors, and the protection of our environment. The economic proposals have rescued our agriculture, coasts, mountains and impoverished urban populations from the developers and rent-seeking predators. We have rescued, although still on a small scale, traditional trades such as agriculture, fishing, arts and crafts. The journey is long and uphill, and it can be rocky, but there has been much noticeable progress.

As people work with others, trust is restored. Trust and hope for the future leads us to our final comments. Authors such as Stiglitz (2013) and Dicken (2011) are convinced that a better world is possible. For it to happen, social inequality must be addressed and reduced considerably, locally and globally.

Rivera Ramos (2012) emphasises the importance of addressing social inequality which underlies the economic crisis and personal debt. He states that trust is an important variable to propel the economy, even in places which do not have strong institutions. He questions the popular belief that economic development rests solely upon the strength of a community's traditional institutions. On another note, Marxuach (2013) emphasises on the relation between inequality and growth. As suggested by Stiglitz (2013), social inequality is a hindrance to economic development. It has an adverse effect on consumption, education, students' school performance, debt, speculation, political stability, mental health, life expectancy, infant mortality, obesity, homicides, incarceration and general quality of life. It lacerates trust and, with it, democracy (Marxuach, 2013). Rivera (2012) states that tackling social inequality is indispensable in recreating trust among citizens. It has serious implications for public policies and developmental plans. If this is assumed as correct then the state, private enterprise, philanthropic organisations, universities, research centres and citizens, among others, can contribute to addressing inequality as being central to future economic and political plans and policies.

On a more macrosocial level, Stiglitz (2013) considers that a better world is possible if plans and policies for more social equality are agreed and implemented. He suggests the following:

- An economic agenda reform which is directed at curbing excesses at the top, curbing the financial sector, enforcing competition laws more strongly and effectively, limiting the power of CEOs, reforming

bankruptcy laws comprehensively, ending government giveaways to the top, ending corporate welfare, implementing legal reforms which democratise access to justice and diminish the arms race, undertaking tax reforms, creating a more progressive income and corporate tax system, and more effectively enforcing the estate tax system to prevent the creation of a new oligarchy.
- Helping the rest: improving access to education, helping ordinary citizens to save, providing healthcare for all, strengthening social protection programmes, and restoring and maintaining full employment.
- Creating a new social compact: supporting workers' and citizens' collective action, and taking affirmative action to eliminate the legacy of discrimination,
- Restoring sustainable and equitable growth: introducing a growth agenda based on public investment, and redirecting investment and innovation to preserve jobs and the environment.

We are aware that these suggestions are resisted by government, and more so by the wealthy. Citizens have become more aware of the threat to the future. They demand participation in government economic decisions yet are still far from these alternatives. Government co-optation is still strong, but the community groups have maintained their struggle and activism, strengthened by alliances among each other. For example, there are regional alliances to develop community enterprises along the ecotourism and food production lines, and the model forest alternative has been approved by government to protect parts of the north coast and mountain areas from development interests at the expense of our natural resources. Resistance leads to a spectrum of actions but it will probably take major social unrest before these alternatives have a real chance.

Dickens (2011, p. 550) suggests that we "must think [of] the kind of world we and our children would want to live [in]". We advocate critical citizen participation which must have this issue on its agenda. Thinking of an alternative future demands consideration of an alternative economy. We propose considering a community economy (Dicken, 2011). It is probably not a matter of globalisation or antiglobalisation, but perhaps to decide how and where to build a sense of place in the world. We need openness and diversity on the global agenda to eradicate poverty.

If we as citizens work to consider these and other proposals, we are already making a better world possible. On a local level, as Marxuach (2013) says,

Puerto Rico is on the route to convert itself into a post-industrial waste land characterized by corruption, crime, unemployment, urban decomposition, and poverty. In order to avoid this destiny, it has to engage in agreements as a country in order to strengthen civic culture, reform government fiscal policies, and build a true economic development strategy.

The future depends on us, as citizens, actively engaging in building our future. We must start with the belief that we depend on the traditional, political and economic institutions which have fostered our despair. As Marxuach (2013) suggests, we must decide to take this journey or leave the colonial relic to whatever destiny has to offer. We believe we can make our destiny. As we face this historic personal debt issue, inevitably we have to go beyond the personal to address history. In doing so we have a chance to initiate a journey to the Puerto Rico that we, and future generations, will want to live in.

References

Acosta Lespier, I (1987). *La mordaza*. San Juan: Editorial Edil.
Bandow, D. (2012). Contributor forbes. *Where to Cut the Federal Budget? Start by Killing Corporate Welfare*. Retrieved on September 29, 2013. http://www.forbes.com/sites/dougbandow/2012/08/20/where-to-cut-the-federal-budgetstart-by-killing-corporate-welfare/.
Bauman, Z. (2003). *En busca de la politica*. Buenos Aires: Fondo de Cultura Econmica.
Beck, U. (2000). *World Risk Society*. Cambridge, UK: Polity Press.
Butler, J. and Athanasiou A. (2013). *Dispossession: The Performative in the Political*. Cambridge, UK: Polity Press.
Caribbean Business (2013). *Puerto Rico's Relationship with the US Federal Government*. September 22.
CEPAL (2005). *Globalización y desarrollo: desafío de Puerto Rico en el siglo XXI*. México, DF: México DF, CEPAL
Cortes Chico, R. (2013). Una deuda con padre y madre. Serie especial. *El Nuevo Día*. 5–7
Delgado, Castro I. (2013). Delirio por comprar. *El Nuevo Día*.7 de septiembre 4–5
Dicken, P. (2011). *Global Shift, Mapping the Changing Contours of the World Economy*. New York: The Guildford Press
Fitch, C., Hamilton, S., Bassett, P. and Davey, R. (2011). The relationship between personal debt and mental health: A systemic review. *Mental Health Review Journal*, 16(4), 153–166.
Ghoroury, E., Hassan, N., Galper, D. I. and Bufta, L. (2012). Stress, coping and barriers to wellness among psychology graduate students. *Training and Education in Professsional Psychology*, 6(2), 122–134.
Giroux, H. (2008). *Against the Terror of Neoliberalism: Politics Beyond the Age of Greed*. Boulder: Paradigm Publisher.

Marxuach, S. (2013). *Despues del 30 de junio*. Center for a New Economy. Grupocne.org /2013/06/30/despues-del-30-de-junio/.

Marxuach, S. (2012). *Cinco prioridades de política económica y fiscal para el nuevo gobernador*. Center for a New Economy. Grpocne.org/2012/12/17/cincpprioridades-de.politica economica.y-fiscal-para-el-nuevo-governador/.

Meltzer, H., Bebbington, P. E., Brugha, T. S., Parrell, M., and Jenkins, R. (2013). The relationship between personal debt and specific common mental disorders. *European Journal of Public Health*, February, 23(1), 108–113. doi:10.1093/epub March 20, 2012.

Negrón de Montilla, A. (1977). *La americanización de Puerto Rico: Sistema de instrucción* (1900–1930). San Juan: Universidad de Puerto Rico Press

Novotney, A. (2013). Facing up to debt. *GradPsych Magazine*. American Psychological Association. January, p. 32

Osuna, J. J. (1949) *A histoy of education in Puerto Rico*. San Juan: Editorial Universidad de Puerto Rico

Povinelli, E. A. (2011). *Economies of Abandonment, Social Belonging and Endurance in Late Liberalism*. Durham and London: Duke University Press.

Rivera Medina, E. and Ramirez, R. (1985). *Del cañaveral a la fábrica*. San Juan: Huracanes Academia.

Rivera Ramos, E. (2012). Mensaje de cierre. *Annual Economic Conference. Center for the New Economy*. Posted February 15.

Stiglitz, J. (2013). *The Price of Inequality*. New York: Norton and Company.

Velazquez, B. (2013). Un salvavidas ante las deudas. *El Nuevo Día*. 7 de junio, 5–7.

Zizek, S. (2012) *The year of living dangerously*. London: Verso.

13
Personal Debt in Third-World Latin American Society

Douglas Marlon Arévalo Mira[1]

> All debtors in El Salvador live under conditions that mean that they will need credit forever. This maintains a state of psychological distress especially in the face of multiple psychosocial challenges which restrict access to basic rights such as housing and health.
>
> (Douglas Mira, 2015)

The cycle of personal debt: A case study

When Chico was young, he began his working life in a factory in the metropolitan area of San Salvador. The factory paid its employees a minimum wage (USD 219.35, EUR 164.21). Chico was single and saved money in the bank, and another portion of his salary was used to support his family. Over time the cost of living and the cost of consumer goods rose. Given this situation and the freezing of wages, he had to resort to borrowing money from co-workers whom he sometimes had to pay back and sometimes did not.

As he got older, Chico acquired new responsibilities, such as paying for a family, food and clothing. The ideal of all Salvadorians is to live better, and to own a home and a car, but the actual economic conditions mean that only 25% of the population have a formal job and only around 18.3% own their home (MINEC, 2007). There are others who achieve lower house prices and better conditions and they are the ones who obtain the facilities that are offered by the programme House for All (Quintanilla, 2010). Hare (1999; cited in Arévalo Mira, 2011) suggests that such circumstances generate dissatisfaction.

In this situation, Chico needed to find other alternatives to improve his living conditions. However, because he could not take care of his large debts, he entered the world of formal credit through a personal loan for the purchase of goods or services, such as household items, business requirements and repairs. His first contact with the banking system was characterised by their lending money immediately, with few requirements, and it involved a limited investment. The offer of loans with minimal requirements and extended balances have proliferated disproportionately in recent years (Ferguson, 2010).

Motivation theory, from the point of view of behaviourism (Pérez Fernández et al., 2005), suggests that the ease with which somebody receives one of the more "powerful" reinforcers (money) reinforces the behaviour of acquiring, when necessary, one or more loans, precisely because this allows people to easily obtain a range of reinforcers such as goods, services or food. Chico discovered that the bank would provide him with certain facilities that would allow him to achieve his "dream", a situation that facilitated his acquisition of more financial products.

Once he had acquired a quick loan for general spending, Chico could request a personal loan for wider projects or a refinance loan to complete a purchase. He was reaching the age when it was expected that he would buy a house for his new family, so this created the need for him to acquire a home loan. Here he moved from a simple to a more complex debt.

The credit conditions changed when Chico got married and took on family responsibilities. This life change led to the uprooting of his family of origin. For some families in El Salvador, debts are assumed by several family members and these must be added to the payment of private hospital services, life insurance and health insurance, which already represent a considerable expense.

In this way for Chico, personal debt would continue growing, including debts to informal groups, the costs of exchanging houses, bank debts, hospital costs, insurance bills, social security and pension payments. While the latter two are not direct debts, they affect purchasing power because they are taken directly from the salary. Some years later, Chico advanced in his factory job (although many will not). Once they have been promoted, people acquire other responsibilities as a result of their changing living conditions related to this new role, such as the acquisition of vehicles, a house in a new residential area, other places for recreation for the family and other schools for the children. Now banks will offer new loan products, new balances on their credit cards and larger loans. At this point, what Chico and others really need is guidance or advice about resource management, costs and saving money but, paradoxically, the institutions that provide credit education are often the banks offering credit. Salvadoran workers are unprotected from the debt spiral partly because they receive an education about spending not from the state but from the institutions that increasingly reduce their income and increase their debt.

Chico's previously friendly relationship with his bank was suspended after a delay in payment occurred. Credit education communication disappeared and then began persecution by telephone, mail or courier, and threats of legal consequences if there were any further delays. This behaviour can be understood by the following popular saying: "tanto fue el cántaro al río que al fin se quebró" (If you keep filling a pitcher with water it will eventually break).

In this situation, Chico could play the role of lender to other employees, allowing a new group of young employees to start their way into loans and credit. With the income that he receives he has the opportunity to meet some of his debt expenses, but as time progresses and the debt increase, he needs to get another job to pay the deficit.

The future, in most cases, is ominous. Chico may move towards a stressful retirement. And while it is true that some people overcome their debts because they take action in time and cancel their credit cards, close credits or group their loans into one account, a great many are less fortunate. For many the debt accompanies them until their retirement. Some banks consider that the debt ceases with the death of the owner, but others assign the debt to guarantors or co-debtors, and so debts are transferred to their families. Thus many are currently carrying inherited debts that will be paid by future generations.

The context of personal debt in El Salvador

The Republic of El Salvador has a territory of 21,041 km² with a population of 6,288,000 inhabitants. According to the United Nations Development Programme (UNDP) (2013), the Human Development Index (HDI) is 0.680, ranking it as 107th of 187 countries. The HDI is a measure of human development potential. It is constructed from three dimensions: the possibility of a long and healthy life, achieving a decent standard of living and access to knowledge-education (UNDP, 2013). These three are closely related to personal indebtedness.

It is important to contextualise personal debt as part of the social processes of a country that is categorised as lower middle income (CECLAC, 2012, p. 8). The 34th session of CECLAC (2012) has allowed a reformulation of some aspects of international support with a view to overcoming poverty. CECLAC considers that in El Salvador it is necessary to address the issues of income per capita, inequality, poverty, investment savings, innovation, infrastructure, education, health, taxation, gender and the environment. With some of these there are no direct indicators of the situation in El Salvador, which represents a challenge when generating the relevant reports to design public policies.

The US has quintupled its income levels compared with the region, showing that the income gap between developed and developing countries has recently been widened. Income in the country, according to the Central Reserve Bank of El Salvador, has declined since 2008 at an average rate of USD 1,481.6 per inhabitant per year (Trujillo, D. 2012), and AOD investment has declined by approximately USD 38 per capita (CECLAC, 2012, p. 12).

So how is income linked to personal debt? It is linked directly to the ability to pay for services and basic needs, such as clothing, food and transportation. Some of these needs for many of the population are being addressed by the Ministerio de Educación Republica (the education department), which announced the Vaso de Leche (Glass of Milk) programme (Núñez, 2013) for 2,400 schools, plus school footwear packages for 1.3 million students (Secretaría de Comunicaciones de la Presidencia, 2013), but this is insufficient in the sense that it equips only a fraction of the country's young people.

The second issue is inequality. According to CECLAC (2012), this encompasses the high concentration of wealth. Comparisons of income deciles suggest that the richest people's incomes exceed those of the poorest people by a factor of 34. This gap is evident in the difference between urban and rural wages, and among the underemployed within the informal and formal sector employees. International market conditions, low investment and dependence on foreign products are some of the factors that are identified as being responsible and that do not allow for the improvement of economic conditions, exacerbating inequitable income distribution (Secretaría de Comunicaciones de la Presidencia, 2013). Those with adverse living conditions suffer an imbalance in comparison with their peers. They begin to think that they must overcome this imbalance, no matter how. In some cases this inequality can be reduced through loan acquisition.

The third issue is poverty, which is particularly pertinent to many of the countries of Latin America. According to the government of El Salvador (Secretaría de Comunicaciones de la Presidencia, 2013) the poverty rate declined from 40.5% in 2011 to 34.5% in 2012, which means that there are now 300,000 people who are no longer poor. It should be noted that according to a IUDOP survey (2013), 36.7% felt that the main achievement of President Mauricio Funes was the improvement in education for 1.3 million people from the poorest areas of the country. However, in some contexts and for some families, a lack of money drives them to be incorporated into the credit world.

Investment and savings in the region are measured by the rate of capital formation, which has been very low in recent years. National saving is also very low, which does not allow the financing of development programmes. In terms of income per capita in El Salvador, there is an uneven distribution of income across the municipalities. When social investment is not generated within certain groups, they are left out of development opportunities and this contributes to their acquisition of credit, loans or credit cards as an easy way to obtain an income.

The research

We conducted a descriptive, transactional survey in which we consulted a group of professionals using the DEPER13 survey to explore the reasons why personal debt starts. Professionals from different areas (lawyers, architects, psychologists, sociologists, designers and journalists) were involved. Some 67.18% of the professionals consulted were between the ages of 26–35 years, 22.72% were 36–45 years and 10.1% were older than 45 years. Of the sample, 59% of the participants were male and 41% female. Considering family composition, 67.18% were living in a nuclear family, 22.72% with their extended family and 10.1% in an assembled family.

According to these characteristics the majority of respondents were of a highly productive age, integrated into their families and with important commitments to the survival of their offspring. The tool DEPER13 consists of 30 questions divided into four general sections, including state of debt, state participation and consumerism. The respondents were asked to fill in an electronic form.

The findings show that 50% of respondents believe that people go into debt due to an imbalance between expenditure and revenue, 18.18% believe that consumerism is the cause, and another 18.18% believe that people go into debt because of the influence of the media. A few also considered bad decisions and financial deception. It is also believed that debts have other consequences, such as encouraging more debt (31.84%), creating a lack of liquidity, reducing fun activities and rendering individuals unable to pay utilities (22.72%). Participants identified personal debt as a common situation, since 67.18% knew 6–10 friends in debt, 22.72% knew 3–5 and 10.1% knew 1–2.

In the research (DEPER13) we inquired about state participation. Over 50% believed that "The economy of a country is related to its personal debt". In addition, 36.36% believed that the consumption of the country generates debt and 24.72% attribute it to poverty. This may well relate to gaps in productivity, innovation, infrastructure and education. If public policies barely touch the infrastructure improvements that are necessary to protect the subjects or to provide independent education on issues that are related to the debt burden that parents leave to children, then the debt spiral will inevitably continue to be reproduced.

Some highlighted the need for a good initiative from the state in order to reduce debt (40.9%) or to provide credit education (31.81%), and 27.29% said that it was necessary to have better regulation of banks. As for the measures or initiatives that are taken by people in debt, 36.36% indicate that they migrate, 27.27% seek to refinance their loans, 18.18% had more than one job and 9.09% end credits and perform illegal actions.

The issue of infrastructure has an impact on public investment, which has affected people in the region despite fiscal adjustments. Many Latin American countries have generated changes in their infrastructure but they have acquired public debt that does not allow them to progress in other areas. In the last four years of government in El Salvador there has been progress in this area, especially in terms of health infrastructure, increasing by 94% the number of health units, and resulting in 1,700 schools being built, repaired or renovated. There are also improvements in infrastructure services such as access to drinking water and a better electricity supply, and the government has repaired or constructed 500 km of roads (Secretaría de Comunicaciones de la Presidencia, 2013).

While these are significant developments in the countries of the region, in El Salvador many of these infrastructure improvements benefit specific groups in society. This is the case with drinking water coverage, which can no longer be managed by the country's water and sewerage association (ANDA), so the supply is provided by private organisations instead. It is currently being discussed whether leaving water access to the purchasing power of people is an effective strategy (Guevara de Ramirios, 2013).

Another issue is education. "A society with high levels of education [has] a better basis for timely incorporation of technical progress, innovation and gains in competitiveness and productivity" (p. 17) to allow new generations to overcome the difficulties that people are facing now. However, the CECLAC report indicates that the average coverage for the region is very close to universal.

In the section of the survey on other actors, when asked about the institutions whose initiatives focus on savings and economics, the answers were universities (36%), the Church (36%), second banks (18.18%) and third ministries of economy and finance (4.55%). In question 23 it was asked to what extent remittances help to reduce debt. Some 54.54% believe "little". We also asked whether cooperatives alleviate the situation, and only 11% were in agreement with this, indicating that they are not yet perceived to be effective.

In the section on media and consumerism respondents were asked: "In the last 6 months have you purchased a product that was not essential?" Some 67.18% replied yes and 32.82% no. When they were asked about the extent to which commercial advertisements enhance debt, 67.18% responded that they did, 22.72% said "a little" and 10.1% said "not at all". The next two questions asked whether debt depended on the purchase of brands and prestigious goods and it was found in both cases that 45.45% agreed with this statement.

Health is the eighth issue considered in the CECLAC report of 2012. In El Salvador there is unequal access to health benefits and this situation increases the inequality between people. Examples are the low levels of investment in infrastructure (Ministry of Communications of the Presidency, 2013), which is evidence by a lack of specialised medicines (Diaz, 2010; EDDH, 2011; Alfaro, 2013), which implies that certain population groups do not have access to these. In the population in general, some people acquire debt as a result of health treatments, and in other cases to pay for health insurance, which is extracted from their salary and so this is particularly relevant to personal debt.

There is a notable tax issue in El Salvador due to a lack of fiscal policies that do not allow for social equality and to reduce the chances of overcoming poverty or encouraging wealth distribution. Although the country has initiated changes in fiscal policy, there is a lack of liquidity and many social projects are subject to state loans. The fiscal deficit from 2009 to 2012 has fallen from 6.3 to 3.4, but the tax burden remains one of the lowest in Latin America (Secretaría de Comunicaciones de la Presidencia, 2013).

Health inequality and the tax gap impact on the population in the most basic way, such as when overcoming health epidemics. Particularly important was the Dengue outbreak in the country which affected many children, which has meant the relaunch of the awareness campaign (EDDH, 2010). In the case of taxation, the tax burden impacts on state institutions in terms of available resources, furnishings, equipment and infrastructure because there must be cash from the state to initiate the necessary purchases to address such health outbreaks.

There is also a gender issue that relates to inequalities in education, social protection and productivity. Mothers with fewer resources have less chance of developing a healthy family environment, especially when they are the head of the household. In the survey, most respondents indicated that the debt was a real problem for a productive middle-class family, and that this affected both men and women.

The environment is the last of the issues presented by CECLAC and it is the one that guarantees sustainability over time. The environment has been considered by several governments. The public discourse of Mauricio Funes, the previous president of El Salvador, highlighted the inclusion of this issue in the portfolio of the Ministry of the Environment and Natural Resources, which has been equipped with a 24-hour observatory to monitor climatic events (Secretaría de Comunicaciones de la Presidencia, 2013).

Considering these CECLAC issues overall from a point of view that most benefits the population requires further reflection on both vulnerability and risks to the conditions of life for residents. If we consider the risks generally, we can say that we have a population that is exposed to several threats, including environmental, but also economic (e.g. loss of employment and stagnating basic salaries) regarding which the population have little guidance, limited say and which frequently puts people at the gates of "economic disaster". In another sense, the environmental problem puts much of the population at risk of significant losses (home, family, property) and, by definition, financial losses. These must be supplemented immediately and this very often occurs through loan applications.

Reviewing these issues shows that savings, innovation, taxation and education are very important challenges for El Salvador. That is to say, when less is spent on social conditions (including education, health and security), the purchasing power of the country's inhabitants is reduced and this impacts on unemployment and GDP. Considering that education is not available to all young people, then logically the development of El Salvador is hindered by the lack of possibilities for its people to overcome their situation.

One item that has not been considered here is violence, and this has been affecting the general population for a number of years. For example, according to Lemus (2010), acts of violence in schools are explained by the authorities as being a consequence of schools being located in risky areas with the presence of gangs. Such conditions cause many families to invest in transportation and, on some occasions, vehicles for the protection of their children. These actions also have to be funded, often through loan applications. According to UNICEF (Sosa, 2015), during the last decade the violence has mostly affected students aged 14–18 years, and mostly adolescent males. In some areas this has led to an increased number of school dropouts, as indicated by recent research from La Prensa Gráfica (Zepeda et al., 2013).

Most of these social structural issues have a part to play in Chico's debt cycle, outlined earlier in this chapter. The fact that so many professionals are unprotected, together with a lack of economic policy that protects against a rapacious credit industry and the risky alternatives to moving out of debt, indicate that the problems are not receding but rather increasing. In the final section we provide a forecast for personal debt should these issues not be addressed.

Conclusion: A personal debt forecast

Everyone has a solution to the problematic social conditions in which they must live. When the expected standard of living does not match their actual living conditions, this balance can lead them to deny or ignore the issue or even to resort to self-inflicted violence (see Hare, 1999; cited in Arévalo Mira, 2011). What happens when people are not offered life-growth opportunities but are reduced to a single way of life that is governed by non-ideal patterns? In these cases, many citizens, when they find this contrast between their aspirations and their reality, find the solution through the acquisition of debt.

The tendency is to believe that new revenues will arrive in the future, and then people will be able to pay off their debts. Hence people buy financial products and services, probably influenced by the information that is available in the media. There are few known projects that support personal finance education, and they are usually found in blogs that specifically address the issue (Lopez, 2013). There are, as mentioned, some initiatives from the banking sector (Sanchez, 2012), but these are potentially problematic since such institutions provide the largest number of credit products (debts) in loans, credit cards and insurance management.

So credit facilities work to enhance the debts that are caused by an imbalance between spending and revenue, which is experienced not only at the domestic but also at the national level (Leiton, 2013). Debt may also be more common among professionals than in previous years due, in part, to the abovementioned issues outlined by CECLAC. The relationship between state policy and citizen debt is clearly evidenced and there are a number of problems and conditions that do not allow poverty, as the central issue, to be overcome.

When conditions are adverse, people consider risky actions, such as migration, refinance and even illegal activities, so personal debt is one of the key factors relating to important social issues such as migration, crime and embezzlement. Indeed, some studies have established that debt and low income are what drive citizens to migrate (Massey et al., 1993, pp. 448–454). We forecast that young professionals, male or female, whose economic opportunities are limited will continue to use credit and loans that have few requirements in order to give them the opportunity to get services and goods that they cannot otherwise afford. So far the picture is not yet alarming, but it may well become so.

Some other expressions of solidarity exist, such as cooperatives, supporting institutions and NGOs, but these do not as yet have a clear role or a strategic hold on the problem. Currently we have identified a social problem, but the experience of the population is that all citizens have debts and loans. This is simply because there is no other way to overcome the imbalance between the cost of living and wages that conditions people's life options and particularly their capacity to afford the essentials. The protagonist of our initial reflection, Chico, is not only at the mercy of credit and payment terms but is offered only one way to address the problem. A key part of the problem is the prevailing culture of consumption that is perpetuated by the media through commercials and that reinforces the acquisition of certain brands and places (Sanzana Palacios, 2011). The media do not educate people on the use of their finances but instead focus on encouraging them to take credit, for both necessary and unnecessary goods.

In our survey, respondents proposed a control of debt spending, where there is no longer a clear imbalance between the price of necessities (e.g. food and fuel) and incomes. There was a proposal to regulate and restrict wage inflation. Here there is a need for a state that creates fair everyday economic conditions so that citizens can maintain a decent standard of living through the regulation of the prices of essential products for everyday survival.

A second proposal was the better availability of information in the media about rates, interest and balances, rather than the overwhelming dominance of the media in creating false beliefs and false expectations, and where people are encouraged to acquire products such as travel, housing and cars, all through credits loans.

People who are financially dependent on creditworthiness often have a future that is likely to see them take on the debts of their parents. Some 30 years ago, credit was granted to senior executives, financiers and professionals, but now it is available to traders, farmers and young people who are just starting work, and it is almost impossible to find people who have no debts or credit that they use to cover the everyday basics of living. Every system depends on the people who constitute it. El Salvador is a country with high unemployment, high underemployment, low coverage by the state of key elements of the social infrastructure as identified by CECLAC, and with most of its people in debt. This places El Salvador in a very worrying position in terms of its sustainable development in the future.

Note

1. Special thanks go to Camilia Carolina Acevedo Paz and Carl Walker, colleagues who helped with the translations used in this chapter.

References

Alfaro, A. (2013, May 10th). Unidad con carencia de medicina especializada. La Prensa Gráfica. From http://www.laprensagrafica.com/unidad-con-carencia-de-medicina-especializada-
Arévalo Mira, D. M. (2011). Aproximación multidisciplinar a la violencia autoinfligida. *Revista de Psicología GEPU*, 2(2), 19–50.
Comisión Económica para América Latina y el Caribe. (2012). Los Países de Renta Media: Un Nuevo Enfoque basado en brechas estructurales. San Salvador: Trigésimo cuarto periodo de sesiones de la CEPAL, 27 al 31 de Agosto.
Díaz, C. (2010, April 11th). Población se queja por falta de medicamentos. El Diario de hoy. From http://www.elsalvador.com/mwedh/nota/nota_completa.asp?idCat=6375&idArt=4687514.
El Diario de Hoy (2010, February 25th). Relanzan campaña escolar contra el dengue. El diario de hoy. From http://www.elsalvador.com/mwedh/nota/nota_completa.asp?idCat=6364&idArt=4552543.
El Diario de Hoy (2011, september 13th). Diabetes, un "enorme desafío" con 366 millones de afectados. Retrieved June http://www.elsalvador.com/mwedh/nota/nota_completa.asp?idCat=47895&idArt=6185457.
Guevara Ramirios, N. (2013). A defender el agua de la privatización. [Blog Internet] from http://www.simpatizantesfmln.org/blog/?p=26018.
Instituto Universitario de Opinión Pública (2013). Boletín de prensa, año XXVII N°2. El Salvador: Vicerrectoría de proyección social, Universidad Centroamericana José Simeón Cañas. From http://www.uca.edu.sv/publica/iudop/archivos/boletin2_2013.pdf.

Leiton, P. (2013). Ingreso en dólares pone en aprietos la estabilidad económica. Costa Rica: Periódico La Nación, sección Economía. Disponible en http://www.nacion.com/2013-01-14/Economia/ingreso-de-dolares-pone-en-aprietos-estabilidad-economica.aspx.

Lemus, E. (2010, 19 de Agosto). El Salvador: Estudiantes bajo riesgo. BBC, Mundo

López, V. (2013). Mi deuda es 25.5 veces más que mi sueldo. Visitado en Enero 2013, disponible en http://economiapersonal.com/mi-deuda-es-25-5-veces-mas-que-mi-sueldo/.

Massey, D. S., Arango, J., Graeme, H., Kouaouci, A., Pellegrino, A. and Taylor, J. E. (1993). Parks theories of international migration. *Population and Development Review*, 19(3), September 1993. Disponible en http://cis.uchicago.edu/outreach/summerinstitute/2011/documents/sti2011-parks-theories_of_international_migration.pdf.

Núñez, Y. (2013, 21 de Enero). Inauguran el año escolar 2013. Diario El Mundo.

Pérez Fernández, V., Gutiérrez Domínguez, M. T., García García, A. and Gómez Bujedo, J. (2005). Procesos psicológicos básicos. España: Pearson Educación, S. A.

Quintanilla, J. (2010, 19 de febrero). Casa para Todos avanza con más de 1900 viviendas. La Prensa Gráfica. Disponible en http://www.laprensagrafica.com/el-salvador/social/94665-casa-para-todos-avanza-con-mas-de-1900-viviendas.

Sánchez, W. (2012). *Elimina tus deudas*. Visitado en Enero 2013, disponible en http://dinero.about.com/od/Deuda/a/Elimina-Tus-Deudas.htm.

Sanzana Palacios, A. (2011). Consumo, endeudamiento y vulnerabilidad a la pobreza. Elementos subjetivos y socioculturales para su compresión. Chile: Universidad de Valparaiso, 1–16.

Secretaria de Comunicaciones de la Presidencia (2013)/Ministry of Communications of the Presidency (2013). Discurso del presidente maurico funes a 4 años de gestión. Retrieved on June 7, 2013.http://www.transparenciaactiva.gob.sv/discurso-del-presidente-mauricio-funes-a-4-anos-de-gestion/.

Sony Pictures Classics, Representational Picture Film, Screen Pass Picture (Producer), and Ferguson, C. (Director) (2010, 25 March 2011). Inside job (trabajo confidencial). [Video/DVD] Sony Picture.

Sosa, B. (2015, January 1st). Exigen mayor atención del estado a la niñez y la adolescencia. La prensa gráfica, from http://www.laprensagrafica.com/2015/01/01/exigen-mayor-atencion-del-estado-a-la-niez-y-la-adolescencia.

Trujillo, D. (2012, 30 de agosto). Ingreso por habitante disminuyo $27 desde 2008. Diario El Mundo.

United Nation of Development Program (2013). Informe sobre Desarrollo Humano El Salvador 2013 El Salvador. Imaginar un nuevo país. Hacerlo posible. Diagnóstico y propuesta. Retrieves June 7 http://www.sv.undp.org/content/dam/el_salvador/docs/povred/UNDP_SV_IDHES-2013.pdf.

Zepeda, A., Flores, R. & Herrera, B. (2013). Alumnos dejan sus estudios. El Salvador: El Diario de Hoy, from http://www.laprensagrafica.com/alumnos-dejan-sus-estudios-por-amenazas.

14
The Personal Debt Industry: Racist Debt Practices and Pasifika Peoples in New Zealand

Bruce Curtis and Cate Curtis

This chapter is based on an analysis of the working poor as flawed consumers. We begin by recognising the generalised and the local/racialised aspects of this concept:

> [The] poor of a consumer society are socially defined, and self-defined, first and foremost as blemished, defective, faulty and deficient – in other words, inadequate – consumers.
>
> (Bauman, 1998, p. 38)

> In Pacific families, in particular, we notice that a number of the mums come in carrying other people's debt. I don't think they do it by choice, they have to, there is an expectation and that's so ingrained that there is no choice...
>
> (Anglican Trust for Women and Children staff member, cited in Families Commission, 2012, p. 15)

In mid-2014 we were fortunate to spend time in the UK, France, the Netherlands, Portugal and Spain as part of research and study leave that was sponsored by our respective universities.[1] During this time, while we enjoyed the privilege of a fully funded sabbatical and worked on our writing projects, including racist debt practices and Pasifika peoples in New Zealand, we were challenged by manifestations of what Bauman has called "flawed consumers". Almost at every corner and certainly in the safest, stereotypical holiday destinations we were confronted by homelessness and begging. Fortunately the happy snaps that we posted on Facebook excise the ammonia tang of urine from a lumpen proletariat living cheek by jowl with transnational tourists. The point here, of course, is that this proximity now occurs in the heart of empire. For us, at least, the beggar in Lyons, whose wares were suppurating wounds, seemed surreal. Regardless, we were forced to acknowledge both our privilege and that – despite New Zealand's 30-year track record as a neoliberal experiment (Kelsey, 1995, 1999) – we had lived sheltered lives after all.

This experience both reinforced and problematised Bauman's flawed consumers. The issue wasn't so much the very dramatic, individualised and embodied flawed consumers as beggars or rough sleepers in the context of austerity, but the all-pervasive, normalised business of "easy loans", "rapid loans", "pay-day loans" aimed at the cash-strapped employed or beneficiaries looking to avoid the humiliation of poverty. It underscored the power of the argument that the poor are pathologised and victimised in contemporary, consumer society. It certainly reinforced our notion that the poor have good reason to borrow, to go into short- and long-term debt to avoid the humiliation of inadequate consumption. But this business element of flawed consumption – the predation on flawed consumers, if you like – somewhat transforms Bauman's insights from primarily a political economy into a statement about handling spoilt identity in consumer society. After Erving Goffman, accruing credit/debt (the two can always be flipped in any discussion) constitutes a means of avoiding stigma. The poor borrow to hide their spoilt identities as consumers, even if, and perhaps because, there is little chance of repaying the principal. The poor borrow to pass as proper consumers (Goffman, 1963).

In more practical terms, the sabbatical allowed us to better contextualise racist debt practices and Pasifika peoples in New Zealand. This means an appreciation of the Global Financial Crisis and how it has played out in neocolonial New Zealand – specifically its racist consequences, but also what this victimisation normalises more generally.

New Zealand is a debtor economy

As a settler colony of the UK, New Zealand has been a debtor economy for much of its history (the country gained formal independence in 1908). However, in recent decades the impacts of debt, and of indebtedness, have been obscured by a neoliberal rhetoric and by its very uneven effects. New Zealand was one of the first movers in the international adoption of neoliberal policies in the latter part of the 20th century and arguably it moved the furthest, at least among the OECD nations.[2]

This chapter will draw particular attention to the racialised aspects of debt, but we do first wish to contextualise debt in terms of the broader economy. One measure of debt is the current account, which measures the balance of trade between imports and exports. New Zealand's current account has been in debt since 1973 and, apart from periods of worldwide prosperity (the "Long Boom") and of war (when New Zealand's exports of food and fibre were needed urgently by the UK), this is the normal state of affairs. Like almost all colonies, even those like New Zealand that enjoyed a somewhat privileged position thanks to its close historical ties to the motherland (i.e. based on colonisation by British settlers), New Zealand lacks a balanced economy. Exports including agricultural produce, tourism and commercialised education are the "core" of the economy. Manufacturing and domestic focused sectors have always occupied a somewhat parlous position and were more or less obliterated in the mid-1980s when successive New Zealand governments embraced neoliberal or "more market" policies. The country had abandoned most tariffs, import quotas and domestic subsidies by the early 1990s to secure the nation as a "free and open trading economy". Neoliberal policies did not much, if at all, improve the state of the current account. Indeed, while the champions of neoliberalism often claim that the economy is healthier with a more market approach, they pay scant regard to the individuals and communities that make up that economy.

There isn't room here to document the many failings of neoliberalism other than to note the following: (1) the sale of state-owned assets to the private sector and user pays has resulted not in a more open and efficient system of delivering services but in a range of monopolies or cartels that are primarily owned by foreign investors (e.g. telecommunications, banking, infrastructure and, increasingly, health); (2) neoliberal policies have locked in a low-wage scenario – by all measures the standard of living for the majority of New Zealanders has fallen with the neoliberal orientation; (3) New Zealand is a far less egalitarian society – the difference between rich and poor has widened significantly. These and other failings paint a gloomy picture and in terms of personal debt the situation is even worse. Indeed, the New Zealand "experiment" with neoliberalism has created the perfect storm for a racialised indebtedness.

First, and most obviously, the low-wage scenario coupled with the decimation of manufacturing and a host of semiskilled jobs since the 1980s means that average wages or social welfare are simply inadequate to meet the needs of individuals and families. Indeed the average working family in New Zealand can only just get by with the aid of Working for

Families, a tax credit scheme (see below). This scheme, more than anything, supports low wages and low-wage-paying employers rather than struggling families. Second, New Zealand has a high level of external debt (approximately 126% of GDP) and a relatively low level of public (state) debt (approximately 39% of GDP). This debt is private (owed mainly by individuals to transnational banks) rather than public. High external debt combined with low state debt reflects New Zealand's early adoption of neoliberalism – what is now called "austerity". Yet the international ratings agencies regard New Zealand very highly. For example, Moody's rates New Zealand in the top flight of current ratings (Aaa). Clearly the capacity of the "rule of law" to secure the servicing of debt is more important to international creditors than the (poor) health of the economy (and by inference, of the people who make up that economy). The result is that debt is at every level a private issue despite the fact that neoliberal policies create this situation with low wages and a high interest policy, and transnational banks that have cornered the market on mortgages for otherwise unaffordable homes. Third, debt – call it the credit industry – is big business and has been unfettered by neoliberalism.

Thus low wages combined with an increasing cost of living have led to increased personal indebtedness, the rise of a burgeoning credit industry and the all-encompassing nature of personal debt (Families and Retirement Commissions, 2008). Legge and Heynes (2009) favour a locus of control argument in terms of taking on debt. However, this seems doubly blind: blind to the issues of social structure in general and to the specifics of personal debt. In the context of a low-wage economy, declining measures of "affordability" and the necessity of (easy) credit, this appears little more than blaming the victims. At the same time, recent decades have seen a proliferation of private finance companies that target the most vulnerable in society. While it is unfair to portray New Zealand's "psychology" in terms of a rehashing of Livingstone and Lunt (1992), a rounded social psychology perspective is definitely lacking (Walker, 2013).

Pasifika peoples and debt

The term Pasifika, or Pasifika peoples, is a collective label that is applied to locally born and migrant people from the nations of the Pacific: Samoa, Fiji, Tonga and Niue, among others. The term has replaced others, in official reporting at least, that are now regarded as offensive or old-fashioned (Pacific Islanders and Polynesians are examples of the latter). The re-emergence of the German-inflected spelling of Pasifika (Germany was a major colonial force in the Pacific prior to the First World War) reflects the open-ended and contested nature of postcolonial efforts at terminology.[3] While the terminology is problematic, the social statistics that it reveals is a straightforward story of structural, racist disadvantage.

Pasifika peoples constitute around 7% of the population of New Zealand. The measurement of ethnicity in New Zealand is a somewhat contentious issue because in official surveys and most others, individuals can self-select multiple identities which when totalled exceed the number of individuals surveyed. This double-counting appears to be most significant for those selecting Māori as part of their ethnic identity. Bearing this in mind, the last census figures indicate that alongside the 7% Pasifika, 71% of the population identified with an European ethnicity, 15% with Māori and 12% with Asian (Statistics New Zealand, 2013a). The Pasifika population is the youngest (by median age), the shortest-lived and the most fertile of the four main ethnic groupings (Curtis and Curtis, 2006).

They are also disproportionately located in Auckland (New Zealand's somewhat sprawling and largest conurbation), especially in its poorest, southern suburbs; located and overcrowded, it should be noted. Pasifika households are the most likely to have insufficient bedrooms: "43% of Pasifika people live in households requiring an extra bedroom, compared to 23% of Māori and 4% of European households" (Henare et al., 2011, p. 34). This overcrowding and the damage that it causes are long documented. For instance, using data drawn from the late 1990s, in a number of presentations in 2003, Chris Bullen from the Clinical Trials Research Unit at the University of Auckland demonstrated a spatial overlap of overcrowding and meningococcal disease cases that was breathtaking in its correlation. Yet rather than spend (what was then a very considerable budget surplus) on social housing to the lasting benefit of the residents of South Auckland, the neoliberal, Labour government of the day preferred to waste several millions of dollars on a botched vaccination campaign, the end result of which was an increased mortality rate from the disease (see Law and Sumner Burstyn, 2006).[4] In these suburbs, poor living conditions and poor nutrition have resulted in increases in illnesses that had been considered third-world problems, such as rheumatic fever, childhood pneumonia and tuberculosis, as well as meningococcal disease, mentioned above (Baker et al., 2003).

Other socioeconomic statistics are equally grim, but they are often hard to locate or are hidden away in the text of official reports, so we will simply run through a recent selection of them. Pasifika peoples have the smallest share of family net worth. Thus,

> Families containing at least one person of Pacific ethnicity had the lowest overall family net worth of all the ethnic groups analysed. Very few families had a level of family net worth that put them in the top family net worth quintile, and 86 percent of Pacific ethnicity one-parent families were in the bottom quintile.
>
> (Statistics New Zealand, 2008, p. 13)

Pasifika workers are the

> lowest-paid ethnic group with an average wage last year [2013] of $20.59 an hour, behind Māori on $22.45, Asians on $23.49 and Europeans on $27.08. That wage gap has hardly changed in a decade. Pacific workers averaged 25 per cent below Europeans in 2004 and 24 per cent below Europeans today.
>
> (Collins, 2014)

Interestingly, Pasifika people are not particularly over-represented in the main benefits (income support payments) that are available to the working-age population. In June 2014 they represented around 7.8% of beneficiaries – roughly in line with their population share (Statistics New Zealand, 2014). When income from all sources (e.g. including social welfare benefits) is considered, Pasifika peoples on average receive 65.94% of the total average income compared with the 80.19% that Māori receive and the 107.59% that the average European receives (Statistics New Zealand, 2013b).

A recent Salvation Army report confirms that this Pasifika "share" of working-age benefits has hovered around population levels, although labour force participation was worsening: "In December 2008, the Pacific labour force participation rate was 67% against a nationwide participation rate of 69.6%. In March 2014, the Pacific participation rate had fallen to just above 62%, while the national rate had climbed back to 69.6% following a decline to 67.5% during the recession" (Tanielu and Johnson, 2014, p. 23). Unsurprisingly, Pasifika families are the most indebted:

> For single families, while mortgage debt-asset ratios are broadly comparable (all less than 50 percent), single Māori, Pacific and other families have high non-mortgage debt-asset ratios. The median single

Pacific family, in particular, appears to hold twice as much nonmortgage debt as assets. This suggests they have very low or negative net worth...
(Families Commission and Retirement Commission, 2008, p.16)

It certainly isn't our intention to add to the stereotypical and racist framings of any ethnicities or to reinscribe essentialist readings, but the socioeconomic statistics suggest that the deprivation that is experienced by Pasifika peoples owes much to that endured by the working poor more generally. We contrast this deprivation, with some trepidation, with accounts from across the political spectrum that emphasise Māoritanga, racism and welfare dependency in New Zealand. We argue that Pasifika peoples, as working poor, have a particular vulnerability to the practices of racialised debt. We argue that because Pasifika people are working poor, hegemonic accounts will emphasise racism by way of explanation. In respect of the former claim, we agree with the main findings of the Families Commission (2012) in *Pacific Families and Problem Debt* and are indebted to that scholarly investigation.

The multiple authors of *Pacific Families and Problem Debt*[5] identify a range of causes for indebtedness from which we extrapolate. We will discuss these next but must first mention racism, which they are somewhat coy about. The disadvantaged position of Pasifika peoples in New Zealand, and their overwhelming status as working poor, constantly in the shadow of the reserve army of labour, is an expression of racism. New Zealand racism is mediated by its settler colonial origins and the displacement of Māori tribal society from the best lands by British capital and migrants. Pasifika peoples are migrants too, encouraged to New Zealand in the boom times of the 1950s and 1960s to fill a range of blue-collar jobs. In this respect, Pasifika benefited from the colonial networks of the British Commonwealth, which facilitated migration to New Zealand (Macpherson, 2004). However, this migration was sharply proscribed by its occupational and locational boundaries. When the "Long Boom" ended and decades of stagnation morphed into an outright, neoliberal attack on working people in the mid-1980s, Pasifika blue-collar workers were hit perhaps hardest of any ethnic grouping.

In the context of an attack – a sustained attack – on the pay and conditions of working people, and increasingly of beneficiaries, it would be hard to imagine the racially victimised Pasifika peoples not having recourse to personal debt. And it would be wrong-headed to invert an explanation for indebtedness in terms of Pasifika cultural practices. These practices are significant, however, and include three main, interlinked, analytical elements:

1. **The enduring significance of kinship networks** A stereotype of Pasifika peoples is that they are more family-centred than their Palagi (European) neighbours. The continued importance of kinship networks is undoubted and informs not just the social life of Pasifika peoples but also almost all academic work and policy initiatives in the area. Multigenerational housing is an obvious expression, and overcrowding is its down-side. Kinship networks are frequently transnational, in terms of both migration to New Zealand (Macpherson, 2004) and familial exchanges, but also remittances. An unknown number of Pasifika families remit money to their senior male relatives in their initial homeland:

> They are principally used, at least initially, to repay debts, to finance migration of kin, and to purchase consumer goods including housing. They often reinforce a traditional set of values that emphasizes the prevailing social hierarchy and strengthens established social organization. Remittances tend to go to senior family members who use them in traditional ways instead of for structural changes such as land tenure reform.
> (Connell and Brown, 2005, pp. 10–11)

2. **Continuing elements of a gift economy** Kinship networks and remittances overlap with continuing elements of the gift economy, which find expression in familial obligations to major events both in New Zealand and their initial homelands (e.g. weddings, funerals, and community- and family-based celebrations). In terms of debt, kinship and the gift economy can result in some family members (it would seem predominantly mothers) holding debt for the benefit of others (e.g. in-laws, male children and husbands).

3. **Relative importance of the Church** The extent to which the Church is a progressive or reactionary force in Pasifika communities is hotly debated and also has great potential for racist demagoguery. The Families Commission report *Pacific Families and Problem Debt* (2012) goes to some trouble to discount tithing as a structural source of indebtedness, which in part reflects the role of Church-based groups in providing community support. We regard the relative importance of the Church, in

combination with kinship and gifting, as significant in securing a trope of respectability in Pasifika communities. By respectability we mean a heightened aversion to the stigma of flawed consumerism (to combine Goffman's and Bauman's imagery).

In summary, we posit that Pasifika peoples are poor, subject to structural racism and over-represented in terms of being working poor, and that these socioeconomic realities are mediated by a culture (or subculture) of respectability and stoicism.

Thank you, Instant Finance

All writing has a start-point, and for us it was a series of staggeringly racist advertisements from the loan company Instant Finance, beginning in 2011. These appeared on TV and radio, in print, on billboards and online. They were tailored for the Pasifika community and featured a high-profile Māori sportsman, Stacey Jones (former captain of the New Zealand Rugby League team).[6] The advertisements emphasised stereotypical/racist portrayals of Pasifika peoples: happy, smiling and naïve; needing easy money for a holiday, a daughter's wedding or to fix up the old banger of a car. The tag line "Thank you Instant Finance" was spoken by a motherly Samoan in stereotypically accented migrant English. We were not alone in being offended. Members of the public made complaints to the Advertising Standards Authority about several loan companies in 2011–2012, including at least five against Instant Finance. The minority that were upheld were on the grounds of non-disclosure of required information rather than targeting the poor and vulnerable (Edmunds, 2012).

This is hardly surprising. Recent years have seen the proliferation of companies that offer unsecured loans at high rates, and often in a misleading fashion. They include Cash Train, offering a NZD 750 loan for ten days at a cost of NZD 128. This includes a one-off administration fee of NZD 53, and interest at NZD 1 per NZD 100 borrowed per day – or 365% per annum (http://www.cashtrain.co.nz/). Payday Loans has advertised rates "as low as 1.38 per cent a day" – equivalent to 503% per annum – while stating that "Pay Day Loans can be a great financial tool to help get you through to your pay day – and can even help save you time and money on things such as bank fees or penalties on bills" (http://www.pay-day-loans.net.nz/). Save My Bacon charges an even higher rate of 547.5% per year. This is explained thus: "But this term is an annualised measure that wasn't devised with Save My Bacon small and urgent loans in mind... Our loans only have a maximum term of 31 days and we do not offer a long-term loan product for a year" (https://www.savemybacon.co.nz/charges). Simple Cash (https://www.simplecash.co.nz) offers a similar explanation, with interest rates of up to 803% per annum.

Several loan companies target Pasifika people through the images that they use, such as Pasifika families attending a wedding. The recent research by the Families Commission (2012) noted that many of the participants commented on tailored advertising strategies, including advertisements on Pasifika-targeted radio stations in Pacific languages. Many Pasifika-focused advertisements explicitly target people with poor credit histories. For example, the Aqua Cars & Finance advertising and website states: "We provide vehicle finance for almost anyone... Even if you think your credit's a bit dented – think again! With Aqua car finance, you could still get a loan for the car you need. It's quick, and it's easy to put yourself in the driver's seat!" (http://www.aquacars.co.nz/).

Our unscientific review of Auckland-based finance companies appears to confirm deliberate targeting. The websites of those based in south Auckland tend to be more informal, suggest that a poor credit history need not be a concern and that loans can be approved quickly, and have a larger number of casually dressed Pasifika, Māori and Asian people in their images. In contrast, companies based in the central business district tend to use more white people and more formal language, and also to advertise investment opportunities.

Perhaps an even greater problem than the ease with which credit can be obtained from finance companies is the increase in "mobile truck shops". These trucks frequent deprived neighbourhoods and sell everything from basic grocery items to lounge suites, on credit and often at high prices. Anecdotal evidence (quoted by Grunwell, 2009) suggests that they often charge three or four times the normal retail price. Some request that consumers complete several automatic payment forms, supposedly so that if one is cancelled by the consumer it can easily be replaced by the company (Waiapu Anglican Social Services, 2010).

Pasifika peoples, flawed consumers and hegemony

Bauman's work on flawed consumers has evolved into a broader discussion of "liquid fear" – the notion that contemporary capitalism is marked by amorphous fears and anxieties. These fears are reified in hegemonic accounts for precisely the same reasons that were long ago identified by Gramsci and the Frankfurt School: to obscure the structural contradictions of capitalism; to destroy class solidarity by stigmatising and scapegoating some fraction of the working class; and to foster false consciousness. In this respect, Pasifika people are the perfect "fall guys". Without racist accounts, indebtedness among Pasifika peoples might be understood in terms that would foster working-class solidarity. The notions that they are working poor, family-centred and respectable just like other working people might in themselves be stereotypes, but they are ones that invite comparison and inclusion. Racist formulations provide the opposite dynamic, simultaneously empowering a form of vulture capitalism which predates precisely on the working poor while inviting explanations that are based on difference and exceptionality.

Respect and deprivation

The desire for respectability – to conceal one's status as a flawed consumer – coupled with a lack of access to resources can only exacerbate the effects of problem debt. Debt has been linked to a variety of mental and physical health problems (Balmer et al., 2006). It can significantly change how people live their lives, induce feelings of uncertainty about what is going to happen next, and engender feelings of stigma and shame. The more debts people have, the more likely they are to have poor mental health, with estimates that nearly half of all adults with debt have a mental disorder (Fitch et al., 2010).

Debt may also have indirect psychological effects on the household as well as those who are directly responsible for managing money. The psychological wellbeing of children may be impacted by parental stress and depression, and result in conflict-based family relationships and potential mental health problems among other family members (Fitch et al., 2010). Debt is also linked to higher rates of domestic violence and relationship breakdown (Balmer et al., 2006).

In addition to the somewhat distal impacts of poverty on physical health mentioned above, such as those related to overcrowding, a range of more immediate impacts occur. Insufficient financial resources may mean that a trip to the doctor is missed in favour of paying rent, and that food choices are made on the basis of cost and how "filling" an item is rather than its nutritional value. Cheer et al. (2002) note that food spending is often the easiest cut to make for those who are living in debt; it is not a fixed expense and non-payment does not result in the repossession of goods. As discussed above, due to a high value being placed on collective responsibility and relatively high religiosity, individual and household needs may take a low priority. In practical terms, such commitments can lead to a lack of food in the ensuing weeks, as shown in these quotes from the work of Cheer et al. (2002, p. 510):

> Our cultural obligations are more important than food and so when something comes up like that then it will be just bread and jam that we eat. Food comes after cultural donation. It's also more important than bills like the power... Every time there is a... function, we are asked to pay. There was only just a wedding and funeral we had to pay for in the same week. Even when the family function is back in Samoa, we still have to donate.

> The kids have gone to school without lunch. I've gotten letters from the school about it asking that I give them lunch every day. The guilt is huge.

These quotes indicate the tensions involved in maintaining respectability while living in poverty, and emphasise the attractiveness of obtaining credit/debt to attempt to address deprivation. In this regard, indebtedness is the last recourse of the respectable, working poor under neoliberalism. We believe it to be a common, potentially unifying experience for working people. For Pasifika peoples it may involve challenging the centrality of the Church and of respectability in favour of foregrounding the dilemmas of being working poor and of confronting racism.

Breaking the debt cycle

Possibilities for reducing debt, and the underlying issues of vulnerability and inequality, may be targeted at the macro- and community (and individual) levels. The Families Commission (2012) offers a range of actions that are aimed specifically at Pasifika families, though many are more broadly applicable. These include financial literacy education (also see Reed and Sutton, 2012); social skills training, including budgeting and communication; intensive case management; advocacy with agencies; and engagement with community leaders and churches. Calls for financial literacy training and coordination across services have been common since the global financial crisis, both in New Zealand and internationally (see e.g. Balmer et al., 2006; Fitch et al., 2010). Some other suggestions for managing debt rely very simply on managing psychological factors within families:

> A better understanding of the interplay between factors in a family decision-making setting is also required. For example, where in a

two-parent family one partner has an internal locus of control and the other an external one, it may be in the family's long-term interests for each to be aware of their tendencies, strengths and weaknesses and to empower the internally focused partner to make decisions about the family's finances.

(Legge and Heynes, 2009, p. 40)

However, it seems unlikely that such an approach will assist the increasing numbers who simply have insufficient money about which to make decisions, even if it were possible to ignore or overcome other factors that come into play within families and from their social contexts. Similarly, as noted by Balmer et al. (2006), improving access to financial and budgeting advice may help people to deal with acute financial crises but it will not change the underlying drivers of poverty and social exclusion. Additionally, disadvantaged groups are likely to experience difficulties (further inequalities) in accessing services, serving to further exacerbate their social and economic marginalisation.

The start-point for addressing racist debt practices in New Zealand undoubtedly lies in small reforms around budgetary advice and access to credit/debt. However, while these policies and programmes may assist some individuals and families, they will at best treat the symptoms resulting from underlying structural issues. At worst they support and perpetuate a "blame the victim" mentality, and reinforce stereotypes. By providing an opportunity to claim that assistance is being afforded, they offer an avenue for government to ignore and obfuscate the drivers of debt and inequality, thus continuing the construction of debtors as a group of careless and/or ignorant individuals. Addressing debt must transcend this sort of small "r" reform if it is to succeed. The endpoint of such initiatives lies in the realm of political economy, in addressing the "neoliberal" attacks on Pasifika peoples and on all working people.

On a fundamental social level, many potential solutions revolve around political change. These include policies around the minimum wage; capping of interest rates and loan fees; further simplification of loan documents; the empowerment of unions, incorporating the reversal of the policies of recent decades which have rendered them all but powerless; a return to progressive taxation, including the removal of Goods and Service Tax (the equivalent of Value Added Tax); the reversal of austerity policies; and the return of tariff and import restrictions to encourage local production beyond dairying.

A combination of developing and evaluating social service programmes, while simultaneously challenging the structural contradictions of capitalism, addressing false consciousness and promoting empowerment, is precisely the raison d'être of CP.

The potential of community psychology approaches

CP is an applied social science that attempts to enhance the life circumstances of groups of people, especially those who are oppressed, stigmatised or otherwise marginalised. Practitioners favour group, community and societal interventions which address the structural factors that maintain oppression and suboptimal health, recognising the limitations and potentially victim-blaming nature of individually focused interventions. The way in which CP has developed in New Zealand owes much to our history, in particular as it pertains to issues of culture, ethnicity and colonisation (Robertson and Masters-Awatere, 2007).

CP, politics and culture In order to discuss the practice of CP, and in particular its approach to culture and inequality, it is necessary to first describe something of local psychology's past and the context in which it arose. Of specific relevance is the history of racism.

Colonisation proceeded in New Zealand in a similar way to other parts of the world. From settlement, the colonial administration governed New Zealand largely as if it had absolute sovereignty. For example, the 1852 Constitution Act established a franchise based on land held in individual title, effectively denying the vote to almost all Māori, for whom land was held collectively.

The last part of the 19th century saw the emergence of a more socially just tradition, albeit it one that focused on the needs of the (largely) British settlers. From the 1890s to the 1910s, successive Liberal Party governments laid down the basis of the welfare state (King, 2003, cited by Robertson and Masters-Awatere, 2007). By the late 19th century, New Zealand had gained a reputation as the "social laboratory of the world". Women gained the vote in 1893 (the first country in the world to enfranchise women); and labour laws that improved conditions for workers were introduced, as was an old-age pension. The government built houses to be rented to workers at affordable rates, and there were significant advancements in public health. The cornerstone of the first Labour government was the 1938 enactment of the Social Security Act, providing assistance "from the cradle to the grave" – a comprehensive package of measures including healthcare, increased access to pensions and social welfare benefits. However, these benefits were not evenly applied. For example, the 1938 act allowed for the payment of benefits at a lower rate "if the maximum benefit is not necessary for the maintenance of the beneficiary". Communal living arrangements were often cited as a reason, but there is evidence of the widespread and unjustifiable practice of reducing the benefits paid to Māori (Baker, 2012).

By the mid-20th century, tensions related to the urbanisation of Māori meant that "race relations" were on the social and political agenda. Previously Māori largely lived in rural settlements, but post-war prosperity led to increased demand for labour in towns and cities. At this time, "race relations" meant a focus on maintaining cordial relationships rather than cultural justice. Rapid changes to the make-up of the New Zealand population were to follow. By the early 1970s, the proportion of New Zealand's foreign-born population who were from countries outside the white British Commonwealth was 30% – twice that of 20 years earlier. As the composition of the population changed, so did attitudes. Civil rights crusades in the USA, independence movements in some British colonies and a renaissance in Māori culture brought social issues to the fore, especially among some psychologists.

Alongside a changing population and changing attitudes came, from the mid-1980s, major changes to social and economic policy. The country had the biggest rise in inequality in OECD member nations in the two decades beginning in the mid-1980s, taking New Zealand from well under the OECD average to well above it (Ministry of Social Development, 2013). A number of measures of social capital indicated a steady decline from this period. For example, the youth suicide rate grew sharply into one of the highest in the developed world (reported by the Ministry of Health; see Curtis and Curtis (2011) for a broader discussion); the number of New Zealanders estimated to be living in poverty grew by at least 35% between 1989 and 1992 (Kelsey, 1999); crime (Ewing, 2001) and the number of food banks (Ballard, 2003) increased dramatically; and the public health system was particularly negatively impacted, leading to a significant deterioration in health standards among not only working- but also middle-class people, as services were rationalised (Bramhall, 2003). The poverty rate for working-age adults living on their own trebled from 1984 (10%) to 2007 (30%) (Ministry of Social Development, 2013).

With this history it is perhaps unsurprising that CP developed in response to the concern of many psychologists that preventing social problems and enhancing the quality of people's lives requires more than behavioural interventions at an individual level. It requires the thorough interrogation of, and intervention in, the broader social and political systems that influence human behaviour, in turn confronting oppression in all forms, including sexism, racism and classism, and addressing the resultant disparities (Department of Psychology, University of Waikato, 2011). Though CP in New Zealand dates from the 1980s, its underpinnings can be found decades earlier.

The notion that psychology in general should not be a culture-free endeavour was embedded in some of the writings of early New Zealand psychologists. Of particular note is the work of Ernest Beaglehole (1906–1965). He was influenced by the founders of psychological anthropology, including Ruth Benedict, Margaret Mead and Edward Sapir, and he published many studies of Pacific Island and Māori communities. His contribution is perhaps most evident in *Mental Health in New Zealand* (1950). In discussing the issues that underlie psychological problems, he emphasised situational factors and emotional stressors, including "strained personal, social and economic conditions, together with unsuitable or unsatisfactory employment" (p. 47). He argued that good health required participation in social networks, feelings of security and connectedness, and being part of a cooperative common life, as well as the fulfilment of practical needs such as good-quality housing. Beaglehole drew a connection between culture and mental health, citing aggressive competition and consumerism as being implicated in mental illness (Robertson and Masters-Awatere, 2007).

CP praxis As is the case elsewhere in the world, since its inception, CP in New Zealand has taken a clear stance in relation to values. In particular, the notion of value-free science is rejected. Instead, values such as social justice, collaboration, diversity and empowerment are emphasised. There is a particular importance placed on the critical analysis of hegemonic practices. As might be expected given its antecedents in cross-cultural and ethnopsychology, CP here has focused particularly on culture and especially institutionalised racism.

Today, CP practitioners can be found in a range of sectors, including health services and promotion, social and welfare services, education, community development, disability services, housing, child protection and addiction. They are employed by government at all levels, by iwi (tribal) organisations, by NGOs and by research companies (Robertson and Masters-Awatere, 2007), and they are well positioned to address issues of indebtedness.

That debt may be both a form of poverty and a way of dealing with poverty makes it a complex topic to deal with. However, CP as an academic discipline has long employed a critique of capitalist hegemony and its impacts on specific groups, especially cultural groups. That critique must include the role of austerity politics in the current entrenchment of racialised debt practices.

Conclusion

New Zealand has been in debt for some decades. Since the adoption of austerity measures in the 1980s, income has decreased while debt has increased. The country had the biggest rise in inequality in OECD member nations in the two decades following the mid-1980s, taking it from well under the OECD average to well above (Ministry of Social Development, 2013). Although many New Zealanders are experiencing significant debt as a result, some groups are more vulnerable than others. We have argued that Pasifika peoples are at particular risk. Whereas much of the New Zealand population is in debt due to high mortgages, Pacific Island families are often borrowing to cover their basic needs – loans to be able to buy groceries and pay for utilities. This is due to a number of sociocultural factors, but also the pernicious behaviour of the credit industry, which targets Pasifika people precisely because they are respectable exemplars of the working poor. In the face of this double burden, or racism and capitalist hegemony, we conclude that the possibilities for justice, fairness and wellbeing require significant economic and political change. In the first instance a response to this crisis of racialised personal and community indebtedness must call forth a response to austerity policies.

Notes

1. This article was also assisted by a grant to Bruce Curtis from the Europe Institute, at the University of Auckland. I am deeply indebted to the Europe Institute for their support of a project that began examining exhortations to politeness in the public sphere and has been expressed here, in part, as an examination of damaged identities.
2. New Zealand was an early adopter of neoliberal policies. This was in part because of the right-wing rhetoric of market efficiencies, monetarism and private- over public-good arguments. This transformation of policy included (1) floating the exchange rate; (2) scrapping import controls and tariffs, and subsidies to domestic manufacturing and farming; (3) selling of state-owned assets (e.g. telecommunications, banking and railways); (4) enforcing the sale by local authorities of airports, harbours, power generation and supply, and other revenue streams; (5) requiring the survival of state-owned enterprises to return a dividend to the state (e.g. postal services, public broadcasting); (6)

deregulating the banking, finance, power, telecommunications infrastructure supply and export agriculture sectors; (7) cutting unemployment and disability benefits; (8) raising the age for pensions; (9) abolishing the legal status of trade unions; and (10) drastically limiting the state's capacity to borrow to fund any fiscal interventions (Curtis, 2001).
3. We use the same definition of Pacific people that is commonly used in New Zealand government reports and by the Ministry of Māori and Pacific Island Affairs: people who claim ethnic links to the island nations of the Pacific.
4. It is unclear whether this public health debacle for Pasifika peoples counted for or against Helen Clark, the prime minister at the time and a former minister of health, in her successful campaign to run the United Nations Development Programme.
5. The Families Commission research team: Dr David Stuart, Janine Couchman, Dr Jeremy Robertson, Karen Stewart, Tofilau Kerupi Tavati, Liz Tanielu and Margaret Retter. The Ministry of Pacific Island Affairs research team: Dr Lana Perese, Dr Ieti Lima, Maiava Carmel Peteru and Analosa Ulugia-Veukiso.
6. Then Prime Minister Helen Clark stated in 2005: "He's the epitome of a New Zealand champion."

References

Baker, M. (2012). *Family Welfare – Welfare, Work and Families, 1918–1945*. Te Ara – the Encyclopedia of New Zealand. Manatū Taonga Ministry for Culture and Heritage, updated 13 July 2012. Retrieved. http://www.teara.govt.nz/en/family-welfare/page-3.

Baker, M., Goodyear, R. and Howden-Chapman, P. (2003). Chapter 5: Household crowding and health. In Statistics New Zealand (ed.) *What Is the Extent of Household Crowding in New Zealand? An Analysis of Crowding in New Zealand Households, 1986–2001*. Wellington: Statistics New Zealand, 58–87.

Ballard, K. (2003). *Inclusion, Exclusion, Poverty, Racism and Education: An Outline of Some Present Issues*. Dunedin: University of Otago.

Balmer, N., Pleasence, P., Buck, A. and Walker, H. C. (2006). Worried sick: The experience of debt problems and their relationship with health, illness and disability. *Social Policy and Society*, 5, 39–51.

Bauman, Z. (1998). *Work, Consumerism and the New Poor*. Maidenhead: Open University Press.

Beaglehole, E. (1950). *Mental Health in New Zealand*. Wellington: University Press.

Bramhall, S. (2003). The New Zealand health care system. Physicians for a national health program. Retrieved. http://www.pnhp.org/news/2003/january/the_new_zealand_heal.php.

Cheer, T., Kearns, R. and Murphy, L. (2002). Housing policy, poverty, and culture: "Discounting" decisions among Pacific peoples in Auckland, New Zealand. *Environment and Planning C: Government and Policy*, 20, 497–516.

Collins, S. (2014). *Closing the Gaps: The Great Ethnic Job Divide*, New Zealand Herald. Retrieved on July 31, 2014. http://www.nzherald.co.nz/nz/news/article.cfm?c_id=1&objected =11220647.

Connell, J. and Brown, R. P. C. (2005). *Remittances in the Pacific: An Overview*. Philippines: Asian Development Bank.

Curtis, B. (2001). Reforming New Zealand agriculture: The WTO way or farmer control? *International Journal of Sociology of Agriculture and Food*, 9(1), 29–42.

Curtis, B. and Curtis, C. (2006). The social setting. In Miller, R. (ed.). *New Zealand Government and Politics (4e)*. Auckland: Oxford University Press, 14–24.

Curtis, C. and Curtis, B. (2011). The operation of a suicidal cohort and its socio-economic origins. In Walker, C., Johnson, K. and Cunningham, L. (eds.). *Community Psychology and The Economics of Mental Health: Global Perspectives*. Houndmills, UK: Palgrave MacMillan, 62–79.

Department of Psychology (2011). *Community Psychology Graduate Handbook*. Hamilton, NZ: Department of Psychology, University of Waikato.

Edmunds, S. (2012). *Costly ads lure Kiwis to high-interest loans*. New Zealand Herald. Retrieved on July 31, 2014. http://www.nzherald.co.nz/business/news/article.cfm?c_id=3&objectid=10855713.

Ewing, I. (July 31, 2001). *Crime in New Zealand*. Wellington: Statistics New Zealand. Retrieved. http://www2.stats.govt.nz/domino/external/pasfull/pasfull.nsf/0/4c2567ef00247c6acc256b970010b936/$FILE/CrimeNZ.pdf.

Families Commission (2012). *Pacific Families and Problem Debt*, Research Report No. 6. Wellington: Families Commission.

Families Commission and Retirement Commission (2008). *Beyond Reasonable Debt: A Background Report on the Indebtedness of New Zealand Families*, Research Report No. 8. Retrieved on July 31, 2014. http://www.familiescommission.org.nz/web/beyond-reasonable-debt/index.html.

Fitch, C., Hamilton, S., Basset, P. and Davey, R. (2010). *Debt and Mental Health: What Do We Know? What Should We Do?* London: Royal College of Psychiatrists, College Research and Training Unit.

Goffman, E. (1963). *Stigma: Notes on the Management of Spoiled Identity*. Englewood Cliffs, NJ: Prentice-Hall.

Grunwell, R. (2009). *Mobile Stores a Bad Deal*. New Zealand Herald. Retrieved on July 31, 2014. http://www.nzherald.co.nz/nz/news/article.cfm?c_id=1&objectid=10616604.

Henare, M., Puckey, A. and Nicholson, A. (2011). *He Ara Hou: The Pathway Forward*. Auckland: Mira Szászy Research Centre, The University of Auckland.

Kelsey, J. (1995). *The New Zealand Experiment: A World Model for Structural Adjustment?* Wellington: Bridget Williams Books.

Kelsey, J. (1999). Life in the economic test tube: New Zealand "experiment" a colossal failure. *Electronic Radical Journal of Organization Theory*, 2(1), 1–5.

Law, R. and Sumner Burstyn, B. (2006). *Why has Meningococcal Death Rate Increased Since the Introduction of Vaccine?* Scoop. Retrieved on July 31, 2014. http://www.scoop.co.nz/stories/GE0611/S00058.htm.

Legge, J. and Heynes, A. (2009). Beyond reasonable debt: A background report on the indebtedness of New Zealand families. *Social Policy Journal of New Zealand*, 35, 27–42.

Livingstone, S. M. and Lunt, P. K. (1992). Predicting personal debt and debt repayment: Psychological, social and economic determinants. *Journal of Economic Psychology*, 13, 111–134.

Macpherson, C. (2004). From Pacific Islanders to Pacific people and beyond. In Spoonley, P., Macpherson, C. and Pearson, D. (eds.). *Tangata Tangata: The Changing Ethnic Contours of New Zealand*. Southbank, Victoria: Thompson, 135–156.

Ministry of Social Development (2013). *2013 Incomes Report: Summary and Overview.* Wellington. Retrieved. http://www.msd.govt.nz/about-msd-and-our-work/publications-resources/monitoring/household-incomes/.

Robertson, N. R. and Masters-Awatere, B. (2007). Community psychology in Aotearoa/New Zealand: Me tiro whakamuri a kia hangai whakamua. In Reich, S. M., Riemer, M., Prilleltensky, I. and Montero, M. (eds.). *The History and Theories of Community Psychology: An International Perspective.* New York: Kluwer Academic Publishers, 140–163.

Statistics New Zealand (2008). *Family Net Worth in New Zealand.* Wellington: Statistics New Zealand.

Statistics New Zealand (2013a). *2013 Census – Major Ethnic Groups in New Zealand,* Wellington: Statistics New Zealand.

Statistics New Zealand (2013b). *New Zealand Income Survey: June 2013 Quarter.* Retrieved. http://www.stats.govt.nz/browse_for_stats/income-and-work/Income/ NZIncomeSurvey_HOTPJun13qtr/Tables.aspx.

Statistics New Zealand (2014). *National Level Data Tables – June 2014: Characteristics of Working-Age Recipients of Main Benefits.* Retrieved on July 31, 2014. https://www.msd.govt.nz/about-msd-and-our-work/publications-resources/statistics/benefit.

Tanielu, R. and Johnson, A. (2014). *This Is Home: An Update on the State of Pasifika People in New Zealand.* Manukau: The Salvation Army Social Policy and Parliamentary Unit.

Waiapu Anglican Social Services (2010). *Waiapu families in debt.* Retrieved on July 31, 2014. http://www.waiapuanglicansocialservices.org.nz/userfiles/file/Debtstories.pdf.

Walker, C. (2013). Manufacturing the right way to be in debt: Can psychologists explore the debt industry? *The Australian Community Psychologist,* 25(1): 49–59.

Conclusion: Thoughts for the Future

Carl Walker

A few years ago some colleagues and I were undertaking research on peoples' experiences of personal debt and how it impacted their mental wellbeing. We decided to talk to a range of people in the South East of England who might know about debt. These included debt clients, bailiffs, debt counsellors, mainstream credit suppliers such as banks and building societies, debt collectors, credit unions, people who worked for national organisations such as the Centre for Responsible Credit and the Lending Standards Board, and people involved in financial education programmes at both a local and a national level. Initially we simply wanted to hear what people had to say about the way in which experiences of financial strain generated suffering to try to get a better understanding of the pathways that linked credit acquisition and mental health and that seemed to be so well established in the academic literature. On carrying out this work there were two key things that surprised me.

The first was that almost everyone, regardless of how they related to personal debt, seemed to agree that the majority of people managed their money well. This was true regardless of which income bracket people came from. It seemed to be generally accepted that the problems that people developed with servicing their debts were often largely beyond their control.

The second surprise was how utterly and comprehensively systemic the issue of debt-related distress really appeared. By this I mean how completely the different actors and organisations that we spoke to depended on each other so that the system could operate. Moreover, most of the people whom I talked to seemed quite aware of this, whether they were working in a bank, as a debt counsellor or as a collector, or whether they were a debt client who was struggling to service their debts. Banks depended on low wages in comparison with living costs so that people would need recourse to the credit (and interest) that allowed these institutions to deliver shareholder profits. Governments depended on banks to make credit available in order to continue to let wages stagnate. Banks depended on lax regulatory regimes so that they could lend as responsibly (or irresponsibly) as they wished. They also depended on debt charities to reform the practices of debtors so that they could resume payment of their debts. Governments, banks and debt charities depended on the financial capability sector to make visible the need for individual responsibility. The financial capability sector, the government and banks depended on the media to make visible stories of personal irresponsibility and personal debt. Everyday people, some of whom worked in the sectors above, depended on access to credit for their everyday survival. And so on. Personal debt in the UK was an industry, and distress and suffering were, for many, irrevocable symptoms of the industry. However, when I looked at the way in which personal debt and the mental health problems that are associated with it were articulated in the policy literature, it appeared that the consensus was that individual people who had mismanaged their money required financial literacy training and education. There was little mention of the majority of people who managed their money well but simply didn't have enough. There was little mention of the existence of an industry with clearly dependent and related actors and agents that operated in conjunction to make possible the growth of a debt-fuelled economy.

As a keen cyclist, and an even keener user of strained metaphors, this focus on education struck me as similar to asking a cyclist to cycle along roads that were littered with nails and then questioning the strength of their tyres when they were inevitably punctured. In the UK we were experts at tyre strength. Great rafts of resources were thrown at the metaphorical tyre sector to find ways to make sure that they could stand up to our nail-strewn roads. Few people seemed very interested in looking at the roads.

The chapters in this book show that people are cycling through streets that are littered with nails in countries all over the world and the response in these countries is overwhelmingly to institute a thorough check of tyres. From El Salvador, to New Zealand, to Croatia, to Puerto Rico, this volume makes clear that the same commonalities emerge – not uniformly, it should be noted. We see specific racialised credit practices that aim to exploit Pasifika people in New Zealand, the debt of Puerto Rican people dependent on historical colonial ties to the USA, the Swiss

Franc loans crisis in Croatia, P2P lending in the USA, debt financed and justified austerity in Greece and Spain, and so on.

What links these countries and their debt industries is that a growing number of people around the world can no longer live without debt. Neoliberal policies and discourses, while geographically and temporally specific, depend on people living in debt.

Debt, and the distress that is associated with it, with the harassment, abuse, shame and guilt and the constant worry of losing everything and then being blamed for it, are increasingly the defining features of neoliberal economies around the world. Suffering and worry are the essence of neoliberal debtfare states, of creditocracies. When you read textbooks about neoliberal capitalism they tend to provide a number of defining features such as free-market fundamentalism, low public spending, discourses of individualisation, small government, privatisation, low tax and a dominant finance sector. What this volume shows is that asset extraction, indebted lives and institutionalised suffering need to be added to this list. The average family from most neoliberal states in the world now live in some form of debt bondage. Debt is the cornerstone of neoliberal discipline. It makes free markets – with their inherent contradictions, monopolies and unchecked abuses – possible. It not only defines the parameters of incorporation and exit from labour markets, but also labour markets themselves, and it reshapes lives in the most profound sense (LeBaron, 2014).

Overindebtedness and growing personal debt are manifestations of a particular model of late modern capitalism where the dominant economic and political mode of organisation demands the increased use of credit to sustain consumer demand. A key element of this organisation has been the mobilisation of a range of ideological and discursive representations of debt that privilege the pathologisation of individuals at the expense of a macroscopic analysis (Martín-Baró, 1984).

The last 30 years have seen the construction of vast bureaucratic international and national apparatuses for the creation and maintenance of debt. These have an undoubted diversity around the world but they also have much in common: the uniform importance of stagnating incomes and growing income inequality, the reshaping of labour markets characterised by precarious and poorly paid jobs, and an increasing share of household income that is now allocated to servicing debt obligations where peoples' decreasing pay is handed to the financial sector through increasingly habitual interest payments (Baragar and Chernomas, 2012). Also endemic is a manufactured sense of hopelessness about any sense of possible alternative future.

Neoliberal capitalism is an economics of perpetual crises. The dominant narrative on neoliberal capitalism positions crisis as a temporary disorder in an otherwise sound mode of politics and economic growth. However, as Schmidt and Hersh (2006) point out, the actual brief periods of sustained and rapid growth which punctuate the crises are the deviations from the norm. Moreover, there will be no solution to the current crisis of neoliberal capitalism and its accompanying practices of systemic asset extraction unless there are constraints on capital that are independent of the logics of financialisation. Inherent in neoliberal finance capitalism is an ethics of nation-state competition. This book exposes this ethic as wholly fallacious. The competition is not, and never was, between countries and national economies but between international finance relays, and their governments and medias, and everyone else. This volume shows that the same problems are occurring in much the same way the world over. Stagnating incomes, attacks on essential public services and security, people living in debtfare and increasingly marauded by collectors, evicted by banks and castigated by pliant national medias, all in the name of one mass-coordinated process of asset extraction.

Practices of resistance

There is already valuable work being undertaken across the globe to address the impacts of neoliberal regimes and the apparatuses that institute austerity, scapegoating, inequality, debt and suffering as a matter of course. Under the intuition that each act of debt service should be regarded as a subtraction from the real economy that creates jobs and funds social spending, Ross (2013) suggests that there is a need to invoke human rights doctrine.

Strike Debt released the *Debt Resistors' Operations Manual* in 2012 to promote practical advice about how to reduce, or free oneself from, debt burden and it launched an effective Rolling Jubilee to buy cheap debt on secondary markets where the profit margin is huge (Ross, 2013). It raised USD 500,000 in a matter of weeks – enough to eliminate almost USD 15 million worth of debt in one year. The Indignados and Occupy movements have reconfigured subterranean politics as forms of civil politics and there have been multiple demonstrations in recent years in Brussels, Wroclaw and Budapest (Pianta and Gerbaudo, 2014). The Fabricas Recuperadas (recovered factories) movement in Argentina resulted in more than 200 successful cooperatives after workers reoccupied workplaces that had been abandoned by their owners after the 2001 economic crisis.

Dear and Dear (2013) highlight further global stories of resistance. The Five More movement in El Salvador brings together human rights and social justice organisations to push for progressive social changes, and it has managed to bring in the abolition of payments for healthcare. In Pakistan there have been protests against the country's unjust debt, and in Europe protests and general strikes across 40 cities in 2013, including 1.5 million people taking to the streets in Portugal. In Egypt and Tunisia, protests in the name of "bread, freedom and social justice" have included demands not to inherit the debts of deposed dictators.

However, despite these, neoliberal market economics is still dominant in the practices of the principal global financial authorities that are charged with addressing global and national economic crises. In Portugal for instance, the IMF is advocating a new austerity drive by repeating the well-worn mantra that unemployment benefit is too prolonged and too high, despite more job losses being on the horizon. In Latvia, austerity has created demographic losses that exceed Stalin's deportations in the 1940s, with huge unemployment and a drastic fall in wages across public and private sectors. This has created a health emergency, with operations being cancelled and 26 hospitals closed, including the largest hospital in the country (Dear and Dear, 2013).

According to Pianta and Gerbaudo (2014), the anti-austerity mobilisations have by and large failed in converging one common vision that might serve as a credible alternative to the neoliberal orthodoxies that constitute the political and economic status quo. In the UK the New Economics Foundation (NEF, 2013) likewise laments the lack of clear coherent challenges. It notes that UK austerity advocates have a clear narrative that is rigidly adhered to by proponents in the media and beyond. This includes the messages that the UK is broke, that austerity is necessary, that people can be understood as strivers or skivers, that welfare is a drug and that big government is bad – in short, the effective discourses that constitute Hall et al.'s (2013) commonsense neoliberalism.

The NEF has suggested that none of the challengers have told good stories with simple messages and powerful images, and that among those who challenged the discourses of austerity there was little unity of purpose. It suggests the need for a new international story that is coherent and consistent, that repositions the casino economies of international financial services, that focuses on what the NEF calls "Big bad banks", "Big guys and little guys (Inequality)" and the "jobs gap (standard of living)". Indeed, these messages and themes cut right to the heart of the international stories of debt sufferance that are provided in this text. There is undoubtedly work to do be done here should there be a coherent movement to remove the "personal" from personal debt.

Avenues for a future social science of debt

Judging by many other books about austerity, inequality, poverty and indebtedness, this should be the point in this volume where we reel off a list of grand narratives about how the world has to be changed to make it a better place. It is a challenge to find a text on modern debt, capitalism or neoliberalism that doesn't outline grand transformational projects that outline ways in which the world needs to change in order to address the range of issues that are considered here – and understandably so. For instance, Stiglitz (2013) suggests that a better world is possible if plans and policies for more social equality are agreed and implemented. He contributes alternatives that include an economic agenda of reform which is directed to curb excesses at the top, controlling the financial sector, stronger and more effectively enforced competition laws, a limit to the power of CEOs, comprehensive reform of bankruptcy laws, and an end to government giveaways to the top and corporate welfare. He outlines legal reforms which democratise access to justice, create more progressive income and corporate tax systems, and restore sustainable and equitable growth – that is, a growth agenda based on public investment, and the redirecting of investment and innovation to preserve jobs and the environment.

In a recent article, some of the authors who were involved in the production of this book suggested that we need conceptual tools that make evident the interconnections between shorter-range improvements and the longer-range transformative projects that are outlined by Stiglitz (2013), that promote linkages between local projects and broader programmes of political change (Walker et al., 2014). Thus far, efforts to address the fallout from personal debt have largely focused on individual financial literacy tuition and individual psychological support for those whose mental health is adversely affected by the entrenched systemic brutalities of the debt industries. It should be noted that while the limitations of such ameliorative literacy and mental health approaches have been clearly outlined in this book, they are often useful. That is, some people need and benefit from financial guidance. That individuals' difficulties are part of a broader system of controlled asset extraction does not negate the fact that support in addressing their debts and in navigating their way round the imposed legal ramifications of their overindebtedness can be profoundly beneficial. That a persons' profound psychological distress may have been made manifest by a regime of sustained abuse from debt collectors does not negate the fact that such support may be useful.

Ameliorative approaches are easier to mount than the "revolutionary" task of changing the system, especially for indebted people and for concerned psychologists whose domain for action is typically limited in scope. The problem, though, is that such interventions not only leave the underlying systemic problems unaddressed but could be argued to perpetuate them by supporting the notion that individual deficits are the solution to systemic economic and political problems.

The challenge is to find ways to tie the two together, linking work with people to political activity for system change, so that collective action and the consciousness that is necessary for it are nurtured (Walker et al., 2014). In the spirit of liberation psychology's critique of an individualising and complicit psychology, Kagan et al. (2011) suggest a more nuanced rethinking about the amelioration/transformation distinction. Their approach is based on the observation that in many cases there are both ameliorative and transformative aspects. Moreover, where social transformation has taken place it has often started from ameliorative action, with the experience gained in the former, such as action research findings, understanding of barriers to action, alliances constructed and conscientisation achieved.

Recent moves such as the establishment of credit unions and cooperatives may have positive effects. Engagement in such movements, though, when linked together regionally, may provide the type of popular education that leads to political activism, with the development of campaigns for more widespread changes in practice – for example, the protests at the high-cost UK credit markets which have recently led to the Financial Conduct Authority introducing an interest rate cap for payday lenders (FCA, 2014).

There is further work to be done in many countries to make feasible financial alternatives to mainstream credit institutions. Debt is big business for banks that need to cast about to deliver ever greater profit margins (Griffiths, 2007). Policy-makers have not only abrogated their responsibility for the growth in consumer debt but have also in many cases actively encouraged it. Governments have traditionally placed more restrictions on credit unions as viable alternatives to banks and possibly over-regulated them (NEF, 2013). All manner of neoliberal consumer capitalist economies demand a steady flow of unregulated credit options, so the potential over-regulation of institutions whose ownership structures encourage long-term and prudent management, and a great focus on the needs of customers than on shareholders, makes sense in this framework. Members of credit unions do not claim on profits and hence managers do not face pressure from owners regarding short-term profits. As a result the loan delinquency rate is markedly lower than it is for commercial banks. Therefore there needs to be support in building national and centralised infrastructures both within and between nation states that are able to be positioned as viable alternatives. Mellor (2010) suggests that local money systems such as credit unions are crucial in the development of an economics that is socially literate.

Harper (2003) laments the tendency to focus work on individual explanations of people who have little or no control over the world's economic resources as opposed to the governments and transnational corporations that do. This book has attempted to look at a range of complex industries that produce poverty and debt, and that reproduce very specific explanations of poverty. However, as useful as the chapters are, there is much work still to be done and this collection only scratches the surface of the interlocking mechanisms which perpetuate and sustain debt-fuelled neoliberal capitalism. Our work as academics needs to explore potentially useful materials such as government press releases, ministerial statements, policy documents and multinational corporation strategies which are too often ignored. Here is a fruitful avenue for further research praxis into understanding the ever-changing roles of the multinational activities and processes that so clearly impact and sustain personal debt but that are rarely the focus of research. These include the complex governance system of international agencies such as the IMF, the World Health Organization, UNICEF and the United Nations; the global bond markets; and the major credit-rating agencies that establish the creditworthiness of sovereign states whose sovereignty has been displaced onto the international creditors but who are rarely considered to be part of the consumer debt solution. Such private mechanisms of global governance frame the context within which the UK government determines fiscal strategy (McGrew, 2010), and impacts and shapes many of the key drivers behind personal debt. As McGrew (2010) notes, more needs to be understood about the actual mechanisms through which global governance reproduces poverty and inequality. To focus research praxis on these institutions is essential if we are to remove the "personal" from personal debt.

As academics, activists, students and interested parties, we need to continue to produce valuable knowledge bases that seek to explore and to challenge the debt industries, precarious work, poverty wages, deregulated barely fit-for-purpose finance sectors, endemic systemic abuses of human rights, the clear limits of financial literacy agendas and the industries which place them there. We need to deconstruct the relationships of power that are manifest in daily life through language forms, myths and symbolic processes, and the dominant categories of speech that misrepresent those in debt (Edelman, 1985).

Moreover, as academics we need to get out and work harder to make our work have an impact. Too often we see important pieces of work submitted to journals or have small local launches of reports that then disappear. It is incumbent on us to ensure genuine, forceful, aggressive dissemination to as many audiences as possible in as many ways as possible as being an inherent part of any work that has something important to say about the maintenance of the systemic violence of indebtedness. Hodgetts et al. (2013) suggests advocacy through direct action events, fostering service developments, presenting public lectures for wealthier community groups, mounting sustained attempts to engage in conversations with government bodies, conducting workshops with key stakeholders where we provide case studies and use them as the basis for discussion about what could be done, and contributing to policy submissions.

As Martin-Baro (1994) noted, academics need to contribute to challenging ideology by introducing into the collective consciousness elements and schemata that can help to dismantle the dominant ideological discourse and practices – to contribute to progressive change in the forms of oppression that are inherent in a social world which is currently shaped by the logics of financialisation, austerity and the brutality of industrial indebtedness.

References

Baragar, F. and Chernomas, R. (2012). Profits from production and profits from exchange: Financialisation, household debt and profitability in 21st century capitalism. *Science & Society*, 76(3), 319–339.

Dear, J., Dear, P., Jones, T. (2013). *Life and Debt: Global Studies of Debt and Resistence*. Jubilee Debt Campaign.

Edelman, M. (1985). *The Symbolic Uses of Politics*. University of Illinois Press.

Financial Conduct Authority (2014). Retrieved on August 20, 2014. http://www.fca.org.uk/news/fca-proposes-price-cap-for-payday-lenders.

Griffiths, M. (2007). Consumer debt in Australia: Why banks will not turn their backs on profit. *International Journal of Consumer Studies*, 31, 230–236.

Hall, S., Massey, D. and Rustin, M. (2013). After Neoliberalism. The Kilburn Manifesto, http://www.lwbooks.co.uk/journals/soundings/pdfs/manifestoframingstatement.pdf.

Harper, D. J. (2003). Poverty and discourse. In Carr, S. C. and Sloan, T. S. (eds.). *Poverty And Psychology: From Global Perspective To Local Practice*. United States: Springer.

Hodgetts, D., Chamberlin, K., Tankel, Y. and Groot, S. (2013). Researching poverty to make a difference: The need for reciprocity and advocacy in community research. *The Australian Community Psychologist*, 25(1), 46–59.

Kagan, C., Burton, M., Duckett, P., Lawthom, R., & Siddiquee, A. (2011). *Critical Community Psychology*. Chichester: Wiley.

LeBaron, G. (2014). Reconceptualizing debt bondage: Debt as a class-based form of labor discipline. *Critical Sociology*, January 31st. 10.1177/0896920513512695.

Martin-Baro, I. (1989). *Writings for a Liberation Psychology*, US: Harvard University Press.

Martin-Baro, I. (1994). *Writings for a Liberation Psychology*. Cambridge, MA: Harvard University Press.

McGrew, T. (2010). *The Links Between Global Governance, UK Poverty and Welfare Policy*. York, UK: The Joseph Rowntree Foundation.

Mellor, M. (2010). *The Future of Money: From Financial Crisis to Public Resource*. Chicago, US: Pluto Press.

NEF. (2013). Framing the economy- the Austerity Story. The New Economics Foundation. http://www.neweconomics.org/publications/entry/framing-the-economy-the-austerity-story

Pianta, M. and Gerbaudo, P. (2014). In search of European alternatives: Anti-austerity protests in Europe. LSE Project on Subterranean politics in Europe.

Ross, A. (2013). *Creditocracy*. London: OR Books.

Schmidt, J. D. and Hersh, J. (2006). Neoliberal globalisation: Workfare without welfare. *Globalizations*, 3(1), 69–89.

Stiglitz, J. (2013). *The Price of Inequality*. New York: Norton and Company.

Walker, C., Burton, M., Akhurst, J. and Degirmencioglu, S. M. (2014). Locked into the system? Critical community psychology approaches to personal debt in the context of crises of capital accumulation. *Journal of Community and Applied Social Psychology*, doi:10.1002/casp.2209. http://onlinelibrary.wiley.com/doi/10.1002/casp.2209/.

Index

ability to pay, 32, 237, 259
acquisition of debt, 264
acquisition of wealth, 196
Apropa't, 94, 95
assembled family, 260
asset–based (backed) securities (ABSs), 3, 4
attribution theory, 54
attributional processes, 146, 151
Auckland, 7, 21, 37, 38, 272, 277, 284, 285, 286, 287
austerity measures, 21, 103, 115, 150, 190, 284
austerity, 6–10, 13, 17, 20–1, 53, 101, 103, 115, 118, 126, 131, 133, 135, 136, 138, 139, 148, 150, 151, 157, 163, 178, 180, 187, 188, 190, 200, 246, 269, 271, 280, 284, 290, 291–3, 296

bad conscience, 146
bailout, 7, 37, 53, 63, 103, 129, 132, 138
balance, 4, 13, 25, 49, 138, 139, 145, 194, 237, 257, 259, 260, 264, 265, 270
bankruptcy, 13, 50, 63, 71, 72, 81, 91, 150
banks, 4, 8, 14, 39, 42, 45, 51, 53–4, 61–6, 68–9, 72–3, 77–82, 86–7, 89, 93, 111, 114, 116, 123, 129–31, 133, 138, 142, 145–6, 167, 181–2, 190, 198–9, 201, 207–8, 211, 216–7, 225–7, 230, 232–3, 237, 247, 249, 257–8, 261–2, 271, 282, 288–9, 291, 294–6
basics of living, 266
behavioural economics, 186, 200, 204
being able to manage money, 183, 192
benefit specific, 261
better condition, 256

black and ethnic minority groups, 187, 190
British Academy, 190

Campaign for a Fair Society, 187
Canada, 127–28
capitalism, 3, 5, 12–4, 37, 81, 92, 130, 140, 157, 163, 165, 176, 241–2, 244–5, 249, 277–8, 281, 290–1, 293, 295–6
care responsibilities, 197
Catalonia, 94
cycle, 11–13, 49, 119, 194, 221, 236, 238, 256, 264, 279, 289
central bank, 103, 129, 133, 136, 138, 150
Centre for Welfare Reform, 187
child dependents, 197
child poverty, 85
children, 26, 28–9, 31–3, 46, 68, 69, 73, 76, 85, 87–8, 90–7, 100, 106–8, 110, 112–3, 153, 159, 178, 186–7, 197, 198, 200, 211, 251, 253, 257, 261, 263–4, 268, 275, 278
choosing financial products, 183, 192
church, 202, 243, 262, 275, 279
see also tithing; religion
Citizens Advice Bureau, 198
clear and culturally benign language, 193
cloud housing, 91, 99
collective, 5, 11, 30, 31, 36, 68, 77, 86, 90, 92, 97, 145–7, 149, 151–3, 155, 158, 163, 165, 171, 192, 251, 253, 271, 278, 281, 294, 296
collective imagination, 90
communication, 1, 69, 74, 77, 79, 96, 139–40, 146, 155, 168, 244, 258, 262, 270, 279, 284–5
community, 8, 11, 14–5, 21, 31, 33, 37–8, 56–8, 60, 92, 94–5, 98, 118–9, 135, 139, 150, 179, 180,

184–5, 191–3, 199, 201–2, 207, 214, 220–1, 240, 250–3, 275–6, 279, 281, 283–4, 286–7, 296–7
community–based educational intervention, 191
community–based project, 11, 180
community organisation, 192–3
community psychology, 15, 40–1, 50, 54–6, 92, 119, 135, 180, 191, 202, 281, 286, 287, 297
co–modification process, 195
conclusion, a personal debt forecast, 264
conscientization, 195
construction industry, 86
consultation process, 191–2
Consultative Group to Assist the Poor, 181, 200
consumer debt, 2, 5, 14–5, 48–9, 57, 59, 167, 171, 200, 220, 240, 294–6
consumerism, 37, 101, 109, 133, 166–7, 178, 214, 260, 262, 276, 283, 285
contagion effect, 48, 90
cooperative, 92, 97, 133, 137
Corporation for Enterprise Development, 182
corruption, 63, 78, 89, 124, 196, 254
counsellors and advice services, 186
credit card, 15, 47, 49, 50, 63, 75, 104, 108–9, 130, 161, 167–8, 172, 194, 199, 208, 213, 215–7, 220–1, 225–6, 240, 249, 257–8, 260, 264
credit card debts, 199
credit facilities, 264
credit unions, 198, 230, 288, 294, 295
credit use, 186, 201, 205, 219
crisis, 1, 3, 8, 10, 14, 48, 58–9, 61–3, 68, 73, 76–7, 79, 85, 88–9, 90–1, 97, 99–100, 102–110, 112, 114–6, 117–9, 129, 137–9, 140–6, 148–9, 150–9, 161–3, 184, 189, 196, 219, 225, 241, 245–6, 249, 251–2, 269, 279, 284, 290–1, 297
Croatia, 8, 62–6, 68, 70–2, 78–9, 80, 81–3, 289, 290
cultural obligations, 31, 279
see also kinship
cumulative impact assessment, 279

descriptive, 260
de–alienation of groups of persons, 196
debt, 1–15, 19–30, 31–77, 78–148, 150–6, 160–79, 182, 184, 186, 188, 190, 192, 194, 196, 196, 198–9, 200–23, 225–30, 232, 234–42, 244–50, 252, 254–66, 268–75, 278–80, 282–90, 291–7
debt cycle, 12–3, 236, 238, 264, 279
debt industry, 9, 11, 13, 15, 21, 34, 121, 124, 126–66, 168–9, 170–2, 174, 176–8, 182, 184, 186, 188, 190, 192, 194, 196, 198–9, 200, 202, 204–10, 212, 214, 216, 218, 220–1, 223, 234, 238, 241, 247, 268, 287
debt subjectivity, 165
debt–collection regimes, 4
debtfare, 2, 4, 6, 290–1
declined, 43, 47, 52, 259, 260
deficit, 21, 35, 125–6, 132–3, 241, 245, 258, 262, 294
dehumanisation of citizens, 129
delay in payment, 258
democracy, 35, 85, 119, 123, 124, 135, 136, 148, 166, 241, 252, 258
developed countries, 199, 228
dialogical approach, 180, 191, 195
Diamandouros, N., 117
disabled people, 134, 188, 190, 192, 200
discrimination, 58, 190, 192, 229, 240, 253
discursive production of, 139
discursive, 6, 35, 138, 139, 146, 151, 155, 156, 169, 206, 208, 213, 214, 216, 219, 290
dominant worldviews, 109

ecological validity, 185, 191, 193
economic circumstances, 192
economic conditions, 3, 126, 204, 206, 225, 256, 259, 265, 283
economic crisis, 62–3, 85, 88–9, 90, 102–8, 117–8, 139–46, 148, 149–52, 155–9, 219, 241, 246, 249, 251–2, 291
economic inequalities, 190

economic, 122
economics, 6, 8, 10, 58, 59, 60, 80, 89, 103, 116, 119, 125, 130, 135, 136, 137, 155, 157, 186, 200, 202, 204, 219–20, 238, 240, 243, 268, 286, 292, 295, 297
education, 11, 47, 51–3, 57, 87–8, 96–7, 101, 103, 119, 130, 143, 145, 157, 165, 167, 179–80, 182, 184, 186–7, 191, 196–7, 199, 200, 201, 204, 207, 211, 212, 213, 216–20, 229, 243, 245–46, 248–9, 252–5, 258–9, 283
ejectments, 84
El Salvador 13, 256–63, 266, 267, 289, 29
emotions, 5, 40, 74, 87, 96, 101, 140, 142, 145, 157, 159, 170
employment, 11, 21, 38, 43, 46, 47, 50, 60, 62, 70, 75–6, 81–2, 86, 90, 101–5, 109, 116–18, 125, 136, 139, 141, 142, 143, 147, 151, 155–8, 165, 187–9, 190, 193, 197, 201, 215, 219, 221, 225, 229, 230, 244, 246–50, 253–4, 263, 266, 283, 285, 292
empowerment, 92, 280, 281, 283
English for Speakers of Other Languages, 197
environment, 60, 87, 90, 97, 101, 107–9, 115, 118, 119, 214, 131, 131, 140, 142, 145, 146, 154, 156, 191, 195, 200, 229–30, 238, 248, 252–3, 259, 263, 285, 293
equality, 8, 11, 15, 21, 39, 40, 42, 48, 52, 56, 59, 86, 95, 117–9, 125, 190, 200, 202, 241, 248, 251–2, 255, 259, 262, 279–80, 281, 284, 290–3, 295, 297
escraches, 93
European Women's Lobby, 189, 200
eviction, 6, 8, 9, 84–7, 90, 93–7, 99, 115, 116, 247, 248
exchanging houses, 257
expenditure and revenue, 260
extended family, 29, 33, 251, 260

facilitating social change, 195
families, 7–9, 19–28, 30, 33–8, 41, 47–8, 51, 56, 58, 69–71, 73, 74, 75, 77, 78, 84, 85, 87, 86, 89, 88, 89, 90, 93–7, 105, 116–8, 123, 134, 140, 149, 203, 213, 219, 241, 247, 250, 251, 257, 258, 260, 264, 268, 271, 273, 274–5, 277, 279, 280, 284–7
finance capital, 4, 291
Financial Access Initiative, 181
financial advice, 184, 186, 201
financial and political freedom, 195
financial capability, 11, 180, 182–7, 190–3, 199–202, 204, 212, 229, 236, 239, 289
financial corruption, 196
financial crash, 84, 93, 129
financial education, 84, 182, 184, 200, 204, 211, 211, 212, 218, 288
financial implications, 196
financial literacy, 5, 171–3, 175, 177, 181, 182, 198, 200–1, 213, 220, 279, 287, 289, 293, 296
financial providers, 180, 184
financial services, 7, 11, 129, 180–4, 200–1, 228, 239, 292
Financial Services Authority (FSA), 182
financialization, 15, 58, 59, 220
flawed consumers, 268–9, 277
food banks, 190, 198, 268, 282
foreclosure, 40, 48, 49, 50, 51, 58, 59, 71, 72, 86, 90, 247
foreign-currency loans, 65
formal credit, 257
Foucauldian discourse analysis, 168, 208
France, 91, 127, 128, 158, 178, 268
fraud, 79, 138, 144, 158, 228, 238, 268
free market, 6, 28, 125, 196, 230, 290
free market economy, 196
free-market fundamentalism, 6, 290
fuel poverty, 8, 90, 91, 97
fundamental rights, 87, 90

gender, 6, 60, 80, 173, 178, 189, 192, 200, 229, 230, 259, 263, 278
Germany, 81, 91, 127–8, 272
Global north, 2, 7

Index   301

Global south, 134
governing, 2, 3, 15, 140, 145, 152, 156, 179, 220
governmentality, 10, 38, 60, 160, 163, 164, 165, 167, 168, 169, 175, 178, 179, 229, 240
Graeber , D., 38
Great Recession, 39, 41, 42, 47, 48, 49, 52, 53
Greece, 9, 101–4, 106–7, 110, 114–9, 127–9, 146, 150–1, 157, 290
group discussions, 192–3, 195
guilt, 126, 128–31, 136–7, 140–1

health, 101–12, 115–119, 125–7, 129, 131, 142, 143, 147, 150, 157, 158, 159, 189, 190, 197, 202, 219, 221, 226, 235, 239, 245, 249, 250, 252–9, 261–3, 270–1, 278, 281
 consequences of, 20
 hegemonic representation of, 131
 high deprivation, 190
higher education, 47, 130, 249
homeownership, 52, 90
household debt, 13, 36, 38–42, 44, 46, 48–49, 57, 82, 104, 118, 127–29, 152, 188, 225–26, 296
housing, 8, 44–6, 48, 51, 57–9, 61, 63–8, 70–1, 74, 76–83, 85–6, 88, 91, 98–9, 116–17, 125, 183, 187, 189, 198, 230, 256, 266, 272, 275, 283, 285
housing loans, 61, 63–8, 70–1, 76–8, 80
housing properties, 85
human development index, 258

indebted man, 138, 146–7, 155–6, 178
indebtedness, 3, 6, 9, 11–4, 41, 48, 52, 54–56, 59, 76, 82, 86, 101–2, 105–08, 111–17, 129, 161–63, 174, 200–01, 207, 212, 214–16, 218–20, 225–27, 229–30, 232, 234, 236–38, 240, 250, 258, 269, 270–71, 274–75, 278–79, 283–84, 286, 290, 293–94, 296
International Monetary Fund (IMF), 103
Iraq War, 134

Ireland, 38, 79, 127–28
immigration legislation, 197
income per capita, 259–60
individualised mode, 199
individualism, 102, 174–77, 207
individualization, 164–65, 178
inequality, 8, 11, 15, 21, 39, 40, 42, 48, 52, 56, 59, 86, 95, 117–119, 125, 190, 200, 241, 248, 251–52, 255, 259, 262, 279–282, 284, 290–93, 295, 297
inequitable income distribution, 259
influence of the media, 260
information, 5, 13, 73–4, 81–2, 89, 96, 98, 124, 144, 178, 183–84, 186, 205, 228–234, 236, 238, 240, 243, 248, 264–65, 276
infrastructure, 63, 130, 244–45, 259, 261–63, 266, 270, 285, 295
innovation, 41, 44–5, 253, 259, 261, 263, 293
institutional support, 95
insufficient, 21, 84, 89, 94, 259, 272, 278, 280
interest rates, 12, 21, 43, 46, 49, 61, 63–6, 79–80, 102, 131, 171, 226, 229, 231, 233, 235–36, 248, 277, 280

job insecurity, 90, 143
Joseph Rowntree Foundation, 14, 117–18, 189, 199, 219, 297

keeping track of finances, 183, 192
Keynesian, 133, 139, 245
kinship, 21, 275–76
 see also cultural obligations

lack of social support, 198
learned helplessness, 87, 100
lending to households, 61, 64
life insurance, 257
life–growth opportunitie, 264
living conditions, 19, 257, 259, 264, 271
Local Government Association, 189, 202
longer poor, 260

302 *Index*

macroeconomics, 125
major depression, 105
management, 5, 12, 15, 25, 35, 79, 89, 91, 96, 129, 131, 133, 140, 155, 158, 167, 170, 172, 204, 212, 213, 218–19, 226–27, 236, 247, 258, 264, 279, 286, 295
  meaning of, 38, 139–40, 186
market, the, 13, 38, 43, 53, 78–9, 102, 116, 124, 181, 230, 237–8, 271
measure of Italian, the, 151
mental distress, 11, 118–19, 180, 191, 202
mental health, 5, 14–15, 31, 34, 50, 101, 105–07, 109–112, 118–19, 142–43, 157, 159, 197, 202, 226, 235, 239, 249–50, 252, 254, 278, 283, 285–86, 288–89, 293
middle–class attitudes, 199
migrate, 246, 261, 265
migration, 202, 250, 265, 267, 274–75
minimun Wage
modernization, 129
monopoly, 124, 135
moral debt, 144
mortgage, 2, 9, 41, 44–46, 49–52, 57–60, 67–68, 70, 72, 76, 78, 81, 82, 84–86, 104, 106, 108, 112, 118, 129, 130, 144, 158, 167, 216, 221, 225, 248, 271, 273–74, 284
Movimiento de los Indignados, 92
municipalities, 260

narratives, 10, 12, 39–40, 43, 52–6, 69, 72–6, 78, 81, 126, 134, 163, 177, 193, 293
neoliberal ideology, 36, 102, 112, 160–61, 202
neoliberalism, 3, 14, 20, 37, 41, 53, 55–6, 119, 165–66, 176–78, 227, 241, 251, 254, 270–71, 279, 292–93, 296
New Zealand, 7, 13, 19–21, 23, 34, 36–8, 268–76, 279–87, 289
non–profit, 226, 237
nuclear family, 260

OECD, 20, 21, 110, 118, 182, 200, 269, 282, 284

offer of loans, 257
online trading platforms, 230
overindebtedness, 12, 76, 174, 207, 212, 216, 218, 220, 225–27, 229–30, 232, 234, 236–38, 290, 294
ownership, 52, 57, 59, 63, 77, 79, 85–6, 90, 295

Pacific (Island/Islander), 22, 30–1, 242, 268, 271–75, 277, 283–86
  see also Pasifika
parasitical relation, 4
parents, 31, 73, 75, 88, 94, 96, 113, 183, 192, 197, 239, 261, 266, 286
participatory methodology, 199
Pasifika, 268–69, 271–80, 284–85, 287, 289
  see also Pacific (Island)
Pathfinder programme, 184
payday loans, 49, 276
peer–to–peer lending (p2p lending), 12, 225, 227–35, 237–40, 290
people go into debt, 260
people seeking asylum, 190, 192, 194, 197
perceived financial strain, 101, 105
personal debt, 1–4, 7, 9, 11–3, 15, 20, 22, 29, 36, 38, 41, 60, 86, 102, 118, 160, 163–4, 179, 188, 199, 202–03, 205–06, 212, 218, 221, 223, 225–26, 228, 230, 232, 234–6, 238, 240–2, 244, 246, 248–250, 252, 254–62, 264–66, 268, 270–2, 274–6, 278, 280, 282, 284, 286, 288, 289, 290, 293, 295, 297
planning ahead, 183, 192, 195
Plataforma de Afectados por la Hipoteca (Platform of People Affected by Mortgages), 84, 98, 100
political awareness, 196
population, 7, 9–11, 58–9, 69, 88–9, 95, 103, 110, 115, 118–9, 130, 134, 143, 145–6, 153, 168, 181, 185, 188, 190, 242–5, 248, 250–2, 256, 258–59, 262–3, 265, 267, 272–3, 282, 284

post–socialist transition, 62
potentially problematic, 264
poverty, 2, 6–9, 14–5, 19–20, 24–5, 28, 31–2, 35, 37–8, 42, 59, 85, 88, 90–1, 94–5, 97, 103, 105, 116, 118, 119, 125, 146, 151, 156–7, 165, 180–1, 185–89, 191–2, 196, 199–200, 202, 219–21, 243–4, 253–4, 259–62, 265, 269, 278–280, 282–3, 285, 293, 295–97
Pratt, A., 119
private hospital, 257
privatization, 79, 81–2
propaganda, 6, 9–10, 123–5, 131–2, 135–6
property culture, 86
psychology, 6, 8, 11, 13–5, 21, 38–41, 48, 50, 52–7, 59, 60, 92, 96, 99, 113, 119, 132, 135, 141, 147, 155–9, 166, 178–180, 184, 186, 191, 196, 201–2, 204–6, 208, 219–21, 240–1, 249–51, 254, 271, 281, 283, 286,–87, 294, 297
psychosocial, 7, 21, 86, 94–5, 97, 101, 105, 147, 256
PSY–complex, 166, 168, 174, 176, 220
public debt, 2, 7, 14, 103, 138, 148, 150–1, 155, 241, 244–5, 261
public expenditure, 103, 129, 187

quality of life, 71, 88, 96, 142, 252
quick loan, 257

racism, 159, 178, 190, 274, 276, 279, 281, 283–5
racist, 268–9, 272, 274–6, 278, 280
research, the, 69, 80, 147–8, 185, 208, 260–1
refinance, 45, 257, 261, 265
refocusing of perspective, 196
refugee status, 190
regulate and restrict, 265
regulation of banks, 261
regulatory intervention, 184
religion, 162, 192
   see also tithing; church
remittances, 262, 275, 285

repayment problems, 8, 62, 69, 72–7, 110
repossession, 68, 71–2, 76, 106, 118, 278
resource management, 257
responsibility, 2, 4, 10–1, 31, 40, 52, 61–2, 76, 93, 99, 102, 113, 142–3, 145–7, 149–50, 152–5, 162, 171–7, 184, 189, 199, 203, 205, 208–18, 227, 235, 245, 247, 258, 278, 289, 294
retail banking, 129
rhetoric of, 145, 180, 209, 284
rights, 8, 38, 56, 87, 88, 90, 92–4, 112, 136, 147, 153, 156, 187, 200–01, 206, 256, 282, 291–2, 296
risk, 8, 44, 45, 47, 50
rural wages, 259

sacrifice, 10, 50, 147, 148, 152–3, 155, 162
salary, 61, 70, 73–4, 80, 108–9, 249, 256–7, 262
Securities and Exchange Commission (SEC), 231
shame, 8, 25, 30, 32, 75, 88, 90, 94, 97, 111–5, 119, 142, 144, 147, 155–6, 159, 198, 278, 290
shared lived experience, 192
single people, 192, 197
Skapinakis, P., 119
social cohesion, 87
social drama, 88
social emergency, 91, 94–5, 97
social exclusion, 21, 37, 87–8, 90, 103, 107, 113, 144, 151, 156, 191, 198–9, 280
social heirarchy (hierarchy), 190, 275
social inclusion, 26, 87, 90, 182–3, 192, 202
social inequality, 95, 190, 241, 251–2
social justice, 92, 95, 133, 187, 249, 283, 292
social lending, 228–9, 232
social movements, 92, 97, 134
social processes, 147, 258
social services, 28, 90, 97, 130, 147, 245, 277, 287
social unrest, 35, 139, 150, 253

social, 2–7, 9–13, 15, 19, 21–2, 26, 28–9, 31, 33, 35, 37–8, 41, 46, 51, 54, 55, 57–60, 62, 68, 77, 79, 81–8, 90–107, 109–19, 123, 125, 129–35, 137–151, 153–168, 173–180, 182–3, 185, 187, 190–2, 195–6, 198–9, 202, 206, 209, 212, 216, 218–221, 225–6, 228–232, 234, 236–245, 249–53, 255–58, 260, 262–8, 270–3, 275, 277, 279
social psychological approach, 191
socioeconomic and environmental factors, 101
sociology, 6, 13–5, 117, 119, 152, 156, 158, 251, 286, 297
solidarity, 115–6, 124, 251, 265, 277–8
Spain, 8, 9, 79, 84–92, 94–5, 99, 127–8, 157, 242, 268, 290
Special Interest Group of Municipal Authorities (SIGOMA), 188, 202
spending on healthcare, 190
state, the, 15, 20, 25, 37, 62, 78–9, 88–9, 97, 102, 116, 133, 138, 146, 152, 167, 184, 204, 217, 235, 249, 251–2, 258, 261, 263, 266, 270, 284–5, 287
staying informed about financial matters, 183, 192
structural violence, 89, 156
student loans, 50, 52, 225, 247, 249
subprime lending, 45, 57–8
suicides, 90, 93, 95, 105
Swiss franc loans, 61–2, 65–6, 68, 73, 76, 81
systemic attention, 199

taxation, 45, 129, 131, 246, 248, 259, 263, 280
territory, 12, 242, 258
Thatcher government, 123
The context of personal debt in EL Salvador, 258
theory of knowledge in context, 191

Thoresen Review of Generic Financial Advice, 184, 201
tithing, 275
see also church; religion
transactional, 260
transformative, 98, 195, 293–4
truck shops, 277

underground economy, 87
unemployment, 11, 47, 60, 62, 75–6, 86, 90, 102–4, 109, 117, 125, 139, 141–3, 151, 155, 165, 197, 201, 215, 225, 244, 246–8, 250, 254, 263, 266, 285, 292
universal credit, 189
Universal Declaration of Human Rights, 92

Vaso De Leche, 259
vested interests, 199
violence, 4, 6, 20, 38, 88–9, 97, 111, 119, 138, 146, 155–6, 189, 243, 251, 263–4, 278, 296

wages, 12–3, 21, 42–3, 46, 48, 50, 56, 59, 86, 102–4, 125, 147, 187, 201, 205, 235, 256, 259, 265, 270–1, 289, 292, 296
welfare, 7, 14, 20–6, 28, 30, 32, 36–8, 41, 46–7, 58, 81, 88, 95, 97, 102, 116, 126, 132, 139, 145–7, 151, 164–5, 167, 178, 187–8, 200, 202, 221, 227, 235, 245, 253, 254, 270, 273–4, 281–3, 285, 292–3, 297
welfare dependency, 274
welfare state, 22, 36, 88, 102, 139, 145, 147, 151, 165, 167, 281
wellbeing, 9, 11, 35, 50–1, 94, 96, 101, 105–7, 109, 111, 115, 121, 134, 140, 142, 151, 190, 223, 278, 284, 288
wider projects, 257
working poor, 26, 268, 274, 276, 278–9, 284

Printed and bound by CPI Group (UK) Ltd, Croydon, CR0 4YY